D's

THE HEYDAY
OF
NATURAL HISTORY
1820–1870

'Monday Afternoon at the Zoological Society's Gardens', by C. J. Staniland

THE HEYDAY
OF
NATURAL HISTORY
1820–1870

◆

BY

LYNN BARBER

JONATHAN CAPE
THIRTY BEDFORD SQUARE LONDON

First published 1980
© Lynn Barber 1980
Jonathan Cape Ltd, 30 Bedford Square, London WC1

British Library Cataloguing in Publication Data

Barber, Lynn
The heyday of natural history.
1. Natural history – Great Britain – History
19th century
I. Title
500.9′41   QH138.A1
ISBN 0–224–01448–X

Printed in Great Britain by
Butler & Tanner Ltd, Frome and London

For My Mother

TABLE OF CONTENTS

◆

		PAGE
COLOUR PLATES	... ...	8
ACKNOWLEDGMENTS	... ...	9

PART ONE: THE SOCIAL BACKGROUND ... 11

| 1 | 'AS INTERESTING AS A NOVEL' ... ... | 13 |
| 2 | 'A NATURALIST MAY BE ANYTHING, EVERYTHING' ... ... | 27 |

PART TWO: THE SCIENTIFIC BACKGROUND ... 45

3	'THE MOST SYSTEMATICAL GENIUS'	47
4	THE DANGEROUS PLEASURE	57
5	BELIEFS ABOUT NATURE	71

PART THREE: THE POPULAR EXPLOSION ... 83

6	'TO MAKE THE ACID GRIN'	85
7	THE ECCENTRIC SQUIRE OF WALTON HALL	99
8	AN INVENTION AND ITS CONSEQUENCES	111
9	THE NATURALIST OF THE BOUDOIR	125
10	THE PIONEER OF ZOOPHAGY	139
11	OMNIUM GATHERUM	152

PART FOUR: UPHOLDERS OF ORTHODOXY ... 169

12	THE BRITISH CUVIER	171
13	THE KING OF SILURIA	184
14	THE FOREIGN PROFESSOR	194

PART FIVE: DISSENTING VOICES ... 207

15	THE ROAD TO DARWIN	209
16	'A MUSING, MEDITATIVE STONE-MASON'	225
17	A CASUALTY OF SCIENCE	239
18	CONFESSING A MURDER	251
19	THE BATTLE FOR DARWINISM	269
20	AFTERMATH	286

NOTES AND REFERENCES	297
PICTURE CREDITS	313
INDEX	315

COLOUR PLATES

———◆———

BETWEEN PAGES 64 AND 65

1 Kuhl's parakeet
2 Brown's parakeet
3 White-bearded puff-bird
4 Helmet manakin
5 Humming-birds

BETWEEN PAGES 96 AND 97

6 Rattlesnake attacking a mocking-bird's nest
7 Rieffer's Amazili
8 Sparrow-hawk
9 Grey fox

BETWEEN PAGES 128 AND 129

10 Land molluscs
11 Frontispiece of *Vegetable Kingdom*
12 Sea-mouse, sea-cucumber, serpulae
13 Great seal

BETWEEN PAGES 160 AND 161

14 Title-page of *Zoological Sketches*

15 Title-page of *Rustic Adornments for Homes of Taste*
16 Hippopotamus
17 Gorilla
18 Red-ruffed lemur
19 Palm of the mountain
20 Black-maned lion
21 Common hare

BETWEEN PAGES 192 AND 193

22 Aquarium and conservatory
23 Hart's-tongue spleenwort
24 Succulent plants

BETWEEN PAGES 224 AND 225

25 Sea-anemones
26 Yellow water-lily
27 Japanese flowers
28 Microscopic illustrations

BETWEEN PAGES 256 AND 257

29 Starfishes
30 *Cychla Argus*
31 Victoria Regia water-lilies

ACKNOWLEDGMENTS

◆

This book is dedicated to my mother, Beryl Olive Barber, and I would like to begin by thanking her, and my father, for their unstinting help throughout its writing. Next, I would like to thank my parents-in-law, Maurice and Leonora Cardiff, for their encouragement, and for giving me the run of their excellent library. The following friends provided moral support and help on points of detail – Marcus Binney, Hugh and Mirabel Cecil, Richard Davies, Virginia Ironside, Tim and Joyce Jeal, Gill Luizos, Don Richards, Michael Sissons, Betty Turner and Sebastian Walker – and my research was made easier by the consistent efficiency of the staff of the London and Zoological Society Libraries. I am extremely grateful to all the staff at Cape, but especially Liz Calder, Jane Hill and Valerie Buckingham, for working so hard and enthusiastically to bring the book to its present form.

For help on the illustrations, I would particularly like to thank Jason Spender, who took most of the photographs, working long hours and in difficult conditions with unfailing patience. I would also like to thank Marlborough Rare Books and Messrs Wheldon and Wesley, who allowed us to photograph rare books from their stock.

And of course the book could not have been written without the constant support and encouragement of my husband, David Cardiff, and the many friends, especially Hazel Weaving, who helped by holding one or both babies while I got on with the research.

PART ONE
THE SOCIAL
BACKGROUND

CHAPTER ONE

'AS INTERESTING AS A NOVEL'

HE WORLD IS all agog – for what? for *Bugs* the size of *Water Melons*,'[1] Audubon reported disgustedly in 1836. He was annoyed because the bugs had stolen the limelight from his own beloved birds and sales of his *Ornithological Biography* were falling. And it was true that the public's tastes in natural history were unpredictable. One year they centred on mosses, the next madrepores. In the decade from 1845 to 1855 they moved successively from seaweeds to ferns to sea-anemones. In the next decade they switched bewilderingly to sea-serpents, gorillas and infusoria. These were all national crazes. There were also purely local ones, like the 'limpet fever' which hit Bangor, Northern Ireland, in the 1820s or the passion for keeping baby alligators which suddenly seized the womanhood of Southport in the 1870s. But underlying these short-lived fads and fancies, there was a deeper, more constant enthusiasm for natural history in all its branches which gathered strength from year to year from the 1820s through to the 1860s, and which touched every section of society from the aristocrats who competed in turning their parks over to elands, beavers or kangaroos, to the artisans who hoarded their pennies to buy the *Entomologist's Weekly Intelligencer*.

Every Victorian young lady, it seemed, could reel off the names of twenty different kinds of fern or fungus, and every Victorian clergyman nurtured a secret ambition to publish a natural history of his parish in imitation of Gilbert White. By the middle of the century, there was hardly a middle-class drawing-room in the country that did not contain an aquarium, a fern-case, a butterfly cabinet, a seaweed album, a shell collection, or some other evidence of a taste for natural history, and at the same period it was impossible to visit the seaside without tripping over parties of earnest ladies and gentlemen, armed with a book by Mr Gosse and a collection of jamjars, standing knee-deep in rock-pools and prodding at sea-anemones. Every newspaper ran a natural history section, and every correspondence column became a periodic battleground for debates about whether swallows could hibernate, or whether toads could live for centuries immured in blocks of stone. Natural history was a national obsession, and books on the subject were only marginally less popular than the novels of Dickens. One quite undistinguished natural history book, *Common Objects of the Country* by the Rev. J.G. Wood, sold 100,000 copies in a week.

Such popular enthusiasm for natural history was quite unprecedented. Until the beginning of the nineteenth century, the subject had been not only neglected, but positively despised. Charles Kingsley recalled that in his youth the naturalist had been regarded as a figure of fun, a 'harmless enthusiast, who went "bug-hunting" simply because he had not the spirit to follow a fox.'[2] Victorian naturalists were keenly aware that, by contrast with their predecessors, they were living in a golden age. 'The day has happily passed away,' chirped E.P. Thomson in 1845, 'in which the votaries of nature were taunted with ridicule, and as addicted to childish fancies ... Natural history has assumed an importance in this country, within the last few years, which it had hitherto never been thought to possess.'[3] And five years later, Dr George Johnston, welcoming new recruits to the study of conchology, assured them that they would find themselves 'surrounded and encouraged by a galaxy of congenial spirits', and that, 'so far from having to bear up against the ridicule which might, at no late period, have been your portion, as it was that of some of our predecessors, you will find ... a tacit acquiescence

'Common Objects at the Seaside', by John Leech, *Punch*, 1857

in the becomingness of the study, and a forbearance, at least, from all censure which might fray even the most sensitive.'[4]

Victorian naturalists rejoiced in their new-found popularity, but they were also secretly rather puzzled by it. Those who tried to account for it came up with conflicting and often insubstantial explanations. One American writer, for instance, claimed that it was all thanks to two inventions, the aquarium and the microscope; but since the aquarium was not invented until 1850, by which time the tide of natural history was running at full flood, and the microscope had been invented two centuries earlier, this explanation is unconvincing. Several writers tried to argue that the reason for natural history's popularity was that there were so many great naturalists alive and so many important new discoveries being made every year. But this again is implausible, since the period of natural history's greatest popularity coincided with a period of singular stagnation in biological progress. Between the publication of Cuvier's *Le Règne Animal* in 1817 and Darwin's *Origin of Species* in 1859, almost no major breakthroughs were made, and the biologists who dominated these years were, as we shall see in later chapters, ones whose names are now almost forgotten. In fact it seems more likely that it was the *lack* of serious scientific advance that made the popular addiction to natural history possible, since it is always easier for the layman to follow a subject when it is not undergoing any revolutions.

Those writers who looked further back in time for the origins of their golden age made a more convincing case. Charles Kingsley claimed that the book 'which turned the tide in favour of Natural History, among the higher classes at least'[5] was Gilbert White's *Natural History of Selborne*, published in 1789, and certainly this was an important source of inspiration for every Victorian amateur naturalist, though whether it alone could have generated a nationwide craze seems doubtful. Looking even further back, many writers mentioned the name of Linnaeus, claiming quite rightly that he had launched the modern study of natural history and rescued it from the doldrums of centuries. His work will be discussed more fully in a later chapter: undoubtedly it was crucial in enabling natural history to become popular, though this is not quite the same thing as explaining why natural history actually became popular when it did. For that, we must look to more intangible factors, like the mood and taste of the times.

Perhaps part of the charm of natural history, to the Victorians, was that it was *not* studied at school. If children learned about it at all, they learned it from their Mama, in the course of nursery lessons, and then quickly forgot it under the onslaught of Latin and Greek at school. Schools not only ignored scientific subjects, but positively discouraged them. Darwin was reprimanded by his headmaster at Shrewsbury for 'wasting his time' on experiments, and Dr George Moberly, the headmaster of Winchester, told the Clarendon Commission on Education in 1862 that 'a scientific fact, either as conveyed by a lecturer, or as reproduced in examination, is a fact which produces nothing in a boy's mind. It is simply a barren fact, which after a few years becomes confused with other facts and is forgotten. It

'Scientific Conversazione at Apothecaries' Hall', from the *Illustrated London News*, 1855

leads to nothing. It does not germinate, it is a perfectly unfruitful fact.'[6] In consequence, those adults who did take up the study of natural history came to it with all the freshness of unalloyed ignorance. Queen Victoria learned only in middle age that kangaroos carried their young in pouches, and some of her courtiers were quite astounded by the news that tadpoles turned into frogs.[7] The microscope was not then the loathed and dreaded piece of schoolroom equipment that it is today: on the contrary, an 'evening at the microscope' was a fashionable form of after-dinner entertainment. When Sir Richard Owen, the zoologist, went to stay with Sir Robert Peel, the Prime Minister, he took his microscope with him and all the guests gathered after lunch to examine the remains of the joint they had just eaten and discuss 'why cold boiled beef sometimes shines like mother-of-pearl when cut'.[8] It was the pinnacle of Owen's social success.

Evenings at the microscope, visits to the new zoological gardens and public aquaria, forays into the rock-pools, and magic lantern lectures on the Life History of the Bee, all came under the heading 'rational amusement', and there was nothing that well-to-do Victorians sought for so avidly as that, in order to fill their seemingly interminable leisure hours. To qualify as rational amusement – as distinct from vulgar or 'mere' amusement, like going to the theatre or reading novels – an activity had to contain some element of useful instruction or moral uplift; preferably both. Natural history fitted the bill perfectly. It was scientific, and there was nothing more useful than science, as everyone knew. It was morally uplifting, because it enabled one to find 'sermons in stones, and good in everything'. It was healthy, since it involved going out of doors. For gentlemen it offered new pretexts to go out and shoot something, and for ladies it offered new subjects for water-colours, for albums, or for embroidery. It also tied in very conveniently with the contemporary mania for forming collections. Sir John Lubbock once remarked with a laugh that now people had even started collecting postage-stamps and Darwin said he was surprised that nobody had started collecting different-shaped biscuits.[9] In fact, they preferred to collect shells, seaweeds and butterflies, which were better adapted to drawing-room display.

However, the idea of studying natural history for pleasure was still new enough to need explanation, and every Victorian popular natural history book began with a weighty preface outlining all the moral, practical and life-enhancing benefits that readers could expect to derive from it. They would become more cheerful, more patient, more alert, more interesting. Their temper would be improved by conversing with Nature; their health would be improved by going out into the fresh air. They would probably live longer ('It is curious to remark the great age which naturalists generally attain')[10] and they would certainly become more virtuous ('A good naturalist cannot be a bad man').[11] Natural history, they would find, 'elevates the mind and expands the heart';[12] it was a study from which 'every class may derive every day many moments of gentle exhilaration'.[13] George Henry Lewes (George Eliot's companion) talked of the difference between a lion that has once feasted on human blood and one that has not and compared it to the difference between 'the man who has once tasted of a noble sea-side passion, once lived with his microscope for a few months on the wealthy shores of some secluded spot, indulging in a new pursuit, and the common man, utterly remote from all such experience, walled out from it by blank negation, incapable of even conceiving the heights and depths of such a passion. Visions of those ecstatic hours for ever accompany the happy man.'[14] He also pointed out that the purchase of a microscope could be an effective cure for bereavement, and told how, when his own pet fish had died, 'I grieved for him, and, as a consolation – dissected him ... I had lost a pet, and gained a "preparation".'[15]

Every writer had different reasons to suggest why the study of natural history was particularly suitable for one section of society or another. Sir William Henry Flower favoured it for 'men of independent fortune' who would, he believed, 'be saved by it from all kinds of evil which want of wholesome occupation engenders'.[16] William Swainson recommended it for 'valetudinarians', even bed-ridden ones, and told the story of how Sir Joseph Banks, the eighteenth-century botanist, when confined to his ship by quarantine regulations at Rio de Janeiro, had nevertheless managed to find several new species of plants merely by rummaging through the fodder supplied to the ship's animals. Any invalid, he suggested, could do the same.[17] Other writers recommended it for artisans, for aristocrats, for country-dwellers, for town-dwellers, for ladies, for children, for old people. J.C. Loudon thought it was particularly suitable for clergymen because,

A taste for Natural History in a clergyman has great advantages, both as respects himself and others. It is superior, in a social point of view, even to a taste for gardening. The sportsman often follows his amusements to the great annoyance of his parishioners; the horticulturalist exercises his gentler

pursuit within his garden; and the classical or indoor student of any kind
secludes himself in his closet or his laboratory; but the naturalist is abroad
in the fields, investigating the habits and searching out the habitats of birds,
insects, or plants, not only invigorating his health, but affording ample opportunity for frequent intercourse with his parishioners. In this way their reci-
procal acquaintance is cultivated, and the clergyman at last becomes an
adviser and friend, as well as a spiritual teacher.[18]

Obviously such arguments were persuasive, since a remarkable number of Victorian clergymen *did* take up natural history, and contributed enormously to its
literature.

While the prefaces of Victorian natural history books invariably stressed the
deep seriousness and usefulness of the study, the texts themselves concentrated
on making the subject as light and amusing as possible, often by jettisoning any
pretence to accuracy. It is by no means rare to find whales included among fishes,
or spiders among insects, sometimes with the lame excuse that 'as spiders are popu-
larly considered insects, it will sufficiently suit our purpose to introduce them here
as such,'[19] but usually with no excuse at all. Then there are the myths that receive
a regular airing: that hedgehogs suck milk from cows, that toads and newts are
poisonous, that moles construct 'castles' underground, that flies are 'spontaneously
generated' from dung-heaps, that snails mate by throwing darts at each other,
that shrews kill cattle by running over their backs, that frogs and fish sometimes
fall to earth in showers of rain and – the most durable one of all – that toads can
live for years, possibly for centuries, enclosed in blocks of stone or coal. (Even
as late as 1862 the International Exhibition featured a frog which was supposed
to have been chipped out of a coalmine, and *The Times* in the same year carried
a letter from a correspondent who claimed to have found a live toad inside the
marble of his fireplace.) In addition, there are the ubiquitous anecdotes which
are offered, in all seriousness, as nuggets of scientific fact. Tales of thieving magpies
and Elephants Who Never Forgot are two-a-penny but there are also more esoteric
ones like 'Canine Revenge' about a dog who secretly murdered its rival and then
dragged the body to a nearby pond to hide the evidence, or 'A Valuable Interior'
about a man who lost some jewellery and then found it in his turkey's gizzard
when he came to eat it. Many of the more popular anecdotes recur in book after
book. Even Darwin, in *The Descent of Man*, uses some of the standard anecdotes
to prove that the higher vertebrates are capable of quasi-human reasoning, and
adds one of his own about a female baboon who, when scratched by a kitten that
she had 'adopted', examined the kitten's feet and bit off its claws, thus proving
that she 'certainly had a fine intellect'.[20]

Writers were admired for their skill in deploying the existing stockpile of anecdotes and for their 'power of bringing out the human side of science, and giving
to seemingly dry disquisitions and animals of the lowest type, by little touches
of pathos and humour, that living and personal interest, to bestow which is gener-

ally the function of the poet.'[21] In practice, this meant their skill in anthropomorphizing every animal they described. And not only animals – the Rev. J.G. Wood in *Common Objects of the Microscope* compares the blood corpuscles in a frog's foot to 'a British crowd entering an exhibition, each one seeming to be elbowing its way to the best place',[22] and Charlotte M. Yonge in *The Herb of the Field* characterizes the polypody moss as 'one of those cheerful, humble things, that seems to have a kindness for what is venerable and excellent, even in decay.'[23] Birds are almost invariably referred to as 'feathered songsters', their courtship as 'mutual caresses', their nest-building as 'home-making' and their eggs as 'the dear fruits of happy love'. Each animal is given a 'character' which is presented with no whit less certitude than its appearance. Thus cockroaches, it is agreed, are 'cunning as the fox; greedy as the glutton; impudent as sin; cruel, treacherous, cowardly scoundrels; addicted to drinking; arrant thieves; and not only eat each other, but even devour with avidity their own legs, when they undergo accidental amputation.'[24] One would expect that such judgments, being highly subjective, would differ from author to author, but in fact Victorian natural history writers achieve a surprisingly high level of agreement about the 'true' character of any given species.

Thus while the prefaces of Victorian natural history books promised every form of weighty and improving instruction, what they actually retailed was fascinating facts, bizarre, curious and extraordinary anecdotes, sentimental interludes, long quotations from 'the Poets' (usually Crabbe, Cowper, Montgomery, Milton, Mrs Hemans and the writers themselves), personal reminiscence, pious homilies – in fact, all the usual ingredients of Victorian light reading. They invariably stressed the most strange and exotic aspects of their subject, as reflected in their titles – *Marvels* of Pond Life, *Wonders* of the Sea Shore, The *Romance* of Natural History – often at the expense of basic information, and although their purpose was ostensibly scientific, their style was that of the novel. Natural history therefore represented the best of both worlds. While it was, on the one hand, serious, educational, morally uplifting and so on, it was, on the other, no less entertaining than mere amusement. The Rev. J.G. Wood assured his readers that field natural history 'is far better than a play, and one gets the fresh air besides',[25] while the editor of the *Entomologist's Annual* claimed, a mite more solemnly, that 'It is as interesting as a novel, but gives the same employment to the higher faculties of the mind as are afforded by the abstruser studies of Political Economy and History.'[26] But while novels and plays carried the stigma of mere pleasure, natural history represented rational amusement, and was therefore a safe and respectable indulgence for the middle classes.

It also offered something to *do* – a hobby – and there was nothing the middle classes needed so badly as something to do. The boredom of the affluent Victorian family is truly frightful to contemplate. All the chores (including child-rearing) were taken over by servants, while the opportunities for social intercourse were limited by the strict bounds of social propriety. Gentlemen had their clubs and their field sports (in season), and ladies their 'fancy work' and charitable endeavours, but that still left huge sections of the day entirely unoccupied. Apparently this boredom was widely admitted, so that when natural history writers came forward and offered an instant panacea they were sure of an attentive audience. The Rev. D. Landsborough, for instance, suggesting the study of sea-weeds as a solution, guaranteed: 'The naturalist knows nothing of that *taedium vitae*, – that vampire, *ennui*, which renders life a burden to thousands. To him every hour is precious.'[27] And William Swainson, in his *Cyclopaedia of Natural History*, put it even more starkly: 'The tediousness of a country life is proverbial; but did we ever hear this complaint from a naturalist? – Never.'[28]

And, as the Rev. J.G. Wood had remarked, 'one gets the fresh air besides.' Victorian boredom was compounded of various ingredients, but one of the most loathed and boring of all was the daily walk. Everyone knew that they *should* take a walk every day, because the ubiquitous home health manuals told them so, but how was this to be achieved? Merely to amble about the countryside smacked of idleness and eccentricity: a gentleman had to carry a gun, or a lady a bowl of soup for the poor if they wanted to strike out across the fields. But the poor so often lived in the wrong direction, or the gun was out of season, and then the walk degenerated into the dreaded 'constitutional' or the hardly less daunting practice of 'pedestrianism' – words which sufficiently convey the full horror of the Victorian attitude to walking. What a blessing, then, if one could find some way of combining walking with amusement, and what more perfect solution than to take up the study of botany, say, or entomology. The *Entomologist's Annual* for 1856 points to this advantage and reflects: 'It is no slight pleasure to find occupation and an object in every country walk. An Entomologist cannot say that –

> A primrose by the river's brim,
> A yellow primrose is to him,
> And it is nothing more.

A primrose conveys to his mind a reminiscence of all the insects that feed on it ... [and] a walk, even when he is not actually looking for insects, becomes a totally different thing from what the same walk would be to another person.'[29] Almost every popular natural history mentions this as an inducement. Other hobbies, such as music or painting, might alleviate indoor boredom, but only natural history could offer relief from outdoor boredom as well.

And just as an interest in botany or entomology provided a means of enduring one's daily walk, so an interest in marine biology provided a means of enduring one's annual seaside holiday where the opportunities for boredom were even more extensive than at home. G.H. Lewes begins his *Sea-side Studies* with a daunting picture of the English on holiday: 'What an air of weariness hangs over almost everybody! After the "visitors" have had their first walk on the beach, their first two or three hours' sail, from which they return looking very green – after they

Sea-side studies, 1868

have seen the sunset once, they relapse into utter novel-reading.'[30] What a picture of depravity! But how easily these lost souls might be saved if they would only hitch up their trousers or petticoats and take a prod around the rock-pools. Then, like Lewes himself, they would 'suffer a sea-change, into something zoological and strange.'[31]

However, if killing boredom were the *only* reason for studying natural history, it would hardly count as rational amusement. In order to be rational, a study had to be either useful or morally uplifting. Useful, in Victorian terms, meant applicable to the wants of man, which ultimately meant convertible into shillings and pence. This was not a very easy case to argue for natural history, though the popular writers did what they could. Entomologists were fond of dwelling on the silkworm, and coleopterists lingered long over cochineal. Even writers on seaweeds contrived to make a case for the absolute indispensability of seaweeds to the prosperity of nations. But, in the long run, it had to be admitted that natural history was not as obviously useful as, say, chemistry or physics, and its advocates were careful never to suggest that this was the only, or even a major, reason for its pursuit.

They did not need to, because natural history had a far superior claim to attention, one that made it automatically more rational and respectable than all the other sciences put together. This was natural theology, the spiritual exercise that enabled one to look 'through Nature up to Nature's God' and to

> Find tongues in trees, books in the running brooks,
> Sermons in stones, and good in everything.

These two quotations – from Pope's *Essay on Man* and from *As You Like It* respectively – are to be found in almost every natural history book published in the first half of the nineteenth century; and they served to remind the reader of what he already knew: that the purpose of studying Nature was to approach a closer knowledge of God. The fullest exposition of natural theology was to be found in William Paley's book of that name, published in 1802 and reprinted almost annually, but

William Paley, from a portrait by Romney

even those lucky few who avoided reading Paley's tome, would have had its ideas dinned into them from the cradle up, and heard them expounded from every pulpit in the land.

Paley's book begins with a famous analogy, 'The Watch on the Heath', which was often referred to in early Victorian natural history works. Since it may not be familiar to modern readers, and since it is basic to an understanding of Victorian natural history writing, it deserves quotation here:

> In crossing a heath, suppose I pitched my foot against a *stone*, and were asked
> how the stone came to be there, I might possibly answer, that, for anything
> I knew to the contrary, it had lain there for ever; nor would it, perhaps, be

very easy to show the absurdity of this answer. But suppose I had found a *watch* upon the ground, and it should be inquired how the watch happened to be in that place, I should hardly think of the answer which I had before given – that, for anything I knew, the watch might have always been there. Yet why should not this answer serve for the watch as well as for the stone? why is it not as admissible in the second case as in the first? For this reason, and for no other, viz., that when we come to inspect the watch, we perceive (what we could not discover in the stone) that its several parts are framed and put together for a purpose, *e.g.* that they are so formed and adjusted as to produce motion, and that motion so regulated as to point out the hour of the day ... The inference, we think, is inevitable, that the watch must have had a maker: that there must have existed, at some time, and at some place or other, an artificer or artificers who formed it for the purpose which we find it actually to answer; who comprehended its construction, and designed its use.[32]

The remainder of Paley's book (and it is a long one) is devoted to applying this analogy to the whole natural world. Whenever we examine a plant or an animal, he argues, we find it possessing various structures or contrivances which enable it to survive and propagate its species. These contrivances are so elaborate that they cannot be the product of mere chance, therefore they must have been *designed* by a Creator. The first purpose of the study of Nature, therefore, is to teach us that God exists. The second is to illustrate God's attributes. For just as, in admiring a well-made watch, we inevitably admire the skill of the watch-maker who made it, so, in admiring the various beauties and perfections of Nature, we are inevitably led to think of the beauty and perfection of God who designed them. This, in brief, is natural theology. Its key concept is Design. Nothing happens by chance (or by natural selection), everything by Design. The more we learn to understand and appreciate Design in Nature, the more closely we approach a knowledge of God.

Obviously this was a convenient peg on which to hang the promotion of natural history, as all the popular writers quickly realized. Natural theology made the study of natural history not only respectable, but almost a pious duty, and there was nothing the Victorians liked so much as a duty. It gave thousands of amateur naturalists an excuse to kill butterflies and uproot rare plants to their hearts' content. Moreover, the Paleyan argument was so familiar, it had only to be invoked, not expounded at length. The occasional reference to Design with a capital D, and Providence with a capital P, along with the prominent quotation of 'sermons in stones' and looking 'through Nature up to Nature's God' sufficed to cast a pious aura over any work of natural history. It was this pious ingredient that gave natural history its unique status in the first half of the nineteenth century. Motives such as killing boredom might supply the *real* reason why so many people took up natural history in that period, but natural theology provided, as it were, the excuse,

London Zoological Gardens on Whit Monday, 1866

and since the Victorians never allowed themselves to do anything merely for fun, an excuse was essential.

In fact, natural theology was not quite as tractable a tool as natural history writers might have wished. Any fool could draw sermons out of beehives, but what moral could one derive from the lemming, or how enthuse about the beauty of the blowfly? Mrs Loudon, a prolific popular writer, found herself temporarily stumped by the design of the leaf-insect which, she had to admit, did not *seem* very sensible. In the end, however, she managed to turn even this to account:

> Whenever an animal is found to deviate in shape from the general system, it is still formed to answer the design of its existence. Thus, this insect having such long legs, could never have sustained itself in the air, had not Providence bestowed on the legs themselves a species of wings to balance their weight. These are instances with which Nature teems and which would make the atheist tremble, would he but contemplate the admirable design and system with which they are characterised.[33]

The trembling atheist might, of course, be tempted to ask why Providence had designed the creature with such long legs in the first place that it needed leg-wings to support them, but such questions were taboo in the cosy world of natural theology.

There is a charming book called *The Journal of a Naturalist*, published in 1830, which illustrates the embarrassments of the amateur natural theologian most clearly. Its author, J.L. Knapp, describes himself as a 'Christian moralizer'[34] and is obviously determined to see sermons in everything, but unfortunately the more deeply he delves, the more frequently he finds phenomena which upset him. He is very bothered, for instance, by the insectivorous plants which, he mistakenly believes, do not *need* the insects they consume and therefore must be motivated by spite. 'Our ignorance,' he admits, 'favours the idea of a wanton cruelty in the herb; but how little of the causes and motives of action of created things do we know! and it must be unlimitable arrogance alone that could question the wisdom of the mechanism of him "that judgeth rightly".'[35] As a naturalist, Knapp wants to ask the proper question, 'Why do insectivorous plants eat insects?' but as a natural theologian, he feels obliged to castigate himself for 'unlimitable arrogance' in questioning the phenomenon at all.

For the plain fact was that natural theology was basically inimical to scientific enquiry. If one *had* to find evidence of beauty and benevolence in everything, one had to suppress many of the facts of Nature, or at least not examine them too closely. Time and again in popular handbooks we find the writer asking, 'Why does such-and-such a phenomenon occur?' and then answering himself with the pious evasion, 'Because God ordains it.' Captain Thomas Brown's *Book of But-terflies, Sphinxes and Moths* furnishes a typical example in its treatment of insect metamorphosis: 'It would be difficult to assign a cause,' writes Brown, 'why insects undergo so many changes before arriving at a state of maturity. Why is it that they do not, like other animals, preserve the same general form from infancy to perfection? This is a question which is not easy to answer, but no doubt the thing was wisely ordered by the Creative Power.'[36] That is all he has to say about insect metamorphosis. He finds it odd; he cannot explain it; he presumes that God knows what He is doing.

This casual surrender of all the claims of scientific enquiry seems, to modern eyes, a shocking aberration in a purportedly scientific work. But it did not seem so to the Victorians. When we talk about the 'clash' between religion and science in the Victorian era, we are talking about the 'clash' between an articulated lorry and a grain of sand. Science counted for absolutely nothing compared to religion. It stood, at best, in the relation of a handmaid to religion but, like a handmaid, it could be sacked if it ever showed signs of becoming uppity. Until the arrival of Darwin, Huxley and Tyndall in the middle of the century, science had no champions who were actually prepared to do battle with religion. Most of the scientists were conventionally pious men who, if they saw a conflict between their scientific and their religious beliefs, would unhesitatingly surrender the former. And at the popular level, there was not even a hint of any such conflict. It was *only* religion, in the shape of natural theology, that made the study of natural history worthwhile. The Victorians saw nothing glorious in the pursuit of knowledge for its own sake. E.P. Thomson in his *Note-book of a Naturalist* draws a firm distinction between the pre-Paleyan study of natural history, which he condemns as 'blind curiosity', and the modern study of natural history inspired by natural theology. 'Natural history,' he claims, 'affords a more extensive moral than would be supposed by a casual observer, and the blind curiosity, which formerly was the principal motive for making collections and studying the science, is now giving way to more noble and estimable ideas.'[37] It was this moral and religious justification for the study of natural history that enabled it to become popular in the early decades of the nineteenth century. If there had been any hint, at that stage, that it could lead to irreligious or anti-religious views, nobody would have dreamed of taking it up.

CHAPTER TWO

'A NATURALIST MAY BE ANYTHING, EVERYTHING'

I T IS TEMPTING to define the word naturalist as 'a person who studies natural history', and leave it at that. But it would be an unhelpful definition, since natural history does not mean quite the same now as it meant in the Victorian period, and it did not mean the same at the beginning of the nineteenth century as it meant at the end. The most important difference is that, in the early decades of the nineteenth century, it still theoretically meant the study of the *three* kingdoms of Nature, animal, vegetable and mineral, and therefore included geology, as much as botany and zoology, in its purview. It was in this sense that Charles Darwin described himself, accurately and sufficiently, as a naturalist, and it was precisely because he did include geology and palaeontology in his researches that he was able to arrive at the theory of evolution by natural selection. But by the time he published the *Origin of Species*, in 1859, such eclecticism was already somewhat rare, and most of the serious scientists were beginning to specialize, and to call themselves by names (botanist, geologist and the like) that indicated their speciality. It was not that they spurned the name of naturalist, but rather that they felt they could not honestly claim it.

The exceptions were those who specialized in the study of animals. They *should* have called themselves zoologists, since the word already existed in the dictionary and would have been readily understood. But for some mysterious reason they never did, and while the grander among them called themselves 'comparative anatomists', the humbler continued to call themselves 'naturalists', even though this implied a familiarity with botany and geology which they often did not possess. By the 1850s, therefore, naturalist was becoming increasingly synonymous with our modern zoologist, although it was still quite often used in its older sense of zoologist-botanist-geologist combined. The same confusion is apparent in general books on 'natural history' published at the middle of the century, some of which contain sections on botany and geology, and some of which do not.

At this juncture, a new element entered with the arrival of 'biology'. The word had been used on the Continent for half a century, but in 1862 it was still apparently new to English readers, since we find G.H. Lewes in his *Studies of Animal Life* explaining: 'The needful term Biology (from *bios*, life, and *logos*, discourse) is now becoming generally adopted in England, as in Germany. It embraces all the separate sciences of Botany, Zoology, Comparative Anatomy, and Physiology.'[1] The word had obvious conveniences, being shorter and more flexible than natural history, and by 1889 the President of the British Association was telling his listeners that 'The happy introduction and general acceptance of the word "biology" … [have] practically eliminated the now vague and indefinite term "natural history" from scientific terminology.'[2] This was in many ways a pity; first, because it marked the final separation of geology from its erstwhile siblings; and second, because it marked, in practice, a caste division between the professional and amateur. By the end of the century, all professionals were calling themselves 'biologists', and 'naturalist' was becoming the hallmark of the sort of sentimental amateur who referred to birds as his feathered friends.

However, in the period with which this book is mainly concerned, up to the 1860s, these invidious distinctions had not yet been invented and the naturalist might be anyone from Darwin down to the lowliest Sunday bug-hunter. In fact, as G.H. Lewes said, 'A naturalist may be anything, everything.'[3] Being an amateur was no disadvantage, or in any way less prestigious than being a professional – rather the reverse, since it meant one had more time to devote to research. Professional posts for naturalists were extremely rare, and such few as there were were ludicrously badly paid. The botanist in charge of the herbarium at Kew was paid less than the clerk who handled correspondence. Salaries for scientific posts were calculated on the basis that anyone holding them must be a gentleman and

'Holiday Time at the Zoo', 1872

therefore must have private means. Those scientists who did not have private means found it extremely difficult to earn a living. Edward Forbes, a brilliant marine zoologist who many people thought would have become a second Darwin had he lived (he died at the age of thirty-nine) had to support himself by taking two uncongenial jobs simultaneously – Professor of Botany at King's College, for which he was paid less than £100 p.a. and Curator to the Geological Society of London, for which he was paid £150. 'People without independence have no business to meddle with science,' he concluded.[4]

Much the same difficulties beset Thomas Henry Huxley in his youth. In order

Thomas Henry Huxley, 1857

to go on the *Rattlesnake* voyage – his personal Voyage of the *Beagle* – he had to join the Navy as an assistant surgeon. When he returned, loaded with scientific honours, he was still unable to get a job, and wrote despondently to his sister, 'There is no chance of living by science. I have been loth to believe it but it is so.'[5] The situation was acute because in the course of the *Rattlesnake* voyage he had become engaged to a girl in Australia, and it would be six years before he could afford to bring her to England and marry her. He warned her gloomily that Richard Owen, the leading comparative anatomist of the day, earned just £300 a year 'which is less than the salary of many a bank clerk'.[6] Owen himself trumpeted his financial woes to anyone who would listen, and Macaulay wrote to Lord Lansdowne on his behalf:

> A poet, a novelist, an historian, a painter, a sculptor, who stood in his own line as high as Owen stands among men of science, could never be in want except by his own fault. But the greatest natural philosopher may starve while his countrymen are boasting of his discoveries, and while foreign Academies are begging for the honour of being allowed to add his name to their list.[7]

All this was true. It was still true in the 1890s when Sir William Henry Flower claimed that natural history was 'about the worst paid and least appreciated of all professions.'[8]

The trouble arose from the fact that natural history was not part of any university degree course. A few universities had professors or readers in natural history, but as they were not equipped with facilities, staff or students, their role was mainly decorative. One zoologist reported that in Cambridge, in the 1840s, 'Natural history is discouraged as much as possible, and regarded as idle trifling.'[9] King's College, London, sacked its Professor of Natural History in 1834 because no students had ever been known to attend his lectures. American universities were slightly more willing to appoint natural history professors, but only if they could turn their hands to teaching a gamut of other subjects as well. Constantine Rafinesque, at the University of Transylvania, had the compendious title of 'Professor of Natural History and Modern Languages', and Spencer Fullerton Baird, at Dickinson, was expected to teach 'Animal Physiology, Natural Theology and Mathematics', all for a paltry $400.

In any case, whether natural history appeared on a university's prospectus or not, there was no way that students could graduate in it, or even earn credit for having studied it. It was always the most optional of options, the most extraneous of extras. The only degree course remotely applicable to the naturalist's needs was medicine, which at least offered a grounding in comparative anatomy and physiology, and also in botany, which had remained in the syllabus ever since the days of herbalism. Darwin, Owen, Huxley and many other naturalists started their careers at medical school, but it needed a strong stomach to study medicine when operations were performed without anaesthetics, and when the bodies used for dissection were frequently putrid, and stolen from the grave. Darwin dropped out after seeing just two operations. In many ways it was easier to study divinity, and become a clergyman, which gave one an assured income and ample leisure time. (Darwin considered this possibility, but decided that his atheism was a drawback.) It is striking how many of the leading naturalists of the period *were* clergymen – Henslow the botanist, Kirby the entomologist, Landsborough the algologist, Buckland, Conybeare and Sedgwick the geologists – and at least one of them, the Rev. J.G. Wood, had no parish or parishioners to distract him from his relentless outpouring of natural history textbooks.

However, the fact that there was no such thing as a 'qualified' naturalist was in many ways an advantage, since it meant that anyone could become a naturalist at any time, whatever his age or educational background. Several people received the call to natural history late in life. Audubon was thirty-five before he realized that he was far more interested in drawing birds than in trying to run his various hopeless business ventures, and he was forty-two by the time his first plates were printed. Margaret Gatty, a Yorkshire clergyman's wife, was thirty-nine and recovering from the birth of her seventh child when she suddenly decided to become an algologist and write a history of British seaweeds, which she forthwith did. Sir Roderick Murchison (see chapter 13) had devoted his entire life to fox-hunting and pheasant-shooting until one day, out in the shooting butts, he received his Saul-like conversion to geology. All one had to do, to become a naturalist, was to say that one wanted to be one, and set about reading the subject up. It was obviously an advantage to join a few learned societies, such as the Linnean or the Zoological, but this was largely a matter of finding the requisite subscription.

Charles Kingsley, in *Glaucus*, lists 'the qualifications required for a perfect naturalist' and they make a rather daunting array. 'Our perfect naturalist,' he maintains, 'should be strong in body; able to haul a dredge, climb a rock, turn a boulder, walk all day, uncertain where he shall eat or rest; ready to face sun and rain, wind and frost, and to eat or drink thankfully anything, however coarse or meagre; he should know how to swim for his life, to pull an oar, sail a boat, and ride the first horse which comes to hand; and, finally, he should be a thoroughly good shot, and a skilful fisherman; and if he go far abroad, be able on occasion to fight for his life.'[10] Obviously Kingsley's perfect naturalist could not be a woman, but other than that he might be almost anyone, since there is nothing about money or training or even literacy to deter any aspirants.

He might even, *mirabile dictu*, be a member of the working class. Admittedly, with an average working week of sixty, seventy, or even eighty hours, plus the appalling Sabbath which had to be passed in chapel, it was hard for any working man to find the time to study anything, but a surprisingly large number managed it. Spitalfields weavers were traditionally famous for their addiction to botany and lepidoptery, and many Lancashire textile workers later followed the same path. George Crabbe's poem *The Borough* includes an account of the

... humble tradesmen in their evening glee
When of some pleasing fancied good possest,
Each grew alert, was busy, and was blest;
Whether the call-bird yield the hour's delight,
Or, magnified in microscope, the mite.[11]

Mrs Gaskell's *Mary Barton* includes a plausible portrait of the working-class naturalist in Job Legh, and Charles Kingsley, in *Glaucus*, presents a type which he obviously felt would be familiar to his readers: 'your douce and portly head-clerk ... your very best man of business', who spends his nights in Epping Forest sugaring the trees for moths, which he preserves in cabinets in his Islington home.[12]

A handful of working-class naturalists even achieved fame in their chosen fields. The most successful by far was Hugh Miller, the Scottish stone-mason who became a best-selling geological writer (see chapter 16), but there were others who contributed almost as much to science, if not to literature. Robert Dick, for instance, the Thurso baker, was an expert on the botany and geology of his neighbourhood, and no geological tour of Scotland was considered complete without a visit to his bakery, where he sketched out the leading formations in flour on his baking-board. Then there was Charles Peach, the 'self-taught naturalist of Cornwall', who regularly delivered important papers on the British zoophytes at the British Association's annual meetings. (The British Association, incidentally, was the usual showcase for these self-taught naturalists. It was open to all comers and prided itself on its democratic spirit.) *Chambers's Edinburgh Journal* devoted a glutinous eulogy to Peach's appearance at the 1844 meeting:

But who is that little intelligent looking man in a faded naval uniform, who is so invariably to be seen in a particular central seat in this section? That, gentle reader, is perhaps one of the most interesting men who attend the British Association. He is only a private in the mounted guard (preventive service) at an obscure part of the Cornwall coast, with four shillings a-day, and a wife, and nine children, most of whose education he has himself to conduct. He never tastes the luxuries which are so common in the middle ranks of life, and even amongst a large portion of the working-classes. He has to mend with his own hands every sort of thing that can break or wear in his house. Yet Mr. Peach is a votary of Natural History; not a student of the science in books, for he cannot afford books; but an investigator by sea and shore, a collector of zoophytes and echinodermata, strange creatures many of which are as yet hardly known to man. These he collects, preserves and describes; and every year does he come up to the British Association with a few novelties of this kind, accompanied by illustrative papers and drawings ... Honest Peach! humble as is thy home, and simple thy bearing, thou art an honour even to this assemblage of nobles and doctors; nay, more, when we consider everything, thou art an honour to human nature itself; for where is the heroism like that of virtuous, intelligent, independent poverty? And such heroism is thine![13]

The same sort of patronizing praise was heaped on another working-class naturalist, Thomas Edward of Banff, who was the subject of a biography by Samuel Smiles, intended to illustrate the virtues of self-help. Edward was a poorly paid Scottish shoemaker whose formal schooling ended when he was six. He worked every day from 6 a.m. to 9 p.m. and spent all of Sunday at prayer, so that his natural history excursions had to be made at night. He would collect as many specimens as he could before dark, and then sleep on the spot in order to collect a few more at dawn. He kept his specimens in his hat and his hat on his head,

Thomas Edward, 1876

and once had the nasty experience of being woken by weasels climbing over his face to steal his treasured trophies. He was far too poor to buy books on natural history but, through the help of a local minister, made contact with other naturalists up and down the country who named his specimens for him, and eventually he became sufficiently well-known to contribute occasional (unpaid) articles to the *Naturalist* and *Zoologist* magazines. Later, when he was too ill to go on night-time rambles, he would send various of his eleven children to collect the debris from fishing-boats, which he searched for marine fauna, and one of his married daughters 'sent home her collection of fish stomachs twice a week by carrier.'[14] Some of his best finds were made in the stomach of cod and haddock. He lived to enjoy the naturalist's consummation of having a species named after him – *Couchia edwardii*, a tiny midge fish. Unfortunately, despite all his obvious worthiness, recounted at such tedious length in Smiles's hagiography, he seems to have been a most repellent man – grim, joyless, and given to endless diatribes against the people he felt should have helped him and didn't. His most bitter vituperations were reserved for members of his own class, and he once wrote an apoplectic letter to the *Banffshire Journal* about the obstinate refusal of 'gamekeepers, gardeners, and farm-servants' to learn the rudiments of natural history: 'I maintain that none have it so well in their power to become acquainted with the works of nature, and to add to our knowledge in that respect, as they have, if they but *would*; and yet they are about as ignorant on the subject, if not more so, than those whose occupations confine them in the house from morning till evening ... And why? Why just because they *will* not.'[15]

Actually, Edward was not the only writer to complain about the apparently wilful ignorance of the rural working classes. They persisted in believing that hedgehogs sucked milk from cows and that toads were poisonous long after most town-dwellers had learned to discount these myths. Their most damaging belief was that almost every living bird and beast constituted 'vermin' and should be killed accordingly. The Rev. Houghton, in his *Country Walks of a Naturalist with his Children*, recounts a conversation he had with a mole-catcher which must have been equally irritating for both participants:

'Good morning, Mr. Mole-catcher ... Do you know what moles eat?'
'Well, sir, I believes they eats worms.'
'Yes, they feed principally on worms, but they also devour wireworms and other creatures which prey upon the farmer's crops. I think moles do more good than harm, and I have examined the stomachs of many, and I am of opinion that it is a mistake to kill them.'
'Lor, sir, you be's a gemman that has seen the inside of a mole's stomach, has you? You may be a cliver sort of a mon, but moles be varmint.'[16]

Obviously, it was important to teach the working classes natural history in order to stop them killing everything in sight, but there was another motive behind the middle-class eagerness to ram natural history down working-class throats. It was a form not only of rational but, more importantly, of *innocent* amusement. It was better for the working-classes to spend their spare time chasing butterflies, than drinking or fighting or gambling or whatever other iniquities they usually got up to. Thomas Edward's patron, the Rev. Mr Boyd, inserted a notice in the

Fraserburgh Advertiser about Thomas Edward's manifold virtues and followed it with the observation:

> Happy would it be, if our tradesmen were to take a leaf out of Mr. Edward's book, and instead of wasting their time, squandering their means, and embittering their existence in the haunts of dissipation, they would sally forth in these calm summer evenings to rural scenes and sylvan solitudes, to woo Nature in her mildest aspect.[17]

Hugh Miller, another dour Scot, but marginally less so than the envenomed Edward, begins his most successful book, *The Old Red Sandstone*, by exhorting working-class readers to follow in his own footsteps, and, in doing so, mentions an idea which may have been at the back of many middle-class minds:

> My advice to young working men desirous of bettering their circumstances, and adding to the amount of their enjoyment is a very simple one. Do not seek happiness in what is misnamed pleasure; seek it rather in what is termed study. Keep your consciences clear, your curiosity fresh, and embrace every opportunity of cultivating your minds. You will gain nothing by attending Chartist meetings. The fellows who speak nonsense with fluency at these assemblies, and deem their nonsense eloquence, are totally unable to help either you or themselves; or, if they do succeed in helping themselves, it will be at your expense. Leave them to harangue unheeded, and set yourselves to occupy your leisure hours in making yourselves wiser men.[18]

No middle-class writer could have put the argument better, but the fact that it came from a man who had spent most of his life as a stone-mason, made it better still. No wonder Hugh Miller was embraced so warmly to the middle-class bosom. No wonder his words were quoted, and his example cited, in every Mechanics' Institute up and down the country. He was the perfect example of the working man made good; one who, by diligent study, temperate habits, and avoiding the snares of Chartism, had risen from lowly origins to become a respected naturalist and author. Why couldn't every working man do the same?

And indeed, by Victorian standards, natural history was an unusually classless pursuit. As William Swainson wrote: 'Natural history has this peculiar advantage – that it can be prosecuted, in one shape or other, by almost every body and under every ordinary circumstance. Of all sciences, it is that which requires, in most of its departments, the fewest materials. It is as much within reach of the cottager as of the professor.'[19] This was broadly true. Most of the naturalist's equipment – nets, jars, pins, collecting boxes – could be assembled by anyone, and even a microscope only cost two or three guineas. The material for study lay freely strewn around the countryside, and access to the countryside was then much easier than it is today. Two hours' walking would bring one into fields, even from the

The Penny Magazine of the Society for the Diffusion of Useful Knowledge

largest cities, and when, towards the end of the century, the cities began to sprawl, the railways provided an enviably cheap and efficient means of escape. Admittedly, the major learned societies were too expensive for working men to join, and many of the metropolitan museums and libraries were shut in the only hours they could use them – deliberately so, in the case of the British Museum – but many provincial museums went out of their way to encourage working-class visitors by opening in the evening or at weekends. William Swainson reported how he had seen three members of the 'operative class' studying the displays in the Manchester Natural History Museum, and how, 'The superior tone and manners of these humble admirers of nature are very striking, and at once show the effect of such tastes upon the inward man.'[20] The Society for Promoting Christian Knowledge and the Society for the Diffusion of Useful Knowledge published many cheap natural history handbooks, and the Mechanics' Institutes and public libraries gave access to more expensive publications. Moreover, the general middle-class approbation for this type of innocent amusement meant that any working man who *did* take up the study of natural history could be sure of encouragement from all the local do-gooders.

Some branches of natural history were, of course, more classless than others. Entomology was genuinely so, because the specimens involved were small enough to find a place in even the most crowded working-class home. It could be prosecuted as well in town as in the country, and it required the bare minimum of equipment. The Entomological Society was well-known for its democratic constitution and low subscription, and, as the editor of the *Entomologist's Annual* remarked, 'Entomologists are not drawn from the wealthy, but rather from the working classes ... An Entomologist is none the less one because he wears fustian, and "labours, working with his hands" ... An observation, if new, is as important by whomsoever made; and a Spitalfields weaver may supply some important gap in our knowledge, which Oxford and Cambridge put together would fail to elucidate.'[21] Ornithology, by contrast, tended to be an aristocratic affair, best pursued by country gentlemen on their own estates. If one wanted to collect birds, or even identify them with certainty, one needed to own a gun and the right to carry it. Marine zoology was obviously confined to those people who lived by the sea, like Mr Charles Peach, and to the middle classes on their annual holidays. Botany tended to be the preserve of ladies and clergymen, because there was no cruelty involved – insects did struggle so gruesomely on the pin, as one lady natural history writer remarked. But these divisions were dictated more by personal choice and by geographical considerations than by any deliberate exclusivity, and in theory it was possible for a working man to take up any branch of natural history he fancied. E.P. Thomson was probably right when he claimed that 'There is a kind of freemasonry in the study or pursuit of natural history.'[22] Naturalists were fond of referring to themselves as 'brothers' – brothers of the net, brothers of the hammer, brothers of the dredge – and were prepared to sink class differences for the sake of their shared enthusiasm.

One of the most useful ways in which the freemasonry operated was the system of correspondence and exchange of specimens between naturalists, helped by the advent of the penny post. In those far-off days it was possible to send a batch of live sea-anemones or snails from one end of Britain to the other by post, and often to receive a reply, or even a return batch, the same day. G.H. Lewes warned that you should not send sea-anemones in a cardboard box, because when he did so and marked it WITH CARE: LIVE ANIMALS! the post-office clerk stamped the box so vigorously that it and its contents were entirely squashed; but this problem could be obviated by the use of tins.[23] Frank Buckland told an amusing anecdote of how he had once sent a bear's foot to a friend as a Christmas present. The friend didn't like the look of it, so forwarded it on to another friend, but without a covering letter. This recipient decided that the now putrefying paw must be 'the foot of some savage' and sent it to an eminent anthropologist. The anthropologist's wife opened the package and immediately summoned the local policeman

'Travellers from Foreign Climes', 1884

who declared that it was indeed a man's foot and that 'he knew the man who had lost it.'[24] Scandals were only averted by the belated arrival of the covering letter. No doubt the police and post office found this sort of traffic undesirable, but it was a great boon to amateur naturalists, expecially those who, by reasons of class or geography, had limited access to museums.

In general, any naturalist, whatever his background, could write to any other naturalist who shared his speciality, without any formal letter of introduction, and be fairly sure of a reply. The usual way of finding a suitable correspondent, with whom to exchange information and specimens, was through the popular natural history magazines. The *Entomologist's Annual*, for instance, carried a regular list of entomologists who were open to correspondence, including some marked with an asterisk who were 'willing to assist young beginners, with specimens or information'. Many of the names listed were quite eminent ones – J.E. Gray, head of Zoology at the British Museum; the Rev. F.O. Morris, author of innumerable popular handbooks; Kirby and Spence, co-authors of the standard *British Entomology*; and H.T. Stainton, the editor of the *Annual*, who advertised himself as being 'At Home to Entomologists every Wednesday Evening after 6 p.m.' In an 'Address to Young Entomologists', Stainton went further and claimed that 'if any young collector (not under fourteen years of age) were to write to me for information, I should be more pleased at receiving his enquiry than he would be at obtaining my answer, and let him not imagine that I am a sedate elderly person with no fellow feeling for a mischievous school boy; I have no sedateness about me, and am as full of fun as anyone.'[25] He advised his young tyros to begin their letters 'Dear Sir', which 'is the *etiquette* among Naturalists', rather than 'Sir', which 'would be considered very stiff and formal',[26] and he warned that exchanges of specimens should not be considered in the light of barter, which would turn the correspondents into 'hucksters and petty tradesmen',[27] but rather in the light of gifts. And indeed, this was the usual practice among naturalists. If they acquired duplicates of specimens which they already had in their collections, they sent them off to whoever might need them, and would probably, but not necessarily, be sent something in return. They preferred to correspond with people living a long way away because they would be able to obtain specimens they could not obtain themselves. Of course, the informal correspondence system could be abused. Anyone who was rash enough to write to Darwin was liable to find himself counting pigeon's feathers for the rest of his life, and when Audubon casually asked Swainson if there was anything he could do for him in America, Swainson replied immediately: 'You asked me what you can do for me in America. I will tell you. Send me a cart load of shells from the Ohio, or from any of the *Rivers near New Orleans*. The *very smallest*, as well as the *very* largest – *all sizes*.'[28] But most naturalists were less demanding, and simply enjoyed sharing their enthusiasms with a like-minded correspondent. The fact that they often did not ever meet their correspondents made it easier to ignore class differences.

However, though the great brotherhood of naturalists was not divided by class or by any amateur-versus-professional distinction, it *was* riven by another great divide across which the two opposing camps regarded each other with little short of hatred. This was the division between field and closet naturalists. Field naturalists, as one might expect, were those who studied living organisms in their natural environments. Closet naturalists studied and dissected dead organisms within the confines of the museum or 'closet'. Their consuming obsession was the naming and classification of species – an obsession so central to pre-Darwinian natural history that it will be discussed more fully in another chapter. Closet men relied on field men to bring them new species for analysis, but beyond that there was almost no contact between the two groups. Broadly speaking, the field belonged to the amateur, and the closet to the professional. Closet naturalists held all the top scientific posts and dominated the learned societies and journals. They rarely even bothered to read accounts of field studies, and were sometimes unable to recognize living animals when they saw them. Joseph Wolf, the zoological illustrator, remarked that closet ornithologists rarely knew the colour of a bird's eyes because they were only used to dealing in skins, and T.H. Huxley damned them all as 'spider-stuffers and hay botanists'.[29] Field naturalists, on the other hand, carried a far more potent appeal to the general public who, not surprisingly, preferred reading the biographies of living animals to bone-by-bone dissections of dead ones. In consequence, the popular books and magazines of the period were almost the only available repository for field-notes and observations, which were studiously ignored by the learned journals.

This total divorce between field and closet research was obviously detrimental to both. There was no point in being a brilliant field observer like, say, Charles Waterton, if no one could ever be quite sure what species you were observing. Waterton's *Wanderings in South America* is full of careful, vivid descriptions of the call notes and flight characteristics of various jungle birds, but as the birds are given only local names, they can never be identified with certainty. Conversely, a simple lack of real-life knowledge often led the closet naturalists into absurd mistakes. There was, for instance, the famous case of the legless Birds of Paradise which arose because all the first Birds of Paradise sent to England had their legs cut off to facilitate packing. Leglessness thereupon became enshrined as a characteristic of the species, and popular writers went into rhapsodies at the thought of the little creatures spending all their lives in the air. Only the eventual arrival of a Bird of Paradise complete with legs put paid to these ethereal fantasies. As late as the 1870s, John Edward Gray, Keeper of Zoology at the British Museum, perpetrated a similar gaffe when he attacked a book on Indian fauna, published by naturalists attached to the Indian service, because it depicted a certain species of mud-turtle without any holes in its flippers. He had examined many museum specimens of the turtle and knew that it always had a hole between the second and third digits and it was, he maintained, negligent of the illustrator not to have noticed this. Whereupon the authors, field naturalists all, replied icily and publicly that, as everyone in India knew, the holes were made by the fishermen who caught the turtles tying their flippers together to prevent them escaping. But obviously a closet man could not be expected to know this.[30]

Closet naturalists rarely bothered to bestow any notice at all on field naturalists, but field naturalists were constantly inveighing against the tyranny of the closet. Philip Gosse, for instance, begins his *A Naturalist's Sojourn in Jamaica* (1851) with a passionate denunciation of the closet approach:

Natural History is far too much a science of dead things; a *necrology*. It is mainly conversant with dry skins furred or feathered, blackened, shrivelled, and hay-stuffed; with objects, some admirably beautiful, some hideously ugly, impaled on pins, and arranged in rows in cork drawers; with uncouth forms, disgusting to sight and smell, bleached and shrunken, suspended by threads and immersed in spirit (in defiance of the aphorism that 'he who is born to be hanged will never be drowned') in glass bottles. These distorted things are described; their scales, plates, feathers counted; their forms copied, all shrivelled and stiffened as they are; their colours, changed and modified by death or partial decay, carefully set down; their limbs, members, and organs measured, and the results recorded in thousandths of an inch; two names are given to every one; the whole is enveloped in a mystic cloud of Graeco-Latino-English phraseology (often barbaric enough); – and this is Natural History![31]

Time and again, popular writers pleaded for more attention to field studies. The Rev. J.G. Wood wrote in his *Common Objects of the Country*, 'It is impossible to form an idea of the real beauty of animal life, without seeing it displayed in a free and unconstrained state; and more real knowledge of natural history will be gained in a single summer spent in personal examination, than by years of book study.'[32] But such pleas were vitiated by the fact that they *only* occurred in books written for the general public, which the closet experts never read. And when the Rev. J.G. Wood went on to say in the next sentence that, in field study, 'The characteristics of creatures come out so strongly; they have such quaint comical little ways with them; such assumptions of dignity and sudden lowering of the same; such clever little cheateries; such funny flirtations and coquetries, that I have many a time forgotten myself, and burst into a laugh that scattered my little friends for the next half-hour,' one can hardly blame the closet man for curling his lip.

The only model to whom field naturalists could turn for inspiration in the early decades of the nineteenth century was Gilbert White, the Hampshire clergyman whose *Natural History of Selborne* was published in 1789. White described himself accurately as an '*out-door naturalist*, one that takes his observations from the subject itself, and not from the writings of others',[33] and he had a hard word to say for 'Faunists' who were 'too apt to acquiesce in bare descriptions, and a few synonyms.'[34] White had no scientific training; he was born and died in Selborne and never travelled further afield than Derbyshire; he had no naturalist friends in his immediate neighbourhood to encourage his interests; and he seems to have had only occasional access to learned publications. Yet his field observations were so accurate as to gain universal respect, and even closet men acknowledged his achievements.

He was the first person to differentiate between the three species of 'willow wren' (the willow warbler, wood warbler and chiff-chaff); the first to describe the British harvest mouse and its nest; the first to observe that swifts copulate on the wing, that earthworms are hermaphrodite, and that male and female chaffinches form separate flocks in winter. He examined many birds' crops and droppings to discover their diet; he noted that owls hoot in B flat and cuckoos mainly in D; he

Gilbert White

shouted at bees through a loud-hailer to test their sense of hearing. He had a fine eye for ecological detail. He described how men riding over close turf are often followed by parties of swallows which seize the small insects thrown up by the horses' hooves; and how cattle, standing in a pond during hot weather, drop dung which nurtures insects 'and so supply food for the fish, which would be poorly subsisted but for this contingency.'[35]

His mistakes were few. The most notorious was his often-quoted suggestion that swallows hibernate, possibly underwater, but, to be fair, he never stated this as a certainty. Indeed, his great virtue as a field observer was that he always distinguished carefully between things he had observed for himself and was sure of, and things he had merely inferred or read about (such as that tortoises spend a month in one act of copulation). When he did speak from personal observation, he was confident, because he knew his observation was thorough. Apropos his notes on bird-song, he explained: 'For many months I carried a list in my pocket of the birds that were to be remarked, and, as I rode or walked about my business, I noted each day the continuance or omission of each bird's song; so that I am as sure of the certainty of my facts as a man can be of any transaction whatsoever.'[36] Once and once only did his correspondent Thomas Pennant catch him out in an unverified statement, and then he was quick to acknowledge his error:

> You put a very shrewd question when you ask me how I know that their [the ring-ousels'] autumnal migration is southwards? Was not candour and openness the very life of natural history, I should pass over this query just as a sly commentator does over a crabbed passage in a classic; but common ingenuousness obliges me to confess, not without some degree of shame, that I only reasoned in that case from analogy. For as all other autumnal birds migrate from the northwards to us ... so I concluded that the ring-ousels did the same.'[37]

White described his aim in *Selborne* as 'an humble attempt to promote a more minute inquiry into natural history; into the life and conversation of animals',[38] and in that he succeeded. But although almost all Victorian naturalists professed to admire Gilbert White, remarkably few succeeded in emulating him. One who did was J.L. Knapp, whose *Journal of a Naturalist* (1830) sets out to describe his own Gloucestershire parish in the same way as White described Selborne. But throughout the book, on almost every page, Knapp finds it necessary to apologize for the dullness and insignificance of the observations he is making, and in his very last paragraph he remarks that the reader 'will probably be surprised that I could take the trouble to register such accounts of such things; and I might think so too, did I not know how much occupation and healthful recreation the seeking out these trifles has afforded me.'[39] In other words, though White himself was respected, the sort of facts he collected were still regarded as 'trifles', and the idea that field observations might actually be important to science seems not to have occurred to anyone.

The reason for the low status of field studies is not far to seek. Even the most ardent fact-collectors have to feel that their facts bear relevance to *some* larger theory or scheme of things, and until the advent of Darwinism, there was no theory to which field studies were relevant. The whole effort of biological enquiry in the first half of the nineteenth century was directed to naming, identifying and classifying species, which was strictly closet work. Living animals and plants merely confused the issue, and although many amateurs and popular writers like Knapp continued to observe them for their own pleasure, and as the basis for entertaining books directed to the general public, there was a widespread tacit acquiescence in the view that this did not represent 'real' science. Although Gilbert White was undoubtedly an important influence in making natural history a popular subject, the other and far more important influence was Linnaeus. And it was Linnaeus, rather than White, who set the pattern that natural history was to take for the entire first half of the nineteenth century.

PART TWO
THE SCIENTIFIC
BACKGROUND

CHAPTER THREE
'THE MOST SYSTEMATICAL GENIUS'

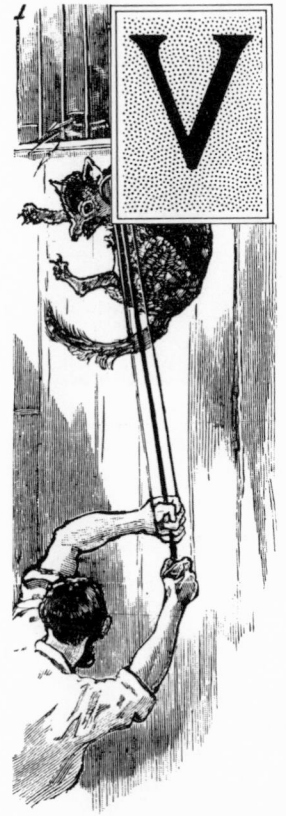

ICTORIAN NATURALISTS BELIEVED that they were living in a golden age, and they dated the dawning of that golden age from the work of Linnaeus in the mid-eighteenth century. W.H. Harvey wrote in his *Sea-Side Book* of 1849,

> It is scarcely more than a century since the several sciences to which we apply the general name of Natural History, began to rouse themselves from a sleep into which they had fallen nearly two thousand years before ... and, instead of the somnambulism of the preceding ages, naturalists, like men newly risen, went forth in their morning strength and ardour to the labour of the day ... The writings of LINNAEUS, composed in a clear and elegant style and offering a systematic arrangement such as all could readily understand, contributed more than those of any other naturalist to the spread of a taste for his favourite science. He was eminently a popular writer ...[1]

Similar tributes to Linnaeus's influence can be found in all the more thoughtful Victorian natural history books. It was an influence that survived undimmed until the advent of Darwinism a full century later, and it was entirely thanks to Linnaeus that natural history was able to enjoy the sunshine of popular favour in the early decades of the nineteenth century. He therefore belongs in this book, although he lived and died in the eighteenth century.

Linnaeus's biography can be quickly disposed of. He was a Swede, born in 1707, the son of a pastor. After medical training and a journey of exploration to Lapland in 1732, he established himself as a serious botanist during visits to Germany, Holland, England and France in the 1730s. In 1741 he was appointed Professor of Medicine and Botany at the University of Uppsala, remaining there until his death in 1778. His most important works are the *Systema Naturae* of 1735, the *Fundamenta Botanica* of 1736, the *Philosophia Botanica* of 1751 and the *Species*

Linnaeus, aged twenty-five, in Lapland dress   Title-page of Linnaeus's *Flora Lapponica*

Plantarum of 1753. D.H. Stoever, his first biographer, called him 'the most *systematical* genius of the age, the most intimate and scrutinizing minion that ever graced the bosom of Nature.'[2]

Linnaeus's enormous and essential contribution to natural history was that he devised a system of classification whereby any plant or animal could be identified and slotted into an overall plan. In the course of expounding his system he also, almost casually, introduced a method of naming species which is still used today. These two innovations may sound unexciting until we try to imagine a scientific world without these fundamental tools. Even such an apparently unambiguous name as robin means quite different things to Americans and Englishmen (*Turdus migratorius* and *Erithacus rubecula* respectively) and of course it means nothing at all to a non-English-speaker. It is obviously crucial that every species should have a name which is the same in all languages and which designates that species and no other. Similarly, it is important to have a universally understood classification, so that when a zoologist wants to discuss, say, the marsupialia, he may do so without having to list every marsupial species individually, and assume that other zoologists will know which animals he refers to. This is only one of the virtues of a classification system – others are information retrieval, predictive value and meaning by association – but it is already clear that it is indispensable.

Indeed, we have only to look at pre-Linnaean natural history books to see the sort of quagmire that lack of a system led to. Thomas Moufet, embarking on a description of grasshoppers and locusts in his *Theatre of Insects*, *c*. 1590, began: 'Some are green, some black, some blue. Some fly with one pair of wings, others with more; those that have no wings they leap, those that cannot either fly or leap, they walk; some have longer shanks, some shorter. Some there are that sing, others are silent. And as there are many kinds of them in nature, so their names were almost infinite, which through the neglect of Naturalists are grown out of use.'[3] Moufet is clearly lost amid the bewildering diversity of nature. Should he sort his locusts according to their colour, their wings, their legs, or their singing capacity? Or should he – as in fact he later does – follow such delusive lights as their relative commonness or rarity, or their size? What Moufet and all the pre-Linnaean naturalists lacked was a plan into which to fit the 'many kinds' occurring in Nature, and some names which other naturalists would understand.

Let us take the names first, although this was a mere by-product of Linnaeus's larger purpose. Linnaeus was the first person to give each species a name consisting of two Latin words. The first defined the genus, and was common to every species within that genus; the second, or 'trivial', name defined the species. Thus our familiar coal-tit is named *Parus ater*, our great tit *Parus major* and our blue tit *Parus caeruleus*, and those specific names will serve to designate the birds to any ornithologist in the world. In using Latin, Linnaeus was simply following the custom of the times (he would have made little impact on the world if he had written in his native Swedish), but in reducing the specific name to two words he made an invaluable break with the past. Previous naturalists (and Linnaeus himself when young) had tried to give specific names which incorporated all the distinguishing features of that species. The humble milfoil, for instance, laboured under the designation *Achillea foliis duplicato-pinnatis glabris, laciniis linearibus acute laciniatis*, which no one could hope to remember. Often these names had to be revised and expanded when similar related species came to light, and anyway they quite commonly differed from author to author. The shell now universally known as *Strombus gigas* L. (the L. standing for Linnaeus) passed under such earlier aliases as *Murice Orecchiuto per il gran labbro che sporge* (Buonanni), *Buccinum ampullaceum striatum, clavicula miricata, apertura leviter purpurascente* (Lister) and Marbled Jamaica Murex with Knotty Twirls (Petiver).[4]

Linnaeus's simple masterstroke was to separate the designatory and descriptive functions. The species was designated by its two-word name; this was then followed by a description which made it clear what species the name referred to. It was largely due to the excellence and precision of Linnaeus's descriptions, whose formal arrangement is still broadly followed today, that his names won such universal acceptance. The two books in which he first used binomial nomenclature consistently were the *Species Plantarum* of 1753 and the tenth edition of the *Systema Naturae* of 1758; these two works are now accepted, by international convention, as the respective starting-points for modern botanical and zoological nomenclatures. All previous names (including those used by Linnaeus himself in earlier works) are dismissed as 'pre-Linnaean' and have no status in modern scientific literature.

Yet the invention of binomial nomenclature, vital as it has come to seem, was trivial by comparison with Linnaeus's main achievement: that of devising a classificatory system for the whole natural world. Of course there had been systems before, starting with Aristotle's, and some of them were probably as good as Linnaeus's, but none of them was as fully worked out, as widely applicable, or as easy to use. Linnaeus began by dividing each natural kingdom (animal, vegetable and mineral) into classes, then subdivided these into orders, the orders into genera and finally genera into species. This hierarchy is still followed today, though with certain additions, such as phylum, family and sub-species.

Linnaeus's zoological classification, first expressed in the *Systema Naturae* of 1735 and fully and finally expressed in the tenth edition of the same book (the former is only fourteen pages, the latter over two thousand pages long), began by dividing animals into six classes: mammals, birds, amphibia, fish, insects and 'worms'. The worms were a hopeless ragbag of assorted invertebrates which had to be totally reorganized by later writers, and his birds and amphibia were awkwardly arranged, but the mammals, defined according to teeth and teats rather than feet, were a vast improvement on the older class of 'quadrupeds' and now gathered in the whales which had previously been classed with fish. (Dr Johnson, incidentally, defined the fish in his dictionary as 'an animal that inhabits the water' – which would include not only whales, but also seals, turtles, shellfish, corals, and many other unfishlike oddments.) Linnaeus took the unusually daring step of placing man in the same genus as the orang-utan (*Homo sapiens* and *Homo troglodytes* respectively), thus earning a rebuke from the Swiss polymath von Haller which antedates the Darwinian controversy by more than a century: 'The unbounded dominion which Linnaeus has assumed in the animal kingdom must upon the whole be abhorrent to many ... He can hardly forbear to make *man a monkey* or *the monkey a man*.'[5]

Linnaeus's botanical classification was more thorough than his zoological, since he was primarily a botanist. For the *Species Plantarum* he examined almost seven thousand species. He divided all flowering plants into twenty-three classes based on their male organs, with a twenty-fourth class, the Cryptogamia, covering all plants which seemed to be flowerless, such as the mosses. These classes were then subdivided into orders based on the female organs. Thus a lily, having six stamens and one stigma, would be placed in the class Hexandria (six men), order Monogynia (one woman). It was such a simple system that anyone with the elementary knowledge to identify the sexual parts of a flower could easily find its place in the Linnaean scheme.

Two features of Linnaeus's botanical classification are important: first, that it was artificial, and second, that it was sexual. The definition of 'artificial' as opposed to 'natural' systems is something that sends modern taxonomists into frenzies of controversy but, broadly, an artificial system is one that classifies organisms according to one key attribute, whereas a natural classification tries to express the totality of resemblances. In the post-Darwinian era, a natural system is also one that reflects phylogeny, i.e. the evolutionary history of the organism, but of course this was not a consideration in Linnaeus's time. We are then forced to ask what *was* the point of a classification system to a pre-Darwinian? If it had no evolutionary rationale, surely it might as well be completely arbitrary – in fact, any arrangement that would suit man's convenience. But Linnaeus and his contemporaries did have a conception of a plan in Nature, based on Aristotelian and Thomist logic, which they strove to reflect in their classifications. All natural organisms formed a ladder, a *scala naturae* or 'great chain of being', grading from lower to higher organisms, with man, of course, at the summit. The appearance

Medallion of Linnaeus, from *Animal Life*

of living things suggested their 'essence' – the idea of the perfect or archetypical organisms that had been in God's mind when He created them. A species consisted of the genus or 'kind of' animal, plus its differentia – the features that made it different from other species within the same genus. In Linnaeus's time there was already some argument about whether the 'kinds' of animals mentioned in the Genesis account of the Creation were genera or species. If they were genera, it allowed one leeway to think in terms of evolution of species, but, at that period, the process was usually characterized as degeneration, i.e. a gradual deterioration of the organism from its perfect genus to the imperfect species, rather than evolution towards more perfect adaptation to environment. In any case, Linnaeus was not a subscriber to such arguments. He believed firmly in special creation and the fixity of species, as he states unequivocally at the beginning of the *Philosophia Botanica* of 1751: '*Species tot numeramus quot diversae formae in principio sunt creatae.*' (We enumerate as many species of diverse appearance as were created in the beginning.)

Linnaeus himself admitted that his botanical system was imperfect and would be improved by later workers – as indeed it was. And yet, despite its artificiality, it survived the advent of Darwinism surprisingly well. This was because the key feature that he chose as his classificatory tool – the reproductive organs – was in fact a fundamental one, and plants which resemble each other in the number and arrangement of their sexual parts do usually resemble each other in many other ways as well. Had he chosen, say, colour, size or habitat as his key, he would have arrived at a less 'natural' classification.

However, the decision to classify plants according to their sexual parts provoked considerable comment in his day. Professor Dillenius, the Oxford Professor of Botany, wrote to Linnaeus in 1837: 'I consider sexual differences altogether useless, superfluous, even misleading, for establishing the character of a plant. What is the point of it all? It is puerile; and it is quite enough that one botanist – Vaillant[6] – should have had his head turned by them.'[7] But Linnaeus clung to his sexual system and even, rather tactlessly, emphasized its metaphorical possibilities. Thus he glossed the Monandria as 'one husband in a marriage', the Diandria as 'Two husbands in the same marriage' and the exciting Polyandria as 'Twenty males or more in the same bed with the female.' He named the flowerless plants cryptogams or 'clandestine marriages'. In his first statement of the system, his undergraduate thesis *Praeludia Sponsaliarum Plantarum*, he made plant reproduction truly erotic:

> Words cannot express the joy that the sun brings to all living things ... Yes, Love comes even to the plants. Males and females, even the hermaphrodites, hold their nuptials (which is the subject that I now propose to discuss), showing by their sexual organs which are males, which females, which hermaphrodites ... The actual petals of a flower contribute nothing to generation, serving only as the bridal bed which the great Creator has so gloriously prepared,

'Elusive Bloom'

adorned with such precious bed-curtains, and perfumed with so many sweet scents in order that the bridegroom and bride may therein celebrate their nuptials with the greater solemnity. When the bed has thus been made ready, then is the time for the bridegroom to embrace his beloved bride and surrender himself to her.[8]

Erasmus Darwin, Charles's grandfather, was sufficiently moved to versify the Linnaean system in a long poem called *The Loves of the Plants* (1789), with a cast of youths, swains, knights, virgins and nymphs. Thus the Turmeric (Curcuma) with its one fertile and four sterile stamens, becomes:

> Woo'd with long care, Curcuma cold and shy
> Meets her fond husband with averted eye:
> *Four* beardless youths the obdurate beauty move
> With soft attentions of Platonic love.[9]

While the difficult truffle consummates her clandestine marriage with suitable vagueness:

> Deep in wide caverns and their shadowy aisles,
> Daughter of Earth, the chaste Truffelia smiles;
> On silvery beds, of soft asbestus wove,
> Meets her Gnome-husband, and avows her love.[10]

Naturally the prudes were not enchanted. Johann Siegesbeck, a St Petersburg academician, called Linnaeus's system 'loathsome harlotry' and laid down the law that, 'God never would, in the vegetable kingdom, have allowed such odious vice as that several males (anthers) should possess one wife (pistil) in common, or that a true husband should, in certain composite flowers, besides its legitimate partner, have near it illegitimate mistresses.'[11] (Linnaeus retaliated by giving the name *Siegesbeckia* to a particularly ugly, stinking weed.) The Rev. Samuel Goodenough, later Bishop of Carlisle, wrote to J.E. Smith, the founder of the English Linnean Society, in 1808: 'To tell you that nothing could equal the gross prurience of Linnaeus's mind is perfectly needless. A literal translation of the first principles of Linnaean botany is enough to shock female modesty. It is possible that many virtuous students might not be able to make out the similitude of *Clitoria*.'[12]

Linnaeus's graphic choice of names for shells also caused distress. The British conchologists W.G. Maton and T. Racket complained in the *Transactions* of the Linnean Society in 1804 that,

A few of these terms, however strongly they may be warranted by the similitudes and analogies which they express, and which when so pointed out are of great advantage to the language of science, are not altogether reconcilable with the delicacy proper to be observed in ordinary discourse; nor are they such, perhaps, as should be employed on any occasions, except those when their original signification is immediately implicated.[13]

Yet, despite all these delicate scruples, Linnaeus's system and nomenclature quickly triumphed over all their rivals, and won almost universal acceptance. They triumphed because they were extremely easy to use, and the fact that they were universally accepted made them even more useful, so that their pre-eminence increased with the passage of time. Naturalists no longer needed to go rummaging in countless old texts to discover all the synonyms for a given species; they could simply refer to Linnaeus. A species not given by Linnaeus could be assumed (though perhaps not always correctly) to be new. In effect, Linnaeus had gathered and collated the work of all previous naturalists, stripped it of its redundancies, renamed it, rearranged it, and presented it in a 'modern' form. Although many parts of his classification had to be revised and rearranged by subsequent naturalists, it continued to provide the framework into which new systems could be slotted. *Deus creavit, Linnaeus disposuit.*

The Linnaean system was particularly strongly embedded in British hearts as a result of an historical chance. After Linnaeus's death (in 1778), his widow wrote to Sir Joseph Banks offering his natural history books and collections for sale. Banks felt that his own collection was already overgrown, but he happened to have a wealthy young protégé, the 24-year-old James Edward Smith, at breakfast with him when he received Fru Linnaea's letter, and he urged Smith to buy the collections. This he did, for the paltry sum of 1,000 guineas, and the Linnaean collections arrived in England – pursued, so the story goes, by a Swedish warship – in 1784. They included about 19,000 sheets of pressed plants, 3,200 insects, 1,500 shells, 2,500 minerals, 2,500 books and about 3,000 letters and manuscripts. In 1788, to honour this material, Smith founded the Linnean Society of London,[14] and became its first President. The Society had as its aim 'the Cultivation of the Science of Natural History in all its branches and more especially of the Natural History of Great Britain and Ireland' and thus attracted all the leading British naturalists. On Smith's death in 1828, the Society acquired Linnaeus's collections as its own property, which they remain today.

By the beginning of the Victorian period, almost all of Linnaeus's zoological, and some parts of his botanical classification were considered by serious scientists to be out of date. Nevertheless they continued to be used by popular writers, for the sound reason that they were simpler than anyone else's, and more accessible to the layman. Linnaeus's own writings, being in Latin and unillustrated, were not designed for a popular audience, but within a few decades they had been translated into countless elementary handbooks which anyone could use. And ladies in particular found that, thanks to Linnaeus, they were now able to take up the study of botany, which had previously seemed so mysterious and difficult. Miss Brightwell of Norwich recorded in her *Life of Linnaeus* of 1858: 'The study of botany was so greatly promoted and facilitated by the easy and pleasant method introduced by Linnaeus, that it is no wonder the ladies acknowledged with gratitude their obligation to the naturalist who first originated a method by which this delightful study could be brought within the attainment of all who loved it.'[15] Linnaeus himself became the subject of numerous sentimental biographies, and even had the doubtful honour of being versified by Mrs Hemans.

When we remember the terrible fears aroused by the 'gross prurience' of Linnaeus's language, and his emphasis on plant sexuality, it is ironic to find him thus cosily enshrined in the female bosom. Even more so, to find him presented to children, but so he was – in Mrs Jane Marcet's *Conversations on Botany* of 1817:

EDWARD: You said something about a very industrious man, who had examined a great many plants.

MOTHER: Yes: – we were speaking of Linnaeus, a celebrated botanist, who did so much to increase our knowledge of the works of nature, that he was called the Father of Natural History ...

EDWARD: When I have examined a plant, mamma, how am I to find out its name?

MOTHER: Before you can do so, you must learn how the vegetables that are known have been arranged; and I will explain to you, as clearly as I can, the system of Linnaeus ...[16]

And so Edward is introduced into the exciting world of clandestine marriages and 'Twenty males or more in the same bed with the female.'

Ladies botanizing, *c.* 1830

CHAPTER FOUR

THE DANGEROUS PLEASURE

LINNAEUS HIMSELF WOULD probably have been the first to admit that classification is only a tool, and not the ultimate purpose, of biological enquiry. But unfortunately this truth was not apparent to his successors and for the next hundred years biologists were to concern themselves with classification almost to the exclusion of everything else. The next most eminent biologist after Linnaeus was another classifier, Georges Cuvier (1769–1832), a French comparative anatomist and palaeontologist who continued the work that Linnaeus had begun in the zoological field. Like Linnaeus, Cuvier was a believer in the fixity of species, and he used his immense influence (he was a Cabinet Minister as well as a scientist) to crush the evolutionary theories of Lamarck as soon as they appeared. Of theories in general, Cuvier wrote: 'I have sought, I have set up some myself, but I have not made them known, because I have ascertained that they were false, as are all those which have been published up to this day ... In the present state of science, it is impossible to discover any [theories].'[1]

This was the tone that 'serious' natural history was to take for the entire first half of the nineteenth century. All facts, however trivial, were revered; all theories, however stimulating, were shunned. And the facts that naturalists were most concerned with were those bearing on the description and classification of species. Finding new species was the highest goal to which they aspired; squabbling about names and priority was an occupational disease; describing, arranging and collecting ever more and more species was the business to which they devoted every minute of their working lives. It was the sort of work which, once embarked on, was never-ending, and ultimately became obsessive.

A species then meant something far more clear-cut than it means today. It was defined as a group of identical animals or plants which could reproduce with themselves but not with outsiders. Modern biologists are careful to stress that a species consists of individuals, no two of which are exactly the same, but pre-

Baron Georges Cuvier

Darwinian systematists did not like individual variations and preferred to ignore them. Instead, they described every species in terms of a standard type – usually an actual specimen preserved in some museum or herbarium – to which it was imagined that all the members of the species exactly conformed. Moreover, species in those pre-Darwinian days were immutable. Leopards did not change their spots, so that once *Panthera pardus* had been properly described and classified, and its skin and skeleton preserved as the 'type' in some established institution, there was no need for any naturalist ever to look at another leopard again. Species were as uniform and stable as, say, postage stamps and, like postage stamps, they were satisfying both to collect and to arrange. The most gratifying achievement of all was to find a 'new' species, a nondescript, something that no one previously had found or described. In fact, it was more than gratifying, it was almost dangerously exhilarating, for, as Charles Kingsley remarked in *Glaucus*,

> The truth is, the pleasure of finding new species is too great; it is morally dangerous; for it brings with it the temptation to look on the thing found as your own possession, all but your own creation; to pride yourself on it, as if God had not known it for ages since; even to squabble jealously for the

right of having it named after you, and of being recorded in the Transactions of I-know-not-what Society as its first discoverer.[2]

One only has to read any naturalist's account of his first encounter with a new species to see the sort of wild excitement it induced. Alfred Russel Wallace, Darwin's co-discoverer of the principle of natural selection, recalled that when he first saw the butterfly *Ornithoptera croesus* during his Malaysian travels, 'My heart began to beat violently, the blood rushed to my head, and I felt much more like fainting than I have done when in apprehension of immediate death. I had a headache the rest of the day.'[3] And when Audubon was working on the *Birds of America* he tore open a letter to his friend Dr Richard Harlan to add the feverish postscript: 'I reopened my letter to say I have Just *now* killed a Large *New Falcon, yes positively a new species of Hawk, almost black about* 25 Inches Long and 4 feet broad tail, square Eye yellowish White, Legs and Feet bare short & strong. – I will skin it!!!'[4] Even Darwin, a much less excitable man, remarked in his *Autobiography* that he could still recall, fifty years later, the exact appearance of certain old tree-stumps and gate-posts where, as an undergraduate, he had found beetles which he believed at the time to be new.

Field naturalists were as much victims of the species obsession as the closet naturalists who dictated it. Many of them, in fact, were little better than suppliers to the closet since their chief aim in going into the field was to find a new species, kill it, and bring it home. Far from patiently observing the habits and behaviour of living organisms, as Gilbert White had done, what they really dreamed of was travelling to some far-off ideal field where new species would start from the undergrowth at every step. They read White with affection, but they were more keenly excited by the accounts of explorer-naturalists, like Charles Waterton's *Wanderings in South America*, H.W. Bates's *A Naturalist on the River Amazons*, A.R. Wallace's *The Malay Archipelago* and Paul du Chaillu's *Explorations in Equatorial Africa*. And of course at this period it *was* quite easy to find a field in which almost every species one encountered would be 'new'. All of China, most of South America, much of western North America, Australia, Russia, Japan, India and Africa were still zoologically and botanically uncharted. Naturalists who could explore these places were almost bound to find dozens of new species which would ensure them a place in the annals of natural history. And the field naturalist's reputation was largely determined by the number of new species he amassed.

However, the pure joy of finding new species did not belong exclusively to the field naturalist, since a species did not officially exist until it was published, and this was work for the closet man. To make sure that a species was indeed new one had to read all the relevant literature from Linnaeus to the present, and examine related specimens in museums and private collections. Much scorn attended the naturalist who published a 'new species' which later turned out to be old. Audubon's collaborator John Bachman warned him as they embarked on the *Viviparous Quadrupeds*:

Don't flatter yourself that the quadrupeds will be child's play. I have studied them all my life. We have much, both in Europe and America, to learn on this subject. The skulls and the teeth must be studied, and colour is as variable as the wind; down, down in the earth they grovel, while we, in digging and studying, may grow old and cross. Our work must be thorough.[5]

Audubon was one of the very few naturalists who both found new species in the field and published them himself (and there are many mistakes in his work as a result). Most field naturalists simply handed their finds over to some acknowledged closet expert to publish. One or two of the experts, notably Richard Owen, used this opportunity to snatch all the credit for the discovery, but most of them were scrupulous in returning honour to the field man. And the best possible way of doing this was to name the new species after the man who had found it. The custom of naming species after individuals became increasingly common in the nineteenth century, although Linnaeus had realized its complimentary possibilities early in his career when he wrote to his tutor, Professor Rudbeck, 'So long as the earth shall survive, and as each spring shall see it covered with flowers, the *Rudbeckia* will preserve your glorious name.'[6]

A few die-hards considered that the use of proper names for species was vulgar, and Charles Waterton thundered in his *Essays*:

Our ornithological nomenclature is much more dignified now-a-days than it was in the olden time. Many a bird, which heretofore would have received its name from some particular spot in which it resides – the *wood*-owl, to wit; or from some peculiar food upon which it was known to feed, – the *carrion*-crow, for example, now bears the name of some individual of the human race, some friendly patron, some modern Croesus, who can assist the author in his journey through an expensive press ... I have my doubts whether this complimentary nomenclature be of any real benefit to the public at large, or to science in general.[7]

But most naturalists enjoyed giving and receiving this type of compliment and, since it was the only reward they could hope to obtain for their labours, it would have been churlish to deny it.

The main role of the closet naturalist was to write up finds which other people sent in from the field, but he could also go hunting for new species himself without ever leaving the confines of the closet. This was because many of the old European collections contained specimens that had been written up in the early eighteenth century, and which, in consequence, were often wrongly labelled and lumped together. The eighteenth-century systematists, for instance, had recognized only one species of elephant and one of rhinoceros, whereas their successors, using the improved techniques of anatomical analysis pioneered by Cuvier, recognized two and six separate species respectively. Thus it was quite possible to find new species merely by re-investigating old ones – a dull exercise, no doubt, but a perfectly legitimate one.

However, there were other, less legitimate, ways of discovering new species. One of the most effective was, simply, to invent them, and the chief proponent of this dashing approach was a French-Greek-German-American naturalist with the suitably exotic name of Constantine Samuel Rafinesque-Schmalz (1783–1840). Rafinesque (he usually dropped the Schmalz) could conjure new species out of the air – literally, since on one occasion he published a paper defining twelve species of thunder and lightning. His mania for species-making was a standing joke among his acquaintances. But he could never quite be dismissed as a crank because some of his new species *were* genuine, especially among the Ohio fishes and bivalves which he studied carefully, and even modern scientific historians have still not finally resolved how seriously Rafinesque ought to be taken. A few of his ideas were extraordinarily forward-looking, especially his statement in the *New Flora of North America* that, 'All species might have been varieties once, and many varieties are gradually becoming species by assuming constant and peculiar characters'[8] – a remark that anticipates Darwin by twenty years.

Rafinesque was born in Constantinople, of a French father and Greek-German mother, and was variously brought up in France, Italy and the Levant. (His father disappeared, romantically, being captured by pirates while *en route* to China.) At the age of nineteen, he went to the United States and worked as a shipping clerk, but three years later returned to Europe and settled in Sicily. There he got a job as manager of a whisky distillery and made a fortune on the side by exporting syrup of squill, a baneful medicine, to America. There also he befriended William Swainson. In 1815 Rafinesque set sail for America, was shipwrecked, and after countless travels and adventures, landed up as Professor of Natural History and Modern Languages at the University of Transylvania in Kentucky. But after a few years he picked a quarrel with the University President and was sacked, leaving the place with curses on it which, he notes gleefully in his autobiography, were effective, since the President immediately died of yellow fever and the University burned down. The remaining years of his life were spent as a medical quack and unsuccessful businessman in Philadelphia, where he promoted schemes for a steam-plough, a submarine boat, an incombustible house, and a savings bank which both loaned and borrowed money at six per cent. He was so poor when he died in 1840 that his landlord tried to sell his body to a medical school in back-payment of rent.

The most vivid portrait of Rafinesque occurs in Audubon's *Ornithological Biography* where he is presented as 'The Eccentric Naturalist'. They met in 1818 when Audubon was working as a storekeeper in Henderson, Ohio, and Rafinesque arrived off a flatboat with a bundle of herbs on his back and a letter of introduction from a mutual friend which read, 'My dear Audubon, I send you an old fish, which you may prove to be undescribed and hope you will do so in your next letter.' Audubon, entombed in the backwoods (this was long before he published the *Birds of America*), was delighted to meet a fellow-naturalist, however uncouth, and he invited Rafinesque to stay in his house. That same night, Audubon recounts, when all the household was asleep,

> Of a sudden I heard a great uproar in the naturalist's room. I got up, reached the place in a few moments, and opened the door, when, to my astonishment, I saw my guest running about the room naked, holding the handle of my favourite violin, the body of which he had battered to pieces against the walls in attempting to kill the bats which had entered by the open window, probably attracted by the insects flying around his candle. I stood amazed, but he continued jumping and running round and round, until he was fairly exhausted, when he begged me to procure one of the animals for him, as he felt convinced that they belonged to 'a new species'. Although I was convinced of the contrary, I took up the bow of my demolished Cremona, and administering a smart tap to each of the bats as it came up, soon got specimens enough. The war ended, I again bade him good night, but could not help observing the state of the room. It was strewed with plants, which it would seem he had arranged into groups, but which were now scattered about in confusion. 'Never mind, Mr. Audubon,' quoth the eccentric naturalist, 'never mind, I'll soon arrange them again. I have the bats, and that's enough.'[9]

Of course, Audubon was not the soul of sobriety himself and, having detected his guest's fatal flaw, he spent the next three weeks playing practical jokes on him. Each day he would show Rafinesque some of his drawings and field-notes, and each day he would include in the pile one 'new species' which he had concocted for the occasion. The best was the 'Devil-Jack Diamond-fish, *Litholepis adamantinus*', which had bullet-proof scales, and which Rafinesque later described in his *Ichthyologia Ohiensis* (1820) as follows:

> This may be reckoned the wonder of the Ohio. It is only found as far up as the falls, and probably lives also in the Mississippi. I have seen it, but only at a distance, and have been shown some of its singular scales … They are conical, pentagonal, and pentahedral with equal sides, from half an inch to one inch in diameter, brown at first, but becoming of the colour of turtle shell when dry: they strike fire with steel! and are ball-proof![10]

No less than ten such 'new species' were reproduced in Rafinesque's *Ohio Fishes*. But the final joke was on Audubon. Under each of the ten spoofs, Rafinesque conscientiously recorded, 'This genus rests altogether upon the authority of Mr. Audubon, who presented me with a drawing of the only species belonging to it.' Unfortunately, the joke was never forgotten by European naturalists who henceforward tended to regard all American new species with the deepest suspicion. Audubon and Rafinesque between them created a reputation for unreliability that was to bedevil all American naturalists in their dealings with Europe for the next two generations.

Rafinesque's sometime friend William Swainson was a species-monger of a different order. His new species were usually someone else's old species renamed and redescribed to fit in with his own private classification system, which he called 'the circular system of affinities'. Others called it the 'quinary system' because it involved a heavy reliance on the quasi-mystical properties of the number five. The system was first propounded by William Sharp Macleay in his *Horae Entomologicae* of 1824, but when Macleay soon afterwards emigrated to Cuba, Swainson took it over and became its chief guru in England. In practice, it meant that every species had to be renamed and rearranged according to its own foggy lights; as Audubon remarked, 'Swainson never goes to bed without describing some new species.'[11]

We know a lot about William Swainson because he includes a very full, though no doubt biased, account of himself in his *Bibliography of Zoology*, published as part of Lardner's *Cyclopaedia* in 1840. Indeed, he devotes no less than fourteen pages to himself – ten more than he gives to Cuvier, and nine more than he gives to Linnaeus. From this we learn that he was born in 1789, the son of a Liverpool customs officer, and spent his early manhood with the British Mediterranean Army stationed in Sicily (which is where he met Rafinesque). Natural history, he says,

William Swainson

Constantine Samuel Rafinesque

was his first and abiding love – 'Sleeping or waking, my thoughts were constantly bent on how I could get abroad, and revel in the zoology of the tropics'[12] – and from 1816 to 1818 he explored Brazil and amassed vast zoological collections. These he wrote up on his return and illustrated himself in several lavish volumes (*Zoological Illustrations, Exotic Conchology* and *Ornithological Drawings*). His illustrations were much admired at the time, though they now seem rather wooden.

In 1826, having married and begun producing numerous children, he found himself pressed for money and hit on an age-old idea: 'At length, it occurred to me that no profession was more honourable than that of an author; that many of my friends found it a source of profit, no less than of fame; and that I might justly turn to pecuniary account that knowledge, to gain which I had sacrificed so much.'[13] So saying, he sat down to the exhausting hack-work of producing an eleven-volume *Cabinet Cyclopaedia of Natural History* for Dr Dionysius Lardner's series of improving home compendia. The *Cyclopaedia*, despite its many eccentricities, remains an important survey of the state of natural history research and institutions in the early part of the nineteenth century. It is most unfairly known as *Lardner's Cyclopaedia*, though Swainson wrote it all.

Unfortunately, while writing the *Cyclopaedia*, Swainson became increasingly ensnared in the coils of his wretched quinary system, and by 1830 was writing to Audubon, with whom he was supposed to be collaborating on the *Ornithological Biography*, 'I have peculiar notions on *Species*, which, as I *believe* them correct, so I do not suffer to be influenced by others.'[14] In return, of course, others did not suffer themselves to be influenced by Swainson, and the quinary system, after a short-lived flurry of general interest, deteriorated into the butt of naturalists' jokes. Charles Waterton, in one of his *Essays on Natural History*, mentions the camichi bird of Guiana which has two peculiar spurs on its wings, and then chortles:

> By the way, who knows but that some scientific closet naturalist may not account for these alar spurs of the camichi, through the medium of that very useful and important discovery, the quinary system. Thus, for example's sake, suppose these said spurs were once normal or typical on the legs; but, by some rather obscure process, having become aberrant, they made an approach or passage to the wings; while the bird itself was progressing in the circle or leading round, in order to inosculate the posteriors of its antecedent. He who clearly comprehends the quinary system, will readily understand this.[15]

The more Swainson propounded his theory of 'types grallatorial, types tenuirostral, types rasorial, and types suctorial',[16] the more his fellows mocked him, and in 1840 he finally gave up the unequal struggle and emigrated to New Zealand. He was never heard of in European zoological circles again.

Yet the memory of the quinary system, and the madness it had induced, loomed as a sort of Awful Warning to aspiring theorizers for many years afterwards, and

1 Kuhl's Parakeet from Edward Lear's *Parrots*, 1832

2 Brown's Parakeet from Edward Lear's *Parrots*, 1832

3 White-bearded Puff-bird, from *Birds of Brazil* by William Swainson, 1841

4 Helmet Manakin, from *Birds of Brazil* by William Swainson, 1841

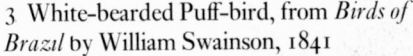

5 Humming-birds, from *Things in the Forest* by Mary and Elizabeth Kirby, 1883

tended to enhance that widespread fear of generalization which bedevilled natural history progress in the early decades of the nineteenth century. Even Darwin was touched by this fear, and referred back to the quinary system in a letter he wrote to Richard Owen a few days after the publication of the *Origin*: 'I have thought that perhaps my book might be a case like Macleay's quinary system. So strongly did I feel this that I resolved to give it all up, as far as I could, if I did not convince at least two or three competent judges.'[17] Of course, far from being another quinary system, Darwin's book turned out to be the key that released the species deadlock and launched biological enquiry into a new era, but it is characteristic of the period that the idea of presenting *any* general theory was one to induce extreme nervousness and a fear of ostracism from the scientific community. That, after all, had been the fate of all the previous theorizers from Lamarck to Swainson, and most naturalists felt quite rightly that it was safer to stick to detail than to make any attempt at synthesis. In particular, they felt safe in the description of species. It was respectable work, and it needed to be done, and many of them were happy to remain on this treadmill throughout their careers.

Not surprisingly, this single-minded concentration on one aspect of natural history did produce an enormous accretion of new species in the scientific literature of the period. The number of known animals increased one hundredfold between 1758, when Linnaeus listed 4,162 species known to him, and 1898 when Mobius listed 415,600. (The current number of known animal species is well over a million, but, as new insects are described at the rate of 6,000 *a year*, no biologist would dream of predicting any final number.) Most of this species explosion occurred between the 1820s and 1860s. Linnaeus had listed 444 species of bird in 1758, and by 1817 Cuvier had brought the number up to 765 – a fairly modest increase over sixty years. But in 1834 the Keeper of Zoology at the British Museum claimed that there were over four thousand species of bird in the world; Johnston's *Physical Atlas* of 1856 (second edition) listed over six thousand species; and Richard Owen in 1862 mentioned a total of over eight thousand species, which meant that they had doubled in less than thirty years. Similar patterns of increase could be traced for all the other classes of animals in the same period – relative stability in the eighteenth century, followed by sudden explosion in the nineteenth. The effect of this was ultimately discouraging. Whereas Linnaeus and his contemporaries had believed that a total classification lay almost within their grasp – it was simply a question of filling a few 'gaps' – nineteenth-century closet naturalists gradually came to realize that no total classification would ever be achieved, because as fast as one 'gap' was filled, new yawning chasms appeared. The reason why species-gathering slowed down after the 1860s was not because the work had reached completion, but simply because Darwin's theories provided a new line of enquiry for naturalists to embark on, so that fewer and fewer of them were prepared to devote their lives to classification.

However, while the species obsession lasted – i.e. for the first half of the nineteenth century – it provided in many ways an encouragement for the popular study

'Botanising – a Bog Plant', from *Hood's Own*

of natural history. In the first place, it was work which the layman could not only understand but even hope to contribute to. Finding new species did not, after all, require any great mental powers, and it was not absolutely necessary to explore unknown continents in order to find them. Any Sunday bug-hunter or botanist might, in the course of his rambles, come across a species or sub-species which, if not 'new to science', was at least 'new to Britain' or 'new to Essex', and would ensure a measure of local recognition. The *Entomologist's Annual* is full of heroic sagas of how this or that new insect was discovered by some patient amateur, practically on his own doorstep. Mr Winter of Brighton, for instance, discovered *Ennomos alniaria* (a tiny moth new to Britain) 'at a gas-lamp outside the Sussex County Hospital',[18] and Mr Brewer of Reigate found his new moth, *Trochilium chrysidiforme*, on a cheap day-return railway outing to Dover. Indeed, the editor of the *Annual* decided that Mr Brewer's adventures were sufficiently momentous to require recounting in full and in his very best literary style:

It so happens that the directors of the South-Eastern Railway had resolved to treat the denizens of Reigate, on that day, [25 June 1855] with an excursion train to Dover; Reigate is a healthy neighbourhood, but still a few hours by the sea-side might be a treat to the inhabitants, and accordingly many of the in-dwellers and out-dwellers of Reigate committed themselves to the safe custody of the South-Eastern Railway, and were in due time transported to Dover. Now at Reigate there lives a Coleopterist of the name of Brewer. Mr. Brewer was one of those who profited by the excursion train to Dover. No doubt he amused himself as the train wended along past Tunbridge, Staplehurst and Ashford, with conjectures of the rare coast beetles he was then about to meet with. But it was not by any Coleopterous insect that that day's excursion was to be immortalized. Sweeping the herbage on the undercliff between Dover and Folkestone, he obtained a transparent-winged moth, and not being learned in Lepidopterology, it struck him as curious. Now a Coleopterist carries no boxes, he carries only a phial with bruised laurel leaves, and in this already sundry *Harpalidae* and *Staphylinidae* were wriggling their legs. Man is an inventive animal; when at a loss for a word he coins one, when at a loss for an implement he uses something not orginally destined for that purpose. Happily for my present subject, Mr. Brewer was a smoker of tobacco, and carried a fusee-box; the clear-winged moth was placed as a curiosity in the fusee-box and carried home.

Now it so happened, that at this time, Mr. Douglas had made out a visit for some days to Mickleham, and being there went over to Reigate to see Mr. Brewer. The conversation, of course, ran principally upon *Coleoptera*, but Mr. Brewer, aware that his Lee correspondent was also a devoted adherent of Lepidopterology, placed the fusee-box in his hand, inquiring if *that* was *of any use to him*, and so *Trochilium chrysidiforme* gladdened the eyes of a Lepidopterist!

From that time the insect found itself duly honoured; it had a special label attached to it, indicating its pedigree, and was exhibited at the Meeting of the Entomological Society of London, where it created a sensation.[19]

And so Mr Brewer of Reigate attains his scientific honours. His triumph might seem puny beside that of A.R. Wallace in the Malay archipelago, or H.W. Bates on the River Amazon, or Paul du Chaillu in darkest Africa, but it was the very stuff of life to readers of the *Entomologist's Annual* and to thousands of other amateur field naturalists who might never set foot outside their native country, but who still might hope to find a morsel of scientific moment in the course of their weekend rambles.

However, even those laymen who never dreamed of going out to find new species themselves often took an armchair interest in such activities. When they opened their newspaper to read of an 'Important New Scientific Discovery' there was no danger of it being something daunting and incomprehensible like a new theory of plant biochemistry – it was almost invariably a new species which, as often as not, would soon be exhibited in the zoological or botanical gardens. Almost every year produced a new sensation – new orchids, humming-birds, pitcher-

The Black Leopard 'Satan' arrives at London Zoo

plants, toucans, bird-eating spiders, giant tortoises, moon moths from Java, the Victoria Regia waterlily which was so large it had to have its own conservatory built to house it – an endless list of ever bigger and better marvels to fire the public imagination. Whenever the supply of new wonders seemed about to flag, something even more extraordinary would turn up. In 1861, for instance, it was the turn of the gorilla – an animal whose existence had been rumoured since classical times, but never previously substantiated. In the next ten years a French missionary to China, Père Armand David, produced no less than three large hitherto-undiscovered animal species, the giant panda, the snow monkey and the 'Père David's deer'. Time and again throughout the century, naturalists predicted that no new large animals remained to be found, and time and again they were proved wrong. The largest carnivore in the world, the Manchurian brown bear, was not discovered until 1898, and the okapi, a horse-sized, zebra-striped animal related to the giraffe, managed to evade the eyes of African explorers until 1901.

The fact that so many new, extraordinary species kept cropping up had a peculiar effect on the popular imagination. While scientists endeavoured to arrive at a more precise understanding of what was possible in Nature, laymen, confronted with their first pitcher-plant or their first giant sloth, increasingly tended to believe that *anything* was possible. In particular, they thought it was only a matter of time before scientists would produce their first authenticated unicorn, mermaid or phoenix. The phoenix, after all, had at least as solid a classical literary background as the gorilla, and the unicorn seemed a lot more zoologically feasible than, say, the duck-billed platypus. Even such a sober naturalist as Philip Gosse predicted, in 1860, that the unicorn would soon be found, and suggested central Africa, north of the Equator and south of Abyssinia (now Ethiopia), as the likeliest habitat.[20] But the most persistently sighted and eagerly sought animal of the nineteenth century was the Great Sea-Serpent. It appeared most frequently off the coasts of New England and Norway, but around the mid-century it seemed that no one could sail anywhere (except, oddly enough, Loch Ness, where it did not establish residence until 1933) without running across it. The most publicized sighting was by several officers of H.M.S. *Daedalus* in 1848. This one was about sixty feet long, dark brown in colour, and moved in the croquet-hoop manner of its kind. In vain did Professor Richard Owen, who was deputed by the Admiralty to investigate all sea-serpent sightings, point out that no animal could move in such a manner. In vain did he argue that, if sea-serpents existed, surely one corpse, or at least one skeleton, or at least one vertebra, would have been washed up by now. His conclusion that the *Daedalus* officers had seen a sea-lion or a sea-elephant found few subscribers, and was generally considered to be in very poor taste.

Charles Kingsley, who was a keen amateur naturalist, summed up the Victorian attitude to improbable beasts when he wrote, in the *Water-Babies*:

> You must not say that this cannot be, or that that is contrary to nature. You do not know what nature is, or what she can do; and nobody knows; not even Sir Roderick Murchison, or Professor Owen, or Professor Sedgwick, or Professor Huxley, or Mr. Darwin, or Professor Faraday, or Mr. Grove ... They are very wise men, and you must listen respectfully to all they say:

Surrey Zoological Gardens

but even if they should say, which I am sure they never would, 'That cannot exist. That is contrary to nature,' you must wait a little, and see; for perhaps even they may be wrong.[21]

Thus laymen were encouraged to maintain an almost medieval credulity about Nature – a credulity which the popular natural history books did nothing to dispel since they consistently stressed the most bizarre types of natural phenomena at the expense of more ordinary ones and never bothered to explain the first principles of their subject. And of course this credulity itself contributed to the popular enthusiasm for natural history, since a subject which could produce Victoria Regia water-lilies one year, gorillas another, and might next year produce unicorns and phoenixes, was a very exciting and wonderful thing.

CHAPTER FIVE

BELIEFS ABOUT NATURE

T THE BEGINNING of the nineteenth century, all laymen and most scientists believed that the Earth and all the species on it had been created by God in six days towards the end of October in the year 4004 B.C. The date had been worked out by Archbishop Ussher, by adding together all the life-spans of all the patriarchs listed in the Mosaic genealogy, and it was frequently printed in the margins of bibles, along-side the Genesis account of the Creation, so that it had all the appearance of scriptural authority. In 4004 B.C. God had created the Earth and in 4004 B.C. He had created every species of plant and animal which now exists on the planet. Every species had been created individually, and every species had remained the same ever since. Anyone who was inclined to doubt this was referred to the findings of Egyptian archaeology which showed that the plants and animals preserved and depicted in the Pyramids were identical to their modern descendants. And the Pyramids were three thousand years old or – literally – 'half as old as Time'.

By the 1840s and 1850s, this belief was already under considerable stress. Several evolutionary theories were aired before Darwin's and one in particular, based on a book called *Vestiges of Creation*, attracted great publicity in the 1840s. At the same time, there was a far more serious debate going on about the age of the Earth, and even by the beginning of Victoria's reign, very few geologists were prepared to accept that the Earth was only 6,000 years old. These two controversies, the major one about the age of the Earth, and the relatively minor one about evolution, were thrashed out in newspapers, in pamphlets, in sermons, in theological and learned journals, and by the 1850s it would have been impossible for any literate layman not to have heard of them.

What is striking, however, is that not one whisper of these controversies found its way into the popular natural history books of the period (except those of Hugh Miller, which will be discussed separately). Popular natural history existed in a peculiar vacuum, deriving its biology from Linnaeus, its philosophy from Paley, and its cosmogony from Archbishop Ussher, long after these ideas had become outmoded. The only works that popular writers seem to have consulted were other books in the same genre by their contemporaries and immediate predecessors. They went on reproducing one another's facts, one another's anecdotes and one another's assumptions about Nature year after year, decade after decade. And in particular they ignored all the great scientific controversies that were waging in the world outside, even though these were ones that directly concerned natural history.

This studious neglect of what seem to us the most important scientific questions of the period is baffling if we suppose that Victorian natural history books were written with the same aim as modern ones – i.e. to teach their readers the facts of natural history. But, of course, they were not. Victorian natural history books were written with the aim of encouraging their readers to see evidence of God's existence and attributes in the natural organisms around them, by means of natural theology. And on this basis it was quite legitimate to pass over any facts which did not immediately illustrate God's goodness or wisdom. Such facts were unproductive. It was not hypocritical to pass over them, it was simply common sense. Even more hastily should one pass over any facts which tended to undermine literal belief in the Scriptures. It was for theologians to work out how best to 'reconcile' geology and Genesis, science and religion, and until they had done so, it would be presumptuous for the layman to comment. In any case, there was no *need* to discuss the controversial issues of the day, since they were all ones that concerned past history – the history of the Earth and of species – and just as one could write a cookery book without embarking on the history of the saucepan, so one could write a description of all the species existing on the Earth without ever asking how those species or how that Earth had been created. And, as there was no need to raise controversial topics, still less was there any desire to, since natural history writers were keenly aware that their subject had only very recently gained respectability, and there was no point in jeopardizing its popularity by embarking on potentially irreligious arguments. That is why, at a later date, there is such a uniform silence in the popular natural history books about Darwinism.

However, while popular natural history writers tended to eschew all the real controversies of the day, they frequently embarked on little pseudo-controversies of their own. One of the favourite questions they asked themselves was *why* had God created so many different species? What was their *use*? For the Victorians saw their God as a hard-headed sensible economist of sound business habits who would not waste his energies in creating things unless they had a purpose. (Only Charles Kingsley was blithe enough to suggest that God had created some species – he nominated the crab – as a joke, but his view of God as a fun-loving prankster was not widely shared.) And popular natural history writers conceived it their duty to try to explain the use of every species of plant and animal whenever possible, in order to justify God's effort in creating them.

The Food Museum, South Kensington, 1859

Ultimately they believed that the purpose of all the other species in creation was to be of benefit to man –

> For me kind Nature wakes her genial power,
> Suckles each herb, and spreads out every flower.[1]

The editor of the *Edinburgh New Philosophical Journal* stated flatly in 1860 that, 'It will not be denied, we presume, that animals were created for the use of mankind.'[2] Most writers did not put it quite so boldly, but the attitude is implicit everywhere, and occasionally emerges with naïve force, as when we find the sheep described as 'that soft and harmless creature, that clothes civilized man everywhere in the colder latitudes with its fleece, – that feeds him with its flesh, – that gives its bowels to be spun into the catgut with which he refits his musical instruments, – whose horns he has learned to fashion into a thousand useful trinkets, – and whose skin, converted into parchment, served to convey to later times the thinking of the first full blow of the human intellect, across the dreary gulf of the middle ages.'[3] And Charlotte M. Yonge, in a popular botany book of the same period, asks in all seriousness, 'Does it not show that oranges were made for our special benefit, that there should be so many without pips, so as to be of no use at all, excepting for food?'[4]

The Victorians saw nothing presumptuous in the idea that everything in Nature was created for man's convenience: on the contrary, it was a subject for celebration, and natural history writers spent some of their happiest hours explaining how this or that natural phenomenon was arranged to suit man's requirements. One writer suggested, for instance, that the reason why herrings annually congregate in shoals and migrate towards the coast is so that men may more easily catch and eat them; and the reason why birds migrate is so that people in different continents may have a chance to enjoy them in turn. Flowers, he maintained, were created so that men would be encouraged to take up gardening and thereby improve their temper since 'their operation on our intellectual facilities and moral emotions is that of a soothing melioration.'[5] Robert Mudie's *A Popular Guide to the Observation of Nature* (1832) is entirely devoted to presenting Nature as a sort of factory, endlessly humming in its efforts to satisfy the mill-owner, man. In springtime, Mudie claims, you can see the buds straining to crack their cases, and the green shoots competing to produce the finest flowers. The birds, he says,

Charlotte M. Yonge, by George Richmond

are all in the act of beautifying nature too: some are plucking the dry grass, so that the fields may look green; others are gathering up the withered sticks; others again, the lost feathers and hairs; and others still are pulling the lichens from the bark of trees. The merles and the mavises [blackbirds and thrushes] are running under the hedges, and the evergreens in the shrubbery, and capturing the snails in their winter habitations, before they have had time to prepare those hordes which would be the pest of the gardeners for the whole season. Other birds are inspecting the buds in the orchard; and picking off every one which contains a caterpillar or a nest of eggs, that would pour forth their destructive horde, and render the whole tree lifeless...

All the countless races of that time of labour and of love, both native and visitant, are busy following their own purpose, or rather the law of their being, for they form no purpose of their own, or they would sometimes commit errors of judgements as we do, but they do not. At the same time the fulfilment of the law of their being works for good to us, just as the law of the being of a bushel of wheat works for good to us, when we cast it upon the earth, and cover it with dust; and come back after a season and find ten bushels.[6]

This vision of springtime as a universal litter-drive has its charms, but the astute reader will already have noticed that there is a worm in Robert Mudie's bud, and a snail in his shrubbery. The merles and the mavises may be following the law of their being by running around killing snails and caterpillars, but what exactly

'March of the Processionary Bombyx', from Pouchet's *The Universe*

are the snails and caterpillars doing in the great bushel-of-wheat scheme of things? Their only purpose in existence seems to be to die. And this, indeed, was the great flaw in the anthropocentric view of Nature, and one over which natural history writers puzzled their heads throughout the period. It was all very well explaining how the sheep, the horse or the herring was intended to be useful to man, but what about those species that were not obviously useful, or which were in fact positively harmful to man? Robert Mudie himself offered a peculiar way round this difficulty:

> When we are properly acquainted with them none of the productions of nature are injurious. It is true, that there are some that would poison us, if we ate them; others would burn the body, if they came in contact with it; and others, again, offend, and even waste and wear our organs of sense. But it is our own fault if we allow them to produce any of these bad effects. We need not swallow arsenic, be bitten by rattlesnakes, offended by the sight of toads or newts, or sickened by noxious effluvia.[7]

Mudie's 'solution' did not, of course, tackle the main problem of why these injurious organisms existed in the first place. The more conventional line, preferred by the majority of natural history writers, was to talk vaguely about the 'balance' or 'harmony' of Nature. Some species were necessary to keep down other species which would otherwise run amok. Insectivorous birds, for instance, were 'commissioned by an all-wise and beneficent Providence to free us from the clouds of insects, which would otherwise infest our dwellings, and destroy the labours of the field.'[8] This was quite a promising line of attack, but, since the state of ecological knowledge was low, and since in any case it was based on the false premise that everything in Nature must be ultimately beneficial to man, it often led to circular arguments. What is the use of ladybirds? one writer asks. Why, to help the gardener, by keeping down aphids. And what is the use of aphids? Why, to feed ladybirds, of course. This solution was deemed sufficient.

We have already seen, apropos of natural theology, that Victorian popular natural history writers did not think it necessary, or even desirable, to attempt to explain everything in Nature. This is apparent when they are discussing the subject of Design, and it is equally apparent when they are discussing the subject of use. If a writer *could* explain the use of an organism, by showing how it was of benefit to man, he did so; if he could not, he fell back on redoubled piety and references to the wonderful and mysterious ways of Providence. Thus J.L. Knapp, in his *Journal of a Naturalist*, describes the elaborate seed-dispersal mechanism of the dandelion and then ponders why God has gone to such lengths to propagate a plant which is of no apparent use to anyone. He can find no answer, but he satisfies himself with the reflection that 'This very circumstance should abate our pride, our assumed pretensions of knowledge, as we may be assured that its existence, though hidden from us, is required in the great scheme of nature, or such elaborate and sufficient contrivances for its continuation and increase would never

have been called into action.'⁹ In other words, the dandelion *must* be useful, otherwise God would not have created it, and the fact that we mortals cannot understand
its use only serves to remind us that God works in a mysterious way. The job
of the naturalist is not to explain everything in Nature, which would be presumptuous and anyway impossible, but to explain what he or she can and leave the
rest to God. Charlotte M. Yonge, after addressing herself to the problem of poisonous fungi and admitting that they do seem to be useless and even injurious to
man, concludes cheerfully, 'I do not think we have a right to call any of the works
of the Creator nasty. I am sure we should not, if we once looked well into them.'¹⁰

The existence of animals harmful to man was a knotty problem (though as we
have seen it was not one that naturalists felt themselves obliged to answer), but
it paled into insignificance compared to the problem posed by fossils. Why had
God created so many species of plants and animals before man had even arrived
on the scene? What possible use could they have fulfilled? The problem had
occurred to Hugh Miller early in his geological career when he wrote to a friend
describing the beauties of a fossil, *cornu ammonis*, and then asked:

> But, why so much beauty when there was no eye of man to see and admire?
> Does it not seem strange that the bays of our coasts should have been speckled
> by fleets of beautiful little animals, with their tiny sails spread to the wind
> and their pearly colours glancing to the sun, when there was no intelligent
> eye to look abroad and delight in their loveliness? Of all the sciences there
> is none which furnishes so many paradoxical facts and appearances as
> geology.¹¹

But by the time he came to write the *Testimony of the Rocks* (1857) he had found
at least a partial answer. The geological ages prior to man's creation constituted,
he believed, a kind of dress rehearsal, during which God was undertaking 'the
gradual fitting up of our earth as a place of habitation for a creature destined to
seek delight for the mind and the eye as certainly as for the grosser senses.'¹²
And as the time of man's arrival drew nearer, God dressed the set more and more
elaborately so that everything should be ready for opening night. Flowers were
created just before man 'to minister to that sense of beauty which distinguishes
him from all the lower creatures' and grasses were thoughtfully provided 'in order,
apparently, that he might enter in favouring circumstances upon his two earliest
avocations, and be in good hope a keeper of herds and a tiller of the ground.'¹³
Even Richard Owen, the leading palaeontologist of the day, supported this view,
and claimed that the horse had been 'predestined and prepared for Man',¹⁴ so
that as soon as Adam appeared he could leap into the saddle.

However, this explanation became less and less tenable as geological knowledge
increased, and in 1866 Charles Kingsley roundly attacked 'the conceited notion
which, making man forsooth the centre of the universe, dares to believe that variety
of forms has existed for countless ages in abysmal sea-depths and untrodden

Charles Kingsley, by L. Dickinson, 1862

forests, only that some few individuals of the western races might, in these latter days, at last discover and admire a corner here and there of the boundless realms of beauty.' As a trained theologian, with a more sophisticated understanding of teleology than the average naturalist, Kingsley exposed the question of usefulness to man for what it was: a red herring. The existence of so many different species in Nature was, he asserted, inexplicable on any anthropocentric basis, but it was 'explicable enough to him who believes that God has created all things for Himself and rejoices in His own handiwork.'[15] And this was, indeed, the orthodox theological line. There was no *need* to prove that everything in Nature was created for man's benefit. There was no scriptural authority for suggesting that it was. Kingsley's explanation was sufficient. God had created everything for His own enjoyment.

Why, then, did so many people believe that everything in Nature was created for man's use? Probably because of a misunderstanding of Paley. Paley had chosen a watch as his example of Design, and laymen tended to assume that because a watch is useful to man, everything in Nature must be so too. What Paley meant to illustrate by the example of the watch was that all the parts of an object (or organism) are carefully designed to serve the purposes *of that object* (or organism). But obviously the idea that everything in Nature was divinely appointed to be useful to man was an attractive one, especially at a period of agricultural and industrial expansion when man was exploiting Nature as never before. Moreover, it offered a congenial intellectual exercise for popular natural history writers who were always seeking to imbue their work with the appearance of philosophical gravity. It was considered nobler, and it was in any case easier, to write little disquisitions about the supposed usefulness of such-and-such an animal to man, than to embark on difficult researches into the actual relations between species which at best could produce 'merely' factual results. Hence their reluctance to abandon the topic, even after Kingsley and other theologians had exposed its essential fraudulence.

Another quite unnecessary problem that popular natural history writers set themselves was the question of whether particular organisms could be considered 'good' or 'not good'. (Natural theology did not allow any organism to be bad, and therefore 'not good' meant one whose goodness had not yet revealed itself to mortals.) Time and again in Victorian natural history books one finds the writer sitting in moral judgment on a species. Mrs Loudon's *Entertaining Naturalist*, for instance, is a sort of extended school report on all the more familiar birds and mammals, in which each animal is awarded Pass or Fail or Could do Better. Here is her verdict on the goose:

> Stupidity in her look, uncouthness in her walk, and heaviness in her flight, are her principal characteristics. But why should we dwell upon these defects? They are not such in the great scale of the creation. Her flesh feeds many, and is not disdained even by the great; her feathers keep us warm; and the very pen I hold in my hand was plucked from her wing.[16]

In other words, what the goose loses in beauty, she gains in tastiness, bedding and penmanship, and therefore passes as demonstrably 'good'.

However, natural theology made it imperative to find as many species 'good' as possible, and writers were prepared to extend the criteria for goodness. Usefulness to man was always the *preferred* criterion, and the one they looked for first, but if a species failed on that test it could then be given a second chance to pass on the basis of intrinsic moral worth, i.e. because it led a virtuous life. Many species of non-edible birds, for instance, were admitted to the category of 'good' because they were monogamous and paired for life. The homing-pigeon was particularly good because it apparently pined when separated from its mate. Writers were prepared to exercise amazing ingenuity in finding evidence of intrinsic goodness in the most unlikely animals. Maria Catlow, in *Popular British Entomology*, remarks that earwigs are generally disliked because they are believed to creep into people's ears, which would seem to condemn them to the ranks of the 'not good', but, she triumphantly reveals, they are wonderfully conscientious mothers who spend hours constructing safe and comfortable nests for their children, and therefore in spite of their uselessness, their inedibility, their ugliness, and their annoying habit of creeping into people's ears, they are nevertheless good, because of their marked maternal care. And since, in fact, most animals show signs of care, or at least provision, for their young, the amateur natural theologian could nearly always produce some pretext for admitting them to the blessed category of the good.

These discussions about the supposed goodness of various animals constitute, as it were, the highest peaks of that anthropomorphism which is such a conspicuous feature of Victorian natural history writing. The device of endowing animals with

George Henry Lewes

human qualities was, of course, a traditional one, but the Victorians used it more pervasively than any of their predecessors, applying it not only to the obvious stereotypes (the noble lion, the cunning fox, the faithful dog, etc.) but also to plants and microscopic organisms. It is hard to know whether to consider this a matter of style purely, or a matter of belief. It seems unlikely that natural history writers really believed that plants and animals are 'just like humans' (though the Rev. J.G. Wood, in *Common Objects of the Country*, defied all the orthodox theology of the day by claiming that animals had immortal souls); on the other hand, they so consistently wrote *as if* they believed it, and so rarely made any disclaimers to the contrary, that the reader is certainly led to believe that they believed it, and in turn to believe it himself. Thus, while anthropomorphism may have been adopted as a purely stylistic conceit, it ultimately had a far-reaching effect on the whole Victorian portrayal of Nature.

One instance is its effect on the discussion of animal instinct. Popular natural history writers knew in theory that instinct was a different thing to human reasoning or volition, and their standard locution for instinctive behaviour, such as courtship rituals, was to talk about animals 'going about their appointed tasks'. However, they could then rarely resist adding an anthropomorphizing adverb such as 'joyfully' or 'willingly' which suggested that the animal could choose whether or not to obey its own instinct, and thus effectively demolished any distinction they had been trying to make. G.H. Lewes pinpointed the intrinsic dangers of the anthropomorphic approach when he wrote in his *Sea-Side Studies*:

> We are incessantly at fault in our tendency to anthropomorphise; a tendency which causes us to interpret the actions of animals according to the analogies of human nature. Wherever we see motion which seems to issue from some internal impulses, and not from an obvious external cause, we cannot help attributing it to 'the will'. No one seeing a bird snap at a fly with its beak, could doubt that the movement was voluntary; but if the bird's head were cut off, and the beak continued to snap, would not this throw a serious doubt on the voluntary nature of the former action?[17]

Serious naturalists would have agreed with Lewes's analysis (if not with his rather doubtful example), but in practice they found it very difficult to avoid the anthropomorphic habit. Even Darwin, in the *Voyage of the Beagle*, has a lizard asking, 'What made you pull my tail?'[18]

Another curious question which this habit gave rise to was that of whether animals are happy. For some reason, it is most frequently marine animals which provoke the fullest discussion of this question. W.H. Harvey, for instance, describes in his *Sea-Side Book* the way in which the sea-urchin's shell gradually expands as it grows and then wonders 'why something similar was not devised to assist the Crab', who has 'to flay itself alive, and then wait, defenceless and naked, till a new coat grows on its back.' This seems dangerously like criticizing the Creator, so Harvey retreats with the observation: 'I suppose happiness is equally distributed, and that what would be death to one animal may be sport to another! Possibly the extraordinary efforts made by the Crab or Lobster in throwing off their shells, may be attended with pleasurable sensations.'[19] George Johnston, in his excellent *Introduction to Conchology*, shows similar concern for the equanimity of oysters, concluding that,

> In the gentle agitation of the water which floats around them, in its varied temperature, in the work of capturing their prey, in the imbibation and expulsion of the fluid necessary to respiration, &c., they will find both business and amusement; and, in due season, love visits even these phlegmatic things, when icy bosoms feel the secret fire![20]

It can be seen from the foregoing that the sort of questions popular natural history writers concerned themselves with were purely philosophical ones. Are animals good? Are they happy? What is their use? Why did God create them? These are the burning issues of the Sea-Side Books and Popular Entomologies, not any debates about the age of the Earth or the origin of species. In fact, one could read dozens of popular Victorian natural history books before one came across any inkling that such debates were going on. Only two popular natural history writers, Hugh Miller and Philip Gosse, ever attempted to deal with them, and it is significant that both these men came to unhappy ends (see chapters 16 and 17). Most natural history writers simply ignored all the scientific controversies of the day. This was partly because they did not want to upset their readers, and perhaps relegate natural history to the oblivion from which it had come, but much more because they were not *primarily* interested in science. They were interested in natural theology, or their own idiosyncratic versions of it, and when they came across any scientific discoveries or facts which could not be fitted into the Paleyan mould, they silently discarded them. Piety was, after all, far more important than accuracy; religion more important than science. And it was not the place of popular natural history books to start raising difficulties or disseminating awkward information which might tend to contradict the Genesis account of the Creation, and all the beliefs about Nature that derived from it.

Charles Kingsley by 'Cecioni', 1872

PART THREE
THE POPULAR EXPLOSION

CHAPTER SIX

'TO MAKE THE ACID GRIN'

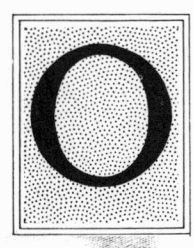

NE OF THE many factors which enhanced natural history's popularity in the early decades of the nineteenth century was its visual appeal. Natural objects were not only beautiful in themselves, but could be imported into the home and used to decorative purpose. Flowers, ferns and seaweeds could be pressed for albums, or mounted into pictures; shells could be displayed as ornaments, either in the house or in the garden; butterflies and beetles could be arranged in kaleidoscopic 'picture cases' to hang on the walls. The serious collector would, of course, have frowned on such frivolity, but most amateurs were happy to show off their little collections as attractively as possible.

The same argument applied to books. Buying a book merely for the sake of its pretty pictures was considered vaguely immoral, or at any rate extravagant, but if those pictures happened to illustrate important and revealing truths about Nature – if they were in fact illustrations of God's benevolent Design – then their purchase was justified. Publishers were quick to exploit this important motive, and it is rare to find a natural history book after the 1840s without any illustrations. In the very cheapest productions, these might consist only of a few poor woodcuts, but in the middle-range books, such as the excellent half-guinea Popular Natural History series published by Lovell Reeve in the 1850s, or the *Naturalist's Library* series edited by William Jardine, numerous good colour illustrations were the rule. Moreover, publishers had a wide range of printing techniques to choose from; the established crafts of etching and engraving, followed at intervals throughout the century by lithography, chromolithography, wood-block colour printing, and, eventually, photography. Even hand-coloured plates were not prohibitively expensive, as the colourists (usually women and children) were so poorly paid.

However, overshadowing the general run of bookshop books, good though this general run was, were the *de luxe* illustrated editions available to subscribers only.

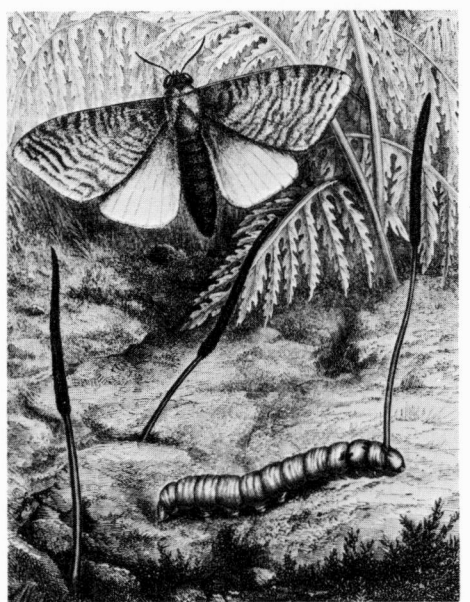

New Zealand Swift-moth and larva with parasite fungus, from Pouchet's *The Universe*

This was a familiar and old-established publishing technique in the nineteenth century, though it is rare enough nowadays to need explanation. It began with the author, artist and publisher (usually all the same man) preparing a specimen part of the proposed work, together with a prospectus outlining its eventual scope and length, and taking this round to potential subscribers who would be asked to commit themselves to buying each instalment of the book as it appeared, at monthly or quarterly intervals, often over several years. The receipts from one instalment would then cover the costs of preparing the next. This was, indeed, the only way of publishing very expensive, large-scale illustrated books, since publishers were not prepared to risk producing them without a guaranteed sale.

And these *were* large-scale books, not only in their eventual length (often ten or twenty volumes), but also in their page dimensions which were enough to demolish any modern coffee-table. Lord Lilford, offering to lend his copy of Gould's *British Birds* to the local schoolmaster, warned him that 'you would require a boy to help you carry them from the house',[1] and John Bateman's atlas folio of the *Orchidaceae of Mexico and Guatemala* (1837–40) has a witty vignette by Cruikshank showing a gang of Lilliputian labourers trying to hoist the huge volume by pulley on to a stand. Such books were also staggeringly expensive – far more expensive in terms of relative incomes than any books published today. Gould's *Birds of Australia*, for instance, cost £115, and Audubon's *Birds of America* cost £182. 14s. or $1,000 in America – well above the yearly income of an average working man. By paying for the work in instalments, of course, subscribers were able to spread the cost over several years, but even so the purchase of such a book represented a considerable capital investment. Moreover, these prices did not include binding, which the purchaser had to arrange for himself and at additional expense.

Obviously, therefore, such books could not be called popular because they were well beyond the reach of any but the wealthiest members of society. And indeed they were often criticized for this reason, especially in America, where they were felt to be 'undemocratic'. Alexander Wilson, while looking for subscribers to his $120 *American Ornithology*, ran into a certain Judge Hustetter who 'took upon himself to say, that such a book as mine ought not to be encouraged; as it was not within the reach of the commonalty; and therefore inconsistent with our Republican institutions!'[2] Audubon met exactly the same criticism twenty years later when his collaborator, William MacGillivray, tactfully advised him that, 'With your celebrity, knowledge, and enthusiasm, you have it in your power to become more *popular* than your glorious pictures can ever make you of themselves, they being too aristocratic and exclusive.'[3] However, books like Audubon's and Wilson's could not have been published in the first place, except as aristocratic and exclusive productions. They eventually became popular when, after the first edition was completed, they were reissued on a smaller and cheaper scale. The 'miniature' edition of Audubon's *Birds of America*, for instance (and actually it was a hefty seven volumes of royal octavo), was published in the 1840s for only $100, as against $1,000 for the first edition, and sold 1,200 copies, as against 150 for the first. By the 1860s it was being reprinted fairly regularly in ever cheaper editions and was well within the reach of any middle-class American family.

The nineteenth century happened to be the era of great bird illustrators, as the eighteenth century had been of flower illustrators, and the greatest of all was undoubtedly John James (or Jean Jacques) Audubon. He was born in the West

J. J. Audubon

Indies in 1785. In later years Audubon was to spin a great web of mystery around his birth, hinting that he was of noble, or possibly even royal, lineage, but the facts, as established by his biographer Francis Hobart Herrick, are straightforward enough: he was the illegitimate son of Jean Audubon, a French naval captain and merchant who at the time was running a sugar plantation in Santo Domingo, and his Creole mistress. When the boy was four, Captain Audubon took him home to his wife in France who, being herself childless, welcomed him as her own son and later formally adopted him, thus making him legitimate. When John James was eighteen, his father sent him to America, to an estate called Mill Grove, near Philadelphia, which he had bought many years before. John James was meant to learn English and to manage his father's estate – in fact, he never really mastered English, as his letters show, and he managed his father's estate so badly that within a few months it was heavily mortgaged and, soon afterwards, sold. Thus began Audubon's rackety and adventurous American career.

For twenty years he pursued a course of unerring failure as a businessman, engaging successively in lead-mining, import-exporting, storekeeping and running a saw-mill, with the same invariably disastrous results. He never succeeded because his heart was never in it. 'Birds were birds then as now,' he wrote later, and 'I seldom passed a day without drawing a bird, or noting something respecting its habits, Rozier [his partner] meantime attending the counter.'[4] It was the desire to find new birds, new wildernesses, as much as the need to escape his creditors, that drove him ever further towards the western frontier. He later remarked cheerfully that if he had been content to stay in Louisville, where he started, he would have made a fortune but 'it was not to be, and who cares.'[5] One of the incidental victims of his business failure was a struggling poet across the Atlantic, John Keats. He had entrusted his small capital to his brother George to invest for him in America, and George had the misfortune to fall for one of Audubon's steamboat schemes. The money disappeared down-river with the boat, and Keats wrote sorrowfully to his brother, 'I cannot help thinking Mr. Audubon a dishonest man. Why did he make you believe him a Man of Property?'[6]

Of course, Audubon *was* a dishonest man, which is what makes him such a difficult subject for the biographer. He wrote numerous accounts of himself in his letters, in his journals, in the *Ornithological Biography* and in *Myself*, an autobiographical fragment intended for his sons, but they were all different. He claimed that his mother lived in Philadelphia, which she never did; he claimed that his father met George Washington, which was quite impossible; and he occasionally claimed that he himself was born in Louisiana, though he never even went there till he was thirty-four. Many of his lies were intended for self-glorification, or to gratify a particular audience, but many, too, seem to have been the product of an amazingly poor memory. He once wrote to tell his wife that he had revisited his old home, Mill Grove, and had stood reverentially in the parlour remembering the happy day sixteen years before when they were married there, when in fact – as Mrs Audubon must have reminded him with some annoyance – they were married at *her* home, Fatland Ford, a few miles away. This miasma of lies and forgettings makes it extremely difficult to disentangle the truth and although, as he himself exclaimed, 'What a curious interesting book a Biographer – well acquainted with my Life could write',[7] he contrived to make the task of that biographer almost impossible.

In particular, it is difficult to sort out the comings and goings of his years as a frontier tradesman. But one event undoubtedly happened in 1810 which was to have an important bearing on his subsequent career. In that year Audubon was (for once) at home minding the store in Louisville, Kentucky, when a grim-faced, middle-aged man with a parrot on his shoulder came in and started showing him a bird book. The man was Alexander Wilson, and the book was his *American Ornithology*, which he had written, illustrated and published himself. Wilson was a Scot, born in 1766, who had left his native land in disgust after being jailed for publishing some libellous verses in imitation of Burns. He had settled in Philadelphia, made his living as a schoolmaster, and devoted all his spare time to drawing and observing birds. One of his few friends (he was a generally unsociable man) was William Bartram, a Quaker naturalist and son of the famous botanist John Bartram, and it was to Bartram that he showed his first bird drawings in 1804 asking him to 'Be pleased to mark on the drawings with a pencil, the names of each bird, as, except three or four, I do not know them.'[8] And indeed at this

Alexander Wilson

period very few people would have known the names of many American birds –
it was Wilson himself who first described and named such familiar species as the
whip-poor-will, the song sparrow, field sparrow, black-billed cuckoo, the canvas
back and ruddy duck, and several dozen of the warblers. Linnaeus had described
the skins of some two hundred American species, but their habits, habitat, range,
song, flight, breeding habits and the rest were still generally unknown. Wilson was
the first field, as opposed to closet, naturalist to cover the American avifauna, and
it is for its lively and accurate field-notes, rather than its pedestrian illustrations,

Great-footed hawk, from Wilson's *American Ornithology*

that his *American Ornithology* is valued today. However, in 1808, when it started
publication, everything about the book must have seemed remarkable: its size (im-
perial quarto), its length (nine volumes), its price ($120), and the fact that every
particle of it, from the typeface to the very rags the paper was made from, was
produced in America. It was a highly patriotic work.

Even so, it was not an easy book to sell, and it is to Wilson's credit that he
eventually found 450 subscribers – more than twice as many as Audubon ever
mustered. At the time he appeared in Audubon's store in 1810 he was engaged
on an arduous 2,000-mile subscriber-finding expedition to Cincinnati, Nashville
and New Orleans, travelling by boat, horse and foot, and Audubon's store must
have been one of hundreds that he called on in the course of his eight-month campaign. What actually happened at this famous meeting of the two great pioneer
American ornithologists is far from clear. Audubon claimed in his *Ornithological*

Biography, published over twenty years later, that he was on the point of buying Wilson's book when his partner, who was also present, reminded him that he had better bird drawings of his own. Wilson then asked to see them, became thoughtful, silent, asked to borrow them. Audubon loaned them gladly, took Wilson shooting, found him specimens, and generally befriended him in the five days he stayed in Louisville. Wilson's version is rather different. It consists only of a laconic entry in his diary that he received not 'one act of civility' in Louisville, and that 'Science or literature has not one friend in this place.'[9] Years later, when Audubon was famous, and Wilson was dead, this diary entry was used by Wilson's friend and executor, George Ord, to blacken Audubon's name, but whatever the exact circumstances of the meeting, there is no doubt that some sort of meeting did occur and, as such, it must have provided Audubon's first intimation that he might one day hope to publish his own bird drawings as a book.

However, he was to spend another nine profitless years in the wilderness before at last, in 1819, the inevitable bankruptcy occurred and he spent some weeks in a debtors' jail. He wrote a terrible account of walking from Henderson to Louisville, penniless and ruined, after his release: 'the only time in my life when the Wild Turkeys that so often crossed my path, and the thousands of lesser birds that enlivened the woods and the prairies, all looked like enemies, and I turned my eyes from them, as if I could have wished that they never existed.'[10] At least the bankruptcy made it legally impossible for him to embark on any more doomed business ventures, so that he was free to concentrate on his 'Great Idea' of drawing every species of bird in America. Of course, he had to earn his living, but he managed that fairly easily, by painting portraits, giving drawing lessons, even dancing lessons, and working for a season as a taxidermist in Dr Drake's Museum in Cincinnati. His wife Lucy gave him every encouragement, setting up a school to support their children, and holding the family together through their long separations. By 1824 Audubon had made enough drawings to take his portfolio to Philadelphia – then the cultural capital of the States – to seek a publisher, but his insistence on having the birds reproduced life-size militated against him, and he was advised to go to England to produce his book. It took him another two years to raise the money, but in 1826, at the age of forty-one, he finally sailed to England.

In fact he never did find a publisher (he published himself) but he soon found an excellent engraver in William Home Lizars of Edinburgh. Lizars was so impressed with Audubon's drawings that he agreed to engrave them as Audubon wanted in 'double elephant folio', the untrimmed sheets measuring $39\frac{1}{2}$ by $29\frac{1}{2}$ inches, with every bird shown in its full natural size. The first plate was ready by November 1826 and publication proper commenced in the Spring of 1827. Audubon prepared a prospectus, explaining that the work would be issued in eighty parts (it eventually ran to eighty-seven) of five plates each, spread over fourteen years, at a cost of two guineas a part, and he busied himself to find subscribers. He was immediately successful. He was invited to address the Royal Society, to exhibit his drawings at the Royal Institution, and to receive the greatest honour that Edinburgh had in its power to bestow: a meeting with Sir Walter Scott. (They found one another charming.) 'My situation in Edinburgh borders on the miraculous,'[11] he wrote to his wife, and he jubilantly signed his letter with all his new-found honours – F.R.S.E. (Fellow of the Royal Society of Edinburgh), F.A.S. (Fellow of the Antiquarian Society), M.W.S.N.H. (Member of the Wernerian Society of Natural History) and M.S.A. (Member of the Society of Arts of Scotland). The social whirl, he remarked, was very tiring but 'those who have my best interests at heart tell me I must *not refuse* a single invitation.'[12] He played the part of the American woodsman to the hilt, striding round Edinburgh in a buckskin jacket, with his long ringlets flowing around his shoulders, and regaling dinner parties with tales of frontier life, encounters with Indians, flatboating on the Ohio, a meeting with Daniel Boone, and all the other anecdotes that he later used in the *Ornithological Biography*. It was at this period, one suspects, that he began experimenting with different versions of his life story; at any rate, he showed a publicist's flair for finding a quotable nugget for every occasion.

No sooner was the book successfully launched than Lizars began to be plagued by colourists' strikes and work on it ground to a halt. Audubon decided to go to London in search of a new printer and he eventually lighted on Robert Havell Junior, then a quite unknown engraver of thirty-four. When he saw Havell's first proofs, he was so excited that he kept shouting in his French accent, 'Ze jig is up! Ze jig is up!' which caused Havell some consternation, but it soon emerged that it meant he was delighted with the results, and Havell henceforth became his printer. Audubon moved to London to supervise the work and find more subscribers. His reception there was not quite the unmitigated triumph that he had enjoyed in Edinburgh. The King refused to see him and he often found himself

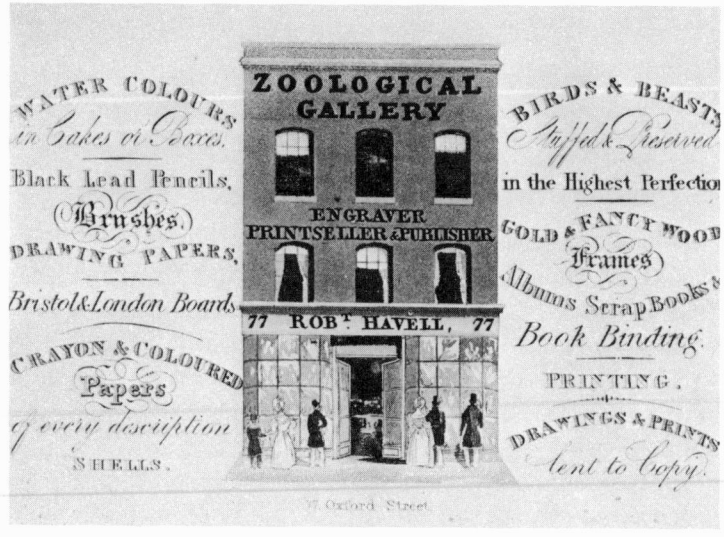

Robert Havell's trade card

'dull as a beetle'.[13] Moreover, he not only had to find new subscribers, but constantly to nurse the ones he had, collecting payments, arranging deliveries, apologizing for delays, and investigating why a piece of beef had been enclosed in a parcel of plates sent to Lord Kinnoull. Many of his subscribers dropped out at various times, on the grounds that the work did not live up to their expectations, and there are in consequence almost as many incomplete sets of the *Birds of America* as there are complete ones. The main complaint seems to have been the colouring – colourists would get slapdash or tired or simply forget to paint certain areas, and then the plates had to be sent back to Havell, washed down, and coloured again, or the subscriber would cancel his subscription.

Audubon was sustained through this trying period by a new friendship, with William Swainson. Swainson at this date was known as an illustrator and hack writer: his addiction to quinarianism had not yet become notorious. He was asked to review the *Birds of America* for Loudon's *Magazine of Natural History* and, with typical opportunism, wrote to ask Audubon to let him have the work at cost price. Audubon replied truthfully that cost price would be considerably more than the published price, but he offered Swainson a reduced rate of 35s. a part, and was rewarded with a laudatory review. The two men met and became friends and that autumn decided to go to Paris together, for Audubon to drum up subscribers, and for Swainson to work in the Jardin des Plantes. But even despite a recommendation from Cuvier, who wrote that his plates were 'equally successful in the drawing, the engraving, and colouring',[14] Audubon could find only thirteen subscribers in France and returned to London disappointed. Swainson was soon asking him for the loan of £80 as proof of his sincere friendship and in order 'that my regard for you may be evinced'.[15]

In 1829 Audubon returned to America, to collect new birds and also to rejoin his wife, whom he had not seen for almost three years. But Havell kept pestering him to return, and at the end of the year, Audubon replied that he was on his way and that, 'I will carry with me some Drawings that I know will make the *graver* and the *Acid* Grin again.'[16] As soon as he returned to London, he set about planning the *Ornithological Biography*, a five-volume text to accompany the *Birds of America* with descriptions of all the birds illustrated, and 'Episodes' narrating his own adventures and scenes of American life. He realized that he would need help on the technical descriptions and also to polish his still Frenchified English, and his first thought was to ask his best friend Swainson. Fortunately for Audubon, Swainson bridled at the idea of becoming a 'ghost', and Audubon thereby escaped being ensnared by the quinary system. He found instead an excellent young Scots naturalist, William MacGillivray, who proved a helpful and business-like collaborator, and the *Ornithological Biography* commenced publication in March 1831, concluding eight years later. The modern reader may occasionally regret MacGillivray's polishing efforts, since Audubon's private letters, in their bad but vigorous English, are far more readable than his sugared public prose, but the style of the *Biography* was much admired at the time.

While in England, Audubon briefly met two young ornithological illustrators who were just then beginning their careers, Edward Lear and John Gould. Lear's subsequent fame as a nonsense writer and, to a lesser extent, as a landscape painter, has tended to overshadow his brief early success as a bird illustrator, but it was in this role that he first become known. Born in 1812, the twentieth child of a family of twenty-one children, Lear was brought up by an elder sister, Ann, and evaded any but the briefest formal schooling. He was 'delicate', short-sighted, and epileptic – the latter a condition to be hidden at all costs because it was regarded by some as a mark of demoniacal possession and by others as a mark of excessive masturbation – and it was probably for this reason that he was ousted from the family home. When he was fifteen, the family fortunes collapsed entirely, and Lear had to support himself and his sister by doing 'uncommon queer shop-sketches – selling them for prices varying from ninepence to four shillings: colouring prints, screens, fans; awhile making morbid disease drawings, for hospitals and certain doctors of physic.'[17] But the next year he was enlisted to provide drawings for Jardine and Selby's *Illustrations of British Ornithology*, and in 1830, at the age of only eighteen, he decided to publish a bird book of his own. He wisely chose the parrots, which were then very fashionable, and of which the Regent's Park Zoo had a good collection. He also decided to print them by the brand new process of lithography, and mastered the art of transferring his own drawings onto the stone. His *Illustrations of the Family of Psittacidae*, which began publishing in November 1830, was extremely well received, and Lear was elected an Associate of the Linnean Society on the strength of it. (He also received the inevitable begging letter from Swainson, asking for the gift of two of the originals 'to hang by the side of a pair by my friend Audubon'.)[18] But, like Audubon, Lear soon found that the publishing side of the business was a perennial headache and 'The tardy paying of many of my subscribers – renders it but too difficult to procure food – & pay for publishing at once',[19] so in 1832, with twelve parts published and two still to go, he abandoned the project.

He had been noticed, however, by John Gould, who was then in the middle of publishing his first book, *A Century of Birds*, and busily planning his second, *The Birds of Europe*, and Lear was asked to provide drawings for both. Gould was a gardener's son, one of those examples of self-made success and tireless industry which the Victorians so much admired. Lear worked for him for six years but said afterwards:

> He was one I never liked really, for in spite of a certain jollity and bonhommie, he was a harsh and violent man. At the Zoological Society at 33 Bruton Street, at Hullmandels [the lithographer's] – at Broad Street ever the same, persevering hard working toiler in his own (ornithological) line, – but ever as unfeeling for those about him. In this earliest phase of his bird-drawing, he owed everything to his excellent wife, & to myself, – without whose help in drawing he had done nothing.[20]

John Gould   Edward Lear

This last is perfectly true. Gould was not so much an illustrator as an illustrators' impresario. Sometimes he did rough sketches himself which were then 'worked up' and transferred to the lithographic stone either by his wife or, after her death, by hired assistants such as William Hart or H.C. Richter, but often he did not even do the sketches. Moreover, he did not always give credit where it was due: many of Lear's plates are subscribed 'J. & E. Gould del et lith' although Lear's signature is visible on the actual drawings. John Gould's main contribution to the books which bear his name was to initiate them, to collect the specimens for illustration, to hire the artists to draw them and colourists to colour them, to arrange publication and printing, to sell them and reap the profits. He was a good businessman with a keen eye for the selling subject and in all he produced 2,999 hand-coloured lithographs of birds in fourteen great folio books, of which the most successful were his *Toucans* (1833–5), his *Humming-Birds* (1849–61) and his *Birds of Great Britain* (1862–73). Among his many other successes, he introduced the budgerigar to Britain in 1840; it is now the most popular cage-bird in the world.

Audubon's son-in-law, John Bachman, once asked him what he thought of Gould and Audubon replied tactfully, 'Gould is a man of great industry and has the advantage of the Zoological Society, museums, gardens, &c., ... His wife makes his drawings on stone. She is a plain, fine woman, and although their works are not quite up to nature, both deserve great credit.'[21] The slightly patronizing tone seems justified. Gould's plates, though much admired by the Victorians, now seem too glossy, too cosmetic and too mechanical. By comparison with Audubon's or Lear's, his birds lack personality. Lear's parrots suggest that if he had continued in that line (he drew his last bird for Gould in 1837, signing off with the excuse that his eyesight was failing) he might have become as great as Audubon, but then the world would have been the poorer by much fine nonsense, so one cannot begrudge him his defection.

Northern Diver, from Gould's *Birds of Europe*

In June 1838, twelve years after its commencement, the 87th and final part of the *Birds of America* was published, and Audubon returned permanently to America, where he found that 'the very streets resound with my name'.[22] Although the first edition of the *Birds* barely covered its costs (only 151 subscribers stayed the full course), the miniature edition, published from 1840 to 1844, represented a solid profit and Audubon was able to buy a fine estate on the Hudson and settle down to planning his next project, *The Viviparous Quadrupeds of North America*, in collaboration with his son-in-law, the Rev. John Bachman. In June 1840 he was surprised by a letter from a 15-year-old-boy who had found a new species of flycatcher which Audubon and every other American ornithologist had missed. The boy was Spencer Fullerton Baird, and he went on to become Secretary of the Smithsonian Institution, organizer of the United States National Museum and the greatest American ornithologist of the post-Audubon era. Audubon immediately enlisted him to find specimens for the *Viviparous Quadrupeds* – 'Please to collect all the Shrews, Mice (field or wood), rats, bats, Squirrels, etc., and put them in a jar in common Rum, not whiskey, brandy or alcohol'[23] – and Baird was soon bombarding him with specimens. But despite Baird's assistance (fittingly

The Mocking Bird. (Male & Female)
TURDUS POLYGLOTTUS.

Rattlesnake.
CROTALUS HORRIDUS.

6 Rattlesnake attacking a mocking-bird's nest, from Audubon's *Birds of America*, 1827–38

7 Rieffer's Amazili, from John Gould's *Humming-birds*, 1861

8 Sparrow-hawk, from Audubon's *Birds of America*, 1827-38

9 Grey Fox, from Audubon's *Viviparous Quadrupeds*, 1845-9

commemorated in the dedication to him of a new species, 'Baird's bunting', in the new edition of the *Birds*), work on the *Viviparous Quadrupeds* did not go smoothly. Audubon had trouble communicating with Bachman, who lived down in Charleston, and trouble obtaining specimens. He even occasionally had to rely on stuffed museum specimens, which he would have considered unthinkable for the *Birds*. He was never as entirely at home with fur as he had been with feathers, and in the end he executed only seventy-six of the one hundred and fifty plates himself. A friend who visited him at his home, Minnie's Land, in 1846 reported:

> The patriarch... had greatly changed since I had last seen him. He wore his hair longer, and it now hung in locks of snowy whiteness over his shoulders. His once piercing gray eyes, though still bright, had already begun to fail him. He could no longer paint with his wonted accuracy, and had at last, most reluctantly, been forced to surrender to his sons the task of completing his Quadrupeds of North America.[24]

He died in 1851, with the text of the *Quadrupeds* still unfinished.

Passenger-pigeons, from Audubon's *Birds of America*

However, it is not for the *Quadrupeds* but for the *Birds of America* that Audubon is remembered. In all it comprises 435 plates representing over a thousand individual birds of 489 species and also several hundred American trees, shrubs, flowers and insects, and in size and scale, quite apart from its beauty, it must constitute one of the greatest publishing feats of all time. Ornithologists, it must be admitted, have never been entirely happy with Audubon's work. They claim that in his efforts to make his birds lifelike and active he occasionally stretched them (he drew from fresh-killed carcases mounted with wires) into unnatural or contorted poses, and that he sometimes showed them in impossible situations. The famous plate of a rattlesnake attacking a mocking-bird's nest was particularly notorious in its day and provoked endless debate about whether rattlesnakes could climb trees (the answer seems to be yes) and whether they would ever attack a mocking-bird's nest (the answer seems to be no). It was also found subsequently that many of Audubon's species were merely immature forms or variants of other species. A more recent criticism comes from conservationists who express horror at Audubon's remark that 'I call birds few, when I shoot less than one hundred per day',[25] but it should be remembered that bird-shooting was an inescapable adjunct of bird-watching in the pre-binocular, pre-camera era. In any case, none of these criticisms can detract from the stunning beauty of the plates which, in their fine and faultless detail and dramatic overall design, seem to possess an almost visionary intensity; the more so if one is able to see them in their original size.

The best summation of Audubon's effect on the viewer was made by a visitor to his very first exhibition in Edinburgh who wrote:

It is a real and palpable vision of the New World, with its atmosphere, its imposing vegetation, and its tribes which know not the yoke of man. The sun shines athwart the clearing in the woods; the swan floats suspended between a cloudless sky and a glittering wave; strange and majestic figures keep pace with the sun, which gleams from the mica sown broadcast on the shores of the Atlantic; and this realization of an entire hemisphere, this picture of a nature so lusty and strong, is due to the brush of a single man; such an unheard of triumph of patience and genius![26]

CHAPTER SEVEN

THE ECCENTRIC SQUIRE OF WALTON HALL

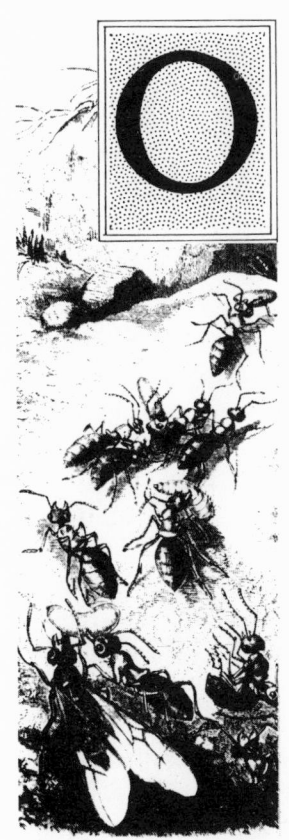

O N 5 NOVEMBER 1826, just a few weeks after he first arrived in Britain and before he had published a single plate of the *Birds of America*, Audubon recorded in his journal that he had received 'a scrubby letter from Charles Waterton'.[1] The scrubby letter no longer survives but one can imagine its contents from what came later. Waterton must have been told to look out for Audubon by his friend and correspondent George Ord of Philadelphia who, as Alexander Wilson's literary executor, was keeping a keen eye on all Audubon's activities, and the letter was presumably by way of being a warning salvo across the bows. Outright warfare did not commence for another five years, and Audubon probably forgot the incident entirely, although no doubt he took the trouble to enquire who this man Charles Waterton was.

He would have been told that Charles Waterton was the author of a bestselling book, the *Wanderings in South America*, which had been published the year before. *Wanderings in South America* is not a title that would nowadays send would-be purchasers panting to the bookshops but in 1825, when it made its debut, it evoked all the most desirable ingredients – exoticism, adventure and the Great Unknown. Wandering, preferably where white man's foot had never trod, was then in vogue and South America was agreed to be the most exciting possible place to wander. It was known to contain humming-birds, orchids, toucans and all the other gaudy extravaganzas of Nature that the English public most admired, and it was also believed to contain the fabled city of El Dorado and a vast inland sea called Lake Parima.

Charles Waterton, in the course of his wanderings, did not actually find El Dorado or Lake Parima, but he came back with traveller's tales almost equally exciting. He had trekked barefoot and alone (apart from a few 'sable slaves') through the jungle, and encouraged vampire bats to suck his toes. He had captured a 14-foot 'Coulacanara' snake alive and carried it, Laocoön-like, in wreaths around

'Sleepers attacked by vampire bats', from Waterton's
Wanderings in South America, 1825

his body. He had dragged a cayman alligator out of the river and ridden along the bank astride its back. 'Should it be asked,' he informed his readers, 'how I managed to keep my seat, I would answer, – I hunted some years with Lord Darlington's fox hounds.'[2] Most impressively of all, he had sought for, and found, the dreaded wourali poison (now known as curare) which the natives used on their blowpipes, and which was supposed to bring death at the merest touch. Waterton believed, on somewhat tenuous grounds, that it would cure hydrophobia, and he brought some back to England to test its powers. He even advertised for volunteers: 'Supposing a person has been bitten by a mad dog... Lose no time in telegraphing for Dr. Sibson, No. 40 Lower Brook Street, London; and for Charles Waterton, Walton Hall, near Wakefield, Yorkshire. We will promptly attend.'[3]

Not surprisingly, some readers were inclined to doubt parts of Waterton's narrative, and one or two reviewers did not scruple to call him a liar, but the controversy served only to sell more copies of the book. So, too, did the vexed question of the 'Nondescript', an ambiguous creature whose portrait forms the frontispiece of the *Wanderings*. It looks like a monkey with an unusually human face. Waterton claimed that he had 'procured' it in the jungle, cut off its head (its body was too heavy to carry), stuffed it, and brought it back to Europe, to adorn his staircase at home. He was not prepared to say what the Nondescript was, though he gave a pretty broad hint: 'In my opinion, his thick coat of hair, and great length of tail, put his species out of all question; but then, his face and head cause the inspector to pause for a moment, before he ventures to pronounce his opinion of the classification.'[4] Several years later, he finally admitted that the Nondescript was made from the skins of two red monkeys, deliberately stretched and distorted to resemble a human face. But meanwhile his readers preferred more sensational explanations. Some claimed that the Nondescript was the head of an Indian whom Waterton had murdered in the jungle, and vociferously demanded an inquest on the remains. Others decided that it was intended as a rude portrait of a certain customs officer who had incurred Waterton's wrath by making him pay heavy import duties on his natural history collections. Anyway, there was sufficient general clamour about the book to make it a bestseller in 1825 and to keep it almost continuously in print for half a century more.

It is not, in fact, a very good book. The style is disjointed and uneven, with many ponderous rhetorical flourishes, and a superfluity of stale Latin tags and absurd Spanish proverbs. It is divided into four Journeys, the first three of which take place mainly in Demerara (modern Guyana), and the fourth in an area which Waterton calls 'the North-West of the United States', though the furthest West he ever reached was Buffalo. The narrative is so digressive that it is impossible now to retrace Waterton's itinerary, and his use of local, rather than Linnaean names for species makes several of them unidentifiable. His field-work is far from thorough and his botanical knowledge does not extend to anything smaller than trees, but his descriptions of the sloth, the 'ant-bear' (great ant-eater) and some of the Demeraran birds are detailed, keen and affectionate. What gives the book its enduring charm are the typically *Boy's Own* adventures – the tussles with the cayman, with the serpent, and the romantic quest for the wourali poison.

Moreover, although the *Wanderings* was written while Waterton was still comparatively young and before he had reached the peak of his eccentricity, there are still enough self-revealing hints in the narrative to suggest that its author was no ordinary man. There is a touching death-bed scene with Sir Joseph Banks when, 'I saw with sorrow that death was going to rob us of him. We talked much of the present mode adopted by all museums in stuffing quadrupeds',[5] and the occasional nice throw-away line: 'About eight years ago, while eating a boiled Toucan...'[6] But it is in the fourth Journey, in the United States, that Waterton really lets himself go. He explains that he arrived at Niagara with a sprained ankle and remembered that the proper treatment for a sprain was to hold the limb under running water. And what more efficacious running water, he decided, than Niagara Falls? He accordingly hobbled down the path and held his foot under the fall, trying to meditate meanwhile 'on the immense difference there was betwixt a house pump and this tremendous cascade of nature, and what effect it might have upon the sprain; but the magnitude of the subject was too overwhelming, and I was obliged to drop it.'[7]

If the *Wanderings* had been written with the deliberate intention of making one want to know more about its author, it could not have been more skilfully done, but it was not until 1838 that Waterton decided to gratify the curiosity he had aroused. In that year he published his first series of *Essays on Natural History* and prefaced it with 'Some Account of the Writer of the Following Essays, by Himself.' This venture into autobiography was so successful that he continued the narrative in the second and third series of *Essays* (published in 1844 and 1857 respectively), at some considerable length. These notes were later collated and elaborated by his friend Sir Norman Moore in his collected edition of the *Essays*. Other biographies followed. The Rev. J.G. Wood, who seems to have known Waterton fairly well though never as an intimate friend, added a 'Biographical

Charles Waterton, by C. W. Peale

Introduction' to his edition of the *Wanderings* published in 1880. And then there was Dr Hobson of Leeds, who was Waterton's personal physician and close friend for the last thirty years of his life, and who published *Charles Waterton: His Home, Habits and Handiwork* in 1866, the year after Waterton's death.

This latter book must be one of the most bizarre biographies ever published. The eccentricity of Waterton's life is at least matched, if not exceeded, by the eccentricity of Dr Hobson's style. In the very first paragraph of the preface, Hobson tells the reader that he is 'determined to clear the decks and take time by the forelock' and his Table of Contents foreshadows the bewildering delights to come:

Special immunity in the female sex from death by lightning;

The Author attaches White Feathers to the Tail of a Swallow to test the Ornithological Knowledge of a Gentleman;

The Ape Searching the Squire's head reminds him of a Cambridge Anecdote;

Securing of Pike by the Bow and Arrow a favourite Amusement of the Squire;

Mr. Waterton 'fairly floored' by Mr. Salvin's clever Imitation of a Pig;

An Allusion to a stench from a dead herring near the Grotto, induces the Squire to relate an incident regarding dead letters;

Explanation why the Squire was able to make his Elbows meet.

Hobson's book is mainly concerned with Waterton's habits in old age, but his earlier life can be reconstructed from the autobiographical notes in the *Essays*. He was born in 1782, the eldest son of an old-established and wealthy family whose seat was Walton Hall, near Wakefield in Yorkshire. But the Watertons were Roman Catholics, and thus debarred from entering Parliament, the Army, or any of the usual careers open to landed aristocrats. After completing his education at Stonyhurst College, therefore, Charles Waterton was sent to Demerara to manage some estates (probably sugar plantations) that the family owned, and he remained there till 1812, even though his father had died in 1806 and he was now the Squire of Walton Hall. Between 1812 and 1824 he divided his time between England and America, where he made the four journeys recounted in the *Wanderings*. He also, in 1817, visited Rome, where he climbed to the top of St Peter's and the Castel Sant'Angelo. Only in 1825, at the age of forty-three, did he finally settle down at Walton Hall, and his wanderings were thereafter confined to annual trips to Scarborough and pilgrimages to certain European shrines.

Dr Hobson recounts in his biography how he was frequently greeted by the sight of the 80-year-old Squire 'actually dancing down the whole length of the broad flagged walk, occasionally throwing one of his loose slippers from his foot high up in the air above his head, and expertly catching it in his hand in its descent.'[8] When the Squire was not dancing out on to the terrace to greet Hobson, it was usually because he was waiting under the hall-table, pretending to be a dog, to bark and snap at the visitor's boots when he came in. He did this so often that Hobson was eventually forced to remonstrate: 'I gently hinted at the fortuitous hazard incurred, stating that many instances were recorded, on undoubted authority, when even permanent aberration of the mind had been the result of such a sudden and unexpected shock to the nervous system.'[9] In addition, Hobson frequently had to watch the septuagenarian Squire climbing high trees in search of birds' nests and, as a party trick, scratching the back part of his head with the big toe of his right foot.

A tour round Walton Hall and park would reveal further marks of eccentricity – the stables designed so that the horses could talk to each other and the woods full of dummy pheasants nailed to the tree-branches to confuse potential poachers. The house was crammed with taxidermic curiosities that Waterton had stuffed himself. The famous Nondescript, of course, had pride of place, but there were also some more elaborate set-pieces designed to shock visitors, such as 'John Bull and the National Debt', and 'The English Reformation Zoologically Illustrated' in which Waterton had worked off his anti-Protestant prejudices by labelling various beetles, toads and snakes with the names of Titus Oates, Cranmer, Bishop

'John Bull and the National Debt'

Burnett and so on. In the course of showing people round his estate, Waterton would expatiate at length about the 'Hanoverian rat' against which he waged unremitting war. This was the brown rat, which had supplanted the native black rat in England about a century before, and Waterton always claimed that it had arrived in the same ships that brought the hated new Protestant dynasty. 'This brute, like the family which first brought it over, exists in round numbers, and demands a most plentiful supply of food.'[10] Almost every one of Waterton's *Essays* contains a reference to the Hanoverian rat, which ranks as one of his major obsessions. After carrying out enormous rebuilding and replumbing works on his house and out-buildings, he was finally able to boast: 'When I am gone to dust, if my ghost should hover o'er the mansion, it will rejoice to hear the remark, that Charles Waterton, in the year of grace 1839, effectually cleared the premises at Walton Hall of every Hanoverian rat, young and old.'[11]

Waterton's personal habits were ascetic. He never touched alcohol and frequently fasted. After his wife's death, he abjured beds and always slept on the bare floor with a wooden block as his pillow. He rose at three, to light his own fire and say his prayers. Incidentally, it is only from Thackeray's brief portrait of 'W. – a friend who belongs to the old religion' in *The Newcomes* that we get a sympathetic account of Waterton's deep piety. Hobson obviously considered the Squire's Roman Catholicism as simply one more symptom of eccentricity. But Waterton began and ended his day with prayers, attended mass regularly, observed all the Church feasts and fasts scrupulously, stayed often with his old teachers at Stonyhurst (and eventually left his natural history collections to them) and made almost annual pilgrimages to Rome or other Catholic centres. His acts of charity were well known in the Walton neighbourhood. He had a standing arrangement with a local cobbler whereby, if Waterton met a barefoot beggar, he would give the beggar a knife and tell him to take it to the cobbler and exchange it for shoes. Waterton would later retrieve the knife and pay for the shoes. Hobson, typically, disapproved of this 'promiscuous charity' and also of Waterton leaving his natural history collections to the Jesuits, and his book ends with a great tirade on the subject and a full transcription of Waterton's will.

Like so many eccentrics, Waterton was a great believer in home medicine. The Niagara treatment for the sprain was a special occasion, but his usual cure for any accident or illness was the operation he referred to as 'tapping the claret', i.e. blood-letting. Of course, this was a standard medical procedure at the time, but Waterton performed it on himself, and with astonishing frequency, telling the Rev. J.G. Wood that he had done it at least 160 times. Not content with endangering his own health, he was always anxious to play the doctor on his tenants, pressing them to take his 'Squire Waterton's Pills' – a concoction of calomel and jalap which he maintained would cure anything. Hobson has a telling anecdote about how once the Squire asked him to lance an abscess for one of his tenants. Hobson replied – with true consideration for the Squire but none at all for the patient – that 'if the case be one of absolute poverty, and the abscess is in the condition and situation you represent, there can be neither difficulty nor impropriety in your opening it.' Having given this quite unwarrantable fiat, Hobson then compounded it with the gift of a surgical knife to perform the operation. 'The Squire's eyes glistened with delight as he admired the form of the knife. He evidently luxuriated in anticipation of the exploit in question.'[12]

One could go on multiplying instances of Waterton's eccentricity for ever (and the reader who wants more is recommended to read Hobson's book), but it is time now to consider his qualities as a naturalist. These can best be gauged from the three series of *Essays on Natural History* and, to a lesser extent, from the *Wanderings* and from his letters and notebooks. He thought of himself primarily as an ornithologist:

> Most men have some favourite pursuit, some well-trained hobby, which they have ridden from the days of their youth. Mine is ornithology; and when the vexations of the world have broken in upon me, I mount it, and go away for an hour or two amongst the birds of the valley; and I seldom fail to return with better feelings than when I first set out.[13]

The situation of Walton Hall, built on a small island in a lake, with woods and swampy ground on its further bank, was particularly propitious for bird-watching, and Waterton made it more so by installing 'an excellent eight-and-twenty-guinea telescope'[14] in his drawing-room window. Furthermore, Waterton was always prepared to shin up any tree, however high, to examine a bird's nest.

In addition – and this is probably Waterton's single most important contribution to the study of natural history – he was one of the first Englishmen (probably *the* first) to turn his park into a nature preserve. He enclosed the whole park in a high wall and forbade his tenants and workers to discharge any firearms within its precincts. He also made a rule that no boats should venture on the lake while the water-birds were breeding. He even built a special tower for jackdaws, starlings and owls to nest in and planted a yew hedge round it to give them privacy. The results were gratifying. In 1849 he wrote to tell his friend George Ord, 'My carrion crows, herons, hawks and magpies have done very well this year and I have had a fine breed of kingfishers. They may thank their stars that they have my park wall to protect them. But for it their race would be extinct in this depraved and demoralized part of Yorkshire.'[15] He was eventually able to record 122 species of birds (including such rarities as the osprey, hobby, hooded crow and crossbill) which had been sighted within the park. This was particularly remarkable because Walton was near a built-up area and within range of pollution from the Wakefield factories. In 1848 Waterton actually sued the owner of a soap and vitriol works whose effluent was polluting his stream and woods, but received only derisory damages.

Waterton's writings on natural history show a characteristic mixture of sound observation and unsound dogmatism. Sometimes he was inspired by the true

Sketch of Walton Hall, by Captain E. Jones

scientific spirit, as when he counted the number of times a blue tit fed her young in the course of a day, or when he examined owls' droppings to discover their diet, and he was good at refuting all the old myths about toads being poisonous, nightjars sucking milk from cows, and the curious idea that herons hung their legs outside the nest when incubating their eggs. His plea that naturalists should pay more attention to field studies and less to closet work was also reasonable, though it was vitiated in his case by his total inability to understand any closet work and his failure to grasp even the first principles of Linnaean taxonomy. But his worst failing was his arrogance. No sooner had Edward Jenner published the first accurate account of how the one-day-old cuckoo pushes its foster siblings out of the nest, than Waterton thundered into print to assert that the thing was impossible and 'The account carries its own condemnation, no matter by whom related and by whom received.'[16] He was to do the same again, more vociferously and more violently, in the case of Audubon's *Birds*.

Audubon, as we have seen, heard the first rumble from Waterton in 1826, but it was not until early 1829, when he and Swainson returned from Paris, that Waterton launched his attack. Swainson wrote to warn Audubon that, 'I have had a most extraordinary letter from Waterton, which will highly amuse you. The man is mad – stark, staring mad.'[17] Swainson already knew Waterton slightly because as a boy he had been instructed by him in taxidermy and they had corresponded for a while on friendly terms, but Waterton had dropped the correspondence when he discovered that Swainson was planning to write a natural history of Demeraran birds, which he regarded as his private property. The 'mad' letter no longer survives, but it was probably inspired by reading Swainson's laudatory review of the *Birds of America* in the *Magazine of Natural History*. At all events, Audubon and Swainson were soon bound together as the objects of Waterton's implacable detestation. 'Those two men ought to be whipped!'[18] he thundered to George Ord.

At this stage, he was still prepared to conduct the warfare in private, but in 1832, when he was already goaded into frenzy by the universal praise for Audubon's *Birds* and for the *Ornithological Biography* which had just commenced publication, he came across an article Audubon had written five years earlier on the 'Habits of the Turkey Buzzard (*Vultur aura*) particularly with the view of exploding the opinion generally entertained of its extraordinary power of Smelling.' Waterton had mentioned vultures, and their power of smelling, in the *Wanderings*, and he chose to read Audubon's article as a deliberate attack on the sacred text. He accordingly dashed off an essay 'On the Faculty of Scent of the Vulture', containing lavish denunciations of Audubon and all his work, for the April 1832 issue of Loudon's *Magazine*. This was the first of nineteen articles attacking Audubon which he was to publish in the next few years. The vulture's nose proved a particularly fertile debating-point, with new champions and opponents, 'Nosarians' and 'Anti-Nosarians', appearing right and left, and Waterton devoted at least three more articles to the theme. Unlike Audubon, he had not actually conducted any experiments to test the vulture's power of smelling but, as in the case of Jenner and the cuckoo, he *knew* that he was right.

Having once tasted blood, Waterton rapidly moved on to other targets: 'The gland on the rump of birds', Audubon's account of the humming-bird, of the passenger-pigeon, and that eternally contentious plate of the rattlesnake attacking the mocking-bird's nest. As his targets multiplied, so too did the violence of his language, and by the time he reached Audubon's humming-bird he was positively galumphing with rage: 'Mr. Audubon tells us that the little pieces of lichen, used in forming the nest of the humming-bird, "are glued together with the saliva of the bird." Fiddle!'[19] But modern ornithologists confirm that Audubon was right and Waterton wrong. In his passenger-pigeon article, Waterton challenged not only Audubon himself but all 'those British naturalists who have volunteered to support a foreigner in his exertions to teach Mr. Bull ornithology in the nineteenth century' and he singled out Swainson for a special snub: 'By the way, I observe at the end of that *Biography* a most laudatory notice by Mr. Swainson. He tells us that Audubon contemplated Nature as she really is, not as she is represented in books: he sought her in her sanctuaries. Well, be it so; I do not dispute his word; still I suspect that, during the search and contemplation, either the dame herself was in liquor, or her wooer in hallucination.'[20]

In 1833 Waterton abandoned guerrilla warfare for a frontal attack: he boldly proclaimed, in the pages of Loudon's *Magazine*, that Audubon was not the author of his own work. 'I request the English reader to weigh well in his own mind what I have stated,' he wrote, 'and I flatter myself that he will agree with me, when I affirm that the correct and elegant style of composition which appears through the *whole of the Biography of Birds* cannot possibly be that of him whose name it bears.'[21] This was sufficiently grave to draw a reply from Victor Audubon, Audubon's son (Audubon himself very sensibly refused to reply to any of Waterton's attacks), and Waterton responded by quoting a letter he had received from George Ord saying that Swainson had been asked to write the *Ornithological Biography* but had declined when he found he was expected to do so under Audubon's name. This was rather a sore point because of course Swainson *had* been asked to do exactly that, and had declined, and his friendship with Audubon had soured as a result. But Swainson, forced to choose between the frying-pan of his minor grudge against Audubon, and the fire of his major grudge against Waterton, wisely decided to stay with the former, and replied immediately in Loudon's *Magazine* in unequivocal terms: 'I was not asked to write the work, nor did Mr. Audubon "insist upon his own name being given to the world as the author" of such parts as he wished me to undertake.'[22] In fact, this may well have been a lie, but it was enough to silence Waterton temporarily, or at least to deter editors from printing any more of his libels.

A slight lull in hostilities ensued, but in 1836 Swainson published a new volume in the *Lardner's Cyclopaedia* series, *The Natural History of Birds*. This presented a somewhat disenchanted view of Audubon's work (his 'scientific descriptions are destitute of that precision and detail which might have been expected in these days')[23] but it contained enough praise of the American to set Waterton off again. He hammered out 'An Ornithological Letter to William Swainson, Esq., F.R.S.'[24] and when he could not find any editor willing to take it, published it as a pamphlet at his own expense. Here he returned to the vulture's nose, the rattlesnake question, and even the authorship dispute: 'You have thought fit to laud one man exceedingly for his zoological acquirements, who, to my certain knowledge, paid other people for the letterpress and drawings which were to appear in his work.' He had also got wind of Swainson's private foible and attacked 'the quinary labyrinth of your fond conceit of circles' and ended by predicting nastily, 'Let me tell you frankly that the admeasurement of ten thousand dried bird-skins, with a subsequent and vastly complicated theory on what you conceive you have drawn from the scientific operation of your compasses, will never raise your name to any permanent altitude.'

This was too much for Swainson. He had borne all the previous attacks in heroic silence, but when his precious quinarianism was at stake, his battle spirit was roused. It happened that the weary progress of Dr Lardner's *Cyclopaedia* had just then brought him to *Fishes* and in an article on the crocodile (which for some reason was included among fishes) he hit at Waterton in his most tender spot:

> The crocodile, in fact, is only dangerous when in the water ... There is no great prowess, therefore, required to ride on the back of a poor cayman after it has been secured, or perhaps wounded; and a modern writer might well

have spared the recital of his feats in this way upon the cayman of Guiana, had he not been influenced, in this and numberless other instances, by the greatest possible love of the marvellous, and a constant propensity to dress truth in the garb of fiction.[25]

Waterton was not the man to resist such provocation and his essay on the cayman[26] is entirely devoted to diatribes against his old enemy. 'Master Swainson', he calls him, 'Swainson, wholesale dealer in closet-zoology', 'this morbid and presumptuous man', 'this dealer in unsound zoology'. He rehearses the whole saga of their quarrel and concludes,

> I thought I had done with him altogether, till 1839, whilst I was in Italy, out came Lardner's volume on Fishes, containing the sweeping extract which I have transcribed at the head of this paper. Swainson was then about to take his final departure to New Zealand. Steam will soon convey him a copy of this. I call upon him to contradict the statements which it contains, or to acknowledge the truth and the propriety of them.

But Swainson never answered the call because in late 1839, worn out by money worries and disappointed by the universal contempt for his quinary system, he had indeed emigrated to New Zealand and was never to appear in English zoological circles again. Yet he had the last word, for in 1840 the final volume of his *Cyclopaedia* appeared, containing potted biographies of all the leading zoologists. Of Audubon he wrote disdainfully, 'A want of precision in his descriptions, and a general ignorance of modern ornithology, sadly disappoint the scientific reader.'[27] But of Waterton he was surprisingly charitable: 'Waterton, Charles – *Traveller*. An unscientific, but a very observing naturalist, whose American travels contain many excellent observations on the animals of Guiana and Demerara.'[28] Even Waterton, in his saner moments, must have realized that this was fair.

CHAPTER EIGHT

AN INVENTION AND ITS CONSEQUENCES

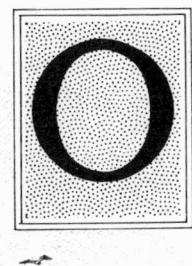

NE DAY IN 1829 a Whitechapel surgeon named Nathaniel Bagshaw Ward who was something of an amateur entomologist found a hawkmoth chrysalis and decided to take it home and try to hatch it. He shut it in a bottle and put it away for the winter. When he came to look at it the next spring, the chrysalis was still unhatched, but he noticed something else alive in the bottle which was in many ways more remarkable. Two tiny seedlings, one a grass and the other a fern, were sprouting from the damp mould on which the chrysalis was lying. What was remarkable about these seedlings was that Ward had not watered them – in fact he had not touched the bottle for many months. He had accidentally discovered the principle that plants enclosed in almost airtight glass cases are virtually self-sustaining. Under sunlight, the plants transpire, moisture condenses on the glass and at night drips back down to the soil. Provided the soil is sufficiently moist to begin with, and provided the case is sufficiently airtight for no moisture to escape, the process can continue more or less indefinitely. It is the principle on which modern bottle gardens are based.

Ward transferred the bottle to his window-ledge and the seedlings continued to grow. (Eventually, having grown and flourished for another two decades, they made an honoured appearance at the Great Exhibition of 1851.) He now decided to experiment. For many years he had been trying to grow ferns in his garden, but in the polluted, smoke-laden atmosphere of Whitechapel they invariably died. This time, however, instead of planting them outdoors, he planted them in bottles on his window-ledge and within three years he had successfully reared no less than thirty different species of fern. He took one of his fern-cases along to the Linnean Society, where it was much admired. He also communicated his discovery to George Loddiges, the owner of a famous nursery at Hackney, who quickly realized its commercial implications. Loddiges packed a consignment of plants in 'Wardian cases' to send on the long and difficult sea-voyage to Australia, and in November 1834 he received word that the plants had arrived safely, alive and thriving.

News of Ward's invention spread slowly. It was mentioned in various popular gardening magazines and in a lecture that Faraday gave to the Royal Institution, but it was not until 1842 that Ward himself wrote up his findings 'On the growth of Plants in Closely Glazed Cases'. As a doctor, he stressed the health benefits to be derived from the introduction of vegetation into the sort of soot-blackened leafless slums that he knew so well from his Whitechapel practice. But at this stage there was still a bar to any widespread adoption of the Wardian case. Glass had been subject to a heavy excise duty ever since the Napoleonic wars, and its high price made it strictly a luxury item. It was only after 1845, when the glass tax was repealed, that the way became clear for Ward's invention to realize its full potential.

The most important and long-lasting effect of the Wardian case was the one already foreshadowed by George Loddiges's Australian experiment. Hitherto it had been commercially impracticable to import plants in any quantity from far-off continents like South America and Australia. The vicissitudes of climate on long sea-voyages and the effects of salt spray usually killed all the seedlings before they arrived. Only those plants that could be successfully imported as seeds had proved worth the nurseryman's while. But now the Wardian case made it possible for growing plants to survive many weeks at sea, even if totally neglected on the voyage. Nurserymen and florists began to place huge orders for 'exotics' from every corner of the globe, and at last the Victorian craving for orchids, pitcher-plants, aspidistras and the like could be fully satisfied. With the repeal of the glass tax, every suburban villa sprouted its greenhouse, 'stove', or conservatory, housing a miniature jungle of foreign plants. But this was only one of the economic benefits. The directors of Kew Gardens began to plan even more large-scale movements of plants and, after a series of experiments with other botanical gardens around the world, when literally millions of plants were ferried to and fro in Wardian cases, they eventually succeeded in establishing tea as a cash-crop in India (from China) and rubber in Malaya (from South America), thus adding two valuable new commodities to the British Empire's resources. Kew's Wardian cases were probably one of the best investments the British Government has ever made, and in fact they were only very recently superseded by the use of polythene bags.

Meanwhile at home a curious fashion was developing. For reasons which are still obscure (despite an excellent analysis in David Elliston Allen's *The Victorian Fern Craze*) the Wardian case gave rise to a passion for ferns and fern-growing which was one of the major fads of the mid-Victorian period and even acquired a title – Pteridomania. In fact it is quite possible to grow ferns without a Wardian case, and it is perfectly possible to grow other plants besides ferns in a Wardian case, but – perhaps for no better reason than that Ward himself had favoured ferns to begin with – Wardian cases quickly became synonymous with ferns in the Victorian mind. Particularly the Victorian *lady's* mind, since the fern craze seems to have been a largely female passion. No doubt the luxuriance and intricacy of ferns appealed to the Gothic taste, as too did their association with ruins and other Udolphian settings. Or perhaps it was the pure seduction of the fern-writers' prose, as surely no one could resist Shirley Hibberd's description of ferns as 'plumy emerald green pets glistening with health and beadings of warm dew'.[1]

At all events, by the middle of the century no fashionable drawing-room was considered complete without its Wardian case full of 'vegetable jewellery' (Shirley Hibberd again) prominently displayed. There were square cases, round cases, table cases, stand cases, Gothic cases, Tintern Abbey cases, Crystal Palace

A Wardian case

cases, 'Oriental' cases – a host of wonderful glittering palaces to house the plumy green pets. An American journalist noted approvingly that the recent fashion for hanging baskets was now giving way to 'the more expensive stand or Wardian case, which being less readily imitated by people of limited means, is likely to continue longer in fashion.'[2] And Charles Kingsley reported patronizingly in *Glaucus*, at the height of the craze, that it was having an entirely beneficial effect on the nation's womenfolk:

> Your daughters, perhaps, have been seized with the prevailing 'Pterido-mania', and are collecting and buying ferns, with Ward's cases wherein to keep them, (for which you have to pay) and wrangling over unpronounceable names of species, (which seem to be different in each new Fern-book that they buy) till the Pteridomania seems to you somewhat of a bore: and yet you cannot deny that they find an enjoyment in it, and are more active, more cheerful, more self-forgetful over it, than they would have been over novels and gossip, crochet and Berlin-wool. At least you will confess that the abomination of 'Fancy work', that standing cloak for dreamy idleness, ... has all but vanished from your drawing-room since the 'Lady-ferns' and 'Venus's hair' appeared.[3]

As usual, Victorian publishers were quick to exploit the new development, and fern books poured from the presses throughout the 1840s and 1850s. The *Phyto-*

'Gathering Ferns', from the *Illustrated London News*, 1871

logist (a fern magazine) reported in 1857 that 'The literature of ferns is in a palmy state . . . It surpasses that of all the other branches of botanical science together.'[4] Many of the books had exceptionally fine illustrations, like those by W.H. Fitch for *A Popular History of the British Ferns* (in the Lovell Reeve half-guinea natural history series) and those by J.E. Sowerby for *The Ferns of Great Britain*. An even more splendid production was the six-guinea *Ferns of Great Britain and Ireland*, *Nature-Printed* with plates printed directly from fern-fronds by Henry Bradbury's patent process. Ladies not content with reading about ferns and growing them could apply themselves to 'spatter-work', a method of stencilling ferns on to fabric and paper. And of course there was the usual glut of fern decoration on china, textiles, woodwork, and wrought-iron garden furniture.

Serious pteridomaniacs went out and gathered ferns for themselves, but there was also a hectic trade in fern supplies for the armchair enthusiast. Visitors to the summit of Snowdon in 1849 were surprised to be greeted by local dealers hawking Holly Ferns at sixpence a root, and fern-sellers could even be found outside the entrance to the Bank of England. One dealer boasted of having removed five tons of ferns in a single foray into Cornwall. The result was as one would expect: by the mid-1860s many rarer species were virtually exterminated and 'even the more common are becoming scarce in localities within easy reach; great quantities being yearly consigned to the London markets.'[5] A lady fern writer commented, with mock concern, that 'The poor Ferns, like the wolves in olden times, have a price set upon their heads, and they in like manner will soon disappear. We must have "Fern laws", and preserve them like game.'[6] But she herself confessed a few pages later that her first reaction on finding a rare fern was to pack up a hamper-full and send it home by rail, and she advised her readers to do the same.

The trouble with fashions, of course, is that once everyone is following them they are no longer really chic, and that was the point that ferns had reached by the mid-1860s. When *every* drawing-room contained a fern-case, they began to seem a little dull, or even – horrid thought! – a little vulgar. The time was ripe for another craze and sure enough it came: the aquarium, the second of the two great inventions inspired by Ward's discovery and made possible by the repeal of the glass tax. But here other people besides Ward were involved. In an early report on his cases to the British Association, Ward had 'directed the attention of the members to the development of animal life upon the same principles'[7] and he followed up his own hint by introducing some ornamental fish into one of his tanks of aquatic plants, and a chameleon and a Jersey toad into his fern house. But he did not make any effort to publicize these events, so it was left to a chemist, Robert Warington, to first fully enunciate the aquarium principle in a paper delivered to the Chemical Society in 1850.

Of course the aquarium was not entirely new – people had been keeping goldfish in glass bowls before this. But the fish usually died rather quickly when their oxygen ran out, or had to be given fresh water every day. One goldfish-owner, Mrs Anna Thynne, had discovered an even more elaborate method; she aerated her tank by having the water poured backwards and forwards every day for half an hour. 'This was doubtless a fatiguing operation,' she reported, 'but I had a little handmaid, who, besides being rather anxious to oblige me, thought it rather an amusement.'[8] Obviously most people did not have such easily amused handmaids, and at this stage aquarium-keeping was an esoteric and generally disappointing hobby.

What made the aquarium craze possible was the discovery that if plants were added to the water they would give off enough oxygen to support animal life. Various people had discovered this accidentally over the years, but Warington was the first person to explain it properly and publicize it. He reported to the Chemical Society how he had kept two small goldfish and a *Valisneria spiralis* plant together in a twelve-gallon tank for almost a year without changing the water. He had also made the useful discovery that pond snails added to the tank would keep the water clear. And three years later he reported in the *Annals of Natural History* that he had carried out similar successful experiments using sea-water. Thus Robert Warington must be considered the official inventor of the aquarium, and his name was duly commemorated (though misspelt) in the 'Warrington Case' which was advertised as an 'Aquatic Plant Case or Parlour Aquarium'.

Parlour aquarium, 1859

Meanwhile, however, Philip Henry Gosse had been independently pursuing exactly the same experiments down in Devon, and it was he, rather than Warington, who precipitated the huge popular craze for the invention. He was a bestselling writer with a faithful public behind him, and it was his *A Naturalist's Rambles on the Devonshire Coast*, published in 1853, that gave the first intimations of what was to come. After describing his own not entirely successful experiments in aquarium-keeping, Gosse remarked,

> Should these experiments be perfected, what would hinder our keeping collections of marine animals for observation and study, even in London and other inland cities? Such a degree of success as I have attained would admit of so desirable a consummation, for even in London no great difficulty would be experienced in having a jar of sea-water brought up once in a couple of months. I hope to see the lovely marine Algae too, that hitherto have been almost unknown except pressed between the leaves of a book, growing in their native health and beauty, and waving their delicate translucent fronds, on the tables of our drawing-rooms and on the shelves of our conservatories.[9]

In an appendix to the book, Gosse added that he had now repeated his sea-water experiments with complete success and had kept various sea-anemones alive for almost a year. He had assisted in the construction and stocking of an aquarium for London Zoo (opened in 1853) and moreover, he reported that a 'Marine Aquarium for the Parlour or Conservatory' was already in the manufacturer's hands, and 'though there are some minor difficulties attendant on the mechanical part of the execution, they are not such as to throw any material doubt on my confident expectation, that in a short time an elegant vase stocked with algae and sea-anemones, and comprising within itself the elements of its constant self-purification, will be before the world.'[10]

Gosse was right. Within a year of the book's publication, the 'elegant vase' was popping up in every drawing-room (sometimes it was the old Wardian case turned upside down) and aquarium suppliers and stockists were setting up shop in every large town. By 1857 one writer reported that, 'It has now become one trade to supply tanks and vases for Aquaria; and another, to collect and supply plants and animals for stocking them.'[11] It was even possible to 'get living Sea-Eggs "*to order*" without stirring from our homes.'[12]

Naturally, handbooks were needed, and the first (and best) was appropriately provided by Gosse in *The Aquarium* of 1854. At this stage the whole concept was so new that Gosse even had to settle the question of its name, and after debating the rival attractions of 'vivarium' and 'aqua-vivarium', he finally resolved, 'Let the word AQUARIUM then be the one selected to indicate these interesting collections of aquatic animals and plants.'[13] He explained how to construct a tank and estimated that a parlour-table-sized one would cost about twenty-one shillings. He suggested that, 'In London, sea-water may be easily obtained, by giving a trifling fee to the master or steward of any of the steamers that ply beyond the mouth of the Thames, charging him to dip it in the clear open sea, beyond the reach of rivers.'[14] (Later on, the railway companies took over the business of supplying sea-water to London aquarium-keepers at a cost of twopence a gallon. Alternatively, there was a patent salt manufactured by Southall Bros and Barclay, to convert freshwater into sea-water.) As an aquarium-stockist, Gosse recommended his friend Mr William Thompson of Weymouth. The efficiency of the railways made it possible to transmit live specimens from the seaside to London within a day.

The Aquarium was the most successful of all Gosse's books and made the then-enormous profit of £900 for its author. Naturally it inspired imitators, one of the first of which was *Glaucus; or the Wonders of the Shore* by Gosse's friend the Rev. Charles Kingsley. *Glaucus* is not particularly helpful on the details of aquarium-keeping (for which it refers the reader to Gosse), but it is a marvellous analysis of the appeal of natural history to the Victorian middle classes. Another follower in Gosse's path was George Eliot's friend George Henry Lewes who plunged into the rock-pools of Ilfracombe and came out with *Sea-side Studies* (1858) which again is full of social insights, though lacking Kingsley's boisterous charm. The accession of two such intellectual heavyweights to the ranks of aquarium-keepers gave lustre to the new hobby, and when it was learned that even Bishop 'Soapy Sam' Wilberforce was an addict, its respectability was assured. In 1855 Gosse followed up his own success with a *Handbook to the Marine Aquarium* which sold two thousand copies in a matter of weeks, and in the summer of the same year he conducted fashionable field-classes in marine zoology at Ilfracombe. 'I recall', wrote Edmund Gosse, 'a long desultory line of persons on a beach of shells, – doubtless at Barricane. At the head of the procession, like Apollo conducting the Muses, my father strides ahead in an immense wide-awake, loose black coat and trousers, and fisherman's boots, with a collecting-basket in one hand, a staff or prod in the other. Then follow gentlemen of every age, all seeming spectacled and old to me, and many ladies in the balloon costume of 1855, with shawls falling in a point from between their shoulders to the edge of their flounced petticoats, each wearing a mushroom hat with streamers.'[15]

Another bestselling book in the same field was G.B. Sowerby's *Popular History of the Aquarium* in the Lovell Reeve series of half-guinea illustrated natural history handbooks. (Incidentally, there is a bewildering profusion of Sowerbys. Ten of them altogether, spread over four generations, appear as botanists, conchologists and illustrators. This one is George Brettingham Sowerby the Second, who was described as 'a mediocre naturalist, a shocking Latinist, but an excellent draughts-man'.)[16] Sowerby gave his readers the essential reassurance they always needed when embarking on a new pursuit: 'Nor is it only for *amusement* that such parlour oceans and lakes are prepared and stocked; they are invaluable as a means of *in-struction*.'[17] He even elaborated the sort of (moral) instruction they were meant to provide: for instance, the ineffective motions of the tentacles of *Virgularia mira-bilis* would serve as a reminder 'that too much independent action among indivi-

'The Aquarium', from *Weekly Welcome*, 1879

dual members of a body politic is unfavourable to the development of corporate power'.[18] and the fact that young polyps die if they leave the polyp-body prematurely should provide 'a salutary example to young people in too great a hurry to become independent of parental care.'[19] After describing the unfortunate tendency of most star-fish to cast their limbs when put into a tank, and so die, he remarks voluptuously, 'Thus a slight dash of melancholy may be introduced occasionally to vary the amusements of a zoological tank.'[20]

Almost all these early aquarium books were pirated in America, which seems to have caught the craze a year or two after Britain. A New York publisher's advertisement of 1858 lists about twenty books on the aquarium and related subjects, all by English authors. The first home-produced American textbook was *Life Beneath the Waters; or the Aquarium in America* by Arthur M. Edwards, published in 1858. From this we learn that 'objects for the purpose of stocking the Aquarium can be now purchased in New York city, and may soon be for sale in other of our large cities',[21] but the author points out that, for the price of a six-cent car ride, New Yorkers can find their own specimens if they will take the trouble to comb the East River shoreline at low tide. Edwards is at pains to stress the fashionability of aquarium-keeping, and he addresses himself particularly to 'the lady part of the community, whom I hope soon to see taking as much delight in the fitting up and management of these beautiful parlor ornaments as their sisters on the other side of the Atlantic.'[22]

All the aquarium books published in the 1850s illustrate the close interconnection of two contemporaneous fashions – the fashion for keeping aquaria and the fashion for dabbling in rock-pools. As with the Wardian case and ferns, the connection was fortuitous rather than essential, but it happened that the aquarium came into existence just as the middle-class habit of taking seaside holidays was losing some of its novelty value, and holidaymakers began to wonder what they should actually *do* once they got to the seaside. Gosse and his followers provided the answer: they should comb the rock-pools in order to find interesting specimens wherewith to stock their new aquaria back home. This was an altogether more earnest pursuit than the old-established custom of beachcombing for pretty shells and seaweeds to make into decorative *objets*. It required special dress and equipment. Mrs Gatty advised the ladies to aim at a sort of 'yachting costume' modified by the addition of boys' shooting boots, short petticoats, stout gloves, and wool stockings. 'Any one really intending to *work* in the matter, must lay aside for a time all thought of conventional appearances,' she warned, and fancy millinery 'must, and will, be laid aside by every rational being who attempts to shore-hunt'.[23]

As for equipment, G.H. Lewes recommended that the serious shore-hunter should carry a largish geological hammer, a cold chisel, an oyster-knife, a paper-knife, a landing-net, a small crowbar, a large, flat-bottomed basket, various phials and bottles from the chemist's ('The short squat bottles, with wooden caps, now sold for tooth-powder, are very convenient')[24] and a selection of jamjars. These were all to take into the field: home equipment would consist of more pots and bottles, an aquarium, and, if possible, a microscope with which to study the smaller organisms. The microscope was another invention that helped the fashion for marine zoology on its way. It was not of course new, but in the 1850s it became much cheaper and more readily available than ever before. A good one cost about four guineas, and an adequate one thirty shillings. A writer in 1861 claimed that 'The microscope is rapidly becoming the companion of every intelligent family that can afford its purchase'[25] and a sudden flurry of popular books on microscopy published in the 1860s seems to bear this out. In fact the minor craze for microscopy may well have been a consequence of the major craze for aquarium-keeping, as Gosse and Lewes and other aquarium-writers recommended their readers to buy a microscope.

According to G.H. Lewes, the twin crazes for aquarium-keeping and rock-pool dabbling achieved their consummation in a passion for sea-anemones which apparently by 1858 had become universal pets. In *Sea-Side Studies* he wrote,

> Since the British mind was all alive and trembling with that zoological fervour excited by the appearance of the hippopotamus in Regent's Park, no animal has touched it to such fine issues and such exuberant enthusiasm as the lovely Sea-Anemone, now the ornament of countless drawing-rooms, studies, and back parlours, as well as the delight of unnumbered amateurs. In glass tanks and elegant vases of various device, in finger-glasses and common tumblers, the lovely creature may be seen expanding its coronal of tentacles, on mimic rocks, amid mimic forests of algae, in mimic oceans – of pump-water and certain mixtures of chlorides and carbonates, regulated by a 'specific gravity' test. Fairy fingers minister to its wants, removing dirt and slime from its body, feeding it with bits of limpet or raw beef; fingers, *not* of fairies, pull it about with the remorseless curiosity of science, and experiment on it, according to the suggestion of the moment. At once pet, ornament, and 'subject for dissection', the Sea-anemone has a well established popularity in the British family-circle; having the advantage over the hippopotamus of being somewhat less expensive, and less troublesome, to keep.[26]

However, by the time every parlour had acquired its aquarium, complete with sea-anemone, the tide of fashion was, of course, beginning to ebb and by 1868 the Rev. J.G. Wood was recording its complete demise:

> Some years ago, a complete aquarium mania ran through the country. Every one must needs have an aquarium, either of sea or fresh water, the former being preferred ... The fashionable lady had magnificent plate-glass aquaria in her drawing-room, and the schoolboy managed to keep an aquarium of lesser pretensions in his study. The odd corners of newspapers were filled with notes on aquaria, and a multitude of shops were opened for the simple

purpose of supplying aquaria and their contents. The feeling, however, was like a hothouse plant, very luxuriant under artificial conditions, but failing when deprived of external assistance ... So, in due course of time, nine out of every ten aquaria were abandoned; many of the shops were given up, because there was no longer any custom; and to all appearance the aquarium fever had run its course, never again to appear, like hundreds of similar epidemics.[27]

Nevertheless, the aquarium craze had one final, if less fervent, phase before it became extinct. The 1870s saw a sudden fashion for huge purpose-built public aquaria, which proved as immediate an attraction as the zoological gardens of the 1830s. London Zoo had opened a small aquarium back in 1853, but it was not on the spectacular scale of the 1870s palaces. The first to be built (though not actually the first to open) was the Brighton Aquarium, which is still the largest such building in Europe. It was designed by Edward Birch (who also designed Hastings Pier) and officially opened in August 1872. An early advertisement puffed it as 'The Largest and most Beautiful Building devoted to Piscatorial Science in the World. Thousands of Fishes and Marine Animals – many of great rarity. The Tanks and Ferneries nightly Illuminated. Promenade Concerts every Saturday at Three o'clock. Band plays thrice daily.'[28]

Crystal Palace Aquarium, 1891

Soon every large town in England was clamouring to have its own aquarium. London's was at Sydenham, where the Crystal Palace building had been moved after the Great Exhibition, and was actually opened a few months before Brighton, although it started building later. Southport opened one in 1874 (at a staggering cost of £90,000), Manchester in the same year, Westminster and Yarmouth in 1876 and Edinburgh in 1878. They competed in offering ever larger or rarer attractions, with white whales, manatees and otters as successive favourites. Southport's star attraction was its baby alligators which, according to Frank Buckland, started an alarming fashion: 'Several of the ladies in Southport,' he reported, 'have purchased pets from among them, and it may be that no Southport lady will consider her establishment perfect without a baby alligator to bask on the hearth-rug, and go out for a walk on the promenade with her. When the pet defuncts, he can be stuffed, gilt, and put in the hat for an ornament, don't you know?'[29]

At the height of the craze, 'the arrival of the octopus had attracted almost as much attention as the visit of a foreign emperor, and the death of a porpoise was mourned as a national calamity.'[30] But the day of the public aquaria, like that of the private, was short-lived. By the 1850s the attractions advertised at Brighton Aquarium consisted of giants, midgets, Zulu chieftains, Javanese temple dancers and Dame Adelina Patti. No hint of 'Piscatorial Science'. Westminster was given over to Laplanders, human canonballs, and Benedetti the sword-swallower, and every other aquarium had made similar adjustments or else closed down. Edmund Gosse, writing in 1890 about his father's role in the development of the aquarium, commented scathingly that, 'When he [Philip Henry Gosse] was eagerly proposing the preservation of marine animals alive in mimic seas, he certainly did not anticipate that within forty years an aquarium would come to mean a place devoted to parachute monkeys, performing bears and aerial queens of the tightrope.'[31]

Why this sudden decline? We must remember that the great motive for the Victorian middle classes was amusement *and* instruction, the two combined. Amusement by itself was always characterized as 'vulgar' and left to the lowest classes. There had to be some element of usefulness to make a pursuit worthwhile, and the aquarium at first had seemed to offer this. When Frank Buckland spoke at the opening of the Crystal Palace in 1872 he made a plea which all his middle-class audience must have approved:

Anemones, soldier crabs, the sensational octopus, barnacles, serpulae, and other non-edible wretches are all very interesting and instructive; but besides, I may say above these, I wish to see several problems of vast national importance solved or attempted to be solved … The Aquarium Company at Sydenham have a great field open to them if they will convert their tanks, some of them at least, into observatories for watching the habits of sea-fish of economic and commercial value. Thus their exhibition will be not only ornamental but practically useful.[32]

But this plea was ignored because, even as it was being made, the scientists were preparing to move elsewhere. In 1873 Anton Dohrn founded the first marine zoological station at Naples and in 1884 Britain opened her own Plymouth Marine Laboratory. These establishments offered superb research facilities, and were generously funded by government grants and institutional fees. They were – for professional scientists – a glorious opportunity. The only trouble was that they were not open to the public or to interested amateurs. They were thus instrumental in that fatal divorce between the layman and the expert that has characterized science since the end of the nineteenth century. For when the lay public could no longer hope to understand, let alone contribute to, the latest developments in marine zoology, they naturally lost all interest in the subject. The public aquaria, deprived of all hope of an instructive rationale, sank into mere vulgar amusement, and the Wardian and Warrington cases, which had promised so much half a century before, were consigned to the attic and forgotten. Nevertheless, the value of Ward's original discovery remains – in the tea plantations of India, the rubber plantations of Malaya, and in a handful of books such as Gosse's which must long outlast the ephemeral craze that inspired them.

Pteris Aquilina, nature-printed by Bradbury

CHAPTER NINE

THE NATURALIST OF THE BOUDOIR

ONE OF THE many remarkable features of the aquarium and fern crazes was that they were almost entirely sustained by women. In the past, feminine interest in natural history had usually been confined to botany, but in the middle of the nineteenth century it expanded into other fields. Women read about natural history, wrote about it, drew it, collected it, and generally enthused about it just as much as men did. Admittedly, their enthusiasm sometimes took odd forms – the German naturalist Humboldt once complained to Murchison that he had been much pestered in his old age by 'letters from pious young ladies, who sought to have the privilege of closing his eyes when he died.'[1] But underlying the freaks and the crazes, there was a solid undercurrent of female support which took tangible form in the shell pictures, seaweed albums, butterfly cases and stuffed birds of the typical Victorian drawing-room.

Charles Kingsley in his *Glaucus* paints a rosy portrait of the Victorian lady naturalist at home. 'I have seen,' he wrote, 'the young London beauty, amid all the excitement and temptation of luxury and flattery, with her heart pure and her mind occupied in a boudoir full of shells and fossils, flowers and sea-weeds, and keeping herself unspotted from the world, by considering the lilies of the field, how they grow.'[2] It is a touching tableau, but one cannot fail to be struck by its essential passivity. The young London beauty is not actually *doing* anything with her shells and fossils, flowers and seaweeds. She may, as Kingsley supposes, be considering the lilies of the field, how they grow, but if she really wanted to understand plant physiology she should be out in the field, or poring over a microscope, not pottering about in her boudoir. Unfortunately, Kingsley's picture is all too accurate. Victorian women rarely translated their genuine enthusiasm for natural history into any purposeful form of research, and a list of their achievements must, as this chapter will reveal, make a poor showing beside the men's.

Illustration was the only form of natural history work in which women really excelled. Marianne North's oil paintings of flowers in the Kew Museum, or Anne Pratt's illustrations of ferns and wild flowers, or Mrs William Buckland's drawings of fossils, or even the young Beatrix Potter's studies of mushrooms can all stand comparison with any male work, and one woman, Mrs Gould, deserves to be ranked only just below Audubon as an ornithological illustrator, since it was she, rather than her husband, who drew the plates for John Gould's *Birds of Europe*. Women were trained to draw well: it was one of the few things they practised and studied consistently from infancy through to adulthood. And in fact one suspects that the list of distinguished women illustrators should be much longer, were it not for the fact that they so often published their work anonymously.

Women also tended to make punctilious collectors. No woman was ever guilty of the crime recorded against a certain nobleman who, having amassed an important collection of trilobite fossils decided that they looked rather dull and had them painted with gold – thereby annihilating their scientific interest for ever.[3] Women's traditional province for collecting was shells, shells being 'so brightly clean, so

Mary Anning

ornamental to a boudoir',[4] but shell-collecting was an expensive hobby by the middle of the nineteenth century, if one wanted to include foreign species, and many women preferred other subjects. The most famous woman collector of the century was Mary Anning of Lyme Regis, who specialized in fossils. She had no training and was barely literate. Her father, a carpenter, died when she was only eleven and she supported herself and her mother by selling natural 'curiosities' (mainly ammonites) to tourists. In 1812, at the age of twelve, she found the first British ichthyosaur. In 1824, she found a plesiosaur, and in 1828, a pterosaur, the first flying reptile ever found in Britain. She had a quite unrivalled skill in recognizing a potentially important fossil from a tiny, exposed fragment of stone and then disinterring it without damage (the plesiosaur took her ten years to dig out) and all the leading geologists of the day took pains to cultivate Mary Anning's acquaintance and keep abreast of her activities. But it is significant that she never made any attempt to publish or even identify her finds herself, while other palaeontologists made their reputations from her work.

Mary Anning's considerable fame inspired many other female fossil collectors, though none achieved quite her eminence. Most of them survive only as names in local natural history museums, but Richard Owen described visiting, in 1842, a Miss Anna Gurney of Norfolk:

> I made a day's delightful excursion to Cromer [he told his sister], to visit an old maiden lady who has been deprived of the power of using her legs from early life, and wheels herself about in a kind of velocipede chair. She is a most cheerful person, as you may well imagine when I tell you that she has saved some men's lives during wrecks on the coast near her cottage. I was told that on stormy nights, when vessels are in danger, she has wheeled herself through the pelting rain or snow to the seaside, and animated the fishermen and others by her example and rewards to exertions, which otherwise they would have shrunk from, but without which the wrecked seamen must have perished. Her attractions to me were a fine collection of the bones from the cliffs and shingle, which she and a sister, now dead, occupied themselves in collecting, and which is now the most instructive one in Norfolk.[5]

The most *scientific* woman collector of the age was not a fossilist but an algologist, Mrs A.W. Griffiths of Torquay. W.H. Harvey, author of the bestselling *Sea-Side Book*, said that 'She is worth ten thousand other collectors; she is a trump',[6] and Charles Kingsley said that British marine botany almost owed its existence to her 'masculine [note the compliment!] powers of research.'[7] One genus and several species of seaweed were named after her, and she is mentioned with respect – almost with awe – by every Victorian writer on seaweeds, but she published nothing in her own name, and now survives only as an acknowledgment in other people's prefaces.

It is particularly galling that Mrs Griffiths should have researched but not written, when unnumbered tribes of other Victorian ladies seem to have written without ever doing an iota of research. Ladies were next in line to clergymen as relentless producers of popular natural history books, able at the rustle of a publisher's contract to launch into endless stories about sticklebacks and beehives, and faithful dogs who rescued their masters from everything under the sun, and elephants Who Never Forgot. Most of their effusions were directed to other ladies or to children (it is often hard to tell which) and characterized by glutinous sentimentality ('I love flowers as forming one of the sweetest lines in the GOD-WRITTEN Poetry of Nature')[8] and an ability to drop into verse at the least provocation:

> No grain of sand
> But moves a bright and million-peopled land,
> And hath its Edens and its Eves, I deem.[9]

Mrs Loudon's *Entertaining Naturalist* is a typical specimen of the genre, and was apparently popular, since it ran into many editions. It consists of illustrations, descriptions and anecdotes about all the more familiar animals, and was presumably intended for mothers to read to their children, although it includes some most unsuitable stories about men being torn to pieces by tigers, and a nasty account of an experiment in which someone cut the feet off his bulldog to see if it would still be pugnacious afterwards. (It was.) The quality of the anecdotes is conveyed by the following which, according to Mrs Loudon, 'is given as a fact, and deserves to be recorded':

An Elephant, disappointed of his reward, out of revenge, killed his governor. The poor man's wife, who beheld the dreadful scene, took her two children and thrust them towards the enraged animal, saying 'Since you have slain my husband, take my life also, as well as those of my children!' The Elephant instantly stopped, relented, and, as if stung with remorse, took the eldest boy in his trunk, placed him on his neck, adopted him for his governor, and would never afterwards allow any other person to mount him.[10]

Quite apart from dubious anecdotes (of which the above is by no means the worst), the *Entertaining Naturalist* perpetrates many errors. The whale is included in the section on fishes, and the auk is placed between the birds and the fishes because it 'is considered by some observers of the wonderful operations of the Creator, a link between the bird and the fish.'[11] Mrs Loudon carefully refutes the old myth about toads being poisonous and then immediately goes on to perpetuate the other old myth about toads being able to live indefinitely inside lumps of coal. She shows the usual Victorian enchantment with statistics: if all the offspring of a single pair of herring were allowed to multiply unmolested for twenty years,

---

10 (*facing page*) Land Molluscs, from *The Royal Natural History*, ed. R. Lydekker, 1896. Drawn by H. Morin.

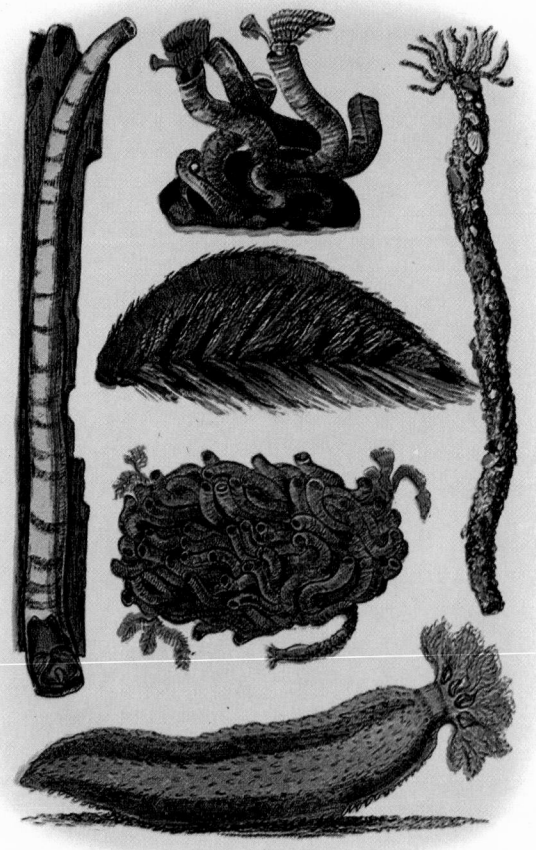

11 *(above)* Frontispiece of *Vegetable Kingdom* by
William Rhind, 1868.

12 *(right)* Sea-mouse, sea-cucumber, serpulae, from
Common Objects of the Sea-shore by the Rev. J. G.
Wood, 1857. Drawn by Sowerby.

13 *Phoca barbata*, the Great Seal, from *The Natural History of British Quadrupeds* by Edward Donovan, 1820

they would 'exhibit a bulk ten times the size of the Earth',[12] and if all the eggs in a single cod's roe were to hatch and attain adulthood they would weigh 26,123 tons and fetch £195,000 in the market. Mingled with such pieces of useless information are handy hints on how to cook and eat kangaroo, bear and opossum, and how to deal with a charging bull: 'When in danger of being attacked by a Bull, the best course is to stand still, and open an umbrella, or flap a shawl, or something of that kind, in the Bull's face; as with all his fierceness he is a great coward and only pursues those who fly from him.'[13] The *Entertaining Naturalist* certainly *is* entertaining, but only at the expense of any accuracy or informational value it might have been supposed to possess. And Mrs Loudon was the wife of J.C. Loudon, the editor of numerous popular natural history magazines, and therefore in a better position than most ladies to keep abreast of current research.

The one woman writer who stands above the *Entertaining Naturalist* crowd is Margaret Gatty, a Yorkshire clergyman's wife who took up the study of natural history at the age of thirty-nine, during a convalescent holiday after the birth of

Margaret Gatty

her seventh child. She eventually produced an authoritative account of British seaweeds, but her most enduring work is *Parables from Nature*, published in five volumes from 1855 to 1871, and re-published well into the twentieth century. These are little tales in the Aesop tradition, using facts and incidents from natural history to inculcate moral lessons. The technique can best be illustrated by giving a précis of one of the stories, 'A Lesson of Faith', which is among the simplest and the best.[14] Its heroine is a green caterpillar (of the species *Pieris rapae*, we are told in the notes) who is charged by a dying butterfly to look after her eggs. The Caterpillar is a conscientious creature who worries about how she will feed them. They will hatch into baby butterflies, she imagines, and want nectar and honey to eat, whereas she can reach no higher than the cabbage leaf on which she lives. She decides to consult the Lark, who can fly very high and see many things. He listens to her problem then flies away to make enquiries, leaving her anxiously pacing her cabbage leaf, with its little clutch of eggs. Eventually he returns. 'News, news, glorious news, friend Caterpillar!' he sings, 'but the worst of it is, you won't believe me.' Oh, says the Caterpillar, like the good Victorian child she is, 'I believe everything I am told.' But of course she does not, because when the Lark tells her that the eggs will hatch into caterpillars like herself, and eat cabbage-leaves, like herself, she thinks he is teasing. And when he announces his even more momentous item of news – '*You will one day be a Butterfly yourself*' – she turns away from him in anger, exclaiming, 'Now you are cruel as well as foolish. Go away! I will ask your advice no more.' But even as she is railing against the Lark, she hears a little movement beside her and turns round to see eight or ten little caterpillars just emerging from the butterfly's eggs. And so she comes to accept that as the Lark's first prophecy has come true, so might the second also, and she spends the rest of her life happily reciting her 'Lesson of Faith' – 'I have known many wonders – I have faith – I can trust even now for what shall come next!'

Many of the other *Parables from Nature* show the same deft interweaving of information about natural history (far more accurate than Mrs Loudon's) and moral instruction, all wrapped up in stories with strong characters and sprightly dialogue. It is perhaps the moralism that prevents them being popular today: Mrs Gatty's child readers are exhorted to be humble, obedient, tidy, clean, polite, well-brushed, God-fearing, nanny-fearing and respectful towards their 'elders and betters' in a way which modern parents might find rather a strain. But many other Victorian nursery classics, with what might seem equally obnoxious morals, are still in print: it seems a pity to let such good children's literature as Mrs Gatty's disappear.

Another woman writer who is interesting (though mainly for historical reasons) is Arabella Buckley, who was probably the first popular writer to translate Darwinian evolution into terms that children could understand. She had worked as Charles Lyell's secretary for many years, and had followed the Darwinian debates from the inside. Her books have disconcerting titles – *The Fairyland of Science*,

Life and Her Children, Winners in Life's Race – and an irritating heroine called 'Life' who replaces the God or Nature of previous writers, but they are scientifically accurate and extremely lucid. *Winners in Life's Race* is an account of vertebrate evolution and was first published in 1882, a time when many of the parents and certainly the grandparents of the children for whom it was intended would still regard Darwinism as controversial, remembering the great debates of the 1860s. But Arabella Buckley's commitment to evolution is uncompromising and she explicitly praises 'the greatest naturalist and thinker of our day, that patient lover and searcher after truth, Charles Darwin, whose genius and earnest labours opened our eyes gradually to a conception so deep, so true, and so grand, that side by side with it the idea of making an animal from time to time, as a sculptor makes a model of clay, seems too weak and paltry ever to have been attributed to an Almighty Power.'[15] Such passages contrast oddly with others in the older sentimental tradition where she praises 'the sweet tender emotions of the little songbirds [who] have learned to fill the world with love and brightness and song',[16] or inveighs against gorillas for being 'degenerate animals, equal neither in beauty, strength, discernment, nor in any of the nobler qualities, to the faithful dog, the courageous lion, or the half-reasoning elephant.'[17] It was one thing to accept the facts of evolution, another to find a style appropriate to them. But despite its odd inconsistencies, *Winners in Life's Race* remained in print as the best child's guide to evolution for at least half a century.

Countless other books by Victorian women could be mentioned as being best-sellers in their day, but a modern reading fails to reveal their attraction. They are nearly all untidy compilations from the work of other authors, and destitute of original observation or research. Writing for children seems to have been considered an excuse for indulging in every sort of inaccuracy and sloppiness, provided it was heavily overlaid with sentiment and piety, and it is rare to find any natural history books by women which are *not* designed for children, or at least for a non-adult mentality. Of course, male writers were also guilty of hack writing, sentimentality, inaccuracy and the rest but one does not find quite the same degree of general mediocrity among them as one does among the ladies. It was obviously perfectly easy for women to get themselves into print, since hundreds of them did so, but they never seem to have aimed at an intelligent audience. Women's education certainly at this period lagged far behind the men's. Another serious handicap was the exclusion of women from learned societies such as the Royal, the Linnean and the Microscopical – a strong disincentive to research, since it was usually only through their various *Transactions* that findings could be published. Had Mrs Griffiths been a man, she would almost certainly have been a member of the Linnean Society and published her algological findings through it. To make matters worse, the societies never gave any reason for excluding women members, so that it was impossible to campaign against the ban.

Local and provincial natural history clubs, however, *did* admit women members, and the Liverpool Naturalists' Field Club actually attributed its success to 'the opportunity it affords of pursuing a pleasing study in company with that sex whose presence doubles the enjoyment both of rural rambles and of scientific investigation.'[18] But even this apparent tribute implies a slur: women were not admitted on the strength of their scientific contribution but rather as a sort of decorative backdrop to 'double the enjoyment' of the men. The presence of ladies always added glamour and excitement to an occasion, but of course glamour and excitement are distracting when the purpose is scientific research. Many field clubs organized special 'ladies' outings' once a year over some particularly docile piece of terrain, with usually a picnic and perhaps a band to enhance the sense of festivity. David Elliston Allen in *The Naturalist in Britain* gives an account of one such outing of the Leicester Literary and Philosophical Society in 1861 when some seventy or eighty members marched into Bradgate Park with a Volunteer Rifle Band at their head, inspected a ruin, drank lemonade, apple wine and sherry, danced, listened to a lecture on 'The Geology of Leicestershire', cheered, had tea, listened to another lecture, danced again and finally went home at dusk thoroughly exhausted.[19] Obviously it was all terrific fun – but it did not bear much relation to serious field study.

One of the reasons why women could never be admitted to scientific societies on an equal footing with the men was the crippling 'delicacy' of the age which

'The Pursuit of Science Under Difficulties' –
a British Association outing, 1865

made it obligatory for them to shy in alarm at the least hint of sex or reproduction. The diary of Caroline Owen, wife of the zoologist Richard Owen, records an odd incident when she was visited by a lady who produced out of her reticule 'a thing which she had been told was an unborn kangaroo'.[20] She (the lady visitor) had brought it to show Richard Owen, but 'she was hesitating about bringing such an "indelicate" subject to a gentleman.' Caroline set her fears at rest by assuring her that the kangaroo had not only been born but had lived for some time, and they then settled down to tea and chat, since Richard was not at home anyway, but it is surely strange that a woman who had no qualms about carrying a dead kangaroo around with her would then start blushing and trembling at the thought of showing it to a gentleman. It reminds us, if we need any reminder, that Victorian delicacy had very little to do with natural modesty and a great deal to do with cultivated prurience. So too does this letter from a well-brought-up young lady (Sophy Horsley, I.K. Brunel's sister-in-law) to her aunt about a visit to London Zoo. Her gentlemen escorts, she reported, had sat down to rest in front of the elephants, and

> I was very glad that they rested themselves in front of a decent animal, for some of them are very indelicate; indeed, the monkeys are so very nasty that I told Thomas Hawes I would rather not look (really, with a gentleman, I think it quite indelicate) at them; he said he quite agreed with me, so we went to the Ottar, while the others remained before the monkeys.[21]

Now obviously, if even the sight of a monkey was alarming, the serious study of zoology became difficult if not impossible. How, for instance, could one talk about mammals when their very name was resonant with indelicate allusions? Richard Owen, who was renowned for his tact in these matters, delivered a lecture at Norwich in which he explained that mammals were characterized 'not only by having living young, but by nourishing their young in a peculiar way.'[22] The 'peculiar way' was not specified so that any of his listeners who did not already know the connection of mammal with breast would remain in the dark. Similar obscurity probably attended another lecture he gave to the British Association when, finding ladies among his audience, he 'modified the reproductive part of the history as delicately as possible.'[23] But a proposed article on parthenogenesis (non-sexual reproduction) for the *Quarterly Review* had to be carefully negotiated beforehand, and Owen wrote to ask the publisher, John Murray,

> Whether your estimable editor of the 'Quarterly' or yourself would regard the details of the reproductive economy and apparatus of a *Rose* and a *Bee* as equally producible in respectable society ... The facts bearing upon this mysterious power of virgin-procreativeness are now so numerous and varied as to form an important body of physiological doctrine, of which the 'Quarterly' ought to take cognizance without squeamishness. For this sensitiveness,

truly akin to the Yankee nether-clothing of the pianoforte legs, is shutting out a vast and rapidly increasing store of most interesting and important knowledge.[24]

This question of whether the reproduction of the bee could be discussed as freely as the reproduction of a rose is an interesting one. When the Linnaean system of botanical classification first appeared, many men assumed that the study of botany would thereafter be debarred to ladies because the sexual terms employed were too gross. Ruskin even begged the 'gentle and happy scholar of flowers' to have nothing to do with 'these obscene processes and prurient apparitions'.[25] But while the men threw up their hands in dismay, the ladies happily embraced the Linnaean system with its cast of concubines and swains and eunuchs and all its supposed 'prurient apparitions' without a murmur. Indeed, more women than ever before took up the study of botany, because Linnaeus had at last made it simple. The same thing might have occurred with zoology, if only the men had allowed it to, but the entrenched idea that women must be shielded from the facts of life was too strong. In the same year (1856) that Owen worried about his parthenogenesis article, Huxley wrote to tell a friend that he had refused an invitation to lecture to ladies at London University, because, 'What on earth should I do among the virgins, young and old, in Bedford Square? ... I should be turned out ... for some forgetful excursions into the theory of Parthenogenesis or worse.'[26] If even a man of Huxley's intelligence could descend to this sort of snigger, one can see that it would take a very brave woman to persist in the study of zoology.

And of course, in natural history as in other fields, there was the usual obstacle that women were not *expected* to achieve anything. The proper limits to which feminine interest was supposed to go were defined by Hugh Miller, the Scottish geologist, in a letter to his fiancée. 'O my own Lydia,' he wrote, 'be careful of yourself. Take little thought and much exercise. Read for amusement only. Set yourself to make a collection of shells, or butterflies, or plants. Do anything that will have interest enough to amuse you without requiring so much attention as to fatigue.'[27] This is strikingly different from the standard *men* set themselves in that hard-working age – Darwin writing the *Origin* while never entirely free from pain for more than twenty minutes at a time, Lyell half-blind in his old age groping his way over the extinct Scottish volcanoes, or Miller himself setting off after a long day's labour in the stone quarry to chisel out the mysteries of a new fossil bed. They would have pooh-poohed the notion of reading 'for amusement only' or of not doing anything that might require so much attention as to fatigue. But women were taught to aim for a lower standard. They were encouraged to pursue an interest such as natural history just so long as it was dilettante; once it verged on real intellectual application it became 'fatiguing' and unhealthy. Hence we arrive back at Kingsley's lady naturalist, playing doll's house with her pretty shells and seaweeds in her boudoir.

But the role of women as encouragers of natural history must not be underrated. It is unlikely that so many local natural history societies, museums, zoological and botanical gardens and public aquaria would have been founded if they could not have relied on regular female support. And women formed one of the prime sections of the audience for public lectures on science, at a time when these constituted almost the only form of scientific education available. In America, women even flocked to hear Agassiz lecture *in French* on Alpine geology, and were reportedly 'lost in admiration of the Alpine glaciers, Alpine peaks, Jura boulders, *roches moutonnées*, and *cailloux striés*, and indeed of the Professor.'[28] It was quite common

'Nature Study', by Goleman, 1860

both in England and America for lecture audiences to be more than half composed of women, and the Lyceum movement, which was the framework of the American lecture circuit, was almost entirely run by women. Lectures, in any case, were one of the few forms of respectable public evening entertainment to which husbands and wives could go together.

As mothers, women encouraged their children to take an interest in natural history at a time when the schools afforded no such encouragement. Even mothers who had no particular affection for the subject themselves believed that natural history was a Good Thing, and conscientiously learned its rudiments in order to pass them on to their children. The huge number of handbooks published for precisely this market from the mid-century onwards indicates that most Victorian matrons included natural history in their nursery lessons, and an article in *The Naturalist's Note Book* for 1867 comments approvingly:

> It is surely a healthy sign of the times when we find our children taking a delight in the study of animal and vegetable life and thereby not only amusing and instructing themselves, but also causing our older heads to become interested in subjects that not many years ago were confined only to scientific professors ... The aquarium, the fern-case, and the microscope, are taking the place of tops, marbles, and Skelt's halfpenny sheets of characters amongst our children, while we have found new and cheerful amusements for our leisure hours.[29]

In many ways, it was a loss to parents when, towards the end of the century, elementary schools took over the responsibility for teaching natural history, and the microscope became an item of school equipment, rather than of home entertainment.

We have mentioned women as writers, as collectors, as illustrators, and as mothers, but there remains yet another role in which some of them contributed a great deal to the advancement of natural history — as wives. One of the incidental pleasures of reading biographies of eminent Victorian naturalists is making the fleeting acquaintance of their wives, whether it be Mrs William Buckland happily presiding over a dinner of ostrich and crocodile, or Mrs Charles Kingsley worrying about the catering arrangements for a visit from the Queen of the Sandwich Islands, whom she believed to be a cannibal,[30] or Mrs Philip Gosse interrupting the din of family prayers to point out a little brown moth that had just come fluttering into the room. ('O! Henry, do you think that can be *Boletobia?*' she asks. 'No! It is only the common Vapourer, *Orgygia antiqua!*' he pronounces and goes back to his Bible.)[31] Wives had to endure many sacrifices in the service of natural history – having their houses overrun with specimens, their holidays turned into field excursions, their evenings given up to sugar rounds. Spencer Fullerton Baird's wife Mary was asked to make an even nobler sacrifice. Her husband took her for a country walk and happened upon some rare fish which he dearly wanted to pre-

'Sea-side Sirens'

serve, whereupon she 'very obligingly lent him her bonnet with which he proceeded to catch the finny treasures.'[32]

The day-to-day trials and tribulations of a naturalist's wife are vividly evoked
in the diary of Caroline Owen, a charming woman who somehow survived marriage
to the appalling Richard Owen. Smells were the most persistent problem, and
the presence of odd animal corpses which were sent over from the Zoo as soon
as they died. The summer of 1847 was rendered particularly foul by 'the presence
of a portion of the defunct elephant on the premises ... I got R. to smoke cigars
all over the house',[33] and another time she had to cope with a dead rhinoceros
which was delivered while Richard was out. Such arrivals must have caused dis-
affection below-stairs, as must the Master's odd insistence on 'having the legs of
a fowl which we had for dinner, to examine the muscles.'[34] Caroline's initiation
into the mysteries of dissection occurred within a few months of her marriage,
when she recorded: 'Richard spent the evening in examining some of the minute
worms found in the muscles of a man. I looked at one or two through the microscope and saw one cut open. I could not get over the smell of the decaying piece
of muscle for hours. Richard only laughed ...'[35] This was all part of a plan which
was revealed a few months later. Caroline was a reasonably proficient draughts-
woman and Richard hoped to turn her into an anatomical illustrator. The first
task he set her was drawing a wombat's brain, which she conscientiously toiled
over for several days. However, 'When R. came in he said it was all wrong, so

I must do it all over again.'[36] She never did become an anatomical illustrator but, almost despite herself, she eventually became a quite competent amateur zoologist, capable of dealing with the various inane queries and putative freaks which people were always sending to her husband. We have already noticed the efficient manner in which she coped with the unborn kangaroo, and she had a similarly brisk way with the inevitable toad supposedly found alive in a lump of coal which seems to have turned up on every naturalist's doorstep from time to time. The toad, she said, did not fit the coal – she had measured it – and the thing was a fraud. Yet, however competent she became, Richard persisted in referring to her as his 'dear little wife' and regarding her as 'an averagely informed member of a "general audience"'[37] when he tried out his scientific lectures on her.

Caroline Owen's diary is not introspective, but one suspects she would have admitted that, despite the smells, the eccentricities, the odd arrivals, her life had been made immeasurably more interesting by science. One cannot claim that this holds true for *all* naturalists' wives, since there is the conspicuous exception of Mrs Charles Darwin who was once overheard in conversation with her husband on their way into a scientific lecture – Charles (*sotto voce*): 'I am afraid this is very wearisome for you.' Emma (out loud): 'Not more than all the rest.'[38] But most women who were exposed to the study of natural history, whether through their husbands, their children, or by some chance circumstance found, perhaps to their surprise, that they enjoyed it. The point was made explicitly by Henrietta Huxley, T.H. Huxley's wife: 'Once we were married,' she wrote, 'the whole atmosphere was scientific – his occupation, his friends, his books – the lectures he gave that I attended … It was a revelation that ennobled the world I lived in, made everything, for me, full of the strangest wonder and interest.'[39] It is unfortunate that more women were not encouraged to discover this 'revelation' for themselves.

'Miss Martha Twinch's Adventures in the Wild-beast Show'

CHAPTER TEN

THE PIONEER OF ZOOPHAGY

THE VICTORIAN LAYMAN'S idea of what the working naturalist should be probably reached its highest pinnacle of fulfilment in the person of Francis (Frank) Trevelyan Buckland. Buckland's four series of *Curiosities of Natural History*, his countless articles in the *Field*, *Land and Water*, and other periodicals, his many lectures, and his on-the-spot enquiries into the state of the English fisheries, brought him constantly before the public and the public was never disappointed. Whether wading waist-deep up a salmon ladder, or nursing a sick otter in a railway waiting-room, or showing visitors round his 'Museum of Economic Fish Culture', or bottle-feeding a porpoise at London Zoo, or striding down Albany Street with a giant on one arm and a lady dwarf on the other, he satisfied every popular expectation. He usually had at least one or two animals about his person. Meeting a Mr Bell in Carlisle who happened to mention that he kept storks, Buckland reported, 'I had no frogs in my pocket to give to the storks' – and the reader who knows his Buckland gasps in disappointment – 'but I had a lucifer-match box full of little toads, about the size of beans.'[1] Probably if Mr Bell had mentioned that he kept ant-eaters, Buckland could just as easily have produced some ants.

Through his regular column in the *Field*, Buckland knew or was known to almost every amateur naturalist in the country. One of his closest friends was Abraham Dee Bartlett, the Superintendent of London Zoo, and to a large extent Buckland acted as the Zoo's unofficial press officer. He also befriended every rat-catcher, bird-dealer, animal-importer, zoo-owner and aquarium-stockist in England. He knew all the travelling showmen with their mermaids and 'Indiarubber dogs' and 'talking fish' and 'Two-headed Nightingales' (the latter a pair of young female Siamese twins who sang very nicely). When the Chief Rabbi wanted to know whether Jews could eat oysters ('Do they creep?' he asked); when the Chinese ambassador wanted to learn how to cast fish; when Lord Bute wanted to introduce beavers on his Scottish estates; when a whale was washed up at Gravesend; when a laughing jackass flew through a Hampstead window – Frank Buckland was always the man to consult.

Even the rural labourers who never normally read a newspaper had heard of Buckland. He was once sent a six-legged kitten (Victorians had a passion for freaks) with the note: 'Sir. I hope you will cuse the liberty in Wrighting But By graite chance I drapped a Cross the kitm I have sent to you. I shoed it to Mr. B——who said it was a good Speriment.'[2] No one would have dared to write to the Olympian Professor Owen in such a strain, and Professor Owen must have missed many a good Speriment (experiment) thereby – had it not been for Buckland.

For Buckland was the perfect and necessary intermediary between the layman and the expert. He fitted that role as no one else could have done. While his own inclinations made him the friend of bird-catchers and kitm-owners throughout the country, his birth gave him access to all the leading scientists of the day. He was the son of William Buckland, a most distinguished and well-loved geologist, Canon of Christ Church Cathedral, Oxford, and later Dean of Westminster. Frank was born in Tom Quad, Oxford, in 1826 and he grew up knowing Owen, Lyell, Sedgwick, Faraday, Forbes and Hooker as intimate family friends. Virtually the only eminent scientist who was *not* part of the Buckland circle was Charles Darwin, who wrote in his *Autobiography* that he knew and liked all the leading geologists, 'with the exception of Buckland, who though very good humoured and good-natured seemed to me a vulgar and almost coarse man. He was incited more by a craving for notoriety, which sometimes made him act like a buffoon, than by a love of science.'[3] This is unusually strong criticism coming from Darwin, but one can understand that the retiring invalid of Down would not be likely to approve the flamboyant Dr Buckland who served ostrich at his dinner-table, who once launched a live turtle into the Tom Quad pond, and who gave his geological lectures on railway trains, pointing out evidence of stratification as they passed through the cuttings.

Dr Buckland and also Mrs Buckland, who was a considerable palaeontologist in her own right, providing several of the drawings for Cuvier's *Ossements Fossiles*, encouraged Frank's love of natural history, giving him his own collecting cabinet when he was only four, taking him bird's-nesting and fossil-hunting, and on visits to the Surrey Zoological Gardens and the British Museum. One day a coachman brought a moribund crocodile to the house and Frank and his brothers were allowed to ride on its back until it died, when the family ate it. When Frank was about four and a half, a Devonshire clergyman came to show Dr Buckland some 'very curious fossils'. The father turned to his son, who was playing nearby, and asked, 'Frankie, what are these?' 'They are the vertebrae of an ichthyosaurus', lisped the child, and the clergyman went away crestfallen.[4]

In 1839 Frank was sent to Winchester where, as he later recalled, 'I dreamed of home, and calculated how big some young ducks I had left in the out-house at home would be when the holidays came round... My father had promised that

Frank Buckland at home

if I was a good boy at my lessons I should cut their heads off when I came home, on the wood block in the tool-house, with the gardener's hatchet. It was made a great treat to my brother and myself to cut a duck's head off while my dear old father held the duck's legs.'[5] Although natural history formed no part of the school curriculum, Frank managed to pursue his hobby outside school hours. He learned how to catch rats, tickle trout, cook fieldmice, and he kept his usual pocket menagerie of guinea-pigs, hedgehogs and adders. He also learned how to skin and stuff animals, and performed a particularly intricate dissection on the eye of the warden's dog. This appetite for dissection gradually crystallized into an ambition to become a surgeon, and in his last few terms at Winchester he haunted the town's hospital, offering fresh eels and trout to the staff in exchange for portions of human anatomy. He gave sixpence to any schoolfellow who would consent to be bled, and terrified one poor boy by muttering in his presence, 'What wouldn't I give for that fellow's skull!'[6]

Dr Buckland approved his son's wish to become a surgeon, but advised him first to take his B.A. degree at Oxford. The course was still exclusively classical,

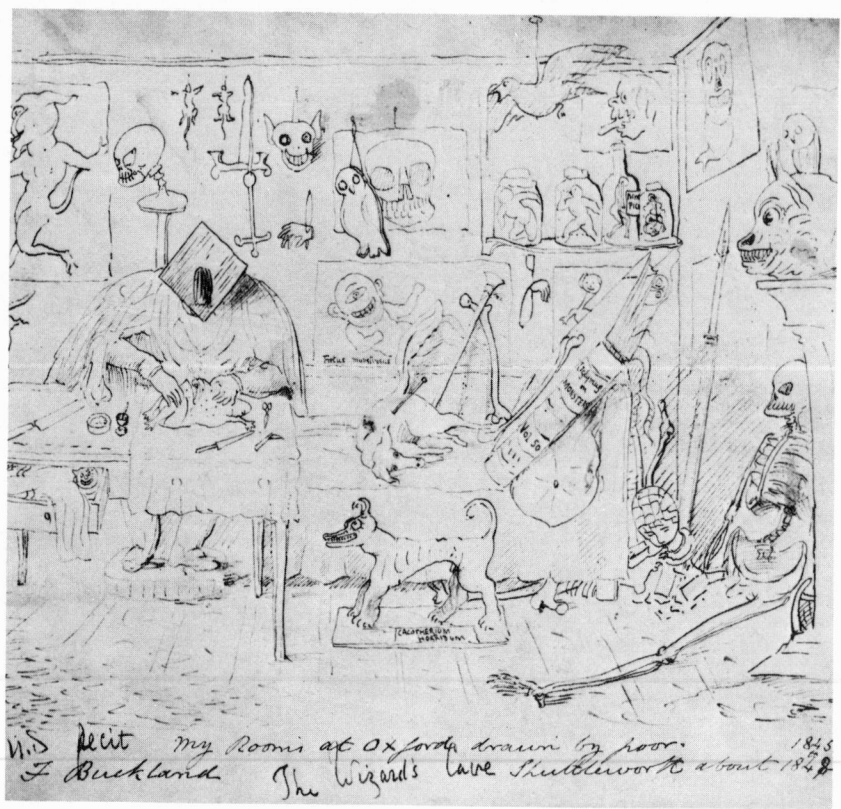

'The Wizard's Cave' – Buckland's rooms at Oxford

but Frank was able to attend extracurricular scientific lectures, including Dr Daubeny's on chemistry, and his father's on geology. Naturally his menagerie accompanied him to Oxford and, as naturally, it expanded. His prize pets were a chameleon, some marmots, an eagle, a jackal and a bear called Tiglath-Pileser. Tiglath, dressed in cap and gown, and accompanied by its owner, attended the Oxford meeting of the British Association in 1847 where Lord Houghton 'attempted to mesmerise him in his corner. This made the bear furious, but he gradually yielded to the influence, and at last fell senseless on the ground.'[7] (Later, Frank's pets were always falling senseless on the ground when he tried out the new miracle of chloroform on them.) Unfortunately the bear, like so many of Frank's pets, had a habit of escaping and the Dean finally pronounced the sentence of rustication. It ended its days in London Zoo.

In 1848 Frank was awarded his B.A. (at the second attempt) and immediately enrolled as a student at St George's Hospital, Knightsbridge. Medical training at the time was hampered by a shortage of bodies for dissection, so Frank seized the opportunity to work at La Charité, Paris, during a cholera epidemic in August 1849, and wrote home delightedly: 'Only think, we have a fresh subject every day, and may perform any operation we like.'[8] He wrote again, a fortnight later,

At 12 the operations. There is a large horrid looking cart which goes round to the Hospitals in the morning and brings in the dead people. I have seen as many as 10 at one time. They are sewn up in coarse cloth. The man pulls them out and the professor chooses one to dissect for which he pays 4 francs. The *teeth* of these poor creatures are the perquisites of the porter and he pulls them all out to sell to the dentists... The subjects are principally old men and women but we have some fine men and pretty women. The thinner they are the better.[9]

In May 1851, Buckland took his M.R.C.S. and a year later was appointed house-surgeon at St George's. One of his colleagues, Charles Lloyd, gives a sketch of him at this time:

As nearly as might be judged at a glance, he was four feet and a half in height and rather more in breadth – what he measured round the chest is not known to mortal man. His chief passion was surgery – elderly maidens called their cats indoors as he passed by and young mothers who lived in the neighbourhood of St. George's Hospital gave their nurses more than ordinarily strict injunctions as to their babies. To a lover of Natural History it was a pleasant sight to see him at dinner with a chicken before him – to watch the scrupulous delicacy with which he removed the leg out of the socket, or examined, after very careful picking, the numerous troublesome little bones which constitute the pinion, and finally to hang over him as he performed a Post Prandium examination of the head – and then to see how, undeterred by foolish prejudices, he devoured the brain.[10]

But exactly a year later, for reasons which none of his biographers can explain, Buckland resigned his house-surgeon's post. Perhaps, after all, he found that operating on live, screaming, unanaesthetized humans was not so enjoyable as dissecting a dead chicken – he fainted at his first operation. Or it may have been connected with his liaison with Hannah Papps, a woman of humble birth by whom he had an illegitimate son in 1851. He eventually married her in 1863, but by then their child was dead, and they never had another.

In any case, a new career was beginning to suggest itself. In the Spring of 1852 he escorted one of his father's friends round the Deanery cellars to show him his pet rats, and discoursed so learnedly and entertainingly on the beasts, that the friend insisted he write it all down in an article. This he did and Buckland's 'Rats' was published in *Bentley's Miscellany* that August. Articles on frogs, cobras, his pet monkey Jacko, and other animal topics quickly followed, and the next year he gave his first public lecture, on 'The House We Live In' (i.e. the body) to an audience of working men. He was soon in wide demand as a journalist and lecturer, and in 1857 he published his first series of *Curiosities of Natural History* which ran into three editions within the year. In 1858 he started running a natural history column in the *Field* and, at the same time, published a new edition of his father's *Bridgewater Treatise* (Dr Buckland had died in 1856) which sold five thousand copies in the first three days. He lectured to working men's institutes and coffee clubs, and took the platform with Professor Owen, Lyon Playfair and T.H. Huxley for a major lecture series at the South Kensington Museum. In 1860 he published a second series of *Curiosities of Natural History* and this too ran into numerous editions. Eventually there were four series, plus the *Notes and Jottings from Animal Life*, published posthumously, which is really a fifth *Curiosities*. He also wrote a *Natural History of British Fishes* (1881) and several manuals on fish-hatching.

By the 1860s he was installed with his wife and numerous pets at 37 Albany Street, which was to be his home for the rest of his life, and an address familiar to all natural history enthusiasts of the period. He was visited there by Mrs Priestly from the *World* magazine, who wrote an account of his domestic arrangements as part of her series on 'Celebrities at Home'. After describing the monkeys, the jaguar, the laughing jackass, the tame mice, the cats, the parrot that kept shouting for cabs out of the window, the rat that could 'sing' and all the various departed pets that, neatly stuffed and mounted, stood around the house, she turned her attention to the kitchen, and remarked,

> Quaint and original must be many of the dishes which issue from Mr. Buckland's kitchen. The long-suffering cook, were she free to speak, might tell some strange tales of mistakes inevitable, of young crocodiles boiled down for stock, of food misapplied, and of diets given to the wrong animals. Mr. Buckland's housekeeping books cover a wide range.[11]

Yes indeed. Mrs Priestly is here alluding to that branch of zoological enquiry which Frank Buckland made peculiarly his own and to which he contributed his most original research – namely, the gastronomy of the subject. Frank Buckland *ate* natural history while other men merely observed it. Even as a schoolboy, he was the acknowledged Boulestin of the pond and garden, specializing in squirrel pie and mice cooked in batter, hedgehogs, frogs and garden snails. 'A roast field mouse – not a house mouse – is a splendid *bonne bouche* for a hungry boy,' he pronounced, 'It eats like a lark.'[12] He complained about earwigs tasting 'so horribly bitter'[13] but wrote encouragingly, 'It is not generally known what excellent eating young rats are.'[14] While at Oxford, he feasted on panther, sent down from the Surrey Zoological Gardens. 'It had, however, been buried a couple of days,' he noted, 'but I got them to dig it up and send me some. *It was not very good.*'[15]

Once he became known as a naturalist, his scope for zoophagy vastly increased. His friendship with the professional bird-catchers gave him unshakable authority in discussing the eating qualities of the British avifauna: wheatears, jackdaws and young rooks were especially recommended. Summoned to Gravesend to examine the whale that had been washed up there, he naturally tasted a portion but 'found it too strong, even when boiled with charcoal.'[16] Lord Wharncliffe sent him some bison which was found to be 'grand eating, with a slight game flavour, a little hard, which perhaps, was my fault in having it broiled.'[17] Mr Bartlett of the London Zoo supplied many delicacies: elephant trunk which he made into soup (rubbery); rhinoceros, which he baked into a huge pie for one of his lecture audiences ('like very tough beef');[18] porpoise, which tasted like 'broiled lamp-wick';[19] and giraffe, which had been cooked on the hoof as a result of a fire in the giraffe house. The latter was one of his few real successes – the meat was white, and tasted like veal. In this it resembled boa constrictor, which was also pleasantly veal-like.

Now admittedly this was a branch of natural history which was then much more widely studied than it is today. Charles Waterton experimented on boiled toucan, armadillo ('strong and rank'), and the large red monkey of Demerara whose only fault was that 'when skinned his appearance is so like that of a young one of our own species that a delicate stomach might possibly revolt at the idea of putting a knife and fork into it.'[20] Spencer Fullerton Baird pursued similar experiments in America, writing to Audubon in 1842, 'I had a fine steak of the wild cat broiled and it tasted like a tender piece of fresh pork. I intend to taste all the Quadrupeds inhabiting this part of the country.'[21]

But Frank Buckland's only serious rival in the field of zoophagy was his own father, the Dean. Dinners at the Deanery frequently featured such dainties as horse's tongue, alligator, puppies, mice, tortoise and ostrich. One guest complained, 'Party at the Deanery; tripe for dinner; don't like crocodile for breakfast.'[22] Dean Buckland even claimed to have eaten the heart of a King – that of Louis XIV, preserved by Lord Harcourt at Nuneham. And when father and son together visited a foreign cathedral which boasted some spots of ever-liquefying 'martyr's blood' on the pavement, it was the father who knelt down, licked, tasted, and pronounced, 'I can tell you what it is; it is bat's urine.'[23]

Buckland equipped as Inspector of Fisheries

But Frank Buckland carried the study of zoophagy one step further than his father had done. He institutionalized it. It all began with the 'Eland Dinner', held in 1859 at the London Tavern, when all the braver naturalists assembled to see if they thought eland should be introduced to the national diet. This occasion was not organized by Buckland but by Professor Owen who, after the meal, gave a speech about 'the benefits which would accrue to us by naturalising animals from foreign parts, animals good for food as well as ornamental to the parks.' He hoped 'that we might one day see troops of elands gracefully galloping over our green sward, and herds of koodoos and other representatives of the antelope family which are so numerous in Africa, enjoying their existence in English parks, and added to the list of food good for the inhabitants of not only England, but Europe in general.'[24] Mr Mitchell of the Zoological Society seconded him and suggested that, although London Zoo had now run out of elands, there were 'plenty more elands in South Africa, to be had for the trouble of importing them', and he 'trusted that this subject might be taken up by those who had convenient pasture-ground for them in England, and would be patriotic enough to further the important cause of the acclimatisation of useful exotic animals in English parks and homesteads.'[25]

Buckland was so charmed by the proceedings that in 1860 he initiated the Acclimatization Society to further the search for new food. A French Société Impériale d'Acclimatation had already been in existence for six years, awarding medals and prizes for domestication of the kangaroo, the Australian emu, the Tibetan kiang, and the South African peetsi. After all, it seemed unsatisfactory to many people that only four new species of animals had been domesticated within historic times – the turkey in the sixteenth century, the musk-duck in the seventeenth, and the golden and silver pheasants in the eighteenth. Sheer patriotism demanded some gustatory return for the vast and rapid expansion of the British Empire: it was absurd that Englishmen in Queen Victoria's glorious reign should still be eating the same monotonous diet as their medieval forefathers. Buckland was thus not alone in his enthusiasm, and he quickly enlisted the Marquis of Breadalbane as President of the Society, and the Hon. Grantley Berkeley as Vice-President, with himself as Secretary.

While Breadalbane and other land-owning members concentrated on breeding the new potential edibles, Buckland devoted himself to tasting them, and on 12 July 1862 he arranged an inaugural dinner for over one hundred guests at Willis's Rooms. The meal began with birds' nest soup, tripang (Japanese sea-slug), and 'Nerfs de Daim', soup, made from the sinews of the Axis deer. All three were remarkably glutinous. The next course was 'Kangaroo steamer' which, as Buckland admitted, was 'a little "gone off", but not bad for all that'.[26] Curried chicken and *ris de veau* followed and were evidently seized with relief by the guests as a brief respite before tackling the main course of kangaroo ham, Chinese lamb, guan, curassow and Honduras turkey. The kangaroo ham was a great success but it emerged afterwards that the waiters had mixed the menu cards, and it was really wild boar. The desserts included sweet potatoes, dried bananas, and various exotic jellies. Lord Stanley made a speech, and the guests retired, in good humour, after midnight.

The Society flourished and produced Annual Reports for about a decade. Lord Breadalbane raised yaks and American bison on his Taymouth estate; Lord Bute stocked his Scottish islands with beavers and thereby killed all the trees for miles; Buckland urged anyone who would listen to turn his park over to kangaroos. A contributor to *All the Year Round* in 1861 told readers that the capybara (a sort of monster guinea-pig) 'strongly tempts the domesticator', explaining that it 'feeds on water weeds, thus converting into wholesome nutriment vegetable substances

Capybara from Brehm's *Thierleben*, 1877

which are turned to no account. It is very prolific, and produces a great quantity of meat in a short space of time.'[27] An entry in the Society's Third Annual Report suggested that the Central American trumpeter bird could be 'trained to watch a flock of poultry, or even to shepherd a flock of sheep'.[28] Inevitably, some anonymous wit printed a fake Annual Report from the Acclimatization Society which was published unsuspectingly by the *Gardener's Chronicle*:

In Birds a great success has been obtained by the Hon. Grantley Berkeley, who has succeeded in producing a hybrid between his celebrated Pintail Drake and a Thames Rat; and the Council consider that this great success alone entitles them to the everlasting gratitude of their countrymen, as this hybrid, both from peculiarity of form and delicacy of flavour (which partakes strongly of the maternal parent) is entirely unique.[29]

One of the more sober aims of the Society was to improve Britain's fisheries and experiment with artificial fish-hatching. Buckland threw himself into this work and set up a small hatchery beside the Thames at Hampton. In January 1863 he organized a fish-hatching exhibition in the windows of the *Field*'s offices in the Strand, which was successful enough to be repeated in July at the Islington Dog Show. He also gave lectures on fish culture to the Royal Institution, the Zoological Society and other learned bodies. In 1864 he turned his attention to oysters which, from having long been a cheap staple of the working classes, were now becoming alarmingly scarce and expensive. He visited La Rochelle to learn how the French managed their oysters, and read a paper on his findings to the British Association. He also visited the Irish salmon fisheries, and assisted James Youl in collecting salmon and trout ova to send to Australia and New Zealand for acclimatization there. It was thus not wholly surprising that in February 1867 Buckland was appointed 'Her Majesty's Inspector of Salmon Fisheries', and retained the post for the rest of his life. His task was to improve the productivity of the English and Welsh salmon fisheries which had been declining for many years as a result of river pollution. In this he achieved considerable success, bringing much energy and initiative to publicizing the problem.

He also, unofficially, made himself responsible for educating the public in the importance of Britain's great fishing industry, and this he did by establishing his own 'Economic Fish Museum' at South Kensington. T.H. Huxley, who succeeded him as Inspector of Fisheries, called it 'poor dear X's rattle-trappery',[30] and certainly its contents were eclectic, ranging from a 'very fine specimen of a man trap' to a tanned boa constrictor's skin. But the main feature of the Museum were the many huge brightly coloured plaster casts of fish which Buckland made himself, in his basement kitchen at home. In one of his *Land and Water* articles, Buckland gave a vivid account of 'How we cast the large Sturgeon' in April 1867:

On Tuesday evening, about 5 p.m., Messrs. Grove of Bond Street sent word that they had a very fine sturgeon on their slab. Of course I went down at once to see it. The fish weighed, I was informed, 212 lbs; it measured 9 feet in length. I was anxious to make a cast of this fine fellow, but I confess the size and weight rather frightened me; however, they offered me the fish *for the night;* he must be back in the shop the next morning by 10 a.m. Determined not to lose the chance, I called a cab, and we tried to get the sturgeon on the top of it, but he was 'too much' for us, and we were obliged to give up all idea of this mode of conveyance of our huge friend from Bond Street to Albany Street. Messrs. Grove then kindly sent him up in a cart, and we got him *out* of the cart easily enough on his arrival at my door, but it was with the greatest difficulty we hauled him up the doorsteps. We then thought of pitching him headlong over the railings into the area below, and thus getting him into the little front kitchen, which, though terribly small, I use as a casting-room; but his back was so slippery and his scales so sharp to the hands, that Master Sturgeon beat us again. However, I was determined to get him down into the kitchen somehow; so, tying a rope to his tail, I let him slide down the stone stairs by his own weight. He started all right, but, 'getting way' on him, I could hold the rope no more, and away he went sliding headlong down the stairs, like an avalanche from Mont Blanc. At the bottom of the stairs is the kitchen door; the sturgeon came against it 'nose on' like an iron battering ram; he smashed the door open in a moment with his snout and slid right into the kitchen, gliding easily along the oil-cloth till at last be brought himself to an anchor under the kitchen table. This sudden and unexpected appearance of the armour-clad sea-monster, bursting open the door – shut purposely to keep out the sight of 'the master's horrid great fish' – instantly created a sensation scene, and great and dire was the commotion. The cook screamed, the housemaid nearly fainted; the cat jumped on the dresser, upsetting the best crockery; the little dog Danny, with his tail between his legs, made a precipitate retreat under the copper and barked furiously; the monkeys went mad with fright, and screamed 'Murder' in monkey language; the sedate parrot's nerves were terribly shaken, and it has never

Buckland's Economic Fish Museum

spoken a word since; and all this bother, because a poor harmless dead sturgeon burst open the kitchen door, and took up his position under the kitchen table.[31]

Buckland's style is often slapdash (he did much of his writing on railway trains, on his way to and from fishery inspections), but always racy and often vastly entertaining. He loved anecdotes and 'fascinating facts' – often more fascinating than factual – and he liked to pass on the curious lore he acquired from bird-dealers, rat-catchers and showmen. His definition of Natural History was a wide one, even for the period, and he included notes on archaeology, local customs and 'human oddities' in his purview. He particularly liked fairs and freak shows and he ends one account of the Islington Cattle Show by confessing that he has a weakness for 'talking fishes', 'elephant horses', 'edible dogs', 'monster pigs, dwarfs and giants', 'indiarubber dogs', 'living skeletons' and all the other dubious fun of the Victorian fair. This low taste was abhorrent to some of his contemporaries and the *Spectator*'s review of the third *Curiosities* derided him for devoting several pages to flea-circuses, but it is precisely this Mayhew-like concern with what was generally considered beneath notice that makes Buckland so valuable today. He cannot be considered a scientific naturalist, nor even a very observant one. He looked on fauna firstly as food, secondly as pets, and thirdly as exhibits – though, to his credit, it should be noted that he frequently exhorted his *Field* readers to observe nature more and shoot at it less. His most useful role was to harvest the very specialized knowledge of bird-catchers, poachers, fishermen, rat-catchers and so on and make it available to science. Darwin even used some of Buckland's *Land and Water* material to support his argument in *The Descent of Man* – an honour which Buckland himself did not appreciate since he loathed Darwinism with all his heart.

Although Buckland's journalism was the part of his work that he himself valued least, it is the part that most endears him today and any of the *Curiosities* can still be read with great pleasure. The *Field*'s obituary, published on Buckland's death in 1880, gives the fairest assessment of his enduring contribution to natural history:

His great merit as a writer was his power of rendering natural history attractive to the multitude; this he did to perfection... Whilst other writers of popular natural history simply compile, Buckland described from his own quaint and singular points of view. His descriptions were therefore vivid, and, if not always consistent, were eminently readable, and doubtless have served their own good turn by attracting many to the study of nature and natural objects.[32]

CHAPTER ELEVEN

OMNIUM GATHERUM

We live in the era of *Omnium Gatherum*; all the world's a museum, and men and women are its students.

Robert Kerr, 1864[1]

THE MODERN CONCEPT of a museum is something that evolved very slowly throughout the nineteenth century. In 1800 such museums as existed were heterogeneous jumbles of 'curiosities' entirely devoid of methodical purpose or arrangement and containing anything from coins to corn-dollies to coleoptera. When the Ashmolean Museum (which contained such doubtful treasures as a dragon's egg and two phoenix feathers) was 'modernized' in the 1820s, it was arranged, not on Linnaean lines, but in accordance with Paley's *Natural Theology* 'to induce a mental habit of associating the view of natural phenomena with the conviction that they are the media of Divine manifestation.'[2] Its usefulness to naturalists was therefore negligible.

The only other two British museums devoted exclusively to natural history in the opening years of the nineteenth century were the Lever and Bullock collections. The former was founded by Sir Ashton Lever, a wealthy Lancashire landowner, whose 'passion for collecting exceeded all bounds of prudence: every subject of zoology or mineralogy he did not possess, was to be purchased, cost what it might.'[3] In 1785 Sir Ashton's collecting mania brought him to insolvency, and he was forced to dispose of his collection. He chose an odd method: a public lottery or raffle for which the prize was the entire museum. It was won by Mr Parkinson, a dentist-surgeon remembered as the discoverer of Parkinson's disease. Parkinson moved the collection from Leicester Square, where it had previously been exhibited, to a purpose-built hall across Blackfriars Bridge. William Swainson, who visited it as a child, remembered it as 'one of the sights for holyday folk, and country cousins',[4] but its unfashionable location proved a drawback and in 1805 Mr Parkinson was forced to sell his strange prize. The auction lasted almost a month and drew naturalists from all the museums of Europe, but not from the British Museum, which was then far too poor to purchase anything.

The 'London Museum of Stuffed Animals' founded by William Bullock, a showman, was exhibited at Egyptian Hall, Piccadilly, from 1809 to 1819 and was generally agreed to be even better than the Lever collection. But it, too, went under the hammer and was mainly dispersed abroad, though some of the ethnological specimens collected by Captain Cook were salvaged for the British Museum, and Lord Derby bought many of the stuffed birds for his private museum at Knowsley Hall. From the demise of the Bullock collection in 1819 until the foundation of the Zoological Society's museum a decade later, Britain had no natural history museum as such. The natural history collections of the British Museum were, at this period, hopelessly inadequate and largely unshown.

The situation in America was rather better since Peale's Museum, Philadelphia, was then at its zenith. For a privately owned museum, Peale's enjoyed an unusually long life (1784 to 1845) and it was an object of envy to European naturalists. Swainson, writing on local or municipal museums in 1840, called it 'the most celebrated of these at present in existence'[5] and Waterton, who visited it in 1824, wrote in the *Wanderings*: 'When you go to Philadelphia, be sure not to forget to visit the Museum. It will afford you a great treat ... To the indefatigable exertions of this gentleman [Mr Peale] is the western world indebted for the possession of this splendid museum.'[6]

Charles Willson Peale, born in 1741, became a museum-keeper almost by accident. He was primarily an artist and by the 1780s was recognized as probably the leading portraitist in America. Like most fashionable painters of the day, he maintained a 'gallery' in his house, where he exhibited his work and received callers, in the hope of stimulating commissions. In 1784 a local naturalist asked him to draw some 'mammoth bones' which he had just acquired, and Peale naturally put them on view in his gallery as an extra attraction. The response was so good that Peale quickly sought other natural curiosities and was gratified with the gift of a large preserved paddle-fish. This and the bones, and his exhibition of 'moving pictures' (a form of diorama), served to keep his name before the public for the next two seasons, but in July 1786 he advertised a more ambitious scheme in the *Pennsylvania Packet*:

MR. PEALE, ever desirous to please and entertain the Public, will make a part of his House a Repository for Natural Curiosities – the Public he hopes will thereby be gratified in the sight of many of the Wonderful Works of Nature which are now closeted and but seldom seen ... MR. PEALE will most thankfully receive the Communications of Friends who will favour him with their Assistance in this Undertaking.[7]

Rather surprisingly, the citizens of Philadelphia rushed to favour him with their assistance and within a few months he had received a French angora cat from Benjamin Franklin and some pheasants from George Washington, as well as numerous gifts from less well-known figures. His sons were despatched to the woods to shoot birds and Peale himself, using trial and error and large, dangerous

Charles Willson Peale in his museum, 1822

bucketsful of arsenic, learned to preserve them. By the autumn he was writing, 'I find that I am getting into a much greater field than I had first expected. I find it very amusing and hope in the end it will be usefull.'⁸ Within a few seasons, museum-keeping had replaced portraiture as his chief occupation. The Quaker citizens of Pennsylvania did not approve of portraits, on grounds of vanity, but they did approve of the rational amusement to be had in a museum, and they seem not to have resented the fact that their donations and admission fees (25 cents a head) were making Peale rich.

In 1801 Peale achieved an even greater coup with his discovery of the mastodon. In that year some gigantic bones belonging to an unknown species were found in upstate New York, and attracted considerable publicity. In fact similar bones had been turning up occasionally for many years (including those which formed the original inspiration for Peale's Museum) but in 1801 the Philadelphia Philosophical Society, of which Peale was a leading member, resolved to find, if possible, a complete skeleton of 'the great American incognitum'. Their motive was more than scientific: it was a patriotic crusade. For half a century American naturalists had been smarting under a slur, first expressed by Buffon and other French writers, that species degenerated in the New World – dogs lost their bark, men their virility, and, in particular, 'All animals are smaller in North America than Europe.'⁹ Jefferson had retaliated with a list of weights and measures of American bears, beavers, otters and martens – all much larger than their European counterparts – and followed up by presenting Buffon with a stuffed American moose. The man who captured it for him apologized that this particular moose happened to have rather small horns, but he thoughtfully provided some elk and deer antlers which, he said, 'could be fixed on'. But even the sight of the moose had not elicited a proper recantation, and American naturalists now felt that the discovery of a truly giant American species was just what was needed to scotch the French slander once and for all.

Accordingly, an expedition was mounted – the first purely scientific expedition in American history – and Peale was put in charge. He went first to New York to drum up publicity, and then sailed up the Hudson to John Masten's farm near Newburgh where the most recent finds had been made. He found the bones spread out in a granary to which Masten admitted the public at a small charge. Many were badly broken, having been dragged out of the earth with chains, but they were enough to convince Peale that they all belonged to one skeleton and the remaining bones must still be buried nearby. He persuaded Masten to sell him the existing bones for $200 and the right to dig for more.

The bones had been found in a water-filled pit of shell marl which Masten and his neighbours used for fertilizer. It was the worst possible site for methodical excavation, but Peale devised an ingenious pump and bucket-chain to clear the water, powered by a man walking inside a tread-wheel. Fortunately the many sightseers who came to the site all wanted to take turns in the tread-wheel, so that part of the work was easily achieved. Peale was enough of a scientist to realize that he should leave the bones in their natural positions until he could make a plan of their arrangement, but the marl proved so slippery and dangerous that in the end he had to snatch out each bone as best he could. Digging continued day and night as thunderstorms rumbled round, but the rain held off long enough for Peale to disinter the foot bones, teeth, part of a tusk, and fragments of the lower jaw, which, together with Masten's original finds, gave him the framework of a complete skeleton. He then prospected other farms in the neighbourhood, using a series of hollow metal rods to test the ground, and eventually unearthed at Peter Millspaw's farm in Orange County another fairly well-preserved skeleton including the part he most needed – a complete lower jaw. Neither the Masten nor the Millspaw skeletons was complete, but together they made up each other's deficiencies. The expedition had taken five months and cost just over $1,000. It was a complete success.

Peale hurried back to Philadelphia and set about repairing and mounting the bones. At that date there was only one other palaeontological reconstruction in existence, a *Megatherium* at Madrid Museum, but of course Peale had never seen it. As with his taxidermy, he had to discover everything for himself by trial and error. He resisted the temptation to cobble the two skeletons together, but instead made two reconstructions, using wood or papier mâché to fill in the missing parts and conscientiously demarcating them with a red line. The Masten skeleton was destined for the Museum: the other was to be taken by his son Rembrandt to Europe to astonish the sceptics and, of course, to make money. (In fact the Old World public proved surprisingly resistant to the New World wonder, and Rembrandt was eventually forced to trundle the monster home again, having failed to find a buyer. It now lies, unmounted, in the American Museum of Natural History.) Peale's reconstructions were remarkably accurate for their time, though he made the creatures longer and taller than modern scientists would allow, and gave them claws and a bison-like hump.

In December, the 'mammoth', as it was always erroneously called, was installed in its own special Mammoth Room in the Museum and Peale invited twelve guests to join him for dinner *inside* the great skeleton, where they sang 'Yankee Doodle' and made patriotic toasts. On Christmas Eve, 'the LARGEST of *terrestrial* beings', 'the ninth wonder of the world!!!' was unveiled to the public (at an extra admission charge of 50c.), and the public was bewitched. 'Mammoth' became the favourite adjective of the decade, with 'mammoth bread', 'mammoth cheese', 'mammoth meals' appearing in every advertisement. All the visitors marvelled at the size of the mammoth, but they must also have pondered an even more remarkable characteristic – the fact that it was extinct. One or two people like Jefferson refused to believe that it *was* extinct – they argued that the vast unexplored regions of Western America might yet conceal living mammoths – but most visitors accepted Peale's explanation that the mammoth was a victim of the Noachian Deluge, and as such bore out the scriptural claim that 'there were giants in the earth in those days'.

The discovery of the mastodon, while it revealed Peale's considerable flair as a showman, also revealed his essential naïvety as a scientist. For in the excitement of exhibiting the creature (and painting its excavation) he quite forgot the scientist's first priority: that of describing, naming and classifying the discovery and thus officially presenting it to science. Peale's announcement of the 'mammoth' as 'the carnivorous elephant of the North' was wrong on every count: it was not a mammoth, not carnivorous and not an elephant. It was left to Cuvier, in 1806, to coin the name *mastodonte* (in reference to its nipple-shaped teeth) and to distinguish it from the true Siberian mammoth. The 'official' discoverer of the mastodon is therefore Cuvier, not Peale.

Of course Peale had no scientific training or background, and such lapses are not surprising, but he did try very hard to make himself a scientist. His dedication is touchingly expressed in the names he gave his sons: the elder boys were christened Raphaelle, Rembrandt, Titian, Rubens and Vandyke, but the two youngest, born after the Museum's inception, were christened Charles Linnaeus and Benjamin Franklin. Some of Peale's scientific aspirations were unusually advanced for his time. In 1796, for instance, he hired a French naturalist, Palisot de Beavois, to arrange and catalogue the specimens on the Linnaean system, and in 1800 he wrote to one of the state legislators: 'I declare that it is only the arrangement and management of a Repository of Subjects of Natural History &c., that can constitute its utility. For if it should be immensely rich in the numbers and value of articles,

Mammoth in the St Petersburg Museum, *c.* 1860

unless they are systematically arranged, and the proper modes of seeing and using them attended to, the advantage of such a store will be of little account to the public.'[10] Of course this is a truism today, but in 1800 it was one which had not yet impressed itself on the curators of, say, the British Museum. In many letters, from the 1790s onwards, Peale expressed the hope that his Museum would become the foundation for a national collection, and he also took pains to emphasize that science, not showmanship, was his guiding star. 'I neglect,' he wrote, 'many little contrivances which might serve to catch the eye of the gaping multitude, but prefer a steady perseverance to execute such improvements as may tend to give a scientific cast, as being most effectual to make deep and lasting impressions on those who come to study the subjects of the Museum.'[11]

However, it is noticeable that Peale's most devout professions of scientific seriousness occur in letters to Jefferson and other legislators, when he was appealing for funds. At the time he was writing the admirable sentiments quoted above, the Museum housed such non-Linnaean curiosities as a collection of monkeys dressed in human clothes, a 'physiognotrace' or machine for drawing silhouettes, a 'whispering tube' which amplified sounds from one room to another, and a five-legged, two-tailed cow. In 1797 an editorial in Cobbett's *Porcupine's Gazette* derided him for showing waxworks – 'Now, Mr. Peale, be so good as to tell me how long *nature* has taken to *work in wax*?'[12] – and the tendency to stray from instruction into entertainment was always apparent.

In 1810, at the age of sixty-nine, Peale officially retired and handed over the management of the Museum to his son Rubens. Rubens was wholeheartedly a showman, untroubled by scientific scruples, and he soon dismantled the Linnaean arrangement, and introduced such crowd-pulling novelties as Signor Hellene, the Pandean Band, and a show called the 'Phantasmagoria' advertised as 'astonishing experiments in natural philosophy...intended to enlighten and guard people against certain superstitious ideas they may have imbibed respecting witches and wizards'.[13] In 1816 he provoked a crisis when he installed gas lighting in the Museum against the wishes of the Museum's landlords, and although Charles Peale managed to smooth things over, the city fathers henceforward looked on the Museum with an unfriendly eye. Peale died in 1827 and Rubens went off to organize rival 'Peale's Museums' in Baltimore and New York, while the youngest son Franklin succeeded as manager. But from then on the Museum was in decline.

The one son who could have saved it – Titian[14] – was too ambitious and too serious a scientist to commit himself wholly to running a museum. In 1817, while still only a teenager, he had drawn the plates for Thomas Say's *American Entomology*, one of the first American scientific publications to win respect in Europe, and later the same year he accompanied Say and George Ord on a collecting expedition to the Florida and Georgia islands. From 1819 to 1821, again with his friend Say, he accompanied the Stephen H. Long expedition to the upper waters of the Missouri, as Assistant Naturalist, and from 1838 to 1841 he was official Naturalist on the Wilkes expedition to the Pacific. Waterton said of him, 'I met no-one in the United States half so knowing or so keen after natural history as Titian Peale',[15] but not surprisingly, his keenness led him into the field rather than the closet, and he never involved himself in the affairs of the Museum.

Anyway, by the late 1820s and 1830s, Peale's Museum had several rivals to contend with. There were Rubens's other 'Peale's Museums', there was Scudder's 'American Museum' in New York, and there was the Western Museum in Cincinnati where Audubon worked briefly as a taxidermist in 1819. In Audubon's time, the Western Museum contained 500 stuffed birds, 200 fishes, 100 mammoth bones, 50 giant sloth bones, besides Egyptian antiquities and an 'elegant organ', but by the mid-1820s it was showing waxworks of the Infernal Regions, including a female figure of Sin who occasionally leaped from her seat and howled at spectators. In 1841 Scudder's American Museum was bought by a then unknown young man, Phineas T. Barnum, who in the next few years introduced new standards of scale, sensationalism and vulgarity to the art of drawing crowds, and eventually swallowed almost every private museum in America into the insatiable maw of his Grand Colossal Museum and Greatest Show on Earth. Peale's Museum was not enough of a 'draw' to compete in the Barnum manner and by the 1840s it had lost whatever scientific importance it had once possessed. It was accordingly sold by the sheriff in 1845, and the collections widely dispersed.

The demise of Peale's Museum (and many similar privately owned museums in Britain and America) was inevitable. The concept of museums was changing and miscellaneous jumbles of 'curiosities' were no longer good enough. A museum, to be useful and important, to be a source of rational amusement, must aim at *completeness*, and only the great national collections could hope to achieve it. Nevertheless it was still possible – just – for a private collector to be comprehensive in a small specialized field, and in the first half of the nineteenth century there were still countless private natural history collections which, in their field, surpassed the national collections. One of the last, and one of the greatest, was the shell collection amassed by the English conchologist Hugh Cuming (1791–1865) which must stand as a representative for all the hundreds of other private collections which flourished in this era.

Some biographers believe Cuming to have been illiterate: certainly he was of humble origins and spent his early manhood working as a sail-maker in Valparaiso, Chile. But by the age of only thirty-five, he had made enough money to retire from business and devote himself full-time to his hobby. In his specially fitted yacht, the *Discoverer*, he toured the islands of Polynesia, the western coast of South America, and the Philippines, scouring their beaches and dredging their shallows. His tours were like royal progresses: he would gather all the natives and children on the beach, show them what he wanted, give them each a bag, and promise to reward the finders of the biggest haul or the rarest specimens. His name was known in all the South American ports, thanks to his sail-making years, and sailors and fishermen would hoard special shells to sell to him on his next visit. Cuming was a dealer as well as a collector. Whenever he heard of a naturalist going out to some conchologically virgin shore, he would offer to pay his expenses in return for shells. The duplicates could be sold to amateurs, or exchanged for better specimens. Of course, Hugh Cuming was lucky in his speciality – shells are small, light, durable, easy to recognize, and need no laborious preparation – but he was also unusually businesslike. And he endeared himself to his closet colleagues by never writing a single scientific paper. While men like G.B. Sowerby II and Lovell Reeve built their reputations by describing the Cuming finds, all Cuming wanted was to bask in the satisfaction of ownership. Albert Gunther of the British Museum recalled seeing him at Zoological Society meetings in the 1860s:

> Cuming attended the meetings regularly, always occupying the same seat, and invariably appearing in evening dress. Poor Martens [Dr Eduard von Martens] was severely reprimanded by him when he appeared as a guest at a meeting with muddy boots. Cuming never uttered a word at any meeting… He lived a solitary widower, always working at his collection of shells, but never describing a species.[16]

In 1846 Cuming believed that he was dying and wrote to the British Museum Trustees offering his collection for £6,000, an absurdly modest price. At that time, it numbered 52,789 specimens, representing at least 18,000 species and including many type specimens and holotypes. This was almost twice as many shells and species as the British Museum then owned, but the Trustees (against the advice of all eminent naturalists) refused the offer, which was perhaps as well since Cuming then survived for another nineteen years, and when the British Museum *did* finally buy the collection from his executors for £6,000 it was even larger and finer than in 1846. No sooner had the collection been moved to the British Museum than Mrs J.E. Gray, wife of the Keeper of Zoology, carried the open drawers of shells across a courtyard in a howling gale and all the labels blew away. The Cuming collection has been a source of vexation and controversy to conchologists ever since.

After Cuming, the only private collector who again aspired to rival the national collections was Walter Rothschild (1868–1937), the son of the first Lord Rothschild and heir to the banking fortune. He used his vast wealth to establish a zoological museum at Tring, to publish his own transactions (the *Novitates Zoologicae*), and to send collectors to every corner of the world. His spendthrift collecting habits were a source of annoyance to the British Museum Trustees since he was always able to outbid them, and on one occasion actually wrote to the Keeper of Zoology re a forthcoming auction, 'I must tell you point blank that for the skins of the varieties of hybrids of grouse I gave an unlimited order to Gerrard before I saw you so, as I should get them anyhow, I shall not give them up.'[17] Other naturalists were also annoyed by his sudden decision in the 1890s to remove every tortoise 'big or little, alive or dead' from the Galapagos Islands (he wanted to 'save them for science', a familiar excuse). But in fact he never seriously dented the pre-

14 Title-page of *Zoological Sketches* by Joseph Wolf,
1861-7

15 Title-page of *Rustic Adornments for Homes of Taste*
by Shirley Hibberd, 1856

16 Hippopotamus, from *Zoological Sketches* by Joseph Wolf, 1861-7

17 The Gorilla, from *Lloyd's Natural History* by
Henry O. Forbes, 1896. Drawn by J. G.
Keulemans.

18 The Red-ruffed Lemur, from *Lloyd's Natural
History* by Henry O. Forbes, 1896

19 Palm of the Mountain, from *The Plant World* by Elizabeth Twining, 1866

20 Black-maned Lion, from *The Naturalist's Library* ed. Sir William Jardine, 1835-52

21 Common hare, from *The Natural History of British Quadrupeds* by Edward Donovan, 1820

eminence of the national collections, of which his Tring Museum now forms a part.

Cuming and Rothschild were really anachronisms in their day, belonging rather to an eighteenth-century tradition. By the middle of the nineteenth century, the hopes of scientists were firmly pinned to the great national collections which were then just getting under way. America benefited enormously from the unlooked-for gift of the Smithsonian Institution. It was formed from the bequest of James Macie Smithson, an English amateur scientist and illegitimate son of the first Duke of Northumberland who was so annoyed at having one of his papers rejected by the Royal Society, and so piqued at being ignored by the English aristocracy to which he felt he belonged, that he left his vast fortune to the American government 'for the increase and diffusion of knowledge among men'. At the same time, Agassiz founded his own Harvard Museum, and began mobilizing that great army of private benefactors which enabled American scientific institutions to move from negligible to enviable in the eyes of their European counterparts in the space of just two generations. Meanwhile, the British Museum Natural History Department was busily contriving to shed whatever vestige of glory it had once possessed. Its history over this period in fact is of such tragi-comic proportions that it deserves recounting here.

The British Museum had been created by Act of Parliament in 1753 and its Natural History Department was formed from collections bequeathed by Sir Hans Sloane (1660–1753) which were important and extensive enough to ensure the Department's respectability for the remainder of the eighteenth century. By the early decades of the nineteenth century, however, most of the Sloane collections had disappeared. Some of them had simply mouldered away from lack of any effort to preserve them, but some had been despatched by more energetic means. Dr George Shaw, for instance, Keeper of Zoology from 1806 to 1813, managed to sell off many specimens to the College of Surgeons. Dr William Elford Leach, Shaw's successor, had an even brisker approach:

> He despised the taxidermy of Sir Hans Sloane's age, and made periodical bonfires of Sloanian specimens. These he was wont to call his 'cremations'. In his time the gardens of the Museum [it was then at Montagu House, Bloomsbury] were still the favourite resort of the Bloomsburians, but the attraction of the terraces and the fragrance of the shrubberies were sadly lessened when a pungent odour of burning snakes was their accompaniment. The stronger the complaints, however, the more apparent became Dr Leach's attachment to his favourite cremations.[18]

By 1833 the Annual Report to the Trustees stated that of the 5,500 insects listed in Sloane's catalogue, literally not a vestige remained.

The chorus of complaints about the Natural History Department in the early decades of the nineteenth century was unanimous. Dr Thomas Stewart Traill wrote in the *Edinburgh Review* in 1825 that the natural history collections were

Grand Staircase, Montagu House

'mouldering or blackening in the crypts of Montagu House, the tomb or charnel-house of unknown treasures' with 'moths, *ptini, dermestes*, busily employed amid the splendours of exotic plumage, or roaring through the fur of animals.'[19] William Swainson, writing in 1840, compared the crypts of Montagu House to 'the catacombs we have seen at Palermo, where one is opened every day in the year, merely to deposit fresh subjects for decay, and to ascertain how the process has gone on during the last year.'[20] And a milder, but even more damning criticism was uttered by Charles Darwin when he wrote to Henslow in 1836, 'I cannot feel, from all I hear, any great respect even for the present state of that establishment.'[21]

The inability of the Natural History Department even to conserve its specimens, let alone display them, was so notorious that the Treasury frequently refused to entrust it with specimens that had been collected at the government's expense. The fruits of Richardson's Arctic researches, for instance, went to the Zoological Society Museum, the Edinburgh Museum, and even into private hands, like Swainson's, rather than into the charnel-house of the British Museum. It was only in 1872, on the return of the *Challenger* expedition, that the government finally ruled that collections made at the nation's expense should go to the nation's museum. And while donations were unlikely, purchases were almost impossible, since the Natural History Department's acquisitions allowance in the first half of the century was generally under £1,000 p.a., and this had to cover geology,

Zoological Gallery, British Museum, 1840

mineralogy and palaeontology, as well as botany and zoology. Entomology, for instance, had just £10 a year to spend on new acquisitions. As a result, many important privately made collections, such as the Lever, Bullock and the Broderip shells, went to other buyers because the British Museum could not afford them.

This was the era when the British Museum Library was achieving its worldwide pre-eminence under the reign of the great Antonio Panizzi. He joined the library staff in 1831, under Sir Henry Ellis, and succeeded Ellis as Principal Librarian (i.e. director of the whole Museum) in 1856. Macaulay said of him that he 'would at any time give three mammoths for an Aldus'[22] and his contempt for the Natural History Department – indeed for science generally – was total. This emerges from his evidence to a Select Committee in 1836. The Committee had been asked to consider whether there should be more scientists on the Board of Trustees, the governing body of the Museum. The fifty-one Trustees were mainly politicians, aristocrats and churchmen with, at most, six scientists among them. Panizzi told the Committee, 'Scientific men are jealous of their authority; they are dogmatical and narrow-minded ... The scientific men would spoil the men of rank, and drive them away from the board. I speak seriously and from experience. An officer would have no chance against a scientific man who should take a crotchet into his head, and they are all crotchety ... I never saw scientific men go right, or view things as other people do.'[23]

With this attitude prevailing among the top administrators, it is not surprising that the Natural History Department languished as long as it did. The fundamental problem was lack of staff. Until 1856 there were only three Keepers (of Zoology, Botany and Geology-Mineralogy) with a handful of assistants. Places went by patronage rather than by merit, and many a well-qualified scientist was rejected because he did not meet the Trustees' notion of a well-educated gentleman. In 1862 there was a public outcry when Arthur O'Shaughnessy, nephew of the mistress of one of the Trustees, was appointed Entomological Assistant over the heads of many internationally recognized entomologists. O'Shaughnessy did not know the difference between a butterfly and a moth; nevertheless, despite protests from the Entomological Society, his appointment was confirmed. The prevailing snobbery was quite shameless. J.E. Gray noticed that when he was appointed Keeper in 1840 he was suddenly referred to as 'John Edward Gray, Esq.' (i.e. a gentleman) whereas before he had been plain Mr Gray. Alexander Agassiz, Louis Agassiz's son, visited the Museum in 1869 and commented, 'What a state of things for the nineteenth century... I cannot imagine how people with any common sense will submit to such caste distinctions and so much nonsense.'[24] Even as late as 1865 it was noticed that G.F. Hampson, who had been struggling in vain to get a formal appointment in the lepidoptery department for the past five years, was suddenly appointed Assistant when he succeeded to a baronetcy.

Such staff as there were were overworked and underpaid and often had to take on outside work to support themselves. There were no pensions, so appointees tended to stay at their posts until they died or went mad, which they did with astonishing frequency. J.E. Gray told a Royal Commission in 1847 that the lack of pensions 'has a very injurious effect on the minds and health of officers and assistants... I need only refer to the fact of the deplorable state of mental disease which has existed among several of the officers.'[25] Gray himself went completely mad only once, in 1832, when he decided to become a Moravian missionary, but most of his colleagues considered him semi-mad all the time. Dr William Elford Leach, who joined the Natural History staff in 1813, started off well but then succumbed to the occupational disease: 'His habits became irregular; he studied during the night, instead of the day; and although much attached to gymnastic exercises, they were violent, uncertain, and not such as would operate gently and effectually on a naturally nervous and irritable temperament. One of these, for instance, was leaping over the back of a stuffed zebra, which was placed in the centre of a large room (now dismantled), over which we have seen him vault with the lightness of a harlequin... It was, if we remember correctly, about the year 1821, that we first remarked an evident change in his health: he had become paler and thinner than usual – highly nervous – and his eyes shone with that unnatural brightness so indicative of the fearful affliction which soon after became apparent to every one, and rendered the care of his friends absolutely essential to his welfare.'[26] Even those staff members who were not actually mad often became highly unbalanced in the pursuit of their pet dogmas. George Shaw, for instance, threatened to put his foot on any shell which was not listed in the 12th edition of Linnaeus's *Systema Naturae*. George Samouelle, a brilliant entomologist, in 1839 deliberately removed all the labels and registration numbers from the entomological cases arranged by his colleague Adam White in a successful attempt to sabotage White's work.

From the evil of understaffing, all other evils arose. For the first three decades of the century, the natural history collections were left unpreserved, uncatalogued, unlabelled, unarranged and therefore unused, because there was no one to perform these essential curatorial tasks. There was thus very little to attract the public to visit them; and indeed, the public was not encouraged to come. The Museum was theoretically open to 'any person of decent appearance' but only on three days a week and only between the hours of 10 and 4, which effectively disbarred any members of the working class. (A further prohibition on babes-in-arms and the absence of any ladies' lavatories provided a second line of defence against working-class women.) This was a situation which the top Museum administrators fully approved. When in 1835 a Select Committee suggested that the Museum might occasionally extend its opening hours to encourage working-class visitors, perhaps during Easter week, Sir Henry Ellis, the Principal Librarian, was aghast: 'The most mischievious portion of the population is abroad and about at such a time...the more vulgar class would crowd into the Museum.' He shudderingly mentioned 'sailors from the dock yards and girls whom they might bring with them', and explained that 'The more important class of the population...would

'Holiday Time at the British Museum', by F. Smith, 1873

'A Dream of the Future' – Sunday opening – from *Judy*, 1885

be discontented.'[27] It was not until 1879 that the Museum was opened daily, and not until 1896, by which time the Natural History Department had moved to South Kensington, that Sunday opening was permitted.

This argument about opening hours – which was *au fond* an argument about whether the working classes should be admitted – waged hotly in all public institutions throughout the nineteenth century. The first museum actually to encourage working-class visitors was the Hancock Museum in Newcastle which, from 1835, held regular open evenings. The Committee reported that 'although the attention of the keeper of the rooms was necessarily divided, it is with pride and pleasure we declare that we are not aware of the injury or abstraction of a single article, although hundreds of interesting objects are necessarily loose and portable.'[28] The idea that working people could visit a museum without necessarily stealing all the contents was still very novel, but slowly and nervously other institutions dared the experiment and were amazed at the response. In 1838, as part of the coronation celebrations, the College of Surgeons Museum and the Edinburgh Museum opened their doors to all comers, attracting 20,000 and 25,000 visitors respectively. In 1840 Professor Richard Owen visited the Leicester and Nottingham Museums on their open days and wrote back to his wife: 'Never saw a better experiment of the amount of danger to be apprehended from indiscriminate admission of English *canaille*, and, so far as we saw and heard, quite successful. All very orderly and all *paws off*; but I found myself the centre of a group whenever I had to take notes of a fossil specimen.'[29] Owen's conversion was an important point because it was under his aegis that the British Museum finally instituted daily opening in 1879.

The British Museum's status in the scientific world began to improve in 1840 when John Edward Gray was appointed Keeper of Zoology. He was not an imaginative or far-sighted man (he compared Darwinism to spiritualism) but he was a hard worker, and by the time he retired, in 1875, he had added over a million specimens to the Museum's collection, at an average cost of less than one shilling apiece. He made international contacts and set up duplicate-exchange systems with colonial museums. He hammered home the lesson (which Peale had learned in 1800) that specimens *must* be arranged and catalogued to be any use, and the two hundred catalogues that the Natural History Department issued under his Keepership – the first that the Department had ever issued – became the model for zoological catalogues throughout the world. Every year he was scolded by the Trustees for overspending his meagre budget, but every year he made the collections more complete.

In 1856 he suffered a bitter blow when Richard Owen was appointed Superintendent of Natural History over his head and proceeded to take the credit for his achievements. But Owen's appointment gave the Natural History Department the prestige it so badly needed and which Gray alone could not have supplied. Almost as soon as he arrived, Owen began to campaign to move the Natural History Department to a separate building. It was absurd, he said, that all the staff should be cramped into one room (called 'the Insect Room') where in winter it was too dark to do microscopic work. And he found an ally in the Principal Librarian, Panizzi, who also wanted the natural history collections to move, simply in order to be rid of them. 'I think it would be a great deal better for the Museum,' he told a Select Committee in 1860, 'that the collection of natural history should not be there; for the fewer persons of this class are attracted as visitors the better.'[30] Many scientists, including Darwin, Huxley and Gray, at first opposed the move.

They still cherished that ideal of Science-and-the-Arts, universal culture, that the Prince Consort had so vigorously demonstrated in the Great Exhibition, and they feared that science would lose status if it were segregated. But by 1869 Parliament had formally accepted the idea of a separation of the collections and in 1881 the new British Museum (Natural History) – only in 1963 did it become, officially, the Natural History Museum – was completed to Alfred Waterhouse's designs. The Victorian public was delighted with its grand new culture palace and 400,000 people a year visited it in the 1880s and 1890s. One or two surviving rooms and showcases (the whales, the dinosaurs, the fossil-fish room and the humming-bird case) give an idea of the visual richness that greeted the Victorian visitor, as does Waterhouse's terracotta façade, with its birds and beasts, including 'Man: the greatest beast of all',[31] put there at Huxley's suggestion, frisking over the gables.

For a few brief years at the end of the nineteenth century the British Museum (Natural History) represented that fusion of scientific vitality and popular entertainment that characterized Victorian natural history at its best. But this ideal was no sooner achieved than dismantled. Owen retired in 1884 and was succeeded as Director by Sir William Henry Flower, an aristocrat and autocrat conspicuously lacking in the common touch. (When his assistants complained that they were so poorly paid that their wives were having to take in washing, Flower said that, yes, he too was feeling the pinch – he had had to tell his wife to restrict the use of her carriage.) *His* great ideal was to separate the collections, into a small generalized representative display to amuse the public, and some private hidden reserve collections to gratify the scientists. The latter, he hoped, would be used by only a very limited number of specialists and if the public did not even know they were there, well, so much the better.

By the end of the century, Flower had achieved this division and it is the principle which all national museums have followed in the twentieth century. Its advantage to museum administrators and to professional researchers is obvious, but for the layman it constitutes a regression from the great Victorian ideal. Once the working heart of a museum is hidden away, its public rooms begin to seem rather lifeless – in Victorian terms, they are suggestive of vulgar, rather than rational, amusement. One remembers the scene in the Leicester Museum in 1840 when Professor Owen found himself the centre of a group whenever he had to take notes of a fossil specimen. For Owen, it was mildly inconvenient; for his audience, it must have been a memorable and stimulating experience, one that made them feel in touch with the scientific discoveries of the age. The problem with museums at the beginning of the nineteenth century was that they were heterogeneous, disorganized and incomplete: by the end of the century they were so specialized, so highly organized, and so vast that they could no longer expose all their treasures to the public, and the layman had to be barred from the inner sanctuaries of the professionals.

PART FOUR
UPHOLDERS OF
ORTHODOXY

CHAPTER TWELVE
THE BRITISH CUVIER

T HIS CHAPTER AND the following two are devoted to describing three important scientists of the Victorian age. Their names are Richard Owen, Roderick Murchison and Louis Agassiz, and the modern reader may be forgiven for not having heard of them, since none of them makes a prominent showing in any history of scientific progress. The reason for that is that their work did not advance scientific progress – they were all reactionaries rather than revolutionaries. What we are trying to do here, however, is to view the scientific galaxy through a Victorian layman's eyes, to describe the scientists who seemed *to him* to be important, and on whom he based his ideas of what a scientist should be. From that viewpoint, Owen, Murchison and Agassiz are more important than Charles Darwin, since the layman would probably not have heard of Darwin until 1859, when the *Origin of Species* appeared, and thereafter would have regarded him with the gravest suspicion. In any case, Darwin never *looked* important. He was not sparkling and dynamic like Agassiz, or pompous and terrifying like Owen. On the contrary, his manner was so quiet and unassuming that, as the illustrator Joseph Wolf remarked, 'A child might have talked to that man.'[1] Most of the time he was rusticated at Down House, an invisible invalid. He was not a Knight, or even a Professor, and although the nation finally bestirred itself to bury its most influential atheist in Westminster Abbey, this was almost the sole mark of national esteem which Darwin ever received.

Owen, Murchison and Agassiz seemed more important than Darwin because they were far more conspicuous. They chaired committees, presided over societies, gave public lectures, founded institutions, wrote regularly to the newspapers, hobnobbed with aristocrats, were consulted by government, and in general acted as public scientists in a way that Darwin did not. And in the Victorian period, this was an important function, since professional scientists were still a new caste and their role in society was not yet established. As Owen, Murchison and Agassiz clambered their way up the social ladder (they were all terrific snobs), the prestige of science clambered with them. Had all the scientists been as self-effacing as Darwin, it is likely that science would still be waiting for its first injection of public money.

The contrast between Darwin and Richard Owen is particularly striking because they were almost exact contemporaries working in more or less the same field. There was no danger of any child wanting to talk to Owen. He spoke slowly, in polysyllables, with all the grandeur and unintelligibility of an oracle. Even his appearance was awe-inspiring: 'He was tall but ungainly in figure, with massive head, lofty forehead, curiously round, prominent, and expressive eyes, high cheek bones, large mouth and projecting chin, long, lank, dark hair.'[2] Everyone who met him commented on his appalling fish-like eyes, and most people found him terrifying. Nevertheless, by the late 1840s, when Darwin was still generally unheard-of, Owen was accepted as the leading biologist of the age, and had earned the title of 'the British Cuvier' because he carried on the work which Cuvier had begun in comparative anatomy. Owen himself disliked the name because he considered himself better than Cuvier. And Huxley disliked it for a different reason – because, he felt, the British Cuvier 'stands in exactly the same relation to the French as British brandy to cognac.'[3] But most scientists, while loathing Owen as a man, recognized him as the leading authority on all matters relating to zoological or palaeontological classification.

Richard Owen was born at Lancaster in 1804, the son of middle-class but not wealthy parents. His father died when he was only five. His mother seems to have been of the doting but unintellectual variety – at least that is the impression one receives from a letter she wrote him in 1830 when he started publishing his Hunterian Catalogue: 'I have, my dear lad, read your Catalogue quite through, *Latin and English*, and have had the pleasure of seeing your name in a philosophical review describing the air-vessels of the gannet ... You may suppose what pleasure such things give me!'[4] Owen attended his local grammar school, Lancaster, which happened to be one of the best in the country, and at the age of sixteen was apprenticed to learn the 'arts, businesses, professions, and mysteries of a surgeon apothecary and man midwife, with every circumstance relating thereto.'[5] This was the poor man's way into the medical profession. Wealthier aspirants simply attended medical school but the Owen family could not run to such expenses. And in fact Owen's apprenticeship gave him an advantage which many more affluent medical students would have envied. His duties included assisting at the post-mortems of any prisoners who died in Lancaster Gaol, and this meant that he had a fairly regular supply of free and fresh corpses on which to practise dissection. This was an unusual luxury at the time. Most medical students had to make do with one corpse a year, or else enter into shady and expensive dealings if they wanted more. But at Lancaster Gaol, while still only a teenager, Owen was able to carve out a precocious knowledge of human anatomy. In later life, he was fond of recounting his many happy hours spent in the Lancaster morgue, and there was one particular

Richard Owen

story – 'The Negro's Head' – which became his standard party-piece. This is the official version, given in his biography:

> My zeal and skill at assisting at *post-mortems* had gained me the rarely be-stowed commendation of the doctor our preceptor. I had already begun to form a small anatomical collection, and had lately added a human cranium to my series of the skulls of dogs and cats and the skeletons of mice and 'such small deer'. It happened also that on the day when a negro patient in the gaol hospital had died, a treatise on the 'Varieties of the Human Race' fell into my hands, and greatly increased my craniological longings. The examination of the body was over and the hurried inquest performed, when, slipping some silver into the hand of the old turnkey as we left the room, I told him I should have to call again that evening to look a little further into the matter, before the coffin was finally screwed down ...
>
> [That evening], provided with a strong brown-paper bag, I sallied forth ... to secure my specimen of the Ethiopian race. I was now an *habitué* of the place, and an attendant was no longer proffered to accompany me. Taking my lantern and keys, I opened every door and gate, duly locking them again after I had passed through ... The gloom of the apartment was just made visible by the light of the lantern, but it served for the business immediately in hand. The various instruments had judiciously been left behind; and when I returned through the gates – the bag under my cloak – the intimation that all was now ready for interment was received with a nod of intelligence by the old turnkey, which assured me that no inquisition nor discovery was to be apprehended on that side of the castle walls.
>
> As soon as I was outside I began to hurry down the hill; but the pavement was coated with a thin sheet of ice, my foot slipped, and, being encumbered with my cloak, I lost my balance and fell forward with a shock which jerked the negro's head out of the bag, and sent it bounding down the slippery surface of the steep descent. As soon as I recovered my legs I raced desperately after it, but was too late to arrest its progress. I saw it bounce against the door of a cottage facing the descent, which flew open and received me at the same time, as I was unable to stop my downward career. I heard shrieks, and saw the whisk of the garment of a female, who had rushed through an inner door; the room was empty; the ghastly head at my feet. I seized it and retreated, wrapping it in my cloak. I suppose I must have closed the door after me, but I never stopped till I reached the surgery.[6]

This story illustrates, if nothing else, Owen's youthful dedication, and it is not surprising that when he finally moved to London in 1825 to take his medical degree, he was noticed by Dr Abernethy, the President of the Royal College of Surgeons, and offered a job at the College's Museum, as assistant curator under William Clift. Owen consolidated his position by marrying Clift's daughter, and was soon effectively in charge of the Museum. The Museum had been founded

The Hunterian Museum, Royal College of Surgeons

from the collections of John Hunter, the great eighteenth-century anatomist and surgeon, but Hunter's executor had burned all the labels and papers relating to the collection, and when Owen moved in he found four thousand unlabelled pickle jars awaiting identification. It was just the sort of work he enjoyed, and by 1830 he was ready to begin publishing his Catalogue of the Hunterian Collections with all the jars carefully organized and labelled. Under his supervision, the Royal College of Surgeons' Museum became a model of what such an institution should be; Swainson described it in 1840 as 'the most beautifully planned and the most conveniently arranged museum perhaps in Europe.'[7]

The Museum remained Owen's base until he moved to the British Museum in 1856, but during his period there he steadily accumulated other appointments, becoming successively lecturer in and then Professor of Comparative Anatomy at St Bartholomew's Hospital, and Hunterian Professor and Professor of Anatomy and Physiology at the Royal College of Surgeons. From 1830 he acted as prosector to London Zoo, which gave him a useful familiarity with many exotic animals, whose anatomy he described in a series of brilliant monographs. Despite these many appointments, he complained loudly and often of his poverty, and was finally awarded a Civil List pension of £200 a year and the gift of a grace-and-favour residence in Richmond Park. (When he died, he was found to have amassed the considerable fortune of £30,000.)

Apart from his teaching and museum work, Owen's fame as the 'British Cuvier' rested on the 400-odd anatomical papers which he published during his long life. It is difficult to convey the importance of these papers to a lay reader, because, as even Huxley complained when faced with the same task, 'Obvious as are the merits of Owen's anatomical and palaeontological work to every expert, it is necessary to be an expert to discern them.'[8] Another difficulty is Owen's style which is at best stupefyingly dull, and at worst, incomprehensible. Even his one or two supposedly 'popular' books are leaden. Owen believed that the poor sales of his books were due to some international conspiracy to suppress his ideas, but anyone who tries to read a page of his prose will find a much simpler explanation. One part of his work, however, did capture the popular imagination and that was his ability to deduce the appearance of a whole animal from a small fragment of bone or, as one of his colleagues put it, to 'make a skeleton out of a single toe-bone, or make species on two toe-bones.'[9]

His most spectacular opportunity for doing this came in 1839 when a sailor brought him a six-inch-long fragment of bone from New Zealand. It was a marrow bone, of immense thickness, which at first suggested that it came from a large quadruped. But Owen noticed various markings on the outside of the bone which reminded him of those he had seen on an ostrich's femur, and after careful examination, he finally decided that the bone fragment must have come from the thigh of a large flightless bird, at least the size of an ostrich. This was a very daring hypothesis, since the bone was not a fossil, and Owen had to assume that these huge conspicuous birds were still running round New Zealand, somehow evading the eyes of its human inhabitants. (Scientists now believe that the moa probably became extinct a few generations before the arrival of the white colonists, but recently enough to be remembered in many Maori legends.) Owen persuaded the Zoological Society, much against their will, to publish his paper, and he sent a hundred copies to New Zealand in the hope of eliciting more information about his putative giant bird. A long, embarrassing silence ensued, but in 1843 Owen suddenly received an enormous box of bones collected by a New Zealand missionary, and although the bones did not amount to a complete skeleton, they *did* amount to confirmation of his hypothesis of a giant flightless bird, and he was able to name the genus *Dinornis* and write a full description of it. The bones exactly corresponded to the predictions he had made on the basis of the first six-inch fragment, and this feat of zoological detective work was widely admired. 'We well remember', wrote a contributor to the *Quarterly Review* in 1852, 'seeing this fragment of the shaft of a femur when it first arrived, and hearing the opinion of the Professor as to the bird to which it must have belonged. He took, in our presence, a piece of paper and drew the outline of what he conceived to be the complete bone ... When a perfect bone arrived and was laid on the paper, it fitted exactly the outline which he had drawn.'[10]

Owen performed a similar piece of imaginative reconstruction on the fossil *Mylodon robustus*, a gigantic extinct sloth unearthed in South America. Since it *was* a sloth, most naturalists assumed that it lived in sloth-like fashion by climbing about in trees. But Owen saw the absurdity of trying to hang an animal the size of an elephant from the branch of a tree, and suggested instead that the mylodon had lived on the ground and used its immense strength to pull down trees or uproot them. In 1842, he received a mylodon skull which, he realized, furnished proof of his hypothesis. The skull was marked by two severe fractures, both of which had healed within the animal's lifetime. Owen argued that if the fractures had been caused by an attack from another animal, the mylodon was not likely to have recovered – the other animal would easily have finished it off. The only other way the wounds could have been inflicted was by a heavy object falling on the mylodon's head, and the most likely heavy object, in the South American jungle, was a tree. And the fact that it had happened twice to the same animal suggested that the animal was often in the vicinity of falling trees – for the simple reason that it felled them itself. Thus Owen, from a single skull, deduced the lifestyle of the extinct mylodon.

In 1853 Owen translated his palaeontological work into truly popular and spectacular form when he supervised the construction of a series of life-sized cement models of extinct animals to inhabit the new Crystal Palace gardens at Sydenham. Owen acted as technical consultant: the actual designer was Waterhouse Hawkins, an eccentric artist and sculptor who seems to have made extinct animals his speciality (he did the palaeontological illustrations for Buckland's *Bridgewater Treatise* and for Owen's book on the Megatherium). Despite Owen's supervision, the models perpetrated many inaccuracies, such as showing the iguanodon as a sort of giant rhinoceros, but they were much admired at the time. Frank Buckland called Hawkins 'the modern Pygmalion'[11] and Charles Waterton claimed that a visit to the Crystal Palace models was 'always a treat of the first order'.[12] When the models were completed, Hawkins invited Owen and other leading scientists to join him for dinner *inside* the iguanodon (perhaps inspired by Peale's celebration inside the mastodon). The invitations were inscribed on the wing-bone of a pterodactyl. Twenty-one guests sat down for dinner inside the concrete model, and another seven sat at side-tables round about. The dinner was a huge success, even though Owen, with his usual charm, made a speech attacking Hawkins for getting the iguanodon wrong. (Hawkins was later invited to New York to make a similar set of models for Central Park, but a certain Judge Hilton attacked the idea as

The Crystal Palace dinosaurs

being 'anti-religious' and the City authorities gradually lost interest in the scheme. In 1871 a gang of vandals, who may or may not have been encouraged by Judge Hilton, broke into Hawkins's studio and smashed all his working-models. He was heartbroken, and spent his remaining years at Princeton painting gigantic murals of his monsters. Meanwhile, the Crystal Palace models had fallen into neglect and dilapidation, and a visitor in the 1890s was heard to opine that 'they were surely placed there with the pious purpose of setting clearly before the eyes of the public, as a terrible warning, the fantastic visions sometimes seen by such as are in the habit of indulging too freely in spirituous liquors.'[13] But in their heyday, in the 1850s, they were a great popular attraction.)

The Crystal Palace project was only one of countless public schemes on which Owen acted as adviser. His career, in fact, illustrates the amazing diversity of duties to which professional scientists could be called in the Victorian period. This was because there were so few professional scientists, and so many schemes requiring scientific advice. The Prince Consort had encouraged the formation of endless committees, institutions and societies devoted to the encouragement of Science-

and-the-Arts, and Owen was a particularly desirable catch for any of these because he was formidable in manner, Olympian in authority, and socially well behaved. He, in turn, enjoyed associating with influential and titled people (his earliest hobby was genealogy) and he was never diffident in accepting invitations. Throughout the 1840s he poked around sewage-works and slaughter-houses for various public health Commissions, and in 1851 he served as a Chairman of Jurors for the Great Exhibition. He performed similar jury service for the Paris Exhibition of 1855 where, rather oddly, his duties included presiding over a wine-tasting. Through his work for the Great Exhibition, he became friends with Prince Albert and was invited to lecture on natural history to the royal children at Windsor. (It was he who first broke the news about tadpoles turning into frogs.) Queen Victoria was one of the very few people who actually *liked* Owen, and it was through her personal intervention that he received the gift of Sheen Lodge, Richmond.

Owen was always willing to stand up as an expert witness, whether or not he had any experience in the relevant field. In 1851, for instance, the Home Secretary asked him to examine Maria Clark, who had been sentenced to death for murdering her child. Owen pronounced her insane, and the woman was reprieved. In the same year, Edwin Chadwick solicited his support for the campaign to abolish window-tax, and Owen responded with some testimony about ventilation being necessary for health. The Duke of Argyll, preparing for a debate in the Lords, asked him whether dogs were suitable as draught animals. Owen replied that though their bodies were strong enough to pull certain loads, their feet tended to suffer.

The Iguanodon dinner, 1854

In 1868 he was subpoenaed as an expert witness in the curious case of the merchant vessel *Dreadnought* which had sustained a three-inch hole in her hull. The insurers claimed that the hole was man-made; the captain claimed that it was the work of a swordfish. Owen supported the swordfish and the insurers had to pay up. In 1879, he again appeared in court, this time as a ballistics expert in a murder case, arguing that it was the accused's revolver that had fired the fatal bullet. Besides these special occasions, Owen regularly advised the Admiralty on all matters relating to sea-serpent sightings, and the London Zoological Society on what animals it should purchase and at what price.

Indeed, Owen seemingly *never* refused to give an opinion (except, as we shall see, on the all-important question of Darwinism). In 1844 he received a letter from a West Country firm of undertakers asking what they should charge for embalming the body of William Beckford, the millionaire author of *Vathek*. 'We are entirely at a loss,' they wrote, 'to know the value, with a family of such wealth, of our process. It has never been done in the West of England.'[14] Back came Owen's answer with the confidence born of a lifetime's experience of embalming millionaires – one hundred guineas.

Like every other Victorian naturalist, Owen was expected to adjudicate on a wide variety of freaks, both animal and human. He visited General Tom Thumb, Joseph Brice the French Giant, the 'Aztec Children' ('very strange beings, and their proprietor seems to be making money')[15] and a man who had a tooth growing through his cheek like a walrus's tusk. He examined the Siamese twins, Chang and Eng, in 1835 and concluded that they could not be safely separated. Almost every month he received some form of animal freak through the post. Faraday offered him the gift of a three-legged frog, and Kingsley sent him 'an adder with two hind legs'.[16] Toads in stones were so common that he left his wife to deal with them. She also had to deal with the 'magnificent, tall American Indian chief in full dress' who suddenly appeared on her doorstep in November 1843. He was wearing war paint and carrying a tomahawk. 'I felt rather staggered,' she confided to her diary, 'but endeavoured to show no signs of it, and so asked the gentleman to sit down in the arm-chair, which he did in a calm, well-bred manner. He was accompanied by a young gentleman, a native of Guernsey, but who had lived some time among the Indians. We were very soon quite at ease with each other.' Owen then returned and escorted the Indian and his interpreter round the Royal College of Surgeons' Museum. On being shown the skeleton of O'Brien, the eight-foot-tall Irish giant, the Indian 'made a remark which, being interpreted, was "This is large".'[17]

In 1855 Owen received an even odder visit from 'a grave Oriental with his interpreter' who showed him an exquisite jewelled ladle which he had brought from the Sultan of Turkey. The bowl of the ladle, he claimed, was made from the beak of a phoenix. After some research, Owen identified the supposed phoenix-beak as the bill of the helmeted hornbill, and sent for a specimen from his museum. In a memoir, Owen recalls:

The head and beak were brought into my study and handed to the Oriental. He examined it very deftly, comparing the beak with the bowl, and then exclaimed with astonishment and reverence, 'God is great! That surely is the bird!' I took a large sheet of paper, and wrote a brief certificate of the nature and country of the bird from which the Sultan's ladle had been made, and gave it to the Turk, requesting the interpreter to write down the name and titles of the individual to whom the precious article had been entrusted. It was as follows: 'Mohammed Abu Said, Chief Spoon and Ladle-Maker to the Commander of the Faithful.'

So much for the phoenix.[18]

While Owen's many and various public duties brought him into close contact with politicians and other leading laymen, his scientific colleagues uniformly avoided him. Indeed they loathed him. Huxley called his politeness 'frightful' and J.E. Gray of the British Museum complained that 'When he is really fulsome, I always think it very disagreeable.'[19] His politeness was usually a cloak for malice. 'It is deeply to be deplored,' wrote Gideon Mantell, the Sussex palaeontologist, 'that this highly eminent and gifted man can never act with candour and liberality.'[20] If Owen could steal the credit for someone else's achievements, he would always do so; if he could not, he would strive to discredit the achievement. Hugh Falconer, the elephant expert, warned Darwin that Owen was 'not only ambitious, very envious and arrogant, but untruthful and dishonest'[21] and Darwin eventually came to see the truth of this assessment, which he repeats in his *Autobiography* along with the comment, 'I often saw Owen whilst living in London, and admired him greatly, but was never able to understand his character, and never became intimate with him. After the publication of the Origin of Species, he became my bitter enemy, not owing to any quarrel between us, but as far as I could judge out of jealousy at its success.'[22]

It was the coming of Darwinism that finally shattered Owen's overweening reputation. As the greatest authority of the age he was naturally expected to give a yea or nay to the new theory, and even Darwin confessed to Lyell, 'How curious I shall be to know what line Owen will take!'[23] But in fact Owen didn't take *any* line, or at least not consistently, and as his pronouncements on the subject became increasingly bizarre and self-contradictory, the public grew at first puzzled, then fretful, and finally dismissive of them. At the same period, Huxley appeared on the public stage, and, since everything Huxley said was cogent, witty and interesting, and since everything Owen said was verbose, humourless and often incomprehensible, Huxley soon took over Owen's role as the voice of Science in the land. The fact that Huxley was an agnostic meant that he could never quite attain Owen's pontifical stature, but he was at least a likable human being.

Although Owen's authority began to decline after the 1860s, the closing decades of his life were by no means wasted. In 1856 he was appointed Superintendent of the Natural History Department of the British Museum, a post specially created

Owen lecturing at the Museum of Practical Geology, 1857

for him, and it was he who effected the Department's move to its own South Kensington Museum in the 1880s. Many of the British Museum staff felt that Owen merely took the credit for improvements which they had made themselves, and on Owen's previous form that seems likely, but it was essential to have one man to speak for the Natural History Department's needs and Owen was the ideal choice. He fought for twenty years to get a separate Natural History Museum, and only when that was accomplished, in 1884, did he finally retire at the age of eighty.

Apart from the South Kensington Natural History Museum, which still retains much of Owen's original arrangement, Owen left very few monuments to posterity. His theories were perceived as absurd even in his own lifetime, and only his small detailed monographs have retained any value. Why, then, was Owen so important? Huxley tried to answer that question in 1894 when he was asked to add an appendix on Owen's scientific achievements to the reverent official biography written by his grandson. It is one of Huxley's least successful essays, and his embarrassment at finding himself in the unaccustomed role of Owen's eulogist is everywhere apparent. After struggling manfully through Owen's theories on homologies, archetypes and parthenogenesis, he finally throws in the sponge:

> I believe I am right in saying that hardly any of these speculations and determinations have stood the test of investigation, or, indeed, that any of them

were ever widely accepted. I am not sure that any one but the historian of anatomical science is ever likely to recur to them; and considering Owen's great capacity, extensive learning, and tireless industry, that seems a singular result of years of strenuous labour.[24]

Owen's trouble, of course, was that he *was* 'the British Cuvier', and fifty years after Cuvier's death was still following a sterile line of biological enquiry. He was the last of the great species-makers, the doyen of the closet, and he lived to become an anachronism. Nevertheless he ruled European biology from the death of Cuvier until the advent of Darwinism, and his very wrongness makes him typical of that period of hiatus in biological process.

CHAPTER THIRTEEN

THE KING OF SILURIA

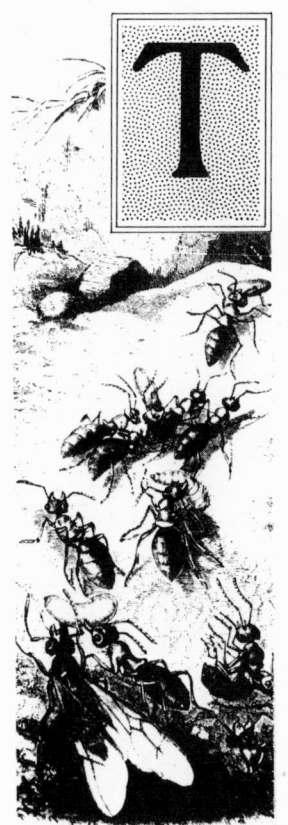

HERE WAS NO figure of authority corresponding to Owen in the geological field. In retrospect, it seems obvious that Charles Lyell should have had that role, but, as with the case of Darwin among biologists, his pre-eminence was by no means clear to his contemporaries. Geologists in any case were notorious for their factions and internecine squabbles; they divided themselves into camps of 'Fluvialists' and 'Diluvialists', 'Catastrophists' and 'Uniformitarians', each of which had scant respect for the others. But while Victorian geologists would have quarrelled endlessly over the respective claims of William Buckland, Adam Sedgwick, William Conybeare or Charles Lyell, depending on which camp they belonged to, laymen would have had no difficulty in naming the greatest geologist of the age. He was Sir Roderick Impey Murchison, and the reason he seemed great was because, like Owen, he was constantly in the public eye. He sat on committees, he chaired meetings, he presided over societies, he was consulted by government commissions, and in short he represented the 'official' voice of geology. Moreover, the fact that his work had absolutely no relevance to any of the great geological controversies of the day was an advantage, since he could be assumed (wrongly, as it turned out) to be impartial.

One of the most fascinating aspects of Murchison's career is the rapidity with which he came to the forefront. Until the age of twenty-nine, he was as innocent of gneiss and trap rocks and mica schists as the babe unborn and, as he freely admitted, 'The noble science of fox-hunting was then my dominant passion.'[1] Eight years later he was President of the Geological Society. Such speed was possible because geology at this period was still a brand new science. In fact it really began only in 1815 with the publication of William Smith's Geological Map of England, which formulated the law of strata identified by fossils. In 1823, when Murchison took up geology, most of the 'founders' of English geology were still alive and, as Murchison's biographer remarks, 'Such was the state

Sir Roderick Impey Murchison

of geological science at the time that a great work could be done by a man with a quick eye, a good judgment, a clear notion of what had already been accomplished, and a stout pair of legs.'[2]

Murchison was born in 1792 into an old Scottish family with vague lairdly pretensions. At thirteen, he was sent to military college and later fought briefly in the Peninsular War under Wellesley – a fact he made much of in later life. Like many another soldier, his ambitions were scotched by the advent of peace in 1815, and in 1816 he married a sensible woman three years older than himself and resigned his commission. At this point he dallied with the idea of becoming a clergyman, for the sound practical reasons that, 'My wife had been brought up to look after the poor, was a good botanist, enjoyed a garden and liked tranquillity; and as parsons then enjoyed a little hunting, shooting, and fishing without being railed at, I thought that I might slide into that sort of comfortable domestic life.'[3] But it was not so easy to slide into, since it required a classical education, which

Murchison had not had. Besides, there was a positive flood of ex-officers into the Church at that time; and perhaps, too, Murchison may have realized that his absence of faith was a disadvantage. A few years later he was to tell Sedgwick that, although he found 'nothing to cavil at'[4] in the teachings of Christ, he could not really believe in His divinity. At all events, he decided to delay his decision by taking a tour on the Continent with his new wife, and by the time he returned to England in 1818, the ordination idea had been quietly dropped.

This sojourn in Italy in 1817–18 gave the first hints that Murchison might have an intellect. He wanted to know about art, so that he could converse about Claude and Raffaello and Salvator Rosa, as a gentleman should. But he studied them all with a quite ungentlemanly seriousness, hurrying to every church and gallery and studio he could find, and taking notes on everything he saw. The notes were un-inspired, but their relentless thoroughness showed that when Murchison wanted to 'get up' a subject, he knew how to set about it. As his biographer remarked, 'Through art he first realized the advantage of a distinctly intellectual life over one of mere desultory gaiety.'[5]

However, when the couple returned to England in 1818, desultory gaiety was again the rule. Murchison sold his Scottish farms, took a house at Melton Mow-bray, and dedicated all his abundant energy to fox-hunting. He kept eight hunters and a hack, hunted six days a week, subscribed £50 a year to a pack of hounds, and contrived to keep financially afloat by speculating in foreign funds. For five years he talked, thought and dreamt of nothing but foxes, and the summit of his ambition was to be known as a 'hard rider' throughout the hunting counties of England.

Then in 1823 his hunting career abruptly ended with a Saul-like conversion. Here is Murchison's own account of what happened:

> In the summer following the hunting season of 1822–3, when revisiting my old friend Morritt of Rokeby, I fell in with Sir Humphry Davy, and experi-enced much gratification in his lively illustrations of great physical truths. As we shot partridges together in the morning, I perceived that a man might pursue philosophy [i.e. science] without abandoning field-sports; and Davy ... encouraged me to come to London and *set to* at science by attending lectures on chemistry, etc. As my wife naturally backed up this advice, and Sir Humphry said he would soon get me into the Royal Society, I was fairly and easily booked.[6]

It was as simple as that. A few weeks later Murchison invited all his hunting cronies to his house, gave them a good dinner with plenty of port, and then led his fine hunters one by one into the dining-room and auctioned them off. He was never to own another hunter again. The following summer he moved to London and began attending lectures on chemistry at the Royal Institution. Within two years, as Davy had promised, he was elected a Fellow of the Royal Society, on

Sir Humphry Davy

the straightforward grounds that 'he was an independent gentleman having a taste
for science, with plenty of time and enough of money to gratify it.'[7]

Davy had no doubt hoped to make Murchison a chemist, like himself, but Mur-
chison was soon drawn into the lively, quarrelsome meetings of the Geological
Society where a liking for the members blossomed into a liking for the subject.
William Buckland immediately took him under his wing, carrying him off to
Oxford to attend one of his horseback geological lectures, and illustrating the anatomy of the Crustacea on the way by dissecting (and eating) a cold crab he had
bought during the coach-stop at Maidenhead. From the summit of Shotover Hill,
Murchison learned to 'read' landscape in geological terms as he had once, as an
Ensign, learned to read it logistically. In the summer of 1825, Murchison under-
took his first geological tour, scrambling along the south coast from Southampton
into Devon, and learning to recognize the leading formations. His wife accom-

panied him and executed careful drawings of the fossils he collected. 'This was perhaps about the happiest period of my life,' Murchison later recalled. 'I had shaken off the vanities of the fashionable world to a good extent – was less anxious to know titled folks and leading sportsmen – and had taken to a career in which excitement in the field carried with it occupation, amusement, and possibly reputation.'[8]

Of course he could not quite shake off his old habits entirely, and old friends kept popping up with invitations to a shooting weekend or the loan of a good hunter which he found impossible to resist. Lord Darlington, his former M.F.H., 'laughed at my new hobby which had converted me into an "earth-stopper"',[9] and as late as 1834 Lord Elcho succeeded in luring him back into the field with the bait of 'a very crack pack of fox-hounds'. Murchison found himself stiff for weeks afterwards, 'not having been accustomed to screw to my seat for the last ten years.'[10] Whenever he could combine geology with shooting he was happy to do so, and he enjoyed the satisfying conjunction of grouse and gneiss in Scotland, but from the late 1820s there was no doubt of where his true enthusiasm lay and by 1830 he could write, 'I was then keen on one scent only, viz., greensands, chalk and tertiary.'[11] The same year he wrote to Sedgwick from Sonthofen: 'Here I am, sticking to my scent like a true fox-hound ... The moment I twigged certain secondary black fossils like lias (in his den near the river) and ascertained that the section was not above a six hours' excursion, the post-wagen was ordered, and off we travelled.'[12]

In 1827 Murchison made a geological tour of Scotland in company with the Rev. Adam Sedgwick, Woodwardian Professor of Geology at Cambridge. Sedgwick's later career was to be handicapped by chronic hypochondria, and he was famous for appearing at the altar-table in vizor and respirator to keep out the cold, and snow-boots to guard against gout, but at this stage he managed to survive the rigours of the field on a regime of 'water-drinking and dephlogisticating.'[13] Murchison had prepared for the tour by making a handbook of useful Gaelic phrases starting with 'Where is the public house?' and by reading up everything that had ever been published on Scottish geology. Between them they made some important researches on Arran island and the northern Conglomerates.

The next year, 1828, Murchison decided to tackle the Continent, specifically the Auvergne and parts of Switzerland and northern Italy, and this time his companion (besides Mrs Murchison) was the young secretary of the Geological Society, Charles Lyell. Lyell had only recently given up his desultory law practice and was still a geological unknown, but this tour was to provide the foundation for his epoch-making *Principles of Geology*, published two years later. Murchison never became a convert to Lyell's theories (and never became as great a geologist as Lyell) but during this tour the two wielded their hammers harmoniously enough. Lyell was impressed by Mrs Murchison, as all who met her were, and wrote, 'She is very diligent, sketching, labelling specimens, and making out shells, in which last she is an invaluable assistant.' Even better, she was 'always desirous of keeping out of the way when she would interfere with the work'[14] – a truly tactful companion!

The tour was conducted at a furious pace, set by Murchison, and after one day's ride of fifty-five miles, Lyell complained of his 'keep-moving, go-it-if-it-kills-you system',[15] but conceded that Murchison, for all his speed, was nevertheless thorough. He also discovered the possible source of Murchison's superhuman energy – drugs. In a letter home, Lyell wrote:

On one occasion we were on an expedition together, and as a stronger dose was necessary than he had with him, I was not a little alarmed at finding there was no pharmacy in the place, but at last went to a nunnery, where Mlle. La Supérieure sold all medicines without profit – positively a young, clever, and rather good-looking lady, who hoped my friend would think better of it, as the quantity would kill six Frenchmen.[16]

The Rev. Adam Sedgwick

Sir Charles Lyell

In 1831, just eight years after he had met Sir Humphry Davy and sold his fox-hunters, Murchison was elected President of the Geological Society. He had studied the geology of Scotland, the Auvergne, the Alps, parts of Germany, Italy and Switzerland, and he had delivered many useful papers. But he had not as yet broken any new ground. His labours had all been among the Secondary formations, as had those of most of his predecessors and contemporaries. Once, hurrying back through Germany and the Low Countries, he complained of the 'interminable grauwacke'[17] which he had to cross to reach anywhere interesting. Now, suddenly, in 1831, he decided to study this grauwacke and make it his own. It was to become his private kingdom of Siluria.

'Grauwacke' or 'greywacke' was an old German miners' term for a special kind of Palaeozoic rock which, through lack of interest on the part of geologists, had come to be applied to almost all the pre-Secondary rocks except coal. Nobody had yet studied these older formations. They were broken and distorted and difficult, and widely (though wrongly) assumed to be destitute of fossils. They did not conform to the neat sandwich-like layers first delineated by William 'Strata' Smith, and they did not appear along the coasts of Hampshire, Dorset and Devon, the training-ground of British geologists. When Murchison decided to sort out the grauwacke he could find no books or papers on the subject, and his only lead was a tip from Buckland that he might find the stuff somewhere up the Wye valley. To the Wye he accordingly went, and from there he tracked his prey across the length and breadth of Wales, up through the border counties and into Cheshire. At the end of his travels, he recorded, 'I may say that it was the most fruitful year of my life, for in it I laid the foundation of my Silurian System. I was then thirty-nine years old, and few could excel me in bodily and mental activity.'[18] The only interruption was a visit to York for the first-ever meeting of the British Association for the Advancement of Science, a society which met for a week every year at a different provincial centre, and in which Murchison was to remain a stalwart to the end of his life.

The next seven years were devoted to 'the perpetual cracking of stones'[19] as he traced the older formations throughout the whole of Britain. It soon became clear that the term grauwacke was inadequate, and in 1835 Murchison proposed his own romantic invention – Siluria – derived from an ancient British tribe, the

Silures, who had inhabited the border county where he had first tracked his quarry. In 1838 he published his two-volume colossus *The Silurian System*, which Hugh Miller described as 'one of those works which form eras in the history of science, and from which, as from the charts of some distinguished voyager, after explorers have learned to shape their course aright, and to recognise as familiar and easily definable, tracts previously unnamed and unknown.'[20] Murchison's next task was to extend his Silurian domain into Europe and eventually into Russia, where he coined the term 'Permian' and analysed vast tracts of country which had never previously felt the geological hammer. These travels resulted in the *Geology of Russia in Europe and the Ural Mountains*, published in 1845. This was the culmination of his career, constituting as it did an outline of the geology of half Europe, much of it previously unknown, and presenting the whole succession of the Palaeozoic rocks.

However, it was effectively his last major piece of original research. In 1854 he published a revised and updated *Siluria* which, as his biographer bluntly remarks, *must* have been useful because it went into four editions in thirteen years 'in spite of its technical character, its total want of literary attractiveness, and its high price.'[21] This book incorporated much work done by other geologists, with-

Murchison lecturing in Dudley Cavern, 1849

out any acknowledgment, but Murchison always considered that anything to do with Siluria was automatically his property. In 1855 he was appointed Director-General of the Geological Survey and School of Mines – his first-ever professional appointment and one he retained for the rest of his life. From then on, he rested comfortably on his laurels as an elder statesman of science. A friend once described him as a man 'born to fill chairs'[22] and that he certainly did, presiding alternately (and sometimes simultaneously) over the affairs of the Geological and Geographical Societies and of the British Association.

No man enjoyed honours more than Murchison. Once, in the middle of one of his Russian expeditions, he suddenly received from the Emperor a four-foot-high, six-foot-round, two-ton vase of Siberian aventurine, bearing on its porphyry plinth the legend,

TO THE GEOLOGIST MURCHISON
IN TESTIMONY OF ITS PARTICULAR ESTEEM.
THE ADMINISTRATION OF MINES
OF RUSSIA.

Many a lesser traveller might have been appalled at such a cumbrous addition to his luggage, but Murchison was entirely delighted, confiding to his diary, 'This is a proud day for me ... How shall I ever render my work worthy of such a largess!'[23] He was annoyed to find, on returning to England, that his exotic Russian decoration, the Knight Grand Cross of Saint Stanislaus, was not recognized at court, and his friends' insistence on addressing him as 'Lord Grauwacke', 'Count Siluria' and so on, only made things worse. Consolation finally came in 1846 with the award of a proper English knighthood, converted in 1866 to a baronetcy.

Darwin gives a most uncharacteristically waspish portrait of Murchison in his *Autobiography*:

> The degree to which he valued rank was ludicrous, and he displayed this feeling and his vanity with the simplicity of a child. He related with the utmost glee to a large circle, including many mere acquaintances, in the rooms of the Geolog. Soc. how the Czar Nicholas, when in London, had patted him on the shoulder and had said, alluding to his geological work, 'Mon ami, Russia is grateful to you'; and then Murchison added, rubbing his hands together, 'The best of it was that Prince Albert heard it all.' He announced one day to the Council of the Geolog. Soc. that his great work on the Silurian system was at last published; and he then looked at all who were present, and said, 'You will every one of you find your name in the Index,' as if this was the height of glory.[24]

Murchison was, in a way, unfortunate in his choice of subject. No one doubted that he was a great geologist, least of all himself, but he happened to live in an

22 Aquarium and conservatory, from *Cassell's Household Guide*, *c.* 1870

23 Hart's-Tongue Spleenwort, from *The Ferns of Great Britain* by Anne Pratt, 1855

24 Succulent plants, from *The Greenhouse, Hot House and Stove* by Charles McIntosh, 1838

age when great geologists were plentiful. Moreover, outside his own Siluria he was slow to recognize new developments. He resisted Lyell's Uniformitarianism to the end of his life, and greeted the dawning of Agassiz's Ice Age with howls of execration. He was, publicly, wise enough to keep quiet about Darwinism, but in private he told friends that 'I look upon it as simply an ingenious piece of sceptical puzzling without the least basis.'[25] The later years of his life (he died in 1871) were therefore devoted to die-hard attempts to crush new theories wherever they dared emerge, and his geological influence was in the end a deleterious one.

His influence on the status of science was, however, wholly beneficial. His snobbishness and his socializing were just what geology needed, especially at a time when most of the other geologists were unworldly and eccentric clergymen. Murchison's grand dinners at Belgrave Square and his shooting sojourns in the great country houses brought a much-needed breath of science to the aristocracy. He pursued the ear of the Prince Consort and the ear of the Prime Minister as sedulously as he had once pursued the fox, and his total reverence for *any* lord or *any* lion, regardless of party, made his contacts eclectic. Bizarre though it may now seem, a solid fox-hunting background was in many ways an ideal qualification for the advancement of science in mid-Victorian Britain.

CHAPTER FOURTEEN

THE FOREIGN PROFESSOR

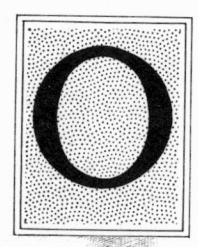

O NE MORE SCIENTIFIC luminary remains to be described, and in some ways he is the most important of the three. He is Louis Agassiz, the Swiss-born comparative anatomist and geologist who, in 1846, at the height of his fame, took up residence in the United States. It is this that makes him so important. Agassiz's arrival marks the coming-of-age of American science, the first date from which America was to have a voice in the world scientific community. Until 1846, very few European scientists had even visited the United States, let alone contemplated living there. They regarded America as a provincial backwater and its naturalists as a doubtful breed of unreliable romancers. The case of Audubon and Rafinesque and the spoof Ohio fishes lingered long in European memories, and as late as 1860 Philip Gosse could still remark, without apparent fear of contradiction, 'We do naturally look with a lurking suspicion on American statements, when they describe unusual or disputed phenomena.'[1] In any case, American scientific publications were hardly ever seen in Europe. Swainson explains, in the introduction to his *Bibliography of Zoology*, published in 1840, that he has had to omit American books because 'they are most imperfectly known in England, where, in fact, they cannot be purchased.'[2] There was an almost total lack of contact between American and European naturalists, and they had very little knowledge of one another's work.

Moreover, American naturalists suffered all the practical disadvantages of living in a 'new' country, which was still at this period less than half-settled and in many places only half-civilized. When Audubon asked Bachman to send collectors into Florida in 1836, Bachman replied that it was impossible – the Seminoles were on the warpath and had 'scalped every woman and child south of St. Augustine.'[3] Much of the South, and all of the West, were devoid of libraries, museums, universities, and all the normal amenities of scientific research. Philadelphia was then the only city that possessed the full complement of university, museum, library,

Louis Agassiz

and academy of natural sciences. Even at Harvard, as late as the 1850s, books were so scarce that when Agassiz's assistant, Jules Marcou, left to go on a year's exploration, Agassiz sent a two-horse carriage round to his house to remove the *Transactions* of the Geological Society of London, the *Reports* of the British Association, and many other standard reference works because they were un-obtainable elsewhere. American naturalists had to waste days and weeks hand-copying extracts from European scientific publications, because there was no hope of being able to buy the books, or borrow them from libraries. The museum situa-tion was even worse. Such few museums as there were – Peale's in Philadelphia, Scudder's in New York, and Drake's in Cincinnati – were miscellaneous jumbles of 'curiosities' rather than systematic collections. Those would come only with the growth of the Smithsonian in the 1850s, and Agassiz's own Harvard Museum of Comparative Zoology in the 1860s. Meanwhile, European museums were unwilling to send specimens to America when they could expect so little in return, and the United States was generally excluded from that network of scientific exchanges which operated in Europe to everyone's mutual benefit. Transatlantic mails were slow, expensive and occasionally hazardous, and European institutions tended to feel that they could manage perfectly well without American exchanges.

In fact, the state of American science was not nearly so hopeless as Europeans liked to imagine. America had, after all, produced Audubon who, whatever his occasional lapses in accuracy, was nevertheless a great ornithologist and a great illustrator. She had also produced a very long line of distinguished botanists, going back to Mark Catesby and the Bartrams in the eighteenth century. More recently, she had begun to breed a generation of excellent geologists, trained in the state geological surveys, who in 1840 banded together to form the first nation-wide scientific organization, the American Association of Geologists. Geology had also begun to attract popular attention, with a series of bestselling handbooks by the Rev. Edward Hitchcock, and two wildly successful lecturing tours made by Charles Lyell in the 1840s. And already by the time Agassiz went to Harvard, there was one American scientist at work there, Asa Gray, who was ultimately to achieve a far greater reputation than his. It was Gray whom Darwin turned to for facts on the geographical distribution of plants for the *Origin of Species*, and it was Gray who was later to become Darwinism's chief advocate in the United States. But to his contemporaries, Gray did not seem as important as Agassiz. In the first place, he was a quiet, self-effacing man – Darwin called him 'a complex cross of lawyer, poet, naturalist and theologian'[4] – who never pushed his own claims or those of science generally. And in the second, he *was* an American, and therefore a prophet without honour in his own country. For by this time American scientists had developed such an inferiority complex, from years of European neglect, that they needed a European to restore their self-esteem and promote their achievements to the world at large.

Agassiz was thirty-nine when he moved to America, and had already achieved a great European reputation. He had studied under Cuvier and, under his aegis, had embarked on the *Poissons Fossiles*, a massive five-volume description with plates of all the 1,700 species of fossil fish then known. Then, in 1840, he published the *Études sur les Glaciers* which formulated for the first time the theory of the Ice Age. In it, he showed that areas like Scotland and Ireland which are now devoid of glaciers must once have been subjected to glacial action, and he suggested that the whole Northern hemisphere must once have lain under a great sheet of ice. Either the theory of the Ice Age or the *Poissons Fossiles* alone would have made a great scientific reputation; the fact that Agassiz published both while still in his thirties (indeed, he embarked on the *Poissons Fossiles* when only twenty-two) made him a giant among naturalists.

Why then, at the height of his fame, did he emigrate to the United States? The short and simple answer is money. The *Poissons Fossiles* had nearly bankrupted him. It had taken thirteen years to write, and over that time he had employed a staff of at least ten assistants and illustrators. He had even founded his own printing press, because he felt he could not entrust the plates to any commercial printer. Meanwhile, his only source of income was his small salary as Professor of Natural

Asa Gray

History in the tiny Swiss-Prussian town of Neuchâtel. It barely provided enough to support his wife and three children, let alone his staff and his printing works. None of this bothered Agassiz unduly. 'He acted, all his life,' wrote his friend and biographer Jules Marcou, 'as if he knew with certainty that a great lump of gold belonging to him was lying somewhere behind an enormous boulder, and that he had only to extend his hand behind the boulder, and fill his pockets with as much as he wanted.'[5] When he happened to have some money in hand, he immediately distributed it among his assistants and conceived even bolder plans for the future; when he had none, which was most of the time, he managed without and so, perforce, did his staff. He had one assistant, Armand Gressly, who was quite brilliant at living on nothing. On fossil-hunting expeditions, he subsisted on nuts and berries and whatever he could beg from the local farmers. He never changed his clothes, and cleaned his fossils by licking them with his tongue. But even had all Agassiz's assistants been like Gressly, they could not have continued living on nothing for ever.

In 1846 Agassiz's creditors brought matters to a head by forcing him to close the printing works, dismiss most of his staff and face the prospect of bankruptcy. The only hope was America, where, as everyone knew, money grew on trees. The English geologist Charles Lyell had recently returned from a lecturing tour there and reported that he had earned enough in six weeks to live on for a year. Agassiz wrote to Lyell, who recommended him to John Amory Lowell, the Boston financier and founder of the Lowell Institute, who immediately offered him $1,500 for a season's lecturing. The fact that Agassiz could barely speak English seems not to have occurred to anyone, and in September 1846, after brief visits to Paris and London, Agassiz embarked on one of the new transatlantic steamships. He spent the long weeks of the voyage regaling the Captain with halting sentences about the anatomy of the vertebrates as he struggled to perfect his English. In theory, he was going to America for a visit only, but he had settled his affairs in Neuchâtel with a thoroughness that suggested permanent exile.

American naturalists waited impatiently for the advent of 'this big geologico-everythingo-French-Swiss gun'[6] and wrote excited reports to one another as soon as they saw him. Emerson reported,

> I saw in the cars a broad-featured, unctuous man, fat and plenteous as some successful politician, and pretty soon divined it must be the foreign professor who has had so marked a success in all our scientific and social circles, having established unquestionable leadership in them all; and it was Agassiz.[7]

Most people were more flattering about his appearance, deciding that his dome-like head and dark expressive eyes were just what one expected in a genius. James Russell Lowell deemed him 'a true male, in all its meaning',[8] and Professor Gilman was reassured to find that 'He was not of that type of scholars whose shrivelled faces and whose withered forms declare the neglect of exercise, and the misuse

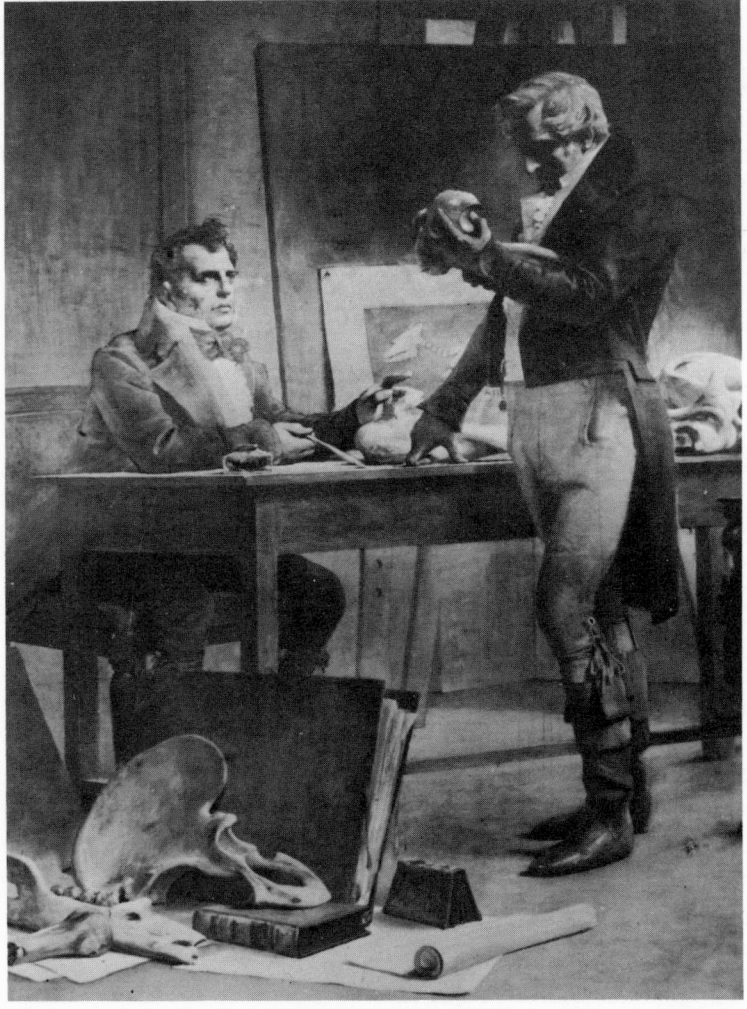

Cuvier lecturing

of food.'[9] Agassiz's manners were generally agreed to be as satisfactory as his appearance and Asa Gray found him at first 'as excellent and pleasant a man as he is a superb naturalist'[10] – an opinion he was to revise dramatically in the coming years. Agassiz in turn was enchanted with his new colleagues and wrote home to his mother:

> I thought myself tolerably familiar with all that is doing in science in the United States, but I was far from anticipating so much that is interesting and important. What is wanting to all these men is neither zeal nor knowledge. In both, they seem to compete with us, and in ardor and activity they even surpass most of our savants.[11]

One month after his arrival, he faced the ordeal of his first public lecture in English. He was astonished at the size of the audience that awaited him in Boston's Tremont Temple – 1,500 people, whereas the most he had ever seen at Cuvier's lectures in Paris was three or four hundred. He was also astonished to see working men and women in the audience. The Lowell Institute sold its tickets cheaply by lottery to whoever wrote in for them, and working men had as good a chance as anyone to get in. It was Agassiz's first exposure to American democracy in action, but on the whole he liked what he saw. He mounted the platform and delivered his account of 'The Plan of Creation in the Animal Kingdom'. Occasionally his English would fail and then 'he would pause and wait patiently, with his peculiar smile and beaming eyes, so characteristic of the man, in the meantime amusing his audience by drawing on the blackboard excellent outlines of animals.'[12] The ladies were entranced by his French accent; the scientists in the audience were impressed by the fact that his lecture included much new material. There had been a fear that Agassiz would talk down to Americans, especially to a lay audience, but that was an error Agassiz never committed. Like Huxley, he possessed the gift of conveying complex ideas in simple and attractive language, and from this first lecture in Boston to his last teaching camp on Penikese Island a few months before his death, he invariably succeeded in captivating his audiences.

Agassiz had been booked for only one season at the Lowell Institute, but soon every state in the Union was clamouring to hear him. In less than six months he earned nearly six thousand dollars. At the same time, the wave of revolutions in Europe made him even less eager to return there, and he began to let it be known that he might be persuaded to stay in the States. Opinions were sounded, strings were pulled, and in November 1847 the *American Journal of Science* announced that 'Professor Agassiz ... has consented to remain in this country in connection with the scientific corps of Harvard ... Every scientific man in America will be rejoiced to hear so unexpected a piece of good news.'[13] Harvard had just opened the Lawrence Scientific School and Agassiz was appointed its first Professor of Zoology and Geology – a post which he was to hold till his death.

However, the Americanization of Agassiz was not without its early tribulations. Soon after his Harvard appointment, Agassiz sacked his secretary, Edward Desor, who had come over with him from Switzerland. Desor retaliated by spreading a tale that Agassiz was guilty of immoral conduct with a maidservant, Jane, who lived in his house. Just at this moment Mrs Agassiz, who had been left behind in Switzerland, died suddenly and Desor added the slander that it was Agassiz's conduct that had killed her. (In fact, Agassiz's marriage had already broken up, which was one of the reasons he was not anxious to return to Europe.) The whole affair blew into such a scandal that Agassiz was obliged to submit it to an informal court of arbitration. Three leading Boston citizens heard evidence from all the members of Agassiz's household respecting his relations with Desor and with the maidservant Jane. Desor's son testified that one night he had gone into Agassiz's room and found Jane and Agassiz together: 'The front of M. Agassiz's trowsers was in disarray; and Jane afterwards told him that she was sewing on a loosened button!'[14] But this was the only serious charge against Agassiz, and the Boston arbitrators had no difficulty in exculpating him. The next year he celebrated his liberation from Desor, Jane, and the deceased Mrs Agassiz by marrying an American lady, Elizabeth Cary, and bringing his children over from Switzerland to live with them.

Soon afterwards Agassiz made a more serious gaffe when he declared publicly that the Caucasian and Negro could not have descended from a common ancestor. He never quite said that they belonged to different species – he talked, rather, of separate 'centres of creation' – but this nuance was lost on most of his readers. Before leaving Europe, he had believed in the unity of the human race, but as soon as he encountered Negroes in Philadelphia, he confided to his mother that the more he saw of 'this degraded and degenerate race' the more impossible it became for him 'to repress the feeling that they are not of the same blood as we are'.[15] In 1847 he visited the South and decided that Negroes were not only marked by physical differences, but by their 'submissive', 'obsequious' and 'imitative' nature.[16] In 1850 he rashly published these views in the *Christian Examiner* and, even more rashly, allowed them to be reprinted and exploited by Dr Josiah Clark Nott of Alabama, a notorious pro-slavery propagandist. For, in this tense pre-Civil-War period, it was but a short step from saying that the Negro was 'different' to saying that he was inferior, and that slavery was justified. To be fair, Agassiz was never guilty of this. He maintained that the Negro 'should be equal to other men before the law'.[17] But by placing the huge weight of his scientific authority behind the theory of separate origins, he naïvely played into the hands of the pro-slavery lobby and went on doing so right up until the outbreak of the Civil War. He never understood the political issues involved, and regarded the war itself as a minor off-stage skirmish. At the very height of the fighting he wrote to the Secretary of War, Edwin M. Stanton:

> Now that the temperature is low enough ... permit me to recall to your memory your promise to let me have the bodies of some Indians ... Direct the surgeon in charge to inject through the carotids a solution of Arsenate of soda. I should like one or two handsome fellows entire and the heads of two or three more.[18]

He wanted the Indians for his Museum, which, from the time of his move to Harvard until his death, was his central preoccupation and obsession. As soon as he arrived at Harvard he started talking about 'the Museum' as though it already existed, and so infectious was his delusion that the Museum quickly materialized. First, the Harvard Board allowed him an old bath-house to store his personal collections. Then they awarded him various grants to help him add to his collections. But it was not long before he was claiming that it was ridiculous that such important and valuable collections should be stored in a bath-house. So finally, in 1860, with funding from Harvard, the State of Massachusetts, and from innumerable private benefactors drummed up by Agassiz, the 'Museum of Comparative Zoology' was opened to the public. A few dissidents scoffed at this 'palace for bugs' but most visitors were impressed by the place which was always known in his lifetime as 'Agassiz's Museum'.

The Museum formed the centre of Agassiz's teaching work and students were immediately drafted as unpaid assistants, curators, labellers, and cataloguers. A few of them resented the work, but many recognized an unprecedented opportunity and were able to benefit from Agassiz's bizarre and informal teaching methods. One of his students, Samuel H. Scudder, later wrote a delightful magazine article called 'In the Laboratory with Agassiz' about his own first days in the museum. He recounts how, when he first arrived at the Museum, Agassiz approached him and asked him what he planned to study. 'Insects,' said Scudder. 'Very well,' said Agassiz, and handed him a large pickle jar containing a fish. 'Take this fish,' said he, 'and look at it; we call it a Haemulon. By and by I will ask you what you have seen.' So saying, Agassiz disappeared for the rest of the day, leaving the unfortunate Scudder alone with the fish. In the late afternoon he returned and asked Scudder what he had seen. Scudder described the fish as best he could. 'You have not looked very carefully,' was the discouraging response. 'Why, you haven't even seen one of the most conspicuous features of the animal, which is as plainly before your eyes as the fish itself. Look again! Look again!' When, at the end of the day, Scudder still found himself unable to describe the fish, Agassiz gave him the night to think it over and Scudder spent the small hours wrestling with his memories of the hated Haemulon. By the morning he had found the answer. 'Do you perhaps mean,' he asked Agassiz, 'that the fish has symmetrical sides with paired organs?' 'Of course, of course!' shouted Agassiz and spent the next half-hour chatting happily and enthusiastically about the importance of this point. Then Scudder asked what he should do next. 'Oh, look at your fish!' said Agassiz, disappearing again.

For three days Scudder was left in solitary communion with his Haemulon, gradually seeing more and more of its structure. On the fourth day he was rewarded with the gift of another fish, a member of the same family, to make comparison. Then he was granted another and another, until finally the whole Haemulon family, in their smelly jars, stood before him. It was eight months before Scudder was finally allowed to leave the fish and concentrate on his chosen speciality – insects – but as he himself came to appreciate, and explained in his magazine article, 'This was the best entomological lesson I ever had – a lesson whose influence has extended to the details of every subsequent study; a legacy that professor has left to me, as he left it to many others, of inestimable value, which we could not buy, with which we cannot part.'[19]

The demands of teaching, and of the Museum, left Agassiz little time for original research. This did not, however, prevent him from conceiving several grand schemes. He always enjoyed launching projects – it was their completion that eluded him. This was true of the Museum where, for many years, his collections lay in disarray because he could never decide how best to arrange them. It was also true of the many books he planned to write in the United States. The first of these, announced in 1863, was a natural history of all the American fishes. Agassiz sent out over six thousand circulars to members of the American Association, the Coastal Survey, the Smithsonian, and all the local natural history societies up and down the country, asking them to send him all the fishes they could find. America set to with a will. Senator Charles Sumner, passing through the Boston fish-market, noticed an unusual specimen on the slab and sent it post-haste to Agassiz's house. Henry David Thoreau sent some live snapping turtles. Barrels and buckets and parcels of fish arrived almost daily. One admirer sent a live bear from Maine which broke into Agassiz's spirit collection and became so violently drunk that it had to be destroyed. But before the Natural History of Fishes could be written, it became subsumed into an even grander project: a natural history of *all* American animals. Those who had sent fishes before were now adjured to send snakes, birds, mammals, toads, insects or anything that took their fancy. A subscription list was launched, and 2,500 subscribers enrolled to receive the projected ten volumes of the *Contributions to the Natural History of the United States* at $120 a set.

But only four of the ten volumes ever appeared, and two of these were taken up with some very recherché notes on the embryology of turtles. The only readable part of the *Contributions* was the preliminary 'Essay on Classification' which constituted Agassiz's fullest statement of his scientific creed. While it pleased many laymen by its frequent and fulsome references to God, it disappointed many scientists by the poverty and outdatedness of its ideas. It was virtually a restatement of Cuvier, and by the 1850s this was not enough. Ironically, it contained a section on embryology and a chapter on the 'Relations between Animals and Plants and the Surrounding World' which positively shrieked with evidence of evolution, but the flatly stated conclusion of the Essay was that evolution was impossible because there was no continuity of species from one geological epoch to the next, and this was the view Agassiz was to persist in two years later when the *Origin of Species* appeared.

In fact, Agassiz produced no original research of any value after his move to America, but that is not to say that his time there was wasted. The very first year he arrived in America he diagnosed what was wrong with the situation, writing to Henri Milne Edwards in Paris, 'What a people! Their look is wholly turned toward the future ... and thus nothing holds them back, unless, perhaps, a consideration for the opinion in which they may be held in Europe.'[20] It was this inferiority complex that Agassiz set himself to dispel. In 1850 he wrote, 'The time has come when American scientific men should aim at establishing their respective standing without reference to Europeans ... Let us make an effort to be what we can without the assistance of anybody, and let me include myself in the list, if I can be welcome.'[21] He gave the proof of his sincerity in 1857 when he was offered

Spencer Fullerton Baird

the top Chair in Palaeontology at the Paris National Museum (the old Jardin des Plantes) and, with maximum publicity, refused it. American science needed him, he said, and he would stay in his adopted country. At the height of the Civil War, and again with maximum publicity, he took out American citizenship to confirm his commitment.

Moreover, he showed a politician's shrewdness in the way he set about enhancing American scientific prestige. On one occasion, Spencer Fullerton Baird of the

Smithsonian Institution wrote to ask him if he had sent some papers off to Europe, and Agassiz replied sharply,

> Thus far I have done nothing towards circulating any of my papers in Europe, as I thought best for the sake of all our doings here, that they [the scientists there] should some day or other find out that there may be something doing in this part of the world, for which it may be worth their while to be on the lookout and also to check the expectation already raised that every thing which is published here is as a matter of course to be presented to them. That will not do in the long run, otherwise it would perpetuate in another form the tributary position in which science in America has been with reference to the old world.[22]

That was a sort of deviousness that would never have occurred to Baird, but it was the right course – within a few years European institutions were begging for American publications, where before they had ignored them.

And of course the fact that Agassiz *was* a European was an enormous advantage. By the time he moved to America, he was already in contact with all the leading European scientists, and he was consistently generous in sharing these contacts with his new American colleagues. His correspondence abounds in job references and letters of introduction designed to put European and American specialists in touch with one another. At the same time, he concentrated on improving the status of science in America itself. He enjoyed being a social lion, he enjoyed hob-nobbing with literati and politicians, and he used his immense personal prestige for the benefit of science. When he dined with businessmen and other influential people, he filled their ears with paeans to science, and they in turn filled the coffers of the museums and universities. When he appeared on the lecture platform, it hardly mattered that the ideas he expounded were years out of date. Audiences were captivated by his flashing eyes, his thrilling delivery, his exotic French accent, and they came away feeling that the study of science was a glorious vocation and a patriotic duty. On his death, hundreds of 'Agassiz Associations' sprang up across the country to encourage field natural history among young people.

Obviously American science would have come of age in the latter half of the nineteenth century even had Agassiz never moved there. The work of men like Spencer Fullerton Baird, Asa Gray, Dwight Dana, and the palaeontologists Cope and Marsh was far too important to be neglected for long. And there were other developments, like the establishment of the Smithsonian Institution and the growth of American universities, which occurred independently of Agassiz and contributed much to the enhancement of American intellectual prestige. But it was Agassiz more than any other individual who brought American naturalists into the world scientific community, and it was he who taught the American public to cherish their scientists and treat them generously. The fairest assessment of Agassiz's achievements was made by one of his assistants, Theodore Lyman, in

1872, the year before Agassiz's death. He wrote:

> There is not a single man in Europe today who could do *all* that he has done. You might find his equal as a naturalist; but then you would also find that he wore a dirty shirt, swallowed his knife, and could only talk German. You might find his equal in social force, but then it would be a man who didn't know the difference between an earth worm and a sparrow ... [Agassiz] has done more to excite and push forward Natural History in the U.S. than any man who was ever there.[23]

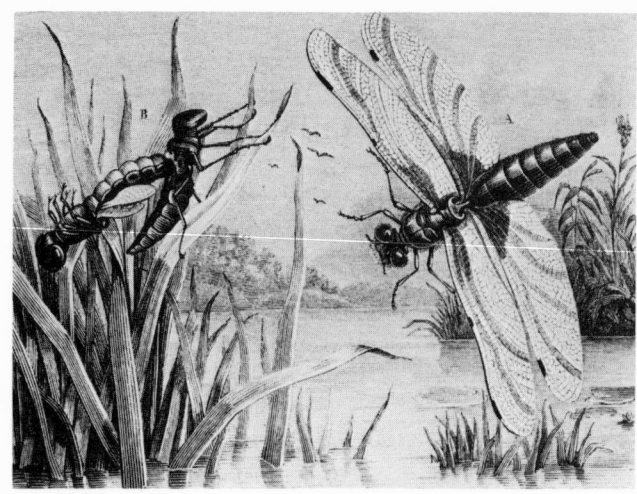

PART FIVE
DISSENTING VOICES

CHAPTER FIFTEEN

THE ROAD TO DARWIN

I cannot understand why you scientific people make such a fuss about Darwin. Why it's all in Lucretius!

Matthew Arnold to John Judd, 1871[1]

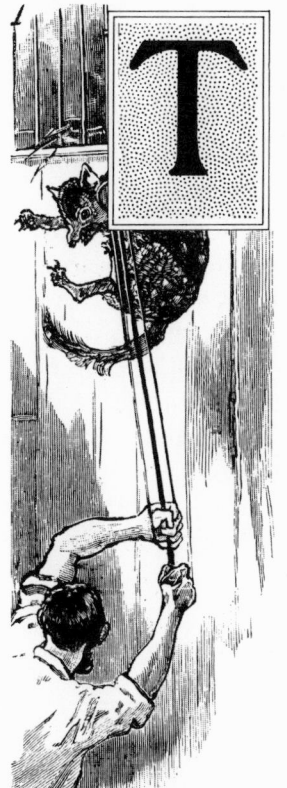

HE ONLY TWO influences which Darwin acknowledged were Lyell's *Principles of Geology* and Malthus's *Essay on Population*, neither of which is a biological work. He claimed that he was not influenced by any other evolutionary theory – particularly Lamarck's, which he detested – and wrote in the *Autobiography*:

It has sometimes been said that the success of the Origin proved 'that the subject was in the air' or 'that men's minds were prepared for it.' I do not think that this is strictly true, for I occasionally sounded not a few naturalists, and never happened to come across a single one who seemed to doubt about the permanence of species.[2]

As we shall see later, this was an extremely disingenuous remark, and the fact that Darwin and Wallace arrived at exactly the same theory at exactly the same time is sufficient proof that *something* was in the air, although it may not have been precisely evolution. The theory of evolution was, in any case, as old as the hills. It occurred frequently in the classics, and also in Chinese philosophy. It was only in the Christian world that it was taboo, because it clashed with the account of the Creation in the Book of Genesis. Nevertheless, intimations of such a theory occur in biological works for at least a century before Darwin. It was not called evolution in those days (it was not called evolution until some time after the *Origin of Species*), but whether presented as the 'descent theory', the 'continuity theory', the 'development hypothesis' or 'transmutation', it rested on the same basic premise that species were *not* immutable, that they could change.

But in the eighteenth century it was no easy matter to publish an idea that conflicted with the Book of Genesis. The French naturalist Buffon (1707–88) was rash enough, quite early in his career, to state the view that the Earth was much older than was generally thought, and in consequence found himself threatened with excommunication and forced to make a public recantation. From then on he was more careful, and when he wanted to discuss the subject of evolution in his *Histoire Naturelle*, he resorted to a peculiar technique, whereby pro-evolutionary statements were immediately contradicted by anti- ones. Talking about the ass and the horse, for instance, he argued, 'But if we once admit that there are families of plants and animals, so that the ass may be of the family of the horse, and that the one may only differ from the other through degeneration from a common ancestor, we might be driven to admit that the ape is of the family of man.' And having once accepted *that*, Buffon continued, ' ... then there is no further limit to be set to the power of nature, and we should not be wrong in supposing that with sufficient time she could have evolved all other organized forms from one primordial type.' At this point, Buffon obviously felt that he had gone as far as he dared, and his next sentence provided the disclaimer: 'But no! It is certain *from revelation* that all animals have alike been favoured with the grace of an act of direct creation, and that the first pair of every species issued full formed from the hands of the Creator.'[3]

Throughout the countless tomes of the *Histoire Naturelle*, Buffon followed the same tortuous technique, seizing every opportunity to discuss questions bearing on evolution (hybridism, artificial breeding, rudimentary organs, geographical distribution of species, etc.) but interlarding them with pious and contradictory references to revelation. As a result, he was dismissed by most of his scientific contemporaries as a dilettante and his work, despite or perhaps because of its enormous lay popularity, was ignored by serious scientists. Darwin did not read it until the 1860s, when he admitted to Huxley, 'I have read Buffon: whole pages are laughably like mine.'[4] However, though Buffon argued as clearly as he dared for the mutability of species, his idea was not the same as Darwin's, because he thought of evolution as a process of degeneration, from a perfect to an imperfect form, rather than a process of specialization.

The first naturalist to state a theory of evolution unequivocally was Erasmus Darwin (1731–1802), Charles's grandfather. In his *Zoonomia; or the Laws of Organic Life* (1794–6) he argued that all species must have originated from the same primitive 'filament' and that they had subsequently developed and differentiated as a result of external influences. He was particularly interested in changes produced by artificial breeding and by climate, and before birth by crossing or mutation, which are precisely the sorts of changes that his grandson studied in arriving at *his* evolutionary theory. However, Erasmus Darwin held so many wild ideas on such a variety of subjects that he was not taken seriously. Coleridge said that he had 'a greater range of knowledge than any other man in Europe', but he also coined the word 'Darwinizing' to mean indulging in far-fetched speculation.[5] Charles Darwin said that he was much impressed by the *Zoonomia* as a child but that when he came to re-read it as a student, 'I was much disappointed, the proportion of speculation being so large to the facts given.' He admitted, however, that 'It is probable that the hearing rather early in life such views maintained and praised may have favoured my upholding them under a different form in my Origin of Species.'[6] The *Zoonomia* was translated into French, German, Russian and Italian, pirated in New York, and placed on the papal Index. It was an important talking-point at the turn of the century, and produced the word 'Darwinism' long before Charles Darwin was even born. It is possible that it influenced our next evolutionist, Lamarck, although as Charles Darwin noted, it did not provide the factual evidence to really impress a scientist.

Erasmus Darwin, by Joseph Wright of Derby, 1770

Jean Baptiste Pierre Antoine de Monet, Chevalier de Lamarck (1744–1829) was, as his long name indicates, a French aristocrat by birth, but an impoverished one. His early manhood was spent as a literary hack and as tutor to Buffon's son. In 1793, he was appointed Professor of Zoology at the Jardin du Roi (which became the Jardin des Plantes) with the task of lecturing on Linnaeus's 'insecta' and 'vermes'. He had no prior experience of this mixed bunch of organisms, being by training a botanist, but by 1801 he had sorted them into a workable order, rescued the spiders and crustaceans from the insects, coined the word 'inverte-brate', and established several of the major modern classes. His taxonomy was based on a belief in Aristotle's 'great chain of being' far more literal than Linnaeus's. He believed that there were no gaps in Nature, and that when species or genera appeared to be widely separated from their nearest neighbours, it was only because man had not yet discovered the missing links. In practice, this belief worked very well because it forced him to consider fossil species alongside living ones, and to think of animate nature as a whole, instead of separating zoology and botany as Linnaeus had done. Indeed, it was Lamarck who coined the word biology, to embrace the study of all living things.

Lamarck published the first statement of his evolutionary theory in *Philosophie Zoologique* in 1809. In it, he argued that all species had evolved in a continuous progression from monad to man, and were still evolving. Changes in structure, he thought, arose in response to new conditions which necessitated new habits: organs developed or atrophied according to how much they were used. The giraffe's long neck, for instance, was produced by the giraffe's habit of craning its neck upwards to reach fresh foliage; the mole's poor sight by its habit of burrow-ing in the earth and neglecting the use of its eyes. In Lamarck's view, organisms contributed to and directed their own evolution. Or, as one Victorian parodist had it,

> Some, wishing to walk, manufactured a limb,
> Some rigged out a fin with a purpose to swim,
> Some opened an eye, some remained dark and dim,
> Which nobody can deny.[7]

The flaw in Lamarck's theory was that it depended on belief in the hereditability of acquired characteristics; a belief now known to be unsound. One giraffe might perhaps, by constant exertion, lengthen its neck by a fraction of an inch but it would *not*, contrary to Lamarck, pass on that extra fraction to its offspring. This was an ignis fatuus that was to mislead evolutionists throughout the nineteenth century. Even Darwin at one point seems to have been seduced by it, and it was not finally disproved until the twentieth century.

It is therefore rather difficult to account for the storm of venomous derision with which Lamarck's theories were greeted by his contemporaries. They after all *did* believe in the hereditability of acquired characteristics and could not disprove Lamarck by reference to Weismann or Mendel. Of course, Lamarck's theory ran contrary to the Church's teachings, but the French, unlike the British, had a healthy tradition of scientific anti-clericalism which should have sustained them. It seems to have been a question of personalities. Lamarck was, like Erasmus Darwin, an eccentric, a dabbler, and an uninhibited theorizer. (He published annual weather forecasts which were most reliably wrong.) His literary style was arid, and he placed his theories before his facts without bothering to anticipate objections, as Darwin did so skilfully in the *Origin*. Most importantly, Cuvier hated him, and in his *Éloge de M. de Lamarck*, delivered to the French Academy in 1832, he dismissed Lamarck's theories for ever: 'A system resting on such foundations may amuse the imagination of a poet ... but it cannot for a moment bear the examination of any one who has dissected the hand, the viscera, or even a feather.'[8]

Cuvier's dismissal was obediently repeated by almost every scientific historian of the nineteenth century. Swainson said in his 1840 *Bibliography of Zoologists* that Lamarck's evolutionary theories 'may be briefly characterised, not merely as

Jean Baptiste de Lamarck

fanciful, but absolutely absurd; leading, in some instances, if legitimately followed
out to their conclusions, to consequences of a very pernicious tendency.'[9] Darwin
inherited the prevailing prejudice, writing to Hooker in 1844: 'Heaven forfend
me from Lamarck nonsense!' and referring to his work as 'veritable rubbish'.[10]
He regarded Lamarck's history as an awful warning of the dangers inherent in
publishing a theory without sufficient supportive evidence.

Nevertheless, despite the utter rejection of Lamarck, the idea of the mutability
of species seems to have enjoyed an increasing currency from the 1820s onwards.
And 1831 saw the publication of a book by one Patrick Mathew which contained
a complete outline of the theory of evolution based on the principle of natural
selection, thus anticipating Darwin by almost thirty years. For instance, Mathew
wrote:

> The self-regulating adaptive disposition of organized life may, in part, be
> traced to the extreme fecundity of Nature, who, as before stated, has, in all
> the varieties of her offspring, a prolific power much beyond (in many cases
> a thousandfold) what is necessary to fill up the vacancies caused by senile
> decay. As the field of existence is limited and pre-occupied, it is only the
> hardier, more robust, better suited to circumstance individuals, who are able
> to struggle forward to maturity, these inhabiting only the situations to which
> they have superior adaptation and greater power of occupancy than any other
> kind; the weaker, less circumstance-suited, being prematurely destroyed.[11]

However, Mr Mathew's suggestive remarks were buried in the Appendix of
a book entitled *Naval Timber and Arboriculture* and although the book was well
reviewed as a contribution to the study of naval timber and arboriculture, its hints
at a theory of evolution were ignored until 1860 when, at the height of the Darwinian furore, Mr Mathew wrote to the *Gardener's Chronicle* and drew attention
to them. The new evolutionists then hastened to their libraries, looked up *Naval
Timber*, and found that lo! Mr Mathew was right. Darwin admitted as much in
later editions of the *Origin* ('The differences of Mr. Mathew's view from mine
are not of much importance ... He clearly saw ... the full force of the principle
of natural selection')[12] and Mr Mathew celebrated by having the words 'Discoverer of the Principle of Natural Selection' engraved on his visiting cards. However, neither Darwin nor any other scientist could be said to have been influenced
by Mathew's book, which remains a rather irritating blind alley off the main road
of evolution.

A very different case was *Vestiges of the Natural History of Creation*, published
anonymously in 1844. This attracted a great hubbub of publicity, went into four
editions within the year (and eight more subsequently) and was widely rumoured
to have been written by Prince Albert. Its author was in fact Robert Chambers
(1802–71) of the *Chambers's Encyclopaedia* family, a journalist, traveller, and
author of a sound though minor geological work on *Ancient Sea-Margins*, although
he did not own up to *Vestiges* until just before his death. The book was bold in

its style, and in its claims. It ascribed the origin of life to a 'chemico–electric process' and suggested that Man was descended from a large frog, which had subsequently become extinct. The 'facts' on which these theories were based were tenuous in the extreme. The modification of species was illustrated by an appeal to the supposed change of fungi into algae, and of wheat and oats into rye. The inevitable inheritance of acquired characteristics was 'proved' with, 'The coarse features and other structural peculiarities of the negro race only continue while these people live amidst the circumstances usually associated with barbarism ... When the same people in the United States of America have enjoyed a within-door life for several generations, they assimilate to the whites amongst whom they live.'[13] And to make matters worse, the author even showed an addiction to Swainson's old foible, the quinary system.

Nevertheless, the book was a success, and scientists were outraged. Sedgwick lambasted it in the *Edinburgh Review* and Huxley reviewed it, as he later admitted, 'with needless savagery'.[14] But of course these strident attacks only served to enhance the book's popularity and 'Mr. Vestiges' with his batrachian origins became the glamorous bogeyman of the decade. Suddenly the 'development hypothesis' was on everyone's lips, a subject for tea-table chatter. The heroine of Disraeli's *Tancred* (1847) has this to say about it:

> You know, all is development. The principle is perpetually going on. First, there was nothing, then there was something; then – I forget the next – I think there were shells, then fishes; then we came – let me see – did we come next? Never mind that; we came at last. And at the next change there will be something very superior to us – something with wings. Ah! that's it: we were fishes, and I believe we shall be crows.[15]

Darwin, like every other competent naturalist, was unimpressed by *Vestiges* but it is perhaps significant that it was in the summer of 1844, soon after the book appeared, that he first wrote out a proper outline of his theory which he asked Mrs Darwin to publish if he should die (as he fully expected to do) before he could complete the work himself. In the 'Historical Sketch of the Recent Progress of Opinion on the Origin of Species' which he prefixed to the third and subsequent editions of the *Origin*, he said of *Vestiges*:

> The work, from its powerful and brilliant style, though displaying in the earlier editions little accurate knowledge and a great want of scientific caution, immediately had a very wide circulation. In my opinion it has done excellent service in this country in calling attention to the subject, in removing prejudice, and in thus preparing the ground for the reception of analogous views.[16]

In other words, *Vestiges*, though worthless in itself, provided a useful stalking-horse for Darwin's *Origin*.

Charles Lyell, by George Richmond, *c.* 1853

This, then, was the point that the theory of evolution had reached at the time Darwin published the *Origin*. It had been aired fairly thoroughly at the beginning of the century, and again in the 1840s with *Vestiges*, and both times it had failed to win scientific acceptance. By the 1850s it was virtually dead, and Darwin was probably honest when he claimed that he never met another naturalist who seemed to doubt the permanence of species. But there was another controversy going on in these years, a geological one, which was in every way more important; ultimately it was a geological theory (Lyell's) that 'prepared men's minds' for the *Origin of Species*. Indeed, it prepared *Darwin*'s mind, as he readily admitted – 'I always feel as if my books come half out of Lyell's brain.'[17] Huxley, too, claimed that 'Lyell, for others as for myself, was the chief agent in smoothing the road for Darwin.'[18] And in a much larger sense the geological controversy of the 1830s, 1840s and 1850s prepared the way for Darwinism by first undermining the literal acceptance of the Book of Genesis which had hitherto hampered all scientific speculation about the origins of the Earth and of species. Darwin's book was to provoke all sorts of other religious difficulties, but the battle of Genesis had already been won.

There were many different geological controversies going on in the early decades of the nineteenth century, but the overriding one, and the one which had bearings on all the others, was about the age of the Earth. Archbishop Ussher, it will be remembered, had dated the Creation to 4004 B.C., but anyone who studied geology at all found it hard to accept that the Earth was only 6,000 years old. Even Linnaeus had once exclaimed, 'I should like to believe that the earth is even older than the Chinese believe it to be, but the Scriptures do not allow this',[19] and Buffon had been threatened with excommunication for suggesting the same thing. By 1785, speculation about the age of the Earth was fairly widespread, or so we gather from Cowper's *The Task*, which includes the sardonic lines:

> ... Some drill and bore
> The solid earth, and from the strata there
> Extract a register, by which we learn
> That He who made it, and revealed its date
> To Moses, was mistaken in its age.[20]

The reason why it was difficult to accept a date of 4004 B.C. was that the Earth had obviously undergone so many upheavals. How could continents split, mountains be forced upwards, other mountains be eroded to dust, all in the space of 6,000 years? And then there were fossils, which showed that there had once been many species of plants and animals on the Earth which no longer exist today. At first, this was not an insuperable problem because it could be explained by Noah's flood. Noah had rescued many species, but had left others to their fate – the 'giants on the earth in those days', like Peale's mammoth, whose fossil bones had been discovered. But this belief was only tenable as long as comparatively few fossil species were known. Once it became apparent that there had been many thousands of different extinct species, a great number of which were by no means giant, it became less plausible. And when a humble canal engineer, William 'Strata' Smith, the father of English geology, showed that these fossils occurred in a regular sequence, in regular strata, 'like slices of bread and butter on a breakfast plate', making their entrances and exits at different geological levels, it became impossible to account for them all by a single Noachian Deluge.

It was at this point that Cuvier enunciated the theory that was to sustain pious geologists for several decades. In his *Recherches sur les Ossements Fossiles*, published in 1812, he outlined the theory that the Earth had undergone a series of catastrophes – he envisaged them as global earthquakes – each of which had changed the entire landscape of the world, and annihilated all the plants and animals then living. After each catastrophe, God had started afresh with a new Creation. The Book of Genesis, Cuvier explained, was only concerned with the last of these Creations, the one in which man appeared. God had not bothered to reveal the previous Creations to Moses, because they did not concern man. Like all the other Creations, this last one was followed by a catastrophe – Noah's flood – but, unlike all the others, had not necessitated a fresh creation because God, acting through Noah, had saved most of the species then alive.

William Buckland, by T. Phillips

The great virtue of Cuvier's explanation was that it did not actually contradict any of the facts given in the Book of Genesis, which is why it met with such immediate acceptance and success in England. It happened that nearly all the leading English geologists of the early decades of the nineteenth century were clergymen, and the need to 'reconcile geology and Genesis' was for them a matter of private conscience as much as an intellectual conundrum. They could not have gone on studying geology if they had felt it conflicted with their belief in the Scriptures. But the Catastrophist theory allowed them to accept the Mosaic account of the Creation, even to accept Archbishop Ussher's dating, and yet to add on a long previous history of the Earth in which to accommodate all those troublesome fossils and geological changes. It gave them the freedom to study their science without interfering with Genesis at all, and, as such, was welcomed as a godsend.

It was the Catastrophist theory, with a few modifications, that William Buckland used as the basis of his 'Bridgewater Treatise' in 1836. The Bridgewater Treatises were an important series of works on natural theology which were published in the 1830s and 1840s as a result of a curious bequest. The Earl of Bridgewater had left £8,000 in his will to be devoted to producing books 'On the Power, Wisdom, and Goodness of God, as manifested in the Creation' in continuation of Paley's great work. The President of the Royal Society, the Archbishop of Canterbury and the Bishop of London were charged with the task of finding suitable authors, and William Buckland, who was Dean of Westminster Abbey as well as an eminent geologist, was the obvious choice for the volume on geology. His 'Bridgewater Treatise' became the standby for pious geologists in the difficult years ahead.

For, inevitably, no sooner had the Catastrophist theory become established than its flaws became apparent. Cuvier himself had suggested that there were probably four or five catastrophes before Noah's flood, but as more and more fossils were found, more and more catastrophes had to be invented to accommodate them, and Cuvier's disciple Alcide d'Orbigny eventually produced no fewer than twenty-seven separate catastrophes and creations. And even then it was difficult to explain how some fossil species reappeared in creation after creation, whereas others made one neat appearance on the stage and then departed, catastrophically, for ever. The problem of the geographical distribution of species was even more trying. Why were some fossils found here but not there, or why were some found almost everywhere and others only in one place? Lost continents were obviously the answer, but then they too began multiplying out of hand, until they were popping up and down like a school of porpoises across the length and breadth of the ocean. Another problem was posed by the archaeologists, who kept finding human bones or human artefacts in association with the bones of extinct animals, suggesting that man himself was older than 6,000 years and must have occurred in a previous creation. Nevertheless, the British geological divines battled manfully to assimilate each awkward new fact as it emerged and were still doing so in 1830 when Charles Lyell produced the theory of Uniformitarianism to upset them all.

Uniformitarianism was (or is, since it is still the basis of modern geology) the belief that the Earth has been shaped into its present contours by processes which are still at work today, and which can be observed. Winds wear away mountains, glaciers transport huge boulders, volcanoes occasionally erupt and wreak topographical change. Valleys are eroded by rivers, cliffs by the sea; the material washed away from them is eventually deposited elsewhere, in the form of beaches, sandbars, and so on. These are all processes which can be observed in action today, and which can be assumed to have acted similarly in the past, and *they alone* are sufficient to account for the shape of the landscape as we know it. It is not necessary to postulate world-shaking catastrophes and supernatural events – unless one believes that the Earth is only 6,000 years old. The assumption underlying Uniformitarianism is that the Earth is millions of years older than that.

Lyell did not 'invent' Uniformitarianism, any more than Darwin invented evolution. The theory was first propounded by the Scottish physician James Hutton in his *Theory of the Earth*, published in 1788. Lyell's contribution, like Darwin's to evolution, was to take an old theory and cram it so full of new supporting facts that it could no longer be ignored. Charles Lyell was born in 1797, the son of a wealthy Scottish landowner and amateur botanist. His mother believed that drunkenness was endemic to Scotland and forced the family to move to Hampshire, where Charles was brought up. At the age of seventeen, he went to Oxford to read Classics and was attracted to the horseback geologizing excursions of the flamboyant Dr Buckland. When he came down from Oxford, he immediately

James Hutton, from *Kay's Scottish Portraits*, 1787

joined the Geological Society. His father had intended him for the legal profession but, like Darwin, Lyell developed a convenient ailment – in his case, weak eyes – which prevented him carrying out this wish and left him free for the far more arduous pursuit of science. The opening of the Continent after the Napoleonic Wars enabled him to make the Grand Tour and he soon became, and remained, the best-travelled English geologist.

It is not known whether Lyell was converted to Uniformitarianism by reading Hutton's book, or simply by the evidence of his own eyes, but in 1817 he was much struck by the signs of cliff erosion which he saw around Cromer, and in 1820 was equally struck by the opposite effect at Rye, where silting has left the erstwhile harbour several miles inland. These are both places where geological changes wreak measurable effects from decade to decade. Certainly by the mid-1820s, Lyell was seeing 'existing causes' everywhere as he whisked around Scotland, the Auvergne and Sicily, and in 1829 he wrote to tell Murchison, his travelling-companion:

> My work is in part written and all planned ... All my geology will come in as illustration of my views on those principles, and as evidence strengthening the system necessarily arising out of the admission of such principles, which, as you know, are neither more nor less than that *no causes whatever* have from the earliest time to which we can look back to the present, ever acted, but those that are *now acting*, and that they never acted with different degrees of energy from that which they now exert.[21]

This was the theory, copiously supported by facts, which he presented in his *Principles of Geology* published in three volumes from 1830 to 1833.

The first volume came out just as Darwin was about to embark on the voyage of the *Beagle*, and Sedgwick, his tutor, sent him a copy with the injunction, 'Take Lyell's new book with you and read it by all means, for it is very interesting, but do not pay attention to it, except in regard to facts, for it is altogether wild as far as theory goes.'[22] Of course, Darwin devoured the book and ignored the injunction, and it was this first volume that made him a Lyellian for life. 'I have always thought,' he said later, 'that the great merit of the *Principles* was that it altered the whole tone of one's mind, and therefore that, when seeing a thing never seen by Lyell one yet saw it partially through his eyes.'[23] As Darwin's geological hammer rang through the Andes, he saw Lyellian Principles everywhere.

He also saw quite early on that the principle of Uniformitarianism could be applied just as well to the organic world as to the inorganic. If, as Lyell so persuasively argued, the Earth was undergoing a slow, but nevertheless continual, process of change, it seemed reasonable to suppose that species might be undergoing the same process, in order to adapt to their constantly changing environment. Lyell himself refused to go this far. He dealt with the species question in his second volume (which Darwin received at Montevideo in 1832) but stuck firmly to a

Cuvierian line, proposing a succession of creations and extinctions. It was only in the tenth edition of the *Principles*, published nine years after the *Origin of Species*, that he changed to a fully evolutionary position.

In fact, Lyell's views on the species question were ambivalent and, like many British scientists, he was prepared to go much further in private than he would in public. In a letter to the astronomer Herschel of 1836, he not only stated his belief in evolution but even offered some suggestions as to how it might be effected, including an outline of the principle of mimicry, which anticipated Bates by many years.[24] When Whewell taxed him with believing that the creation of new species was going on all the time, he replied, 'It was impossible, I think, for anyone to read my work and not to perceive that my notion of uniformity in the existing causes of change always implied that they must for ever produce an endless variety of effects, both *in the animate* and in the inanimate world.'[25]

But Lyell did not publish these views. He felt, quite sensibly, that he did not want to obstruct the acceptance of his geological theories by embarking on contentious arguments on biological questions which were really outside his province. He was a man who cared deeply about social niceties (Darwin recounts in his *Autobiography* how Lyell and Lady Lyell used to spend hours debating the merits of every invitation) and he was not eager for martyrdom. He said of his predecessor Hutton, 'I think he ran unnecessarily counter to the feelings and prejudices of the age.'[26] And he said of his own book, 'If I had stated ... the possibility of the introduction or origination of fresh species being a natural, in contra-distinction to a miraculous process, I should have raised a host of prejudices against me, which are unfortunately opposed at every step to any philosopher who attempts to address the public on these mysterious subjects.'[27] Darwin was disappointed by what he considered Lyell's timidity, but it was most unfair of him to complain because he was to exercise the same sort of reticence himself in dealing with the question of man in the *Origin*.

In any case, in 1830 when *Principles of Geology* first appeared, it was hard enough to win acceptance for geological Uniformitarianism, let alone biological. Lyell told his friend and reviewer Scrope, as he launched the book, 'Full *half* of my history and comments was cut out, and even many facts, because either I, or Stokes, or Broderip, felt that it was anticipating twenty or thirty years of the march of honest feeling to declare it undisguisedly.'[28] But all his tact was wasted on the geological divines, who could recognize an anti-Mosaic principle when they saw it, and realized immediately that there was no possible way of reconciling Lyell's Uniformitarianism with a literal belief in the Book of Genesis. For many of them, it was the most bitter crisis of their lives. Their intellects told them that Lyell's book was a masterpiece: their consciences told them that they could not accept it. They ostracized Lyell and tried to forget that they had ever befriended him.

In fact, the furore that greeted Lyell's *Principles* was hardly less vociferous than the furore that greeted Darwin's *Origin of Species* a generation later. Historians have tended to eclipse the former, but people who lived through both intellectual crises, the geological one of the 1830s and the evolutionary one of the 1860s, were inclined to give them equal weight. Huxley remarked in his old age:

> At the present time, it is difficult to persuade serious scientific enquirers to occupy themselves, in any way, with the Noachian Deluge. They look at you with a smile and a shrug, and say they have more important matters to attend to than mere antiquarianism. But it was not so in my youth. At that time geologists and biologists could hardly follow to the end any path of enquiry without finding the way blocked by Noah and his ark, or by the first chapter of Genesis; and it was a serious matter, in this country at any rate, for a man to be suspected of doubting the literal truth of the Diluvial or any other Pentateuchal history.[29]

'Scene of the Geological Discoveries at Swanage, Dorset', 1857

Moreover, this situation continued for many years after Lyell's book. In the 1850s the Torquay Natural History Society refused to publish a paper about an archaeological excavation which showed man-made stone tools alongside the bones of extinct animals, and an advertisement for 'Sopwith's Geological Models' in 1858 added the cautious note that 'It may be proper to observe, that the train of investigation which is required to study these models is wholly apart from the theoretical researches which extend to the original formation of rocks.'[30] From every pulpit in the land, clergymen denounced the new theories, promising hell-fire for anyone who listened to them, and a Dublin newspaper claimed quite simply that 'Geology has the devil for its author.'[31] Of the countless pamphlets published on this theme, one entitled 'A Brief and Complete Refutation of the Anti-Scriptural Theory of Geologists' by 'a Clergyman of the Church of England' may be taken as typical. It spoke of the 'HORRID BLASPHEMIES of geologists' which were causing 'immense mischief ... *especially among the lower classes.*' Its method of refuting geological facts was simple. They were not facts; they were all lies. Fossils were not *really* fossils; they were merely bits of stone that happened to look like organic forms. As for coprolites (fossilized faeces):

> We cannot believe in such things as coprolites. They are only a curious form of matter commanded by Him who has made the flower to assume all shapes ... The geological assertion that the Creator of this world formed it in some parts of coprolites savours very much of Satan or Beelzebub, the god of dung. Geologists could scarcely have made a more unfortunate self-refuting assertion than this.[32]

The effect of all this controversy on the layman was confusing. Geology had for some time been a fairly popular science and was becoming more so every year, with geological societies and even geological shops springing up in every large town. Many laymen, like the students in Tennyson's *Princess*, liked to spend their spare time,

> Hammering and clinking, chattering stony names
> Of shale and hornblende, rag and trap and tuff.[33]

They would have found Lyell's book, with its exceptionally clear and elegant style, easy to read and to understand. But *should* they understand it? Should they allow themselves to be seduced by its anti-Pentateuchal theories? Their pastors and their consciences told them that they should not. Even to read the new geology smacked of heresy: to believe it carried the risk of damnation. In consequence, geology acquired the reputation of a 'dangerous' science, and only very brave amateurs were tempted to continue with it. The geological debate was thrashed out among theologians and professional scientists, in the Church newspapers and learned journals of the day. It was not discussed in the popular natural histories because it was too 'serious' a subject, and until the advent of Hugh Miller (whom we shall be meeting in the next chapter) most popular writers avoided mentioning any geological topics at all. For, unlike the row about *Vestiges* in the mid-1840s, the geological controversy was not a nine days' wonder. It went on rumbling throughout the 1830s, 1840s and 1850s, and was still rumbling in 1859 when it was subsumed into the far wider controversy about Darwinism.

25 Sea-anemones, from *Actinologia Britannica* by P. H. Gosse, 1860

26 Yellow Water Lily, from *Wild Flowers* by Anne Pratt, 1852

27 Japanese flowers, oil painting by Marianne North, 1875

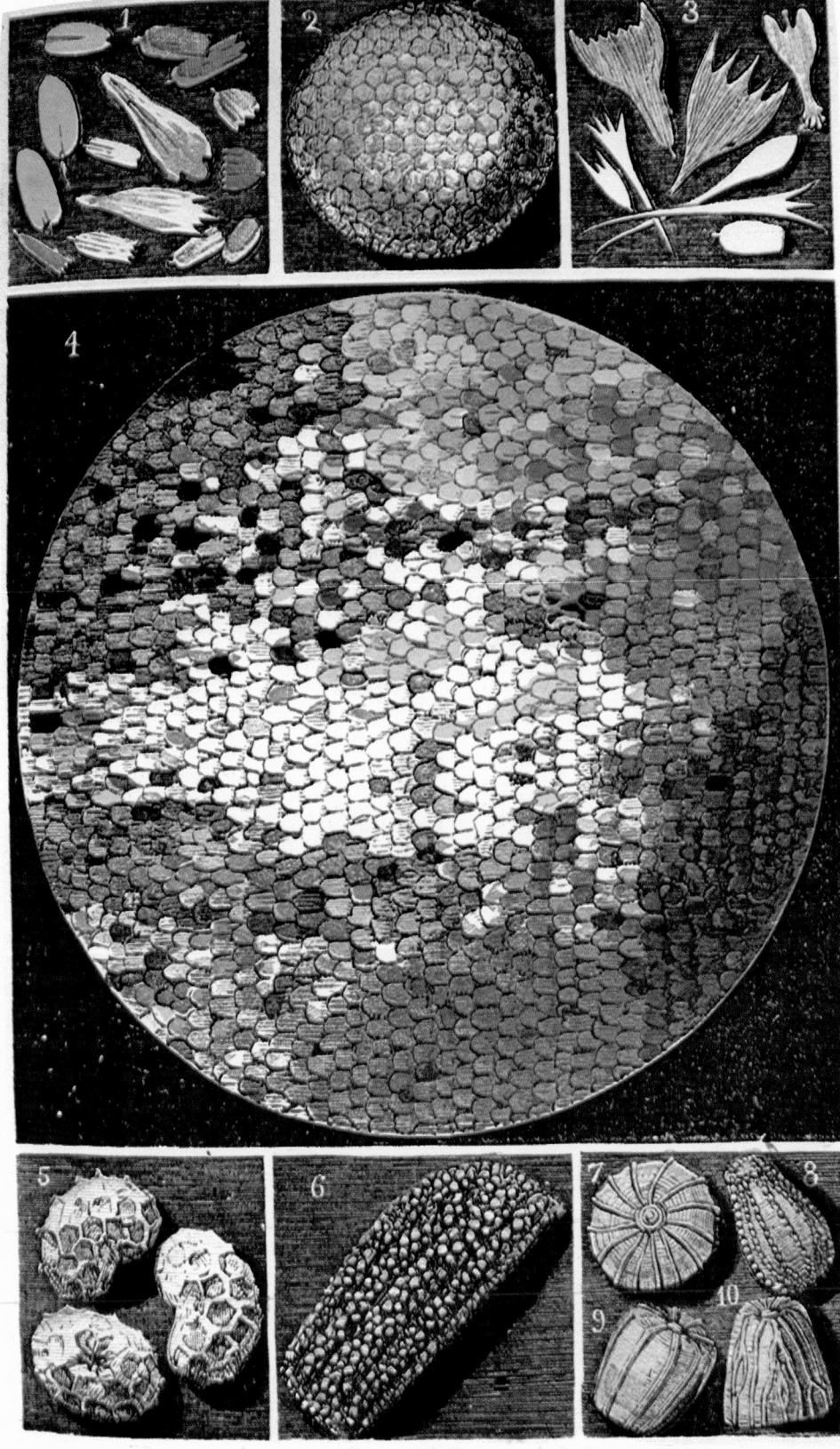

CHAPTER SIXTEEN

'A MUSING, MEDITATIVE STONE-MASON'

T IS QUITE likely that after the upheavals of the 1830s, popular interest in geology might have died out entirely, had it not been for the influence of one man, Hugh Miller. Miller bravely faced the dangers that other writers shunned, and led his readers safely through the thickets of geological controversy, with a fossil fish in one hand and the Book of Genesis in the other. The route he chose was a kind of modified Catastrophism, and he wrote as though Lyell's *Principles* had never existed. He was pious, he was sincere, and above all he was *safe*. Even fundamentalists found that they could read Miller's geological expositions without hearing any distant crackling from the flames of hell-fire.

Moreover, Hugh Miller was a member of the working class, which lent him a quite extraordinary charisma in Victorian eyes. He was the son of a Scottish sailor, and had spent most of his adult life as a stone-mason. He dressed in a plaid, carried a pistol at his belt, and spoke in an almost impenetrable brogue. One of his most famous speeches, about an ancient Scottish forest, was remembered for its ringing finale: 'The exe hed been buzzy in its gleds.'[1] His appearance was hirsute and shaggy and a friend compared it to 'the noblest of the dog tribe, such as Landseer loves to paint'.[2] Yet despite his uncouth looks and manners, he managed to impress Sir Roderick Murchison when he came to Glasgow for the British Association meeting in 1840, and it is to Murchison's enduring credit that he recognized the talents of this 'musing, meditative stone-mason'[3] and urged him to write a geological book. The book, *The Old Red Sandstone*, was to bring Miller a fame and popularity far surpassing Murchison's, and make him one of the most admired writers of the Victorian age.

The story of how the obscure stone-mason became a geologist and writer can be read fully in Miller's autobiography, *My Schools and Schoolmasters*, but it is more movingly sketched in *The Old Red Sandstone*. When Hugh Miller was only five, his father died at sea, and he was brought up by two Shandyan uncles, one

28 (*facing page*) Microscopic illustrations, from *Common Objects of the Country* by the Rev. J.G. Wood, 1858

Hugh Miller

a harness-maker and the other a cartwright. They wanted him to go to university, and would have scraped to send him there, but Hugh Miller refused. He said he had no wish to become a doctor, a lawyer, or that most terrible thing to the Calvinist conscience, a minister without a vocation. His uncles shook their heads and agreed. 'Better be anything honest,' they chorused, 'than an *uncalled* minister.'⁴ And so he became an apprentice mason. He chose that particular trade because he knew that the work was seasonal, and he planned to devote his unemployed winters to writing poetry. He did not yet know of the occupational hazard of the mason's trade – silicosis, which killed most masons before their forty-fifth year – but he knew that the life would be hard enough.

In the first chapter of *The Old Red Sandstone*, Miller recounts his feelings on the first day of his apprenticeship. He set out before dawn to walk to the quarry, and his thoughts as he plodded through the darkness were wholly pessimistic:

> I had been a wanderer among rocks and woods, a reader of curious books when I could get them, a gleaner of old traditionary stories; and now I was going to exchange all my day-dreams, and all my amusements, for the kind of life in which men toil every day that they may be enabled to eat, and eat every day that they may be enabled to toil!

But the quarry, when he arrived there, was a surprise. It was cut into the Old Red Sandstone (though of course he did not know the term then) on the shore of an inland bay, with a stream on one side and a thick fir wood on the other, and it was beautiful. The work was not as heavy as he had expected, and the occasional gunpowder explosions were wildly exciting. So absorbed was he in admiring his surroundings and learning the proper use of the pick, that he was surprised, and even slightly disappointed, when the foreman told him that it was time to go home. 'This was no very formidable beginning of the course of life I had so much dreaded,' he decided. 'To be sure, my hands were a little sore, and I felt nearly as much fatigued as if I had been climbing among the rocks; but I had wrought and been useful, and had yet enjoyed the day fully as much as usual.'⁵

The next day, in sparkling winter sunshine, the scene was even more glorious.

> There was not a wrinkle on the water, nor a cloud in the sky, and the branches were as moveless in the calm as if they had been traced on canvas. From a wooded promontory that stretched half-way across the frith there ascended a thin column of smoke. It rose straight as the line of a plummet for more than a thousand yards, and then, on reaching a thinner stratum of air, spread out equally on every side, like the foliage of a stately tree. Ben Wyvis rose to the west, white with the yet unwasted snows of winter, and as sharply defined in the clear atmosphere as if all its sunny slopes and blue retiring hollows had been chiselled in marble.⁶

In the afternoon, the foreman used gunpowder again and when the rock fell away, Miller noticed that the newly exposed surface was ribbed and furrowed like a bank of sand that had been left by the tide only an hour before. And the loose stones at the top of the quarry were rounded and water-worn as if they had been rolled in the sea for hundreds of years. 'But what had become,' Miller wondered, 'of the waves that had thus fretted the solid rock, or of what element had they been composed? I felt as completely at fault as Robinson Crusoe did on his discovering the print of the man's foot on the sand … I was lost in conjecture, and found I had food enough for thought that evening, without once thinking of the unhappiness of a life of labour.'[7]

A week or two later, the team moved to another quarry and within hours Miller had found his first fossil. 'I picked up a nodular mass of blue limestone, and laid it open by a stroke of the hammer. Wonderful to relate, it contained inside a beautifully finished piece of sculpture, – one of the volutes, apparently, of an Ionic capital.' He opened another nodule, and another, and another, and each of them contained a different fossil. 'Of all Nature's riddles, these seemed to me to be at once the most interesting and the most difficult to expound. I treasured them carefully up … '[8]

And so be became, simultaneously, a mason and a student of geology, and continued thus for the next fifteen years. It was a rough sort of life, even by the labouring standards of the day, especially when the masons had to live together in barns or 'bothys' with leaking roofs and water-logged floors. Miller was once woken in the night by a scream from his bedmate – a rat had bitten off his earlobe. The men lived on porridge, with only the occasional luxury of some milk to wet it. Anyone who burned the porridge, or otherwise annoyed his companions, was given a 'ramming' – lifted up bodily and driven head-foremost against the wall. A serious deprivation for Miller was the lack of privacy in the bothy and of any light by which to read. Eventually the lung pains of incipient silicosis forced him to leave the well-paid but brutish bothy life of the building trade and set up alone as a carver of gravestones. Commissions were hard to come by and poorly paid, but at least he now had time to pursue his studies.

For, throughout all these years, his geological enthusiasm was growing. As he points out in *The Old Red Sandstone*, being a stone-mason was the best possible training for becoming a geologist. His hammer and mallet were always to hand, and his 'sections' were ready-made in the quarries where he worked. Moreover, his geological skill enhanced his usefulness as a mason: often he was able to predict where good building stone might be found, simply by scanning the lie of the country. His work took him from one end of Scotland to the other, and he became familiar with many different rock formations. But the one that engaged him most – perhaps because it was the one he had first looked at – was the Old Red Sandstone, and he began making a systematic collection of the various fish fossils that he found in it.

He bought books on 'oryctology' (the old name for the study of fossils) but was surprised to find no mention of the Old Red fishes in them. By pure chance, he had stumbled on a geological *terra incognita*. One thing in particular bothered him. The fish-parts he found were all external – great back-plates and head-shields like armour – but with no sign of an internal skeleton to support them. He began to wonder if the internal parts could have been constituted not of bone but of cartilage, which would not have survived the fossilization process. He had read widely enough by this stage to know the name of the one man living who could solve the problem – Louis Agassiz, the great palaeontologist and specialist in fossil fishes who was then still living in Switzerland. But how could he, an unknown Scottish stone-mason, ever hope to meet or to consult the great Swiss panjandrum? It was, he felt, 'a contingency rather to be wished than hoped for', an almost impossible dream.[9]

Of course, the story had a happy ending. Miller did meet Agassiz, who duly confirmed that his cartilage theory was correct. But that was not until 1840, and Miller's career had first to undergo many changes. It will be remembered that he originally chose the mason's trade because it would allow him time to write, and he had been practising his writing ever since he left school. In 1829 he published some *Poems written in the Leisure Hours of a Journeyman Mason* which served the invaluable purpose of convincing him that he was not cut out to be a poet, and from that date onwards he devoted his leisure hours more fruitfully to prose. He studied the art of composition as carefully as he studied the Old Red fishes. Addison, Steele and Goldsmith were his models, and it is their fine clarity that emerges in the best of Miller's mature prose. In 1835 he published a volume of *Scenes and Legends of the North of Scotland* which, unlike the poems, was well reviewed and widely sold. He began contributing articles to various newspapers, especially to Robert Chambers's *Edinburgh Journal*. But it was polemics that finally made him a full-time writer. In 1839 Lord Brougham made a speech in the House of Lords denying the long-cherished right of Scottish congregations to choose their own pastors, and Hugh Miller dashed off a pamphlet *Letter to Lord Brougham* stating the opposite, 'anti-intrusionist', case. It found an enormous circulation in Scotland and even influenced English politicians. Gladstone commented, 'The Church question has been discussed in a great variety of pamphlets, some of them very long and very able, others of them very long without being particularly able, and one of them particularly able without being long; I mean the elegant and masculine production of Hugh Miller.'[10]

The pamphlet also drew the attention of various leaders of the Scottish Church who were then in the process of forming a newspaper, the *Witness*, to support the anti-intrusionist cause. Their efforts had hitherto been hampered by their inability to find an editor but now, in Hugh Miller, they recognized their man, and summoned him to Edinburgh to discuss 'some literario–Christian objects'.[11] Miller launched the paper in January 1840, and within a few issues made it one of the most influential papers in Scotland. But then came the summer, with its usual dearth of news, and Miller began padding out the polemics with articles on his own favourite subject, geology. It was these articles which caught Murchison's eye when he came to Scotland, and which led him to seek out their author and invite him to attend the British Association meeting at Glasgow in September.

And so we come to the great day, Wednesday, 23 September 1840, on which Hugh Miller, the erstwhile stone-mason, found himself sharing the platform with Murchison, Buckland, and his long-time hero, Agassiz. The *Report of the Proceedings of the Association* tells what happened:

> Mr. Murchison gave an account of the investigations and discoveries of Mr. Hugh Miller of Cromarty (now Editor of the 'Witness') in the Old Red Sandstone ... He spoke in the highest terms of Mr. Miller's perseverance and ingenuity as a geologist. With no other advantage than a common education, by a careful use of his means, he had been able to give himself an excellent education, and to elevate himself to a position which any man in any sphere of life might well envy. Mr. Murchison added, that he had seen some of Mr. Miller's papers on Geology, written in a style so beautiful and poetical, as to throw plain geologists like himself into the shade. (Cheers.)

Dr Buckland then stood up and announced that

> he had never been so much astonished in his life by the powers of any man as he had been by the geological descriptions of Mr. Miller, which had been shown to him in the 'Witness' newspaper by his friend Sir C. Menteath. That wonderful man described these objects with a facility which made him ashamed of the comparative meagreness and poverty of his own description in the 'Bridgewater Treatise', which had cost him hours and days of labour. He [Dr Buckland] would give his left hand to possess such powers of description as this man; and if it pleased Providence to spare his useful life, he, if any one, would certainly render the science attractive and popular, and do equal service to Theology and Geology.[12]

However, it was Agassiz who provided the climax. Hugh Miller had brought some of his fossil fishes with him to the meeting and Agassiz looked them over. One of them, he said, was a species never seen before: it was 'new to science'. Murchison then invited him to exercise his prerogative as world authority on the subject and name the new species. Agassiz stood up and proposed to the meeting that henceforward the fish should be called *Pterichthys Milleri* – Miller's winged fish. It was the consummation of Hugh Miller's dreams.

The next year his geological articles from the *Witness* were published in book form as *The Old Red Sandstone*, and Miller's name was known in every Victorian parlour. Never, surely, has there been a bestseller with a less inviting title. The Old Red Sandstone is one of the dullest formations in the whole geological calendar. Its fossils consist only of fishes and a few seaweedy plants, none of them very large or very beautiful. Its age disqualifies it from any of the geological plums – no hope of dinosaurs, no glimmering of early man, no trace of gold or even of coal. And yet Hugh Miller's book *was* a bestseller, on a scale barely surpassed by *Uncle Tom's Cabin*, and reading it today, one can still understand why. His style is lucid, always finding the exact happy simile, often a homely one, for the most abstruse details of fossil structure. The ventral fins of *Holyptichius* are compared to a woman's pouched apron pockets; its double row of teeth to 'officers on horseback seen over the heads of their foot-soldiers in front.'[13] By the end of the book, the reader finds that he or she has painlessly acquired a thorough knowledge of Old Red Sandstone fishes, while being constantly entertained and diverted along the way. But even more remarkable is Miller's ability to convert dead fossils into living animals. He once defined geology as 'Natural History extended over all ages'[14] and it is precisely as a field naturalist setting out on an exploring expedition that he enters the geological past. Here, for instance, he imagines himself approaching the coastline of Europe during the Carboniferous era:

Land, from the mast-head! land! land! – a low shore thickly covered with vegetation. Huge trees of wonderful form stand out far into the water. There seems no intervening beach. A thick hedge of reeds, tall as the masts of pinnaces, runs along the deeper bays, like water-flags at the edge of a lake. A

Landscape of the Carboniferous Era, from Figuier's *La Terre Avant le Déluge*, 1864

river of vast volume comes rolling from the interior, darkening the water for leagues with its slime and mud, and bearing with it to the open sea, reeds, and fern, and cones of the pine, and immense floats of leaves, and now and then some bulky tree, undermined and uprooted by the current. We near the coast, and now enter the opening of the stream ...

Scarce can the current make way through the thickets of aquatic plants that rise thick from the muddy bottom; and though the sunshine falls bright on the upper boughs of the tangled forest beyond, not a ray penetrates the more than twilight gloom that broods over the marshy platform below. The rank steam of decaying vegetation forms a thick blue haze, that partially obscures the underwood; deadly lakes of carbonic acid gas have accumulated in the hollows; there is silence all around, uninterrupted save by the sudden splash of some reptile fish that has risen to the surface in pursuit of its prey, or when a sudden breeze stirs the hot air, and shakes the fronds of the giant ferns or the catkins of the reeds.[15]

Even those like Buckland and Conybeare who had spent a lifetime studying the fossils of the Coal Formations had never visualized them as powerfully as this. Geology was always called the 'stony science': nobody had ever tried to breathe sensuous life into it before. But Miller's explorations of the different landscapes of the geological past had all the colour and romance of Bates's or Waterton's descriptions of the South American jungle, and geologists as much as laymen found them a revelation. Carlyle said of the book, 'There is right genial fire, everywhere nobly tempered down with peaceful radical heat, which is very beautiful to see. Luminous, memorable; all wholesome, strong, fresh and breezy, like the "Old Red Sandstone" mountains in a sunny summer day.'[16]

None of Miller's subsequent books is quite as good, though several of them enjoyed in their time an equal or even greater popularity. As a man of deep religious faith (all the stronger for having been a sceptic in his youth) it was inevitable that he should have been drawn into the religio–scientific controversies of the day, and several of his later books are taken up with arguments which now have only historic interest. The fullest statement of his views on the 'Genesis-versus-geology' question occurs in his last book, *The Testimony of the Rocks*, published in 1857. He begins by explaining that the Earth must be far older than 6,000 years but that nevertheless 'geology, rightly understood, does not conflict with revelation.'[17] His method of reconciling the two is ingenious. The Genesis account of the Creation *is* accurate, he maintains, provided we interpret the six 'days' of Creation as six long geological eras, and provided we imagine that God vouchsafed the history to Moses in a vision – 'It was, let us suppose, a diorama'[18] – rather than in words. This would explain Moses' failure to notice the existence of the fishes on the second day: they were hidden in the sea. He then goes on to deal with points of detail. Discussing the recent archaeological finds of human bones and artefacts in conjunction with extinct animals, he decides that these can be explained by the human custom of burying the dead, which produces archaeological confusion. Man, he claims, *is* only 6,000 years old because the Book of Genesis says so. He is equally firm in dealing with a dreadful heresy that was being voiced then in America: the idea that Adam and Eve were *black*. 'Adam, the father of mankind,' he thunders, 'was no squalid savage of doubtful humanity, but a noble specimen of man; and Eve a soft Circassian beauty but exquisitely lovely beyond the lot of fallen humanity.'[19] And if anyone should wonder what a soft Circassian beauty looks like, he refers them to 'the high-bred aristocracy of England' who, he maintains, represent the best expression of the type.[20]

Miller also deals at length with the 'Noah's Ark problem' which had arisen as a result of the species explosion of recent years. Back in the eighteenth century, when the number of known animal species in the world had been counted in hundreds, it was easy to fit them all into the Ark, but by the beginning of Victoria's reign, the number of known species of mammals had increased to 1,000, of birds to 6,000 and of reptiles and amphibia to 1,500, and they continued to increase every year. It then became extremely difficult to fit two of each, with enough food to sustain them, into a three-storey Ark measuring 300 cubits long by 50 cubits broad. The definition of a cubit was slightly elastic but was generally agreed to be around one and a half feet, giving a floor area of 450 feet by 75 feet times three (for the number of storeys) which, as one Victorian pundit helpfully calculated, was exactly one-seventh of the floor area of the Great Exhibition. A few die-hard fundamentalists thought that it could still be done. Dr Hamilton of Mobile, for instance, wrote, 'It must not be forgotten that of all these [species], the vastly greater proportion are small; and that numbers of them could be placed together in the same compartment of the Ark.'[21] But by the 1850s most realistic thinkers, including Miller himself, agreed that it was not possible to fit all the known animals into the Ark, and the best solution was to make Noah's flood purely local in extent, and to confine it to an area somewhere around the Caspian. The 'Noah's Ark problem' now seems the most absurd of all the nineteenth-century religio–scientific debates, but to many Victorians it was the most real. Theories about the age of the Earth or the origin of species could be dismissed by non-scientists as 'speculation', but a visitor to any zoological garden could see the difficulty of fitting so many animals into an area one-seventh the size of the Great Exhibition, and for many laymen this was the first hint that the Book of Genesis could not always be taken at face value.

In *Footprints of the Creator* (which has the helpful subtitle, 'Or the Asterolepis of Stromness') Miller addresses himself to another controversial subject – evolution, or the development hypothesis, which had recently reappeared in *Vestiges of Creation*. Miller had opposed the development hypothesis ever since he first came across it in an obscure French version, de Maillet's *Telliamed*, and he was alarmed to see it apparently becoming popular again. He would have been very surprised to learn that the *Vestiges* was written by Robert Chambers, the editor who had first encouraged his journalistic talents, and a man he still thought of as his friend. In his autobiography Miller pays a lengthy tribute to Chambers, and it is obvious that he never suspected his secret.

In the preface to *Footprints*, Miller explains why he considers *Vestiges* worth refuting. 'The development doctrines,' he warns, 'are doing much harm on both sides of the Atlantic, especially among intelligent mechanics, and a class of young men engaged in the subordinate departments of trade and the law. And the harm, thus considerable in amount, must be necessarily more than merely considerable in degree. For it invariably happens, that when persons in these walks become materialists, they become also turbulent subjects and bad men.'[22] In the second chapter, he brilliantly outlines the dangers to be anticipated from a widespread belief in evolution. He begins by stating that the development hypothesis is not *per se* atheistical. God could have decreed that animals should evolve, as easily as he could have created them individually. But, Miller goes on, if we believe that

'A Saurian' – pun on Gideon Mantell, a noted palaeontologist

Man evolved from the lower animals, 'we must hold either the monstrous belief, that all the vitalities, whether those of monads or of mites, of fishes or of reptiles, of birds or of beasts, are individually and inherently immortal and undying, or that human souls are *not* so.' Obviously we cannot believe that all animals have immortal souls, and so we are led to the belief that human souls are not immortal. 'And thus,' he concludes, 'though the development theory be not atheistic, it is at least practically tantamount to atheism. For, if man be a dying creature, re-stricted in his existence to the present scene of things, what does it really matter to him, for any one moral purpose, whether there be a God or no?'[23]

And, in the same chapter, Miller goes on to warn that the Churches are totally unprepared to meet this new threat:

> The clergy as a class suffer themselves to linger far in the rear of an intelligent and accomplished laity – a full age behind the requirements of the time. Let them not shut their eyes to the danger which is obviously coming. The battle of the Evidences will have as certainly to be fought on the field of physical science, as it was contested in the last age on that of the metaphysics. And on this new arena the combatants will have to employ new weapons, which it will be the privilege of the challenger to choose.[24]

When this rebuttal of *Vestiges* first appeared, in 1849, many of its more intelli-gent readers must have thought that Miller was paying too serious attention to what was, after all, a work of pseudo-science whose arguments leaked at every seam. But ten years later, when Darwinism sprang phoenix-like from the ashes of all the previous development hypotheses, people turned to Miller's *Footprints* as to an oracle. All its predictions had come true. The evolution theory *was* attract-ing widespread belief. It *was* atheistic in its implications (even more so with the new Darwinian ingredient of natural selection). The Churches *were* totally un-prepared to meet it. But unfortunately, though the predictions of *Footprints* were correct, its scientific arguments were useless against the onslaught of Darwinism. They had been designed for a far weaker target, and by the time the *Origin of Species* appeared, many of them were outmoded. 'Was Darwin right?' moaned the *Methodist Recorder*, and 'Were Moses, Plato, Lord Bacon and Hugh Miller wrong?'[25]

The modern reader may well be amazed to find Hugh Miller's name given in such company, but Hugh Miller, from the publication of *The Old Red Sandstone* until his death, enjoyed a quite extraordinary measure of popular approval. He seemed, by his life and by his writings, to be the very pattern-book of Victorian virtues. The working classes approved of him because he was one of themselves. The middle classes approved of him because he told the working classes not to put their faith in Chartism, but to rely on self-education and self-help. He exempli-fied the message that the popular natural history books perennially taught: that anyone, by reading and observing carefully, could master a scientific subject and

contribute important new findings to it. He was the hero of the Mechanics' Institutes; the living inspiration of the Lyceum movement. In the United States

'Labyrinthodon', from Figuier's *La Terre Avant le Déluge*, 1864

he was, if possible, even more popular than in Britain. 'His books,' according to
Archibald Geikie, 'were to be found in the remotest log-hut of the Far West, and
on both sides of the Atlantic, ideas of the nature and scope of geology were largely
drawn from them.'[26] Hugh Miller did more in his lifetime to make geology popular, pious and respectable, than all the previous geological writers put together.

References to death occur in Hugh Miller's writings with astonishing frequency.
Even in private letters to his young children he always qualified talk of future
plans with the proviso, 'if you survive'. And in a letter written to his fiancée when
she was mildly ill, he vividly imagined the scene of her grave and himself mourning
over it. He was deeply superstitious, believing in ghosts, omens and portents, and
often told the story of how, at the time of his father's death when he was a boy
of five, he opened the door to find a disembodied hand beckoning to him. Probably
it was his father's death, coupled with a Calvinist upbringing, which first awakened
his morbidity, but by middle age it seems to have darkened into an obsession.

One of his last published papers is a farewell address he gave to the Royal Physical Society of Edinburgh when he completed his term of office as President. It was reprinted as an appendix to later editions of *The Old Red Sandstone*. Its title is 'The Fossiliferous Deposits of Scotland' and the first four-fifths of the paper give an able and matter-of-fact exposition of the subject. But then, gradually, there comes a change. Miller talks of the gaps that still remain in the fossil record, and the gaps that mark the end of one geological era and the beginning of another. These gaps, he says, serve to remind us that 'to every species that ever lived in the old geologic ages there came a "last day" [and] that as all the species of the past have died, so it is destined for all the species of the present also to die.'[27]

And then comes an extraordinary passage of eschatological foreboding: 'There are peculiarities, too, in the visitations of the present time, suited to suggest many a pregnant thought in conjunction with this curious and surely not unimportant subject. I travelled by railway, in middle autumn, two years ago, for about a hundred miles, through a series of well-cultivated fields; and found almost all their potatoes, constituting about one-fifth of the entire produce of the district, killed by a mysterious disease, and exhaling a heavy odour of death and decay that infected the air mile after mile.' Not only potatoes, he says, but now the vineyards of the South are being ravaged by a mysterious disease, and the human species, too, has recently been decimated by 'a new and terrible disease' – cholera – that has killed more than a hundred million people. 'Read in the light of geologic history,' he warns, 'with its irrefragable evidence of the often-repeated extinction of entire creations, these visitations of the age assume a peculiar significancy.' Potatoes? Vineyards? Visitations? Miller apparently sensed his listeners growing restive, for he cuts himself short with a curt, 'But the subject is one which I must not pursue.'[28]

He then makes the proper thanks and courtesies to the members of the Society for electing him their President and for putting up with his shortcomings. It seems his address is drawing to its predictable close. But talking of the Presidency reminds him of something else. The man chosen to succeed him was Edward Forbes, a young and brilliant naturalist, universally admired – 'But, alas! Death reigns.' News of Forbes's sudden death at the age of thirty-nine has just reached him. And so Miller surges again into the theme of death, and when he finally comes to an end it is with a sombre reminder to his listeners, 'that to each and all that "night cometh" at an uncertain hour, under whose dense and unbroken shadow "no man can work".'[29]

A few months later, on Christmas Eve, 1856, Hugh Miller shot himself. His friends and relatives who attended the inquest were at pains to prove (as with all Victorian suicides) that he was suffering temporary insanity. His doctor gave evidence that he had been suffering from 'head-symptoms' recently, for which he had prescribed a haircut.[30] His wife recounted how he had become obsessed with a fear of burglars and had planted a man-trap (a humane one – that caught the felon without injuring him) in front of the house and had slept with firearms at his pillow. In the last few nights he had suffered terrible dreams, and believed that he had walked in his sleep. In the mornings he would examine his clothes feverishly to see if they bore signs of his supposed nocturnal wanderings. And the note that he left for his much-loved wife before he pulled up his heavy sweater and shot himself through the chest was conclusive:

> Dearest Lydia, My brain burns. I *must* have *walked*; and a fearful dream rises upon me. I cannot bear the horrible thought. God and Father of the Lord Jesus Christ, have mercy upon me. Dearest Lydia, dear children, farewell. My brain burns as the recollection grows. My dear, dear wife, farewell.[31]

The inquest gave the necessary verdict of temporary insanity and Hugh Miller's body received Christian burial. The book that he had just completed, *The Testimony of the Rocks*, was published and duly praised by all the critics. Dickens, Carlyle and Ruskin wrote notes of condolence to the widow. But to the great mass of the general public, Hugh Miller's suicide effectively annihilated all the laborious arguments of his books. He had tried to teach that geology was safe, was respectable, was reconcilable with Christianity, and in his lifetime he had succeeded. But his suicide swept all those lessons away. It proved, on the contrary, that geology was just as dangerous as laymen had always suspected: if *this* was the fate of the Christian geologist, people thought, better to shun the science altogether. Many a country parson and diligent mechanic who had taken up the geological hammer under the benign influence of *The Old Red Sandstone* put it away in dismay when he heard of Miller's end. And though Miller's books were still read for their delightful style, their influence was never to be important again. Within four years they were to be swept into irrelevance by the advent of Darwinism, and the problems of reconciling geology and Genesis were to seem puny indeed beside the insurmountable difficulty of accepting natural selection.

CHAPTER SEVENTEEN

A CASUALTY OF SCIENCE

IT IS VERY easy, and it is very wrong, to envisage the mid-nineteenth century battles about science and religion as taking place in the public arena between one group representing science and another group representing religion. Histories often unwittingly enhance this impression because they rely on written records, mainly from newspapers, which tend to align themselves with one side or the other. But for the great majority of Victorians, the conflict between science and religion was a *personal* one, fought out in their own consciences. Of course, they looked to their religious leaders for advice (and often failed to find it) but ultimately they had to decide for themselves whether to follow the intellectual persuasions of science or the spiritual promptings of faith. And because this was for most people a private matter, we have very few records of what it entailed, although there are occasional hints, like Sir Leslie Stephen's remark that he became an atheist as a result of reading the *Origin of Species*, which suggest the spiritual crisis that every Christian believer must have suffered to some degree in the middle years of the nineteenth century. There is, however, one very full record of one man's experience in these years – Philip Gosse's – which, although it cannot be taken as absolutely typical, serves as a useful reminder that the decisions people came to on scientific issues were ones that affected not only their belief, but the day-to-day conduct of their lives.

Gosse's life is unusually well documented, partly through the autobiographical details given in some of his own published works, but largely through the two biographies written by his son Edmund Gosse: the 'public' or official *Life of Philip Henry Gosse* of 1890, and the private, anonymously published *Father and Son* of 1907. Both books are written with apparent fairness and quite startling candour by the standards of their day. It is only when we turn to Philip Gosse's own writings and illustrations that we suspect that Edmund Gosse has not told the whole story – that his father had a charm, a *joie de vivre* and a sense of poetry which are entirely missing from the portrait of the joyless Puritan father in *Father and Son*.

Philip Henry Gosse was born in 1810, the son of an itinerant miniature-painter, and raised in a state of 'reputable subgentility' in Poole, Dorset.[1] The family funds were insufficient to keep him at school after the age of fourteen, and he was apprenticed as a counting-house clerk. At seventeen he was packed off on a six-year clerical indentureship to the port of Carbonear, Newfoundland, where life was dominated by the annual despatch and return of the seal- and cod-fishing fleets, and harried by packs of wild dogs and even wilder Irishmen. His first few years there were uneventful enough but in 1832, his son records, 'Philip Gosse, suddenly and consciously, became a naturalist and a Christian.'[2]

The occasion of the former was his purchase, at auction, of Adams's *Essays on the Microscope* which made him resolve to collect insects. The occasion of the latter was news from England that his only sister Elizabeth was critically ill. As he anxiously awaited his passage home, he made a private vow that if God would spare his sister's life, he, Philip Gosse, would live the rest of his life as an active Christian. He carried out this vow, as we shall see, and when he returned to England he found his sister fully recovered. He was then free to devote all his holiday to entomology and he made the acquaintance of a local amateur, Samuel Harrison, who agreed to supply him with notes and references on his return to Newfoundland, in exchange for specimens. Such an arrangement was crucial to Gosse because he had no access to books or libraries in Carbonear.

He returned to Newfoundland in late 1832 bursting with enthusiasm to pin every native bug and butterfly, and by the end of the next year was able to record in his diary, 'One year of my entomological researches in this country has passed away. It has been to me a pleasant and a profitable one.'[3] Newfoundland insect-life was sufficiently intriguing to keep him in the country for a further two years after his indentureship was completed, but by late 1834 he had virtually exhausted the entomology of Newfoundland and decided to move to Canada with some friends, the Jaqueses, to try an experiment in communal farming. He wrote to his younger brother in England encouraging him to join him: 'We would have all things common; we could entomologize together in the noble forest, and, in the peaceful and happy pursuits of agriculture, forget the toils and anxieties of commerce ... I have learned to stuff birds, and there are beauties in Canada. We could make a nice museum.'[4]

But the experiment failed. The farm proved infertile, the Jaqueses quarrelsome, and the Utopian dream a nightmare of profitless drudgery. By November 1837 Gosse was writing to his sister, 'Could any employment be obtained at home? I am tired of more than ten years' exile, far from friends and kindred.'[5] Yet there was one substantial consolation. In the dreary winter of 1835–6 he had written up his Newfoundland notes into a book, 'The Entomology of Newfoundland' and he was now at work on journals which would be published as *The Canadian Naturalist*. He was elected a corresponding member of the Quebec and Montreal Natural History Societies, and his little insect cabinet was full to overflowing. Although, as his son remarked in the *Life*, 'He was twenty-eight years of age, and he was not possessed, when all his property was told, of so many pounds',[6] he had at last acquired an interest, a direction in life.

In March 1838 he sold up his share of the farm and moved southwards to the States. The journey was tragic for him because as the carriage rumbled along he watched his little insect cabinet being shaken to pieces, but in Philadelphia he met Titian Peale, Thomas Nuttall and many other stalwarts of the Academy of Natural Science. He made pilgrimages to the house and haunts of Alexander Wilson, and even met an old man who claimed to have known the great ornithologist a quarter of a century before. But there was no work in Philadelphia and he moved on southwards till he found a job as a village schoolmaster in Alabama. Here the loneliness of his life seems to have provoked some kind of nervous crisis, and the last day of 1838 found him at Mobile, awaiting a passage back to England. His twelve years' exile was over, and his career was just beginning, for, on the five weeks' voyage home, he wrote the text of *The Canadian Naturalist* from his notes.

The book was accepted by Van Voorst, who specialized in scientific works, and published to respectable acclaim in February 1840. It is the least readable of Gosse's books, being written in the form of a pseudo-dialogue between father and son, and its sales were not substantial enough to tempt Gosse into writing full-time. Instead, he spent the next three years as a schoolmaster in Hackney. It was only by chance that in 1843 the Society for Promoting Christian Knowledge heard of him through Van Voorst and commissioned him to write a popular *Introduction to Zoology*. At first he was reluctant, feeling himself inadequate to the task, but his timidity soon gave way to enthusiasm, and he completed the two volumes to the S.P.C.K.'s satisfaction in less than a year. His researches took him frequently to the British Museum Natural History Department where, for the first time, he began meeting other naturalists and contributing to scientific periodicals. One of his new confrères, J.W. Whymper, suggested he write a book on the new marine fauna recently discovered by Sir James Ross's expedition to the Pacific, and the result, *The Ocean*, was published by the S.P.C.K. in 1845.

The success of this book amazed even its publishers: it went through countless editions and was still being reissued in the 1880s. In America it was published as *Mysteries* (later *Wonders*) *of the Great Deep* and proved equally durable. Part of the attraction lay in the copious illustrations, engraved by Whymper from drawings by Gosse, and in its relaxed and readable style. But Gosse was not in England to enjoy his sudden success. Early in 1844 his friends in the British Museum had suggested that Jamaica was virgin ground for the entomologist and badly needed a collector. Hugh Cuming, the shell-collector and dealer, offered to pay his expenses in return for shells, and by October 1844 Gosse was on his way to the tropics. In Jamaica he found

> ... birds, insects, flowers, trees, the tone of the whole, the sunlight, the suffused sky, the balmy atmosphere, the variety of the foliage, the massive light and shadow, the dark, deep openings in the forest, all new, rich, and strange;

– not only new individually, but quite new and strange in character, quite unlike anything that I had seen before ... I gazed around, bewildered and entranced, almost, with the variety of charming objects, all at once appealing for attention; the remembrance of which, protracted as it was through eighteen months' duration, with scarcely any abatement, has given in my habitual feelings, a kind of paradisaical association with lovely Jamaica.[7]

He recorded this paradise in three books: *A Naturalist's Sojourn in Jamaica* (1851), *Birds of Jamaica* (1847) and the separately published *Illustrations of the Birds of Jamaica* (1849). The *Sojourn* was a popular success – it is a truly delightful book and marks the beginning of Gosse's mature style – and the *Birds* and *Illustrations* made his reputation among serious ornithologists. On his return to England, he was elected a member of the Microscopical Society and the Linnean, and at last settled into the career of a professional natural history writer. He was now thirty-six, and, as his son records,

From a belated youth he had slipped rather suddenly into premature middle age ... He was under middle size; slight, and almost slim, when he had left England, he returned from Jamaica thick-set and heavy-limbed, troubled

Sea-serpent from Gosse's *The Romance of Natural History*

with a corpulence that was not quite healthy. His face was large and massive, extremely pallid, with great strength in the chin, and long, tightly compressed lips; decidedly grim in expression, but lighted up by hazel eyes of extraordinary size and fulness... His smile was rare, but when it came it was exquisite.[8]

The return to England was followed by important changes in Gosse's personal, as well as his professional, life. Hitherto, in Canada, in England and in Jamaica, he had worshipped with the Wesleyans, and had even at one point applied to become a Wesleyan minister but had been turned down on grounds of age. Now, however, in 1847, he met some members of a recently formed group known to outsiders (though it was not a name they used themselves) as the Plymouth Brethren. In their total rejection of all ritual, ministers and hierarchy, their utter dependence on the self-interpreted text of Holy Writ, he recognized the sort of primitive Christianity he had long been seeking, and immediately committed himself to the sect. The next year he married Emily Bowes, a fellow-member of the Brethren, and writer of numerous gospel tracts. Their only son, Edmund, was born in 1849 and Philip Gosse recorded the event in his diary thus: 'E. delivered of a son. Received green swallow from Jamaica.'[9]

The next decade was almost unbelievably prolific. Edmund Gosse recalls how his father was 'for ever in his study, writing, drawing, dissecting; sitting, no doubt, as I grew afterwards accustomed to see him, absolutely motionless, with his eye glued to the microscope, for twenty minutes at a time.'[10] His labours resulted in a five-volume popular *Natural History* for the S.P.C.K., a *Textbook of Zoology for Schools*, a *Popular British Ornithology*, a *Manual of Marine Zoology for the British Isles* and also in the more informal and delightful works, *A Naturalist's Rambles on the Devonshire Coast* (1853), *Seaside Pleasure* (1853), *The Aquarium* (1854), *Tenby: a Sea-side Holiday* (1856), *Evenings at the Microscope* (1859) and *The Romance of Natural History* (1860).

It is in these latter books that his special charms emerge. He has a relaxed quality, a willingness to stop and enthuse about the particular glories of a particular view or a particular Spring day, and a really astonishing ability to describe the minutest things vividly and dramatically. Edmund Gosse complained that his father 'saw everything through a lens, nothing in the immensity of nature'[11] but for most readers it is precisely this lens-eye view that makes Gosse so appealing. Through his lens we make the acquaintance of the *Stephanoceros* whose 'small pear-shaped body, with rich green and brown hues glowing beneath a glistening surface, is lightly perched on a tapering stalk, and crowned with a diadem of the daintiest plumes; while the whole is set in a clouded crystal vase of quaint shape and delicate texture.'[12] Through Gosse's lens, the small barnacles and sea-anemones, soldier crabs and Aesop's prawns of the rock-pool become gorgeously attired heroes, colossi, in their busy, brightly coloured underwater world. We see him at his happiest on the sea-shore, poking along the tide-line or clambering into rock-pools, dressed in his rusty black suit and wide-awake hat, cluttered with baskets, collecting jars and hammers (for, as he frequently warns in his books, you must never dislodge the seaweed from its base but always chip off a piece of the rock to which it is anchored), stooping, probing, watching, waiting and finally gathering up a few select specimens to add to his marvellous new invention – the aquarium – at home. He makes even the modern reader share this excitement, and it was very largely thanks to Gosse that the Victorian middle classes suddenly took to the rock-pools at the middle of the century.

Not only could Gosse describe the wonderful things he saw through his lens, but he could also paint them exquisitely in glowing illustrations. His skill in microscopic accuracy was no doubt inherited, if not learnt, from his father the miniaturist, and his feeling for warm, sensuous colour was probably liberated by his work on the Jamaican birds. When Victorian readers first saw the almost Fauvist pinks, greens and mauves of his rock-pool illustrations they were apparently incredulous that anything so exotic could exist on the drab British sea-shore – they had only seen *dead* seaweed and *dead* sea-anemones – but a glance into one of the new aquaria would confirm that Gosse was right. And Gosse was one of the first popular natural history writers to offer colour illustrations in a book priced for the mass market. He tried it first in *A Naturalist's Rambles on the Devonshire Coast* but was disappointed at the discrepancy between his own water-colour originals and the printed results, so for his next book, *The Aquarium* (1854), he supervised every stage in the colour printing process himself and learned to make his own drawings on the lithographic stone. The result is a superb example of early chromolithography – it is almost impossible to believe that the plates are not hand-coloured – and it is not surprising that the book was an immediate bestseller. So, too, were most of his subsequent books. *The Romance of Natural History*, for instance, went into at least thirteen editions spanning thirty years. And while producing almost annual bestsellers, Gosse still continued with serious scientific research. In 1856 he was elected Fellow of the Royal Society, and from 1858 to 1860 he published his important study of the *Actinologia Britannica*, the British sea-anemones and corals.

However, Gosse's career was not to continue in unabated triumph. We have already mentioned that he became a member of the Plymouth Brethren, and in *Father and Son* we see exactly what this meant for the family's daily life. Endless prayers, a complete ban on fiction, poetry, theatre-going and secular song, no social life outside the brotherhood, and the need to 'testify' loudly, publicly and often to the redemptive power of the Blood of the Lamb. The testifying is occasionally apparent in Gosse's books – in *The Aquarium*, for instance, where he suddenly whisks us from the rock-pool to the celestial regions by comparing the bristle arrangement on the foot-jaw of the Hairy Broad-Claw crab to 'the Gospel net, mentioned by our Lord, which is "cast into the sea and gathers of every kind; which, when it is full, they draw to shore, and sit down, and gather the good into vessels, but cast the bad away."' This leads into the sermon: 'Persons of all sorts are gathered into the Church here on earth; it is an indiscriminate collection that

Philip and Edmund Gosse, 1857

determines nothing as to the eternal conditions of those who are embraced by it: the selection is to be made "at the end of the age", when it will be found that not every one that saith Lord, Lord! shall enter into the kingdom of heaven. May both the writer and the reader be robed in the righteousness of Christ, that "wedding garment", without which the Christian name and profession will bring only a deeper condemnation!'[13]

It is rare in fact to find a popular natural history book of the period *without* some sort of pious interjections, and Gosse's are only slightly more frequent and fervent than most. There was another element in being a Plymouth Brother, however, which affected not only Gosse's writing, but ultimately his whole career. Like many dissenting sects, but even more so than most, the Plymouth Brethren relied heavily, almost exclusively, on the literal truth of the Bible. They read it as a statement of fact. And hence when Philip Gosse began to follow the implications of the new geological discoveries, particularly the fossil evidence which suggested a much greater antiquity of the Earth than the Book of Genesis allowed, he faced a crisis of conscience. It is this crisis which Edmund Gosse describes so vividly in *Father and Son*. His account errs, perhaps, in attributing too much to Darwinism and too little to the Lyellian controversy about the age of the Earth, but whatever the exact precipitating factor, the crisis is one which many serious-minded Victorians must have shared to some degree. It is therefore worth giving Edmund Gosse's account at length:

So, through my Father's brain, in that year of scientific crisis, 1857, there rushed two kinds of thought, each absorbing, each convincing, yet totally irreconcilable. There is a peculiar agony in the paradox that truth has two forms, each of them indisputable, yet each antagonistic to the other. It was this discovery, that there were two theories of physical life, each of which was true, but the truth of each incompatible with the truth of the other, which shook the spirit of my Father with perturbation. It was not, really, a paradox, it was a fallacy, if he could only have known it, but he allowed the turbid volume of superstition to drown the delicate stream of reason. He took one step in the service of truth, and then he drew back in an agony, and accepted the servitude of error ...

In this period of intellectual ferment, as when a great political revolution is being planned, many possible adherents were confidentially tested with hints and encouraged to reveal their bias in a whisper. It was the notion of Lyell, himself a great mover of men, that, before the doctrine of natural selection was given to a world which would be sure to lift up at it a howl of execration, a certain body-guard of sound and experienced naturalists, expert in the description of species, should be privately made aware of its tenour. Among those who were thus initiated, or approached with a view towards possible illumination, was my Father. He was spoken to by Hooker, and later on by Darwin, after meetings of the Royal Society in the summer of 1857.

My Father's attitude towards the theory of natural selection was critical in his career, and oddly enough, it exercised an immense influence on my own experience as a child. Let it be admitted at once, mournful as the admission is, that every instinct in his intelligence went out at first to greet the new light. It had hardly done so, when a recollection of the opening chapter of Genesis checked it at the outset. He consulted with Carpenter [William Carpenter, the physiologist and naturalist], a great investigator, but one who was fully as incapable as himself of remodelling his ideas with regard to the old, accepted hypotheses. They both determined, on various grounds, to have nothing to do with the terrible theory, but to hold steadily to the law of the fixity of species. It was exactly at this juncture that we left London, and the slight and occasional, but always extremely salutary personal intercourse with men of scientific leading which my Father had enjoyed at the British Museum and at the Royal Society came to an end. His next act was to burn his ships, down to the last beam and log out of which a raft could have been made.

By a strange act of wilfulness, he closed the doors upon himself for ever.[14]

The 'strange act of wilfulness' was the publication, in 1857, of his *Omphalos: An Attempt to Untie the Geological Knot*. It was Gosse's contribution to the continuing quest for a reconciliation between Genesis and geology. But it was a contribution which even the most ardent reconcilers found difficult to accept, and Edmund Gosse merely reflected the general view when he called it 'this curious, this obstinate, this fanatical volume'.[15] On the question of the mutability of species, Gosse was painfully explicit:

> I assume that each organism which the Creator educed was stamped with an indelible specific character, which made it what it was, and distinguished it from everything else, however near or like. I assume that such character has been, and is, indelible and immutable; that the characters which distinguish species from species *now*, were as definite at the first instant of their creation as now, and are as distinct now as they were then. If any choose to maintain, as many do, that species were gradually brought to their present maturity from humbler forms, – whether by the force of appetency in individuals, or by progressive development in generations – he is welcome to his hypothesis, but I have nothing to do with it. These pages will not touch him.[16]

So much for evolution. But it is Gosse's attempt to untie the geological knot which dominates the book and gives it its curious and fanatical flavour. His solution is a theory of his own which he calls 'prochronism'. Nature is cyclical, he argues – the chicken produces the egg that produces the chicken – and the Act of Creation must necessarily have interrupted this cycle at some point. But if we look at a chicken, we imagine the egg that hatched it, or if we look at an egg, we imagine the hen that laid it: every organism carries evidence of an *implied* past. However, if the chicken we are looking at happened to have been created by God just a minute ago, its implied past – the putative egg from which it hatched – is prochronic, i.e. outside Time.

The full madness of prochronism is not unleashed until the very end of the book. Gosse devotes many long and tedious chapters to illustrating the familiar thesis that Nature is cyclical and that most living organisms display visible evidence of their own past. For three hundred pages, he plods steadily through tree-rings and tortoise-shells and horse's teeth, and the reader is lulled into the belief that *Omphalos* is merely an exceptionally dull exposition of a lot of quite unexceptionable facts. Only then does Gosse embark on his wild surmise. Fossils, he says, are the exact equivalent of the tree-rings in the trees in the Garden of Eden, or of Adam's navel. They are prochronic. They are evidence put in the Earth by the Creator to *suggest* that the Earth had a prior history, when in fact it did not. God created the world in six days in the year 4004 B.C. as the Book of Genesis

Philip Gosse in retirement

says, but He implanted it with fossils to make it *seem* older and to confuse later geologists. 'Who will say,' Gosse thunders on page 347, 'who will dare to say that such a suggestion is a self-evident absurdity?'[17]

Of course every single reviewer dared say it. Even his friends dared say it. The Rev. Charles Kingsley, himself a rock-pool enthusiast and an old intimate of Gosse's, was forced to write to him that he could not 'give up the painful and slow conclusion of five and twenty years' study of geology, and believe that God has written on the rocks one enormous and superfluous lie.'[18] And later he made the rejection public by adding a footnote to his *Glaucus* in which he said:

> It is with real pain that I have seen my friend Mr. Gosse, make a step in the direction of obscurantism, which I can only call desperate, by publishing a book called *Omphalos*. In it he tries to vindicate what he thinks (though very few good Christians do so now) to be the teaching of Scripture about Creation by the supposition that fossils are not the remains of plants and animals which have actually existed, but may have been created as they are, for the satisfaction of the Divine mind; and that therefore the whole science, not only of palaeontology, but (as he seems to forget) of geognosy also is based on a mistake, and cannot truly exist, save as a play of the fancy. It seems to me that such a notion is more likely to make infidels than to cure them. For what rational man, who knows even a little of geology, will not be tempted to say – If Scripture can only be vindicated by such an outrage to common sense and fact, then I will give up Scripture, and stand by common sense.[19]

Poor Gosse! His son records the utter dejection that followed.

> In the course of that dismal winter, as the post began to bring in private letters, few and chilly, and public reviews, many and scornful, my Father looked in vain for the approval of the churches, and in vain for the acquiescence of the scientific societies, and in vain for the gratitude of those 'thousands of thinking persons' which he had rashly assured himself of receiving ... A gloom, cold and dismal, descended upon our morning teacups. It was what the poets mean by an 'inspissated' gloom; it thickened day by day, as hope and self-confidence evaporated in thin clouds of disappointment. My Father was not prepared for such a fate. He had been the spoiled darling of the public, the constant favourite of the press, and now, like the dark angels of old,
>
> > so huge a rout
> > Encumbered him with ruin.
>
> He could not recover from amazement at having offended everybody by an enterprise which had been undertaken in the cause of universal reconciliation.[20]

Gosse continued with his *Actinologia* and took refuge in *The Romance of Natural History* – a great success because it included a long section on sea-serpents, an obsession with the Victorians – but after 1860 and the ascendancy of Darwinism, his enthusiasm for natural history seems to have waned. His last popular natural history book was *A Year at the Shore*, published in 1865. From then on his pen was turned to tracts – 'The Revelation: How Is It To Be Interpreted?'; 'The

High Numbers of the Pentateuch: Are They Trustworthy?'; 'The Antichrist: Who or What Is He?' He became mildly interested in coloured stars – no vexed question of species among those natural bodies – and buried himself in the Rotifera or wheel-animalcules. Ironically, he even took up Darwin's favourite hobby, cultivating orchids, and exchanged some quite friendly correspondence with the infidel on the problems of fertilizing *Stanhopea oculata*.[21]

Gosse died in 1888, respected, respectable, but far outstripped by the scientific luminaries of his own generation. He had been in virtual retirement for a quarter of a century. Edmund Gosse recounts in *Father and Son*, how, once, his wife urged him to rejoin the main current:

> My mother wished him to give lectures, to go to London, to read papers before the Royal Society, to enter into controversy with foreign *savants*, to conduct classes of out-door zoology at fashionable watering-places. I held my breath with admiration as she poured forth her scheme, so daring, so brilliant, so sure to cover our great man with glory. He listened to her with an ambiguous smile, and shook his head at us, and resumed the reading of his Bible.[22]

Philip Henry Gosse

CHAPTER EIGHTEEN

CONFESSING A MURDER

ARWIN, AS WE have seen, was not by any means the first person to produce a theory of evolution. The question then arises: why was he, a comparatively unknown amateur, able to win acceptance for the theory when so many of his predecessors had failed? First, because he gave the theory a new ingredient, natural selection, which explained the mechanism by which evolution could have occurred. It is this contribution to the theory which was uniquely Darwin's, and it is this that is usually meant by the term 'Darwinism'. Secondly, Darwin supported the idea of evolution with a greater body of facts than any of his predecessors had ever accumulated. He researched the *Origin of Species* for over twenty years, and when he did finally produce the 500-page opus he still thought of it as a mere abstract of his ideas, a foretaste of the far larger book he had yet to write. He published some parts of this larger book later on – *The Variation of Animals and Plants under Domestication* (1867), *The Descent of Man* (1871) and *The Effects of Cross- and Self-Fertilisation in the Vegetable Kingdom* (1876) – but the stunned public on whom the *Origin* burst in 1859 were not disposed to complain that Darwin had written too sketchily or without sufficient research. On the contrary, they could only marvel at the extraordinary amount of factual detail which he had crammed into his tightly written argument.
As one commentator remarked, 'It was never possible to guess what amount of evidence Mr. Darwin had in reserve behind the few words which marked a mere step in an argument,'[1] but those critics who did try to test Darwin on points of detail usually found that he could support every least assertion with a hundred more facts from his notebooks for which he had not found space in the published book. It was not only that his knowledge went so deep, but that it ranged so wide. Darwin seemed equally at home in geology, palaeontology, botany, zoology, comparative anatomy, embryology, or any other branch of natural history one cared to name. Most professional scientists by this period were forced to specialize, and very few of them could match Darwin's eclecticism. In consequence, very few

felt competent to criticize the *Origin* as a whole because large sections of it were outside their province.

Darwin's thoroughness was not simply a useful deterrent to criticism; it was absolutely essential to the success of the book. For the *Origin of Species* marked, not only a revolution in scientific ideas, but a revolution in scientific *method* and an extension of its domain into areas previously reserved to theology. Darwin needed to show that every living organism could be explained as a product of evolution working through natural selection, because if he left one single gap in the chain of cause-and-effect, he could be quite sure that the theologians would fill it, as they always did, with special creations and miraculous occurrences. He had already seen, in the field of geology, how, once you admitted one supernatural event, like a Cuvierian catastrophe, you were liable to end up with twenty or thirty. Wherever science failed, religion stepped in, welcoming lacunae in knowledge as evidence of divine intervention. But Darwin believed that supernatural explanations were not explanations at all, and that true science consisted in closing all the gaps. He *was* thorough and he *did* close the gaps, and the theologians were duly outraged. 'Their [the Darwinians'] whole occupation is to trace every fact to some immediate antecedent cause,' complained the *Patriot* newspaper, 'and they are so anxious to establish regularity of sequence and uniformity of law, that they cannot bear the idea of the Creator stepping in.'[2] That is precisely what Darwin was about, and although he did not set out to write the *Origin* with the aim of attacking religion, he found in the end that the pursuit of true science was inimical to the cause of true religion.

And *because* Darwin's book was anti-religious in effect, the character of its author became of crucial significance. Had Darwin been a known atheist, an immoralist, a drunkard, a sensationalist, a fortune-seeker, or even a mild eccentric like his grandfather, his book could have been dismissed whatever its intrinsic merits. (Anyone who doubts this is referred to the case of Wallace, who put forward the same ideas as Darwin but was dismissed as a crank because he also happened to be addicted to spiritualism.) Darwin, however, was a very pillar of Victorian respectability. Happily married, neatly dressed, of independent income, quiet in his habits, abstemious, an invalid – even those Victorians who hated the *Origin* could not find any fault with its author. Even Philip Gosse, when he met Darwin, 'was captivated at once, as all who met him were, by the simplicity, frankness, and cordiality of this great and charming man.'[3] Published tributes to Darwin's character often read like hagiography. 'Whatever is great and whatever is beautiful in human nature,' wrote Romanes, 'found in him so luxuriant a development, that no place or chance was left for any other growth, and in the result we beheld a magnificence which, unless actually realised, we should scarcely have been able to imagine.'[4]

One is slightly surprised on turning to Darwin's *Autobiography* to find that his remarks about his friends are judicious rather than affectionate, and the character that emerges is a cold one. But Darwin wrote the *Autobiography* in his late sixties when, as he felt and regretted himself, certain parts of his personality had shrivelled. 'My mind seems to have become a kind of machine for grinding general laws out of large collections of facts,'[5] he lamented. In any case, his warmth or lack of it, had no bearing on the reception of the *Origin*. For that, it was his probity that mattered, and in that he was irreproachable. One cannot say that the Victorians accepted the theory of evolution because its author was known to be a good man, but one can certainly say that they would have rejected it if he had been known to be a bad man.

None of Darwin's later magnificence was apparent in his childhood. When he left school in 1825 he was considered a very ordinary boy of slightly below-average intelligence, and his father gloomily pronounced, 'You care for nothing but shooting, dogs and rat-catching, and you will be a disgrace to yourself and all your family.'[6] Shooting was indeed his consuming passion. 'I do not believe that any one could have shown more zeal for the most holy cause than I did for shooting birds,' he says in the *Autobiography*.[7] Natural history was a secondary interest at best. He enjoyed bird-watching, botanizing, and collecting stones and pebbles, but no more than any other schoolboy. At the age of ten, he 'almost' decided to start an entomological collection, but was deterred by a humane unwillingness to kill any insects.

In fact, he seems to have been quite destitute of any ambition, and it was his awe-inspiring (six foot two, twenty-four stone) father who decided he should become a doctor like himself. He was accordingly sent, in October 1825, to Edinburgh University, where he yawned his way through all the lectures, including Professor Jameson's on Geology and Zoology. Jameson had studied under Werner, the great Saxon geologist, and was considered one of the top British scientists of the day, but his lectures were so dull that Darwin recalled, 'The sole effect they produced on me was the determination never as long as I lived to read a book on geology or in any way to study the science.'[8] However, at Edinburgh Darwin attended meetings of the Wernerian Natural History Society, where he once heard Audubon lecture, and the Plinian, where he even delivered a paper himself on marine zoology. He talked natural history with MacGillivray, Audubon's collaborator, and with two competent zoologists, Drs Coldstream and Grant. It was the latter who one day surprised him by praising Lamarck, and stimulated him to re-read his grandfather's *Zoonomia* – though to little effect.

As an inevitable part of his medical training, Darwin attended two operations, both 'very bad' and one on a child. The memories haunted him for years and made him resolve never to attend another. Darwin thus joined that very large band of Victorian naturalists who opted out of medicine when they first encountered pre-anaesthetic surgery. One suspects that if chloroform had been invented a few decades earlier, nineteenth-century biology might have been considerably the poorer. At about the same time, Darwin deduced that his father would allow him an independent income, and this belief was, as he admitted, 'sufficient to check any strenuous effort to learn medicine.'[9]

Accordingly, his father took him away from Edinburgh and decided instead that his son should become a clergyman. Since we know from the *Autobiography* that Dr Darwin was a non-believer, this choice may perhaps seem surprising, but it was a conventional middle-class career and Charles was an apparently conventional young man. At any rate, it was better than becoming 'an idle sporting man'[10] which is what he seemed most disposed to do. Darwin asked for some time to consider the matter, read Pearson on the Creed, and found that he could subscribe to the requisite beliefs. As he remarked half a century later, 'It never struck me how illogical it was to say that I believed in what I could not understand and what is in fact unintelligible.'[11] This is one of the passages that was expurgated from published editions of the *Autobiography* until Lady Barlow's edition of 1958. Darwin did not, like Huxley, publicly declare himself to be an agnostic, and it was just as well for the success of the *Origin* that he did not. He even concealed the full extent of his apostasy from his immediate family. But in the expurgated passages of the *Autobiography* he described the gradual development of his disbelief and his eventual conclusion, 'I can indeed hardly see how anyone ought to wish Christianity to be true; for if so, the plain language of the text seems to show that the men who do not believe, and this would include my Father, Brother and almost all my best friends, will be everlastingly punished. And this is a damnable doctrine.'[12] But as a teenager he succumbed to his father's desire that he should train to be a clergyman.

The first step was to attend one of the English universities, and after some preliminary cramming, Darwin went up to Cambridge in 1828. He did sufficient work to gain a respectable B.A. three years later. His main preoccupation was still shooting, and he spent hours practising his aim in front of a mirror, but he also acquired a new passion – coleoptery – and recorded in the *Autobiography*: 'No poet ever felt more delight at seeing his first poem published than I did at seeing in Stephen's *Illustrations of British Insects* the magic words "captured by C. Darwin, Esq."'[13] At this stage it was still pure collecting mania, unaccompanied by any essays in dissection or even proper description, that consumed him. A far more important development was his friendship with J.S. Henslow, the Professor of Botany, which Darwin later said influenced his career more than any other. Henslow was his senior by thirteen years, a clergyman, and a scientist of international reputation, so Darwin must have begun to show *some* sort of promise to become known as 'the man who walks with Henslow'.[14] Henslow in turn introduced him to Adam Sedgwick, another clergyman, Professor of Geology and Fellow of the Royal Society, and Sedgwick too took Darwin seriously, inviting him to join him on a geological tour of Wales. Darwin found the tour instructive, but he nevertheless abandoned it at Capel Curig to reach his uncle's house in time for the shooting – 'For at that time I should have thought myself mad to give up the first days of partridge-shooting for geology or any other science.'[15]

When Darwin came down from Cambridge in 1831 he was still an essentially undistinguished young man with no clear sense of purpose in life. But through

Henslow's influence, he was shortly offered the post of unpaid naturalist on an expedition under Captain FitzRoy to survey the South American coast and circumnavigate the world. Even then he dithered, as his ever-influential father opposed the idea, and it was only the brisk action of his uncle Josiah Wedgwood that persuaded Charles to go and his father to agree. 'The voyage of the Beagle has been by far the most important event in my life and has determined my whole career,' Darwin said afterwards. 'I have always felt that I owe to the Voyage the first real training or education of my mind.'[16]

One can trace this education by reading Darwin's *Journal of Researches into the Natural History and Geology of the countries visited during the voyage of H.M.S.*

John Stevens Henslow

Beagle round the world, published in 1839. It is Darwin's most personal, and for the general reader his most enjoyable, book and he himself always felt a special affection for it. Parts of it, such as the account of the earthquake at Concepción, or the encounters with the natives on Tierra del Fuego, are gripping, but even more exciting is the insight it gives into the making of a scientist and of a scientific theory. The theory is not stated or even outlined in the *Journal*, but the observations which Darwin found so striking and which led ultimately to the *Origin of Species* are presented with a suggestive force that can hardly fail to impress the reader. It is like reading a detective story which gives all the clues but no dénouement.

Darwin's small cabin bookshelf on the *Beagle* contained, alongside Milton and the Bible, his brand new copy of Lyell's *Principles*, and as soon as the ship touched land, Darwin was eagerly away to test Lyell's theories. Suddenly geology was more exciting than gambling ('I often mentally cry out 3 to 1 tertiary against primitive'),[17] more exciting even than shooting. 'There is nothing like geology,' he wrote home to his sister Catherine; 'the pleasure of the first day's partridge shooting or the first day's hunting cannot be compared to finding a fine group of fossil bones, which tell their story of former times with almost a living tongue.'[18] And everything he saw only tended to confirm his belief in Lyell's Uniformitarianism. In Patagonia he was at first incredulous that its vast shingle and sedimentary beds could have been built up purely by gradual deposition – where could so many pebbles have come from? But then he climbed the Cordillera and saw its worn-down ravines and heard the rattle-rattle-rattle of countless thousands of pebbles tumbling down its mountain torrents and reflected that that rattle had gone on, day in, day out, for hundreds of thousands of years, and wondered instead how any mountains could survive such waste. 'It was like thinking on time ...' he wrote.[19]

He had accepted Lyell's *Principles* already on an intellectual level, but now he was applying those ideas to his own work, looking always for the present-day causes that could explain vast geological changes over eons of time. At Buenos Aires he listened to accounts of the recent great drought, which had been followed by a season of torrential rains. He heard how, during the drought, the animals had all congregated on the river-banks, predator and prey together, and how they eventually died there when the last trickle of water dried up. Soon afterwards, the rains came and churned the banks into morasses of mud, swallowing all the putrefying corpses together. 'What would be the opinion of a geologist,' he asked, 'viewing such an enormous collection of bones, of all kinds of animals and of all ages, thus embedded in one thick earthy mass? Would he not attribute it to a flood having swept over the surface of the land, rather than to the common order of things?'[20] But he, Darwin, now understood than no Noachian catastrophe was necessary: rather, that one bad drought followed by one heavy rainy season could

29 Starfishes, from *The Aquarium* by P. H. Gosse, 1854

30 *Cychla Argus*, from *Fishes of British Guiana* (part of *The Naturalist's Library* series), 1852

31 Victoria Regia water-lilies, from *Curtis's Botanical Magazine*, 1847

produce the necessary conditions for the formation of a fossil tomb that would look, to future geologists, like the death of an epoch.

At Keeling Island, Darwin applied the touchstone of 'the common order of things' to the question of coral islands. The coral-building polyp can live only in shallow water, and yet most of the coral atolls rise from a seabed hundreds of fathoms deep. How could this happen? Darwin noted that the structure of coral atolls was essentially identical to that of barrier reefs, except that they were not allied to any coastline. But was it not possible, he argued, that the atolls had once been barrier reefs surrounding islands, and that the islands – in fact, the whole Pacific seabed – had subsequently sunk, not suddenly in a great catastrophe, but inch by inch over the centuries? And as the seabed slowly sank, so the coral polyps slowly built, no longer basing their structures on the seabed itself, but adding layer on layer to their own reef to keep abreast of the gradually rising sea-level. Eventually, he postulated, the island that originally hosted them had sunk beneath the waves, but by then the coral ramparts were tall and massy enough to become islands in their own right – the characteristic ring-shaped atolls of the Pacific. Even Lyell was amazed when he read this explanation (he had thought that atolls were the coral-encrusted tips of submerged volcanic craters) but it was only his own Uniformitarianism applied to a new subject. Darwin's study of coral islands was his first major scientific publication after his return to England, and it served to establish his reputation among geologists.

For the first few months of the voyage, Darwin was entirely preoccupied with geology, but by the time he reached Rio he had added a new interest. 'I am become quite devoted to Nat. History,' he wrote home; 'you cannot imagine what a fine miserlike pleasure I enjoy when examining an animal differing widely from any known genus.'[21] He packed up 1,500 specimens in spirits of wine. But Darwin, unlike so many of his contemporaries, did not stop at the fine miserlike pleasure of species-gathering. He noticed as well how animals lived, what they fed on, and how they behaved. Most importantly, he noticed *where* they lived. The facts he collected on the geographical distribution of species were to provide some of the most telling evidence for the *Origin*.

We are now so used to thinking in evolutionary terms that we take it for granted that every continent has its own characteristic species, but this was an awkward and indigestible fact in the first half of the nineteenth century. If one believed that species were specially created, one would expect to find identical species wherever the soil, climate and other environmental conditions were similar. Every warm grassy plain should have its zebra, and every cold mountain-top its chamois. Similarly, if one believed that *fossil* species had also been specially created, and later annihilated by a catastrophe, there was no particular reason why the fossils found in one region should resemble the living inhabitants of that region more than any other. There was supposed to be no genealogical connection between them: God had wiped the slate clean.

As the *Beagle* sailed slowly round the world, Darwin collected all the data he could on the distribution of species, both extinct and extant. Quite early on, at Punta Alta in Argentina, he found a great tomb of fossil bones in a low gravel bank on the beach, including parts of a megatherium, megalonyx, scedlidotherium, toxodon, mylodon and macrauchenia. What struck him about these fossils was that they were all giant versions of animals currently existing on, and unique to, the South American continent. There was a giant sloth, a giant armadillo and a giant guanaco, all clearly related to their smaller modern counterparts, and all unique to that region. 'This wonderful relationship in the same continent between the dead and the living, will, I do not doubt, hereafter throw more light on the appearance of organic beings on our earth, and their disappearance from it, than any other class of facts,'[22] Darwin promised in the *Journal*.

Yet it was the living inhabitants of the Galapagos Islands that provided his most startling evidence. He arrived at those black, treeless volcanic domes in September 1835 and soon met their most conspicuous fauna, the giant tortoises. They

Galapagan tortoises from Brehm's *Thierleben*, 1877

lumbered among the cacti and leafless shrubs, pounding well-beaten tracks across the black basaltic lava. It was an ecology dominated by reptiles where, as Herman Melville later remarked, 'the chief sound of life is a hiss'. To find a similar ecology one had to go back in geological time to the Secondary epochs when giant saurians roamed the Earth. The ubiquitous volcanic domes and craters, the well-marked boundaries of the lava streams, showed that the Galapagos had only recently been thrown up from the seabed – 'Hence, both in space and time, we seem to be brought somewhat near to that great fact – that mystery of mysteries – the first appearance of new beings on this earth.'[23]

The first observation Darwin made was that almost all the Galapagan animals and at least half its plants were unique species, found nowhere else in the world. This was sufficiently surprising, but even more so was their obvious resemblance to South American species. Of course, the Galapagos Islands were *near* South America, but their soil and climate were quite different; according to the special creation theory there was no reason why one group of species should resemble another simply because they happened to inhabit neighbouring areas. In the *Journal* Darwin did not attempt any explanation, but continued with his findings on the finches – thirteen species unique to the Galapagos with beaks ranging from hawfinch down to warbler size, and eating habits varying accordingly. 'Seeing this gradation and diversity of structure in one small, intimately related group of birds, one might really fancy', Darwin remarked innocently in the *Journal*, 'that from an original paucity of birds in this archipelago, one species had been taken and modified for different ends.'[24] It is obvious at this point, if not before, that the *Origin of Species* was already germinating.

Finally, just as the *Beagle* was about to sail and leave the Galapagos Islands for ever, Darwin discovered the most significant fact of all. The Vice-Governor had remarked casually one day that he could tell at a glance which island any given tortoise came from, but Darwin had not paid sufficient attention, and had gone on labelling his specimens indiscriminately 'Galapagos'. Then suddenly it struck him. Many of the indigenous species were not just unique to the Galapagos group but actually unique to one particular island in that group, even though the islands were tiny and nowhere more than fifty or sixty miles apart! In his last few hours ashore, Darwin frantically collected evidence. He was too late to sort out the finches, which he had jumbled irretrievably together, but he had just time to recheck the mocking-thrushes and find that, yes indeed, one species was unique to Charles Island, one to Albemarle, and one to James and Chatham. Fortunately, he had labelled his plants precisely, and here his results were quite conclusive. Of the thirty-eight exclusively Galapagan species found on James Island, no fewer than thirty were unique to that one island; on Albemarle twenty-two out of twenty-six species were unique and on Chatham twelve out of sixteen. He accounted for this by noting that the islands were separated by deep, fast sea-channels and were almost entirely free from wind, so that seeds could not be dispersed from one island to the next. Nevertheless, as he remarked in the *Journal*, 'One is astonished at the amount of creative force, if such an expression may be used, displayed on these small, barren, and rocky islands; and still more so, at its diverse yet analogous action on points so near each other.'[25]

'Creative force' – the term is deliberately vague. If his readers wanted to imagine a God so thriftlessly prolific that He had invented separate species for each of these tiny barren insignificant islands in the middle of nowhere, Darwin was not yet ready to disabuse them, but he was already thinking in terms of evolution. The creative force *he* was astonished by was the power of variations to diverge and evolve into new species, but it was to be another quarter of a century before he dared to say so.

When Darwin returned to England in October 1836, his friends immediately noticed a change in his character, and his father exclaimed, 'Why, the shape of his head is quite altered!'[26] Darwin was still young (twenty-seven), sociable, high-spirited, but now he had a serious purpose in life and he preferred studying even to shooting. He was delighted to find that eminent scientists, including Lyell, were as eager to meet him as he was to meet them. Henslow had read some of his letters to the Cambridge Philosophical Society, and the Punta Alta fossils had made a great stir among palaeontologists. Darwin was invited to join the Geological Society, and soon became its Secretary. He was welcomed into London scientific circles as an able and promising young naturalist of whom much might be expected.

The facts which had so much struck him on the *Beagle* voyage clamoured to be explained, and the summer after his return he opened his first notebook on 'the species question'. But many more distractions were to be endured before he could throw himself wholly into this work. First, he had to write up his *Beagle* journal for publication, and prepare his thesis on coral islands. Then in 1838 a more personal distraction intervened. Looking round his cold, cheerless London rooms one evening, he coolly weighed up the advantages and disadvantages of marriage, listing among the former 'children (if it please God) – constant companion (& friend in old age) – charms of music & female chit-chat', and among the latter, 'terrible loss of time'. Nevertheless with his strong domestic instincts, the charms of children and chit-chat prevailed over the risk of time-wasting, and he concluded, 'Marry, marry, marry, Q.E.D.'[27] Having thus decided to marry, it only remained to find a wife, and fortunately there was one already to hand – his cousin Emma Wedgwood, whom his family had always intended for him. She was his age (thirty), musical, attractive, and as sensible and plain-spoken as himself. (Once asked whether she liked Tennyson's *Queen Mary*, she replied devastatingly, 'It is not nearly so tiresome as Shakespeare.')[28] Darwin proposed and was surprised to find himself accepted. They married in January 1839 and by the end of that year had produced the first of their ten children. In 1842, to make their domestic bliss complete,.they moved to Down House in Kent,[29] where they remained for the rest of their long lives. They both preferred the country, and it was supposed to be better for Darwin's health.

Darwin's health – or rather, his ill-health – is a mystery that will probably now never be resolved. During the *Beagle* years he was obviously as fit as anyone, with only the usual quota of fevers and stomach-upsets. But soon after his marriage he became an invalid and remained so until his death at the age of seventy-three. His symptoms included boils, eczema, fainting fits, headaches, arthritis, palpitations, catarrh, nausea, flatulence and insomnia. He claimed that he could never

Charles Darwin, 1847

write for more than twenty minutes without pain, and that visitors, long conversations and excitement only exacerbated his illness. Whether this illness was real or imaginary, it certainly had the convenient result of leaving him free to study, and soon after the move to Down he established that pattern of relentless and unremitting work that sustained him into his seventies.

During these research years, and despite his unsociable routine, Darwin none the less acquired that band of loyal friends who would prove so invaluable when the *Origin* storm broke. Lyell was the first of the group (Darwin dedicated his *Beagle* narrative to him) though Darwin became disappointed when Lyell refused to take a public stand on the species question, and, from the mid-1840s, turned increasingly to Joseph Dalton Hooker, the son of Sir William Hooker, the Director

Emma Darwin

of Kew Gardens, and an eminent botanist in his own right. Darwin pumped Hooker mercilessly to supply botanical data for the *Origin*, preparing great piles of question slips for him to answer whenever he visited Down. Another extremely useful friendship in this period, although Darwin neglects to mention it in the *Autobiography*, was that with Asa Gray, the American botanist. Botany was Darwin's weakest point, and Gray was an expert on the geographical distribution of plants. When the *Origin* came out, Gray acted as Darwin's American champion, against the overweening opposition of Agassiz, but he was not as pugnacious as Darwin could have wished (he was not a Huxley) and he also betrayed a rather irritating addiction to Christianity, which perhaps explains his exclusion from the *Autobiography*. A latecomer to this charmed circle, but eventually the most important, was Thomas Henry Huxley, Darwin's self-appointed 'bulldog'. Unlike the others, Huxley did not contribute any very important facts to the making of the *Origin*, but, once it was published, he devoted all his formidable powers to promoting it. We shall be meeting him again in the next chapter.

Meanwhile, the notebooks on species were growing into fat portfolios, but there was still one more distraction to be endured. In writing up the zoology of the *Beagle* collections, Darwin had found one barnacle which obstinately refused to be classified. The reason must be, as he reluctantly recognized, that the current classification of the cirripedia (barnacles) was wrong. And so he decided to re-

Darwin's study at Down House

arrange the genera slightly, which of course meant studying other barnacles. In the end, he spent eight years on the problem, analysing over 10,000 barnacles and reclassifying the whole order. Barnacles were so much a part of his life that one of his children, visiting a friend's house at this period, was heard to ask, 'But where does Mr. —— do his barnacles?'[30] Darwin later admitted that this long excursion into taxonomy had been wasted time, but in fact it gave him a necessary respectability among closet naturalists which proved useful in the post-*Origin* furore. He dated his own qualification as a 'thorough naturalist' from the barnacle work.

J. D. Hooker collecting plants in the Himalayas

Then at last he was free to concentrate on the species question, and sift the huge piles of notes he had accumulated over the years. 'I worked on true Baconian principles, and without any theory collected facts on a whole-sale scale,'[31] he claimed in the *Autobiography*, but of course this was never true. He had the basis of the theory before he even disembarked from the *Beagle*. His early notes were admittedly vague, but in 1838 he read Thomas Malthus's *Essay on the Principle of Population* and suddenly saw the full force of the battle for survival and the consequence that must arise from it – natural selection or 'the survival of the fittest'. This at last was the key to explain *how* evolution worked.

But how could one explain how natural selection worked? How describe the stages in a process whose effects were only measurable over thousands of years? It was here that Darwin showed the mettle of his creative imagination. *Natural* selection could never be observed in action but *artificial* selection could, since it was really a speeded-up form of natural selection with all the random factors taken out. And so Darwin began associating with dog-breeders, bloodstock experts, pigeon-fanciers and horticulturalists. He joined two London Pigeon Clubs and found that the fanciers had, by tinkering with the mating arrangements of the common rock-pigeon (*Columba livia*), produced at least twenty varieties which, if they occurred in the wild, would be deemed species. 'Few would readily believe,' he remarked admiringly, 'in the natural capacity and years of practice requisite to become even a skilful pigeon-fancier.'[32] But of course Darwin's aim was more serious than to become a skilful fancier, and he bombarded his new acquaintances with questions. 'At what age do nestling pigeons have their tail feathers sufficiently developed to be counted?'[33] he asked one correspondent, and, to a dog-breeder, 'Did you ever see black greyhound (or any sub-breed) with tan feet, and a tan coloured spot over inner corner of each eye? I want such cases, and such *must* exist because theory tells me it ought.'[34] (So much for true Baconian principles!) In his quiet, modest way, Darwin was quite ruthless about picking people's brains, often sending pages of questions at a time. And such was his charm that the answers invariably came winging back as fast and fully as he desired. Sometimes he even sent printed circulars. He scanned the pages of the popular journals to find the sorts of specialists he needed and as soon as he pinpointed his man, out would go the letters and the exhausting correspondence would begin. Many naturalists and breeders up and down the country must have groaned when they received a letter with the Downe postmark.

The notebooks had been started in July 1837. In June 1842 Darwin first 'allowed himself the satisfaction' (his own expression) of pencilling a 35-page abstract of his theory, and in 1844 (probably prompted by the publication of *Vestiges*) he expanded this into a 230-page outline with instructions for Mrs Darwin to hire an editor, preferably Hooker, to publish it if he should die. At the same time, he wrote to Hooker, 'At last gleams of light have come, and I am almost convinced (quite contrary to the opinion I started with) that species are not (it is like confessing a murder) immutable.'[35] But it was not until 1846 that he began writing his

Big Book on a scale three or four times larger than the eventual published version of the *Origin*. It was *such* a big book that he would probably never have finished it, and it was perhaps just as well that Wallace appeared at this point to hurry him into print.

Alfred Russel Wallace was then a youngish naturalist (born in 1823) little known in England because he had spent most of his adult life abroad. He had no private means and had worked as a land-surveyor and teacher before investing all his savings in an expedition up the Amazon with H.W. Bates. Since 1854 he had been living in Malaysia. Like Darwin, he had been deeply impressed by Lyell's *Principles*; unlike Darwin, he had also been stimulated by the *Vestiges*. In September 1855 he published a paper in the *Annals and Magazine of Natural History* which concluded, 'Every species has come into existence coincident both in space and time with a pre-existing closely allied species.'[36] This was Darwin's first warning that someone else was working in his field, and he wrote to Lyell, 'I rather hate the idea of writing for priority, yet I certainly would be vexed if any one were to publish my doctrines before me.'[37] Lyell urged him to hurry up with his own book. Then in May 1857 Wallace wrote directly to Darwin from the Celebes asking for information on some details of selective breeding. Darwin gave the information and added cautiously, 'I can plainly see that we have thought much alike and to a certain extent have come to similar conclusions.'[38] He also told the younger man that he had been working on the species question for twenty years, as a hint to warn him off. A second letter from Wallace that December contained a brief outline of evolution supported by evidence from geographical distribution similar to Darwin's but without the magic ingredient of natural selection. Darwin must have heaved an inner sigh of relief as he replied dismissively, 'Though agreeing with you on your conclusions ... I believe I go much further than you; but it is too long a subject to enter on my speculative notions.'[39]

A few months later, in the Spring of 1858, Wallace was lying sick of malarial fever at Ternate in the Moluccas when he suddenly remembered Malthus's *Essay on Population* which he had read twelve years earlier. 'In a sudden flash of insight'[40] – his own words – he arrived at the theory of natural selection and dashed off an outline, sending it to Darwin with a request for him to show it to Lyell if he thought it any good. Darwin could hardly fail to think that it was good: it was a lucid statement of exactly the theories he had been working on for the past twenty years. He was appalled. He immediately wrote to Lyell, enclosing Wallace's essay, and swallowing his disappointment as best he could:

> I never saw a more striking coincidence; if Wallace had my MS. sketch written out in 1842, he could not have made a better short abstract! Even his terms now stand as heads of my chapters. Please return me the MS., which he does not say he wishes me to publish, but I shall, of course, at once write and offer to send to any journal. So all my originality, whatever it may amount to, will be smashed.[41]

What could he do? He could hardly suppress Wallace's paper, but how could he then publish his own? Again, he consulted Lyell in what he called 'a trumpery letter, influenced by trumpery feelings', swinging almost hysterically between hopes and desperation. 'I would far rather burn my whole book,' he wrote, 'than that he or any other man should think that I have behaved in a paltry spirit.'[42] Things might have remained at this impasse, had not another blow intervened. Darwin's family was suddenly stricken with diphtheria and scarlet fever and within a few days his beloved infant daughter was dead. Darwin was prostrated with grief. For once the claims of science took second place, and he handed the whole problem over to Lyell and Hooker. The honourable solution they devised was to publish Wallace's paper together with Darwin's 1844 sketch (which established his

Alfred Russel Wallace

priority) and a recent letter to Asa Gray which gave the later developments of his theory.

Wallace accepted the solution gracefully and settled into the role of moon to Darwin's sun which he was to play for the remainder of his life. When he wrote his popular account of evolution in 1889 he entitled it, without irony, *Darwinism*, and he supplied many facts for Darwin's theory-grinding mill. He (together with H.W. Bates) devised the doctrine of mimicry to explain why some animals have markings closely resembling those of other species – it is to warn off predators to whom the mimicked species are distasteful, a sort of sheep-in-wolf's-clothing syndrome. He offered many observations on sexual selection and on the geographical distribution of species, especially in Malaysia, which was his expert territory. In the 1870s, when Darwin showed signs of backsliding into Lamarckism, it was Wallace who maintained the pure natural selection faith. But Darwin never entirely accepted Wallace as an ally and he was furious in 1869 when Wallace published an article in the *Quarterly Review* saying that natural selection alone was not sufficient to account for the human mind – that God, or as Wallace preferred, disembodied spirits must be involved. This was just the ammunition that the anti-Darwinians had been waiting for, and to get it from the man who co-discovered Darwinism exceeded their wildest hopes. Darwin's attitude to Wallace cooled from this point and continued to cool when, in later years, Wallace began embracing all the silliest flights of spiritualism and phrenology.

Too much can be made of Wallace's tragedy. As he was the first to admit, he had based his theory on one week's thought whereas Darwin had based it on twenty years of scrupulous research. And thoroughness, as we have seen, was essential to make the theory critic-proof and also theology-proof. Wallace's eccentricity and belief in spiritualism must also have told against him. Indeed, it even told against Darwin since J.E. Gray, the Keeper of Zoology at the British Museum, put about a rumour that *all* Darwinians were spiritualists – a slander if ever there was one. Wallace, had he published before Darwin, would probably have joined that long line of evolutionists whose theories were read with mild interest and then buried out of sight. But the good grace with which he accepted his secondary role must always be admired.

The joint Wallace–Darwin paper was read to a meeting of the Linnean Society on 1 July 1858. Darwin was still grief-stricken and could not attend, but Hooker reported back, 'The interest excited was intense; but the subject was too novel and too ominous for the old school to enter the lists, before armouring.'[43] Actually, Hooker was being tactful: the paper fell completely flat. But it hardly mattered because now at last Darwin was writing the *Origin of Species*. He started it in the summer of 1858 and finished it thirteen months and ten days later. The first edition of 1,250 copies (which Darwin thought too large) was published on 24 November 1859 and sold out the same day. It was followed early in the new year by a second edition of 3,000 copies. Darwin told John Murray, his publisher, 'I am infinitely pleased and proud at the appearance of my child.'[44]

CHAPTER NINETEEN

THE BATTLE FOR DARWINISM

Society must fall to pieces if Darwinism be true.
Family Herald, 20 May 1871

EFORE PLUNGING INTO the hurly-burly of the public reaction to the *Origin*, it is worth pausing a moment to see what the book really said. The full title is *On the Origin of Species by means of Natural Selection, or the Preservation of Favoured Races in the Struggle for Life*. The word evolution does not occur. Darwin preferred the formula 'descent with modification', while commentators tended to talk about 'transmutation', the 'descent theory' or, more starkly, the 'ape theory'. Many familiar Darwinist phrases like 'survival of the fittest' and 'missing link' are also absent from the first edition. The book is long (over 500 pages), fairly dull, and crammed solid with facts. Its method is speculative rather than inductive: Darwin presents a series of facts and then shows that they can be explained by the evolution–natural selection hypothesis and by no other. He is careful, as he goes along, to anticipate (and deflate) possible objections to his theory and he judiciously avoids pointing the moral that man, too, is a product of natural selection. His only reference to man comes in the closing paragraphs: 'In the distant future I see open fields for far more important researches ... Light will be thrown on the origin of man and his history.'[1] That is all. At no point does Darwin say that man is descended from the apes, although the point could be inferred, and invariably *was* inferred, by any intelligent reader.

Darwin's presentation of the case for evolution is chiefly remarkable for the mass of facts with which it is supported, especially facts relating to the geographical distribution of species. The revolutionary part of the book, however, is the theory of natural selection, the *method* by which evolution could have occurred. Darwin explains that all individuals are born with slight differences (variations) from other members of their species. Most of these variations are neutral in effect, but a few will tend to give their possessors an advantage in the struggle for existence, while others will prove a disadvantage. This struggle is so harsh (as Malthus had demonstrated) that only a few individuals in any given generation will survive to maturity.

Individuals with a disadvantageous variation are most likely to die prematurely, while those with an advantageous variation are more likely to survive long enough to breed and so pass on their advantage to the next generation. Natural selection is therefore a weeding-out process which sifts the many millions of variations occurring constantly in Nature and ensures that the 'fittest', i.e. the ones most useful in the prevailing environment, will be perpetuated. And these variations, continued and consolidated through many generations, will eventually become so marked as to constitute new species.

'Thus, from the war of nature, from famine and death,' Darwin concludes, 'the most exalted object which we are capable of conceiving, namely, the production of the higher animals, directly follows. There is grandeur in this view of life, with its several powers, having been originally breathed by the Creator into a few forms or into one.'[2] But even despite the tactful reference to the Creator, almost no one could see the grandeur in this view of life except Darwin. Huxley warned him while the book was still in the press that it would provoke outrage:

> I trust you will not allow yourself to be in any way disgusted or annoyed by the considerable abuse and misrepresentation which, unless I greatly mistake, is in store for you. Depend on it you have earned the lasting gratitude of all thoughtful men. As to the curs which bark and yelp, you must recollect that some of your friends, at any rate, are endowed with a combatitiveness which, (though you have often and justly rebuked it) may stand you in good stead. I am sharpening up my claws and beak in readiness.[3]

What claws and what a beak! Darwin could not possibly have found a better champion than Huxley. As he affirmed in his *Autobiography*, 'His [Huxley's] mind is as quick as a flash of lightning and as sharp as a razor. He is the best talker whom I have known. He never says and never writes anything flat ... He is a splendid man and has worked well for the good of mankind.'[4] Huxley's fire, his oratory, and his devastating intellect would almost single-handedly serve to carry the Darwinian message against the mighty weight of theological disapproval and public prejudice which opposed it. Darwin himself, nursing his ailments on a sofa, took absolutely no part in promulgating his views to a larger public. He had written his book: let them learn from it who would. It was Huxley alone who had to parry the slings and arrows of outraged churchmen, and he alone had the intellectual courage to do it.

Thomas Henry Huxley was born in Ealing in 1825, the son of a schoolmaster. He attended his father's school for just two years and later said that the society he met there was the worst he had ever encountered, with bullying the least of its vices. When he was ten, the school closed down, and from then on he was left to educate himself by reading whatever he chose. He mainly chose German and mechanics. But the family's circumstances were too straitened to allow him any choice of career and, as two of his brothers-in-law were doctors, he was apprenticed at the early age of sixteen to a Rotherhithe practitioner. There he saw scenes of poverty, people dying through sheer inanition, which haunted him all his life. Although he completed his medical training, and took an M.B. at London University, he never felt any vocation for the work, and said afterwards that he was 'occasionally horrified to think how very little I ever knew or cared about Medicine as the art of healing.'[5] He always thought of himself as a mechanic *manqué*, and said that the only part of his medical training which interested him was physiology, or the mechanics of human engineering. But while still a student, he published his first scientific paper, on a hitherto-undescribed structure in the human hair-sheath, which is still known as 'Huxley's layer'.

Thomas Henry Huxley

Unlike Darwin, Huxley needed to earn his living, and soon after graduating he applied for a post as assistant-surgeon in the Navy. He was accepted and assigned to H.M.S. *Rattlesnake*, under Captain Owen Stanley, to survey the waters of Australasia. The four years of the *Rattlesnake* voyage were Huxley's equivalent of Darwin's *Beagle*. His duties as assistant-surgeon were not onerous and he spent his ample free time studying the *Medusae* or jellyfish, because they were abundant and had not been much studied before. He sent back countless papers to the Linnean Society and finally a more elaborate monograph to the Royal Society. But he heard not a word of response until he returned to England in 1850, and found that his *Medusae* was published, and he was known. Soon afterwards he was elected a Fellow of the Royal Society and awarded its Royal Medal, at the extremely young age of twenty-seven. (Darwin was forty-four when he received the Royal.)

During a shore-leave at Sydney, Huxley had fallen in love with Miss Henrietta Heathorn, and his immediate concern on returning to England was to find a job on which he could support a wife. But scientific posts were almost non-existent, especially if one insisted on living in London, which Huxley did. It took him four years to find a proper job, and when he was interviewed for the post of lecturer in Palaeontology and Natural History at the Government School of Mines, he almost ruined it all by declaring, with his usual candour, that 'I did not care for fossils, and that I should give up Natural History as soon as I could get a physiological post.'[6] In the event, he retained the job for thirty-one years, and grew to care for fossils as much as any man. In 1855, eight years after their meeting, he asked his fiancée to come to England and marry him. She was ill on arrival, and he took her to a doctor who told him she had only six months to live. But they got married anyway, and lived happily together for another forty years, she outliving him.

Some time in the early 1850s, Huxley made Darwin's acquaintance. They liked and respected one another from the start, but at this stage Huxley was not converted to, or even very interested in, any evolutionary hypothesis. His inclination was 'to say to both Mosaists and Evolutionists "a plague on both your houses", and ... to turn aside from an interminable and apparently fruitless discussion, to labour in the fertile fields of ascertainable fact.'[7] Even when he read the *Origin*, he did not immediately become a convert, as he explained to Lyell in 1859: 'I by no means suppose that the transmutation hypothesis is proved or anything like it – but I view it as a powerful instrument of research – Follow it out & it will lead us somewhere – while the other notion is like all the modifications of "final causation" a "barren virgin".'[8] In particular, he did not want to see the *Origin* crushed by a lot of prejudiced churchmen with no respect for scientific method. Huxley could never resist the chance to eat a bishop, and the greater the theological opposition to Darwinism, the more eager his own defence of it grew.

However, his mighty claws and beak were not needed immediately. The first reviews of the *Origin*, in the winter of 1859–60, were quiet, serious and respectful. They discussed the scientific merits and demerits of the book and, though generally concluding with the judgment, 'not proven', paid tribute to Darwin's thoroughness and range of knowledge. By a curious fluke, *The Times*'s review was written by Huxley himself. The book had been allocated to one of their staff writers, a Mr Lucas, but he, being 'as innocent of any knowledge of science as a babe',[9] found it heavy going and searched desperately for a stand-in. His choice happily lit upon Huxley, who dashed off a brilliant and entirely laudatory review. Within a few months, *The Times* was to become the mouthpiece for Darwin's bitterest opponents, but Huxley won this first round effortlessly. It was not until the spring of 1860, when the second edition was printed, that churchmen and opinion-formers became alerted to this seditious book, and discussion of the *Origin* moved from the scientific coterie out into the wider world.

The first real battle took place at the Oxford meeting of the British Association in June 1860. Darwin of course was too ill to attend, but Huxley was there, and so was Sir Richard Owen. Owen was already known to be the author of an anonymous denunciatory notice which had appeared in the *Edinburgh Review*. On June 28, the Oxford Professor of Botany, Dr Charles Daubeny, read a paper on the sexuality of plants with special reference to Darwin's theories. Huxley was invited to contribute to the discussion afterwards but refused to do so in front of 'a general audience, in which sentiment would unduly interfere with intellect.'[10] Owen thereupon stood up and wreathed the subject in his usual brand of magisterial double-talk. Most of what he said was unintelligible, but at one point he stated that the brain of a gorilla more closely resembled that of the lowest quadruman than it did that of man. This was untrue and Huxley knew it. He stood up and gave Owen's assertion 'a direct and unqualified contradiction', promising to 'justify that unusual procedure elsewhere' and then sat down again.[11] He felt, probably rightly, that the excitable and essentially amateur setting of a British Association meeting was not the right place to discuss minute technical details of comparative anatomy, but the effect was as though he had struck Owen in the face. The audience buzzed with excitement – which probably they would not have done if they had had to listen to a full exposition of the *hippocampus minor* organ. Huxley's justification did not appear till the following January.

But it was the Saturday meeting of the Association that brought matters to a head. Huxley had been planning to leave on the Friday, and was actually on the point of doing so when Robert Chambers, the (still anonymous) author of *Vestiges*, persuaded him to stay. Seven hundred people arrived for the Saturday meeting and a new hall had to be found to accommodate them all. The audience included many clergymen and a rabble of undergraduates eager to show their enthusiasm for 'the monkey theory'. The official speaker was an American, Dr J.W. Draper, but hardly anyone listened to him. They were waiting for the anti-Darwinian attack to be led by 'Soapy Sam' Wilberforce, the Bishop of Oxford. Huxley believed that he had been specially crammed for the occasion by Richard Owen. There is some doubt about what Wilberforce actually said in his speech: contemporary accounts differ. But at some point he undoubtedly made a remark about

apes and grandmothers which induced Huxley to mutter, 'The Lord hath delivered him into mine hands!'[12]

Wilberforce eventually sat down to the cooing applause of his audience. The
Chairman then invited Huxley to speak. Here is his own account of his speech,
written to his friend Dyster a few days after the event:

Samuel thought it was a fine opportunity for chaffing a savan – However he
performed the operation vulgarly & I determined to punish him – partly on
that account and partly because he talked pretentious nonsense. So when I
got up I spoke pretty much to the effect – that I had listened with great attention to the Lord Bishops speech but had been unable to discover either a
new fact or a new argument in it – except indeed the question raised as to
my personal predilections in the matter of ancestry – That it would not have
occurred to me to bring forward such a topic as that for discussion myself,
but that I was quite ready to meet the Right Revd. prelate even on that ground
– If then, said I, the question is put to me would I rather have a miserable

Bishop Wilberforce, caricatured by 'Ape', 1869

ape for a grandfather or a man highly endowed by nature and possessed of great means of influence & yet who employs those faculties & that influence for the mere purpose of introducing ridicule into a grave scientific discussion – I unhesitatingly affirm my preference for the ape.[13]

The reaction, according to Huxley, was a great thunderclap of laughter and applause, and he jubilantly concluded, 'I was the most popular man in Oxford for full four & twenty hours afterwards.[14] Darwin chuckled delightedly when he heard the news at Downe: 'How durst you attack a live bishop in that fashion? I am quite ashamed of you! Have you no respect for fine lawn sleeves? By Jove, you seem to have done it well.'[15]

Perhaps the single most important effect of this confrontation was that it made Huxley value the art of public speaking. Hitherto, he told Hooker, he had rather hated speaking in public, but now he had tasted the pleasure of swinging an audience to his side, he determined to cultivate it and improve his skill. He did so to such good effect that within a year or two he became the most-demanded public speaker in England. Even people who hated his ideas – such as bishops – could never bear to forgo the pleasure of listening to him. Whether lecturing to mechanics (whom he considered his best audience), or to eminent scientists and churchmen, he was always compelling, lucid, witty and powerful. A student who attended a series of medical lectures that Huxley gave at Edinburgh in 1876 recalled that his arguments were so close-knit they left the listener exhausted afterwards, but 'I would not miss them, even if they were ten times as difficult. They are something glorious, sublime.'[16] Huxley could lecture on literally *anything* and make it fascinating (his most famous lecture is 'On a piece of chalk') – no wonder, then, that during the 1860s, when most of his lectures were devoted to aspects of Darwinism, he made converts by the thousand. He reported to his wife, apropos one lecture series to mechanics, 'My working men stick by me wonderfully, the house being fuller than ever last night. By next Friday evening, they will all be convinced that they are monkeys.'[17]

The 1860 meeting also marked the first awareness of Darwinism among the general public. From now on, the newspapers would be full of it, even the popular press which normally eschewed scientific topics. There was very little *exposition* of Darwin's ideas, and natural selection was barely mentioned, but by the end of 1860 most literate laymen knew that a Mr Darwin had written a book in which he claimed that animals changed into other animals and, in particular, that monkeys changed into men. It was all very shocking, or hilariously absurd, depending on one's temperament.

In 1861 the controversy was augmented by the arrival of two new talking-points – Huxley's *hippocampus minor* and du Chaillu's gorillas. The gorillas were not, strictly speaking, relevant, but they were apes and newspapers at this time could never mention apes without mentioning Darwin. The *hippocampus* controversy, although more relevant and ultimately more durable, involved a lot of hard words and even harder facts, and editors could be forgiven, in the spring and summer of 1861, for finding du Chaillu and his gorillas better copy.

The gorilla had been sketchily known to science since 1847 when two American missionaries working in Gabon found a large curious painted skull which the natives worshipped as a fetish. They realized that it belonged to an unknown species, and eventually succeeded in obtaining other gorilla skulls, which led to the new species *Gorilla gorilla?* being tentatively incorporated in the textbooks. But no Westerner had yet *seen* the creature[18] and, as far as the general public was concerned, it existed in the same faery hinterland as unicorns and mermaids. Until, that is, the beginning of 1861 when Paul Belloni du Chaillu (1835–1903) and his sensational book, *Explorations and Adventures in Equatorial Africa*, arrived in England. Du Chaillu claimed not merely to have *seen* gorillas, but to have done battle with them face to face, alone but for his trusty sable bearer (of course he was armed) in their native forests. He was an American of French extraction who had lived some time in West Africa as a child and had recently returned there with a grant from the Philadelphia Academy of Natural Sciences to explore and report. Unfortunately, like his compatriot Audubon, he could never resist mixing fiction with fact, or at least colouring his narratives in the deepest shade of purple. All du Chaillu's gorillas remind one of King Kong:

His eyes began to flash fiercer fire as we stood motionless on the defensive, and the crest of short hair which stands on his forehead began to twitch rapidly up and down, while his powerful fangs were shown as he again sent forth a thunderous roar. And now truly he reminded me of nothing but some hellish dream creature – a being of that hideous order, half-man, half-beast, which we find pictured by old artists in some representations of the infernal regions. He advanced a few steps – then stopped to utter that hideous roar again – advanced again, and finally stopped when at a distance of about six yards from us. And here, just as he began another of his roars, beating his breast with rage, we fired, and killed him.[19]

On the evidence of the book alone, du Chaillu might easily have been dismissed as a romancer, but he arrived in England with no fewer than twenty stuffed gorillas, skins, skulls and skeletons, which he exhibited at his numerous public lectures. Mrs Owen attended one at the Royal Institution and reported, 'A tremendous crowd filled the theatre, Sir Roderick Murchison in the chair. M. du Chaillu gave a very quaint, clear, and interesting account of his travels in Africa, and his meeting with the gorillas, a row of which hideous creatures was overhead: some skulls were before the lecturer, who traced his progress on a large map as the lecture proceeded.'[20] Everyone wanted to see the gorillas, and the man who claimed to have shot them, to judge if they were genuine. J.E. Gray of the British Museum claimed publicly that du Chaillu was a fake, that he had certainly never shot a gorilla, probably never seen one, and possibly never been in Africa at all. Abraham Bartlett of London Zoo discovered that one of the gorilla skins was painted. There was much forensic discussion of bullet-holes to show that du Chaillu could not have shot the gorillas from in front, as he claimed, but in the back, when they were fleeing. Charles Waterton thundered to the attack with his usual disregard for libel, claiming that 'Audubon is immaculate when compared to du Chaillu' and that 'His adventures with the gorilla are most formidable and false ... I suspect strongly that the traveller has been nothing but a trader on the western coast of Africa; possibly engaged in kidnapping negroes.'[21] But Professor Owen supported du Chaillu, Huxley did not oppose him, and all reputable zoologists agreed that du Chaillu's skins and skeletons were genuine, however he had acquired them.

All this really had nothing to do with Darwinism; except that the press kept dragging Darwin in. The *Daily Telegraph*, for instance, tried to adopt a blasé tone:

> Two questions of stupendous importance are just now before the world. Is M. DU CHAILLU the modern MUNCHAUSEN? and is the gorilla allied or not allied to the human species? These are the problems which are now agitating certain classes of society and, unless they are speedily solved, the most disastrous consequences to the national peace will, it is to be feared, ensue ... Even if Mr. DARWIN and his friends could persuade us that our distant ancestors were guinea pigs or caterpillars, people would not, we are inclined to think, found a new system of ethics on the discovery. We should still be more interested in our present and our future than in our past. But human dignity and human feeling both revolt against the absurdities of the would-be scientific men.[22]

Moreover, du Chaillu's gorillas gave a certain spine-tingling vividness to the idea that man was descended from the monkeys. Professor Owen had stated that the gorilla resembled man more closely than did any other ape. Translated into journalese, this meant that man was descended from the gorilla, and gorillas, as the public suddenly learned from du Chaillu and from second-hand accounts like Philip Gosse's in *The Romance of Natural History*, were 'demon-like in hideousness' and murderous in habit. 'Two negroes,' Gosse assured his readers, 'will be walking through one of the woodland paths, unsuspicious of evil, when in an instant one misses his companion, or turns to see him drawn up in the air with a convulsed choking cry; and in a few minutes dropped to the ground a strangled corpse. The terrified survivor gazes up, and meets the grin and glare of the fiendish giant, who, watching his opportunity, had suddenly put down his immense hind-hand, caught the wretch by the neck with resistless power, and dropped him only when he ceased to struggle.'[23] This implausible scene was engraved as the frontispiece to Gosse's book, and it was of such murderous gorillas that the public thought when asked to imagine their simian ancestry.

Du Chaillu was something of a nine days' wonder and soon disappeared into Africa again, whereupon Huxley moved back into centre-stage. At the Oxford meeting, he had promised to produce evidence for his assertion that Owen was wrong about the dissimilarity of ape and human brains, and he did so in the first issue of a new magazine called the *Natural History Review*. Owen had argued that the human brain contained an organ, the *hippocampus minor*, which was unique to humans. Huxley proved definitively that the same organ occurred in the brain of the anthropoid apes. Owen was rash enough to reply, and the dispute raged backwards and forwards across the newspaper columns for months. It was even taken up by *Punch* whose contributor 'Gorilla' pondered:

> Say am I a man and a brother,
> Or only an anthropoid ape?
> Your judgment, be't one way or t'other,
> *Do* put into positive shape.
> Must I humbly take rank as quadruman
> As OWEN maintains that I ought:
> Or rise into brotherhood human,
> As HUXLEY has flatt'ringly taught?[24]

'The Darwinian Theory – a Sketch in the Monkey House', from the *Graphic*, 1871

But there was little doubt about the outcome, since the *hippocampus* demonstrably existed. Huxley's victory was all the more overwhelming since it was on Owen's home ground, comparative anatomy. An anonymous burlesque pamphlet entitled 'Report of a SAD CASE recently tried before the Lord Mayor' described Owen's pounding in the language of the police-court: '*Policeman X* – He behaved uncommon plucky, though his heart seemed broke. He tried to give Huxley as good as he gave, but he could not, and some people cried "Shame," and "he's had enough," and so on. Never saw a man so mauled before. 'Twas the monkey that worrited him, and Huxley's crying out, "There they are – bone for bone, tooth for tooth, foot for foot, and their brains one as good as t'other." '[25] Even children in their nurseries heard of the *hippocampus* controversy when Charles Kingsley's *Water Babies* told of the professor who 'had even got up once at the British Association, and declared that apes had hippopotamus majors in their brains just as men have. Which was a shocking thing to say; for, if it were so, what would become of the faith, hope and charity of immortal millions?'[26] Kingsley was rare among clerics in being able to take a cheerful view of the matter.

Owen, clearly worsted in the *hippocampus* battle, retired to the mountain peaks of metaphysics where mere facts were powerless to touch him. From time to time he would utter one of his Delphic pronouncements and the orthodox press would swoon in rapture – 'How cheering to listen to words such as these of Britain's greatest anatomist, which are not more lofty in their wisdom than exemplary in their humility!'[27] But it had to be admitted that Owen's total unintelligibility made it difficult to spread his views to a wider public, and these views in any case shifted with dizzying frequency. When, in 1861, the British Association asked him to define the distinction between man and the lower animals, 'He confessed his entire ignorance of the mode in which it had pleased our Creator to establish our species, as it was said, "out of the dust of the earth." By what marvellous process all that might be accomplished was not told us, nor need it be.'[28] Soon afterwards, however, he came near to expounding a counter-theory to Darwinism in what he called the Law of Derivation or 'the ordained becoming of living things' which had the merit of meaning anything one wanted it to. But in 1866, to make sure that no one could ever accuse him of consistency, he astonishingly announced that the theory of evolution *was* true, and that he had invented it himself, at the earlier date of 1850. The *London Review*, which received this announcement, commented acidly, 'So far as we can gather from his communication, he denies the Darwinian doctrine, admits the accuracy of its basis, and claims to be the first to point out the truth of the principle on which it is founded.'[29] The press, even the violently anti-Darwinian press, grew increasingly impatient with their supposed champion, and in 1872 the *Popular Science Review* finally summed up Owen's position: 'We may not call Professor Owen a Darwinian, but if we could take Mr. Darwin's name from the doctrine, we doubt not Professor Owen would hold to it.'[30]

In America, early discussion of the *Origin* was more muted than in England, because it was eclipsed by the outbreak of the Civil War. Asa Gray was the chief spokesman for Darwinism and Louis Agassiz against, and they thrashed out the matter in a series of public debates in Boston in the spring of 1860, but the confrontation was less dramatic than that between Huxley and Owen, and neither Gray nor Agassiz was on his best form. Gray saw the value of the *Origin* as a scientific theory (indeed, he had contributed important data to it) but he was a committed Christian and he saw from the start that Darwinism spelt the death of natural theology. In consequence, he could never quite support it with the same wholehearted glee as Huxley, who positively relished its anti-religious implications. Agassiz's problem was simply that he could not understand Darwinism. As Gray reported to Hooker, he 'growls over it, like a well-cudgelled dog – is very much annoyed by it',[31] but he was too old and too set in his ways (after all, he had studied under Cuvier) to follow through its details. He contented himself with writing lazy and dismissive critiques for the popular press, airily telling readers of the *Atlantic Monthly* that, 'The world has arisen in some way or another. How it originated is the great question, and Darwin's theory, like all other attempts to explain the origin of life, is thus far mere conjectural. I believe he has not even made the best conjecture possible in the present state of our knowledge.'[32] Like Owen, he enjoyed hinting that he had a better theory up his sleeve but, also like Owen, he was never prepared to divulge it.

With this sort of attitude endemic among many established scientists, it is not surprising that the anti-Darwinians had to rely almost exclusively on emotional and theological argument to refute the new heresy. After the first reviews of the *Origin*, the merits of Darwinism were hardly ever argued on purely scientific grounds. This was partly because there was no scientist equipped or willing to follow Owen into the dragon Huxley's lair, but even more because the subject was really *too serious* to be discussed rationally. The *Family Herald's* reaction – 'Society must fall to pieces if Darwinism be true'[33] – exactly expresses the tone of the opposition. Darwinism could not be *allowed* to be true, because its implications were so dire. It was an abominable heresy which must be crushed and rooted out at source. To try to refute it with a lot of scientific fiddle-faddle facts was already granting it more respectability than it deserved. It must be silenced *tout court*.

Darwin had remarked optimistically in the closing pages of the *Origin*, 'I see no good reason why the views given in this volume should shock the religious feelings of anyone.'[34] But that only showed the extent of his own naïvety or apostasy. Both his ideas – evolution and natural selection – were deeply offensive to established religion. As Hugh Miller had brilliantly foretold in his *Footprints of the Creator*, the theory of evolution when applied to man was 'tantamount to atheism' because it denied the existence of an immortal soul. Darwin had realized this difficulty and chosen to omit man from the *Origin*, telling Wallace, 'I think I shall avoid the whole subject, as so surrounded with prejudices',[35] but his tact was entirely wasted since public discussion of the book and of evolution concentrated on man to the exclusion of all other species.

The orthodox theological position shifted continuously throughout the 1860s and 1870s as churchmen redrew their defences in the light of each new scientific discovery. As the *Origin* debate opened, they were still manning the Cuvierian ramparts, claiming that man had been created in 4004 B.C. when the Book of Genesis starts. (This was itself, of course, a retreat from the earlier nineteenth-century position that the whole world had been created in 4004 B.C.) Then in 1863 Lyell published *The Antiquity of Man*, proving that man was much more than 6,000 years old and had coexisted with various extinct 'ante-diluvian' animals. Theologians thereupon abandoned the last vestiges of Cuvierianism, and the date 4004 B.C., but clung to a special creation for man. They were much fortified in this last redoubt by finding Wallace suddenly on their side when in 1869 he published his *Quarterly* essay claiming that natural selection could not have produced the human mind. But then came Darwin's *The Descent of Man* in 1871 with conclusive evidence that man had evolved from the apes, and even this last bastion crumbled. By the 1880s Huxley found that there were no more bishops left to eat. 'There must be *some* position,' he grumbled plaintively, 'from which the reconcilers of Genesis will not retreat,'[36] but in fact there was not, and the Church's final position – that physical man had evolved, but immortal man (the soul) had been implanted by the Creator at a later date – was impregnable to scientific attack, since it was not susceptible to proof or disproof.

'Suggested Illustration for Dr. Darwin's Movements and Habits of Climbing Plants', by Sambourne, 1875

Of course, Darwinism was not the only threat to religious orthodoxy in the mid-Victorian period. Strauss's *Leben Jesu*, translated by George Eliot in 1846, inaugurated a new era of biblical scholarship, much of which tended to undermine the literal acceptance of the Scriptures. Historians, philologists and archaeologists, just as much as scientists, were beginning to trespass on holy ground, and show up inaccuracies in the sacred texts. And, among younger churchmen, there was a widespread desire to separate the facts of Christ's life and teaching from the myths surrounding them. In 1860 a group of liberal theologians, including Jowett, published a volume of *Essays and Reviews* which discussed the Bible in the light of modern scholarship. They were tried for heresy by the Judicial Committee of the Privy Council, and the case dragged on for months. At the same time, Bishop Colenso (1814–83) of Natal arrived in England, having been publicly denounced and excommunicated by his metropolitan for uttering heretical views. In the course of translating the Bible into Zulu, he had come across certain discrepancies, and in his book *The Pentateuch and the Book of Joshua Critically Examined* (1862–79) he proved that many chronological and genealogical statements in the Old Testament were self-contradictory and inaccurate. Colenso, also, was tried before the Privy Council, and newspaper coverage of the two heresy cases consumed many more column inches than the Darwinian debate. Colenso won many sympathizers for his attitude that 'the "scandal" they complain of is not caused by me, but by those who maintain a state of things in the Church opposed to the plainest results of modern science.'[37] Eventually, both cases ended in acquittal, with the crucial ruling that, although Scripture contains the Word of God, it is not itself the Word of God, and therefore can be sometimes wrong. Discussions of the cases and the issues they raised prevented the Church presenting a united front against Darwinism.

The Darwinian debate rumbled more or less continuously throughout the 1860s, being revitalized occasionally by new pro- or anti-Darwinian books.[38] Most of the British Association meetings of this decade were devoted to Darwinism, which proved a great crowd-puller. Attendance at the meetings increased from an average of 1,400 in the 1850s to 2,300 in the 1860s. But 1871 saw a certain deterioration when Sir William Thomson, the President for the year, told the assembly that life had come to this planet from outer space, carried on 'countless seed-bearing meteoric stones'[39] and the 1872 meeting, according to the *Daily Telegraph*, 'disappointed the ladies in striking no new Darwinian vein.'[40] From about the mid-1870s press and public discussion of Darwinism dwindled into silence. This was not because the scientific difficulties had been resolved, nor because pious opponents had been converted, but because all possible opinions had been aired. It was clear that there could be no final compromise between the defenders of Darwinism and its opponents. It was simply a matter of waiting for the die-hards to die.

The general public remained rather vague about what had happened and probably never mastered the ins and outs of Darwin's theories. By the 1870s most educated laymen, and nearly all scientists, accepted evolution as fact, while doubting or more often ignoring the theory of natural selection. By the time Darwin died in 1883 he was considered respectable and non-controversial enough to be buried in Westminster Abbey, where his son Willy showed a truly Darwinian respect for health by placing his gloves on his bald head throughout the ceremony to keep off a draught.

Yet, in fact, the *scientific* flaws in Darwin's theory had tended to grow sharper rather than weaker with the passage of time. The flaw that the public always took most interest in, as it was the only one regularly discussed in the newspapers, was the absence of 'missing links'. If Darwin's theory were true, they argued, one would expect to find whole series of transitional forms linking one species to the next. As regards present-day species, the Darwinian answer was simple: all modern species are, if you like, 'missing links' between their less-evolved predecessors and the more-evolved forms that will succeed them. Primitive and

Huxley opening the Fisheries Exhibition, 1883

'improved' forms do not coexist because the latter supersede the former. But when it came to fossil species, Darwin was on weaker ground. In fossils, one *would* expect to see transitional forms between modern species and their predecessors. Darwin's only answer, at the time of writing the *Origin*, was to point to 'The Imperfection of the Geological Record', which was the title of one of his chapters. Fossils were only formed in exceptional circumstances, they were only found in exceptional circumstances, and the whole science of palaeontology was less than a century old. But Darwin himself admitted in the *Origin* that this absence of fossil inter-mediate forms was 'the most obvious of the many objections which may be urged against my views',[41] and it was invariably the one the newspapers exploited. 'We defy any one, from Mr. Darwin downwards,' snorted the *Family Herald*, 'to show us the link between the fish and the man. Let them catch a mermaid, and they will find the missing link.'[42] The *Pall Mall* more wittily demanded to be shown 'the stages by which a polypus is finally developed into a professor, and a bed of oysters by the force of "natural selection" into a gathering of the British Association.'[43]

By a very happy stroke of luck, the hue-and-cry for a missing link had hardly been raised before one came to light. In 1862, in a Bavarian coal-mine, Professor Wagner found the most famous fossil of all time – *Archaeopteryx*, a reptile-bird or bird-reptile, with lizard-like tail, claws on its wings, and beak with teeth. Darwin had hypothesized that birds must have evolved from reptiles, and *Archaeopteryx* neatly illustrated the mid-point in that transition. At about the same time, Professor Othniel Marsh in the United States collected a perfect series of fossils illustrating the evolution of the horse from the cat-sized, four-toed *Eohippus* to its modern form. It was Professor Marsh's horses, which he saw when he visited the States in 1876, that finally convinced Huxley that evolution was a fact and not merely a valuable working hypothesis.

But *Archaeopteryx* and *Eohippus* were still not enough to satisfy the general public. They wanted to see evolution taking place before their very eyes. And increasingly their demands centred not on *a* missing link, but on *the* missing link – the perfect transitional form between ape and man. Haeckel had already given it a name, *Pithecanthropus*, but no trace of it had yet been found. The Neanderthal skull, discovered near Dusseldorf in 1856, was certainly primitive but it was clearly a man, and therefore not an ape-man. When Darwin went to collect his honorary LL.D. from Cambridge in 1877, the undergraduates hung a stuffed monkey and a huge ring from the ceiling to remind him that the missing link was still missing. The perfect ape–human missing link has still not been found but the discovery of Java Man by Dubois in 1890 went a considerable way towards satisfying Victorian doubts.

Meanwhile, however, the attention of scientists was increasingly drawn to the *real* weakness of Darwin's theory: his inability to explain why variations occur and how, having occurred, they could be perpetuated. These questions have only begun to be answered in the twentieth century: for Darwin and his contemporaries they were unanswerable. Darwin flatly admitted in the *Origin*, 'The laws governing inheritance are quite unknown.'[44] In so far as they *were* known, or were thought to be known, they made the preservation of variations quite impossible. The Victorians thought of inheritance as a blending process ('mixing of blood' was the usual metaphor) whereby the offspring represented a compromise between the characteristics of both its parents. Thus, if an individual was born with a favourable variation, it would only pass on half the strength of that variation to its offspring, who in turn would only pass on half, so that any variations would be lost by dilution within a very few generations, and the successors would 'revert to type'. In artificial breeding, this tendency could be checked by controlling the choice of mates, but in nature no such controls were exercised.

Darwin saw the difficulty and tried to relieve it, in his *Variation of Animals and Plants under Domestication* (1868), by postulating a theory of 'pangenesis' which had every organ in the body giving off 'gemmules' to transmit its characteristics to the next generation. This was virtually Lamarckianism, and no one was very impressed. In the same book, in a section 'On Certain Characters not Blending', Darwin listed examples of what he considered exceptions to his theory. 'When grey and white mice are paired,' he noted, 'the young are piebald, or pure white or grey, but not of an intermediate tint.'[45] He even described some esperiments he had made in crossing sweet-pea strains and their consistent refusal to blend, but he failed to draw the proper genetic conclusions. He still thought of these as exceptional cases.

In fact the solution to all Darwin's difficulties had already been published by an Austrian monk who had carried out almost identical experiments on peas and sweet-peas in his monastery garden, and drawn the proper conclusions. Gregor Mendel showed that heredity is carried by genes, some of which are dominant, others recessive, and that far from all blending into an homogeneous mix, they retain their integrity and potential for expression through generation after generation. Mendel's findings were delivered to the Natural History Society of Brunn, in Austrian Silesia, in 1866, but attracted only local attention. Soon afterwards, Mendel was appointed abbot of his monastery and found himself too busy to continue his experiments. He died in 1884 with his epoch-making work still unrecognized. It was not until 1900 that three eminent botanists, working independently, rediscovered Mendel's paper and delivered it to the world. The modern science of genetics was then fairly launched, but too late for Darwin who had died with this mighty puzzle still unresolved. It is ironic that he, who cared so passionately for facts, should have formulated a theory whose most fundamental assumptions were, at the time, unsupported by any factual evidence whatsoever.

CHAPTER TWENTY

AFTERMATH

THE PUBLICATION OF the *Origin of Species* had no immediate effect on the popular enthusiasm for natural history. The aquarium and fern crazes were then at their height; a new craze for microscopy was just beginning; and these ran their appointed courses without interruption. In 1861, the paper tax was repealed and a new flood of cheap, popular handbooks appeared on the market, some of them enlivened by colour illustrations in the new technique of chromolithography. The top natural history bestsellers of 1860 were Philip Gosse's *The Romance of Natural History* and Frank Buckland's second *Curiosities of Natural History*. Most of the subsequent bestsellers of the 1860s were written either by Frank Buckland or by the Rev. J.G. Wood who was then at the peak of his always prolific output. Yet neither Wood nor Buckland nor any other popular natural history writer of the 1860s tried to discuss Darwinism or explain it to their readers. If they mentioned it at all, it was to brush it aside in a paragraph, usually in connection with a joking reference to monkeys. The tendency of popular natural history books to run behind the times was always strong, and never more so than in the 1860s when they devoted more space to a new flurry of toad-in-coal sightings than to the greatest breakthrough in biology of the century. In fact, one would not suspect from them that any such breakthrough had occurred.

The effects of the *Origin* had to filter down through the professional scientists before they reached the layman, and the first was wholly beneficial: an end to the obsession with species which had clogged biological enquiry for almost a century. Darwin showed that species were never clear-cut. They shaded off into varieties, into races, into sub-species and ultimately into individuals. Historically, they were never stable; the varieties of today might be the species of tomorrow; the species of today might tomorrow be extinct. This sudden blurring of the sharp edges of species was a bitter blow to the closet naturalists. They could no longer feel that once a species had been named, described and preserved in a museum, it was finished, and they could no longer even dream of achieving any full and final classification. There would be no tidiness in species ever again and, if no tidiness, then no satisfaction for the closet men who were, by nature, tidy-minded.

Instead, the new generation of naturalists would turn their attention to the field, that long-neglected arena which had been for so many years the preserve of amateurs. They wanted to study living organisms, not dead ones, and they wanted to study them, not in cages or laboratories, but in their natural environment. In fact, they wanted to study ecology, and although the word itself (spelt oecology) did not appear until 1873, the science was launched in the *Origin* of 1859 with its constant stress on the inter-relations between species and the dependence of species on their environment. Indeed, the last paragraph of the *Origin*, with its evocation of 'an entangled bank, clothed with many plants of many kinds, with birds singing on the bushes, with various insects flitting about, and with worms crawling through the damp earth ... [all] dependent upon each other in so complex a manner'[1] is virtually a definition of what the study of ecology is all about, and elsewhere throughout the book there are countless examples of ecological thinking. At one point, Darwin gives a precise example of how an ecological chain-reaction works. Red clover, he explains, is fertilized by humble-bees; bees are destroyed by fieldmice; mice are destroyed by cats. 'Hence,' he concludes, 'it is quite credible that the presence of a feline animal in large numbers in a district might determine, through the intervention first of mice and then of bees, the frequency of certain flowers in that district!'[2] What is so remarkable about this otherwise unremarkable observation is that in 1859 it was so novel and apparently far-fetched as to need an exclamation mark, but scientists quickly saw that it was precisely this kind of chain-reaction which must be studied in order to evaluate the theory of natural selection, and that such chain-reactions could only be studied in the field.

The new attention to field studies was helped on its way by a string of technological advances which tended to make field studies more precise and therefore more rewarding. The first prism binoculars were patented in 1859 and soon replaced the gun as essential equipment for the ornithologist. Several popular bird books published in the 1880s, such as Charles Dixon's *Rural Bird Life*, W. Warde Fowler's *Year with the Birds* and Florence A. Merriam's *Birds Through an Opera Glass* stressed the virtues of bird-watching as against bird-shooting and advised on the use of binoculars, 'hides' and notebooks. At about the same time, photography made its first contribution to field studies. Early cameras had required too long an exposure to make them suitable for recording living animals (though someone did successfully photograph a fish in London Zoo in the 1850s) but by the mid-1880s it was possible to photograph birds in flight and animals in motion. Within the next decade, the invention of film, flashlight and telephoto lens vastly extended the usefulness of photography, and in 1889 Ludwig Koch made the first recording of bird-song on an Edison wax cylinder at Frankfurt am Main. These techniques – sound recording and photography – made it possible to record animal behaviour objectively, hence making field study a serious scientific discipline.

And of course this acceptance provided a much-needed boost for the nascent conservation movement. Scientists realized that the survival of a species was intimately dependent on the survival of its environment. Marsh birds would die if their marshes were drained; river fish would die if their rivers were polluted. It was not enough merely to stop people killing them: the only way to conserve species effectively was to conserve their natural habitat. Nature reserves, not zoos, were the answer, and the bigger the better. But even more important was to conserve the *whole* environment, by preventing pollution. The coming of Darwinism marked a very profound change in people's attitude to Nature. For centuries, man had regarded himself as the appointed overlord of Nature, with a God-given right to exploit it at his will. But now he saw himself as only one species among many, coexisting in a fragile harmony, and dependent like all the others on the maintenance of that harmony. Conservationists no longer had to appeal to sentimental

'How to photograph birds' nests in high hedges', from R. Kearton's *Wild Life at Home*, 1899

motives: they could argue that it was in man's own best interests to preserve the natural *status quo*.

Thus far, all the results of the *Origin* seem beneficial, but we now come to those which had a less happy effect on the popular enthusiasm for natural history. We have already mentioned that the *Origin of Species* was an exceptionally dense and fact-packed book and that it introduced a new rigour into scientific method. Professional scientists found this new rigour stimulating, but for laymen it was alarming. If one had to be able to explain *every* phenomenon, *every* link in the chain of cause and effect, it was almost impossible for amateurs to keep up. One could no longer gloss over areas of ignorance with pious references to the Creator and His mysterious ways, or account for gaps in knowledge by postulating miracles and supernatural events. Moreover, post-Darwinian natural history, with its stress on processes and inter-relations, was infinitely more complex than the old species

'Ascending a Thick Tree' and 'Photographing from a Hide', from Kearton's *Wild Life at Home*

work. In the past, an amateur had been able to make himself expert in, say, coleoptery without ever necessarily doing anything more than collecting a very large number of dead beetles. But now the coleopterist was expected to know, not only what his beetles looked like, but where they lived, how they behaved, what they ate, how they digested, how they bred, and how they related to all the other species which shared their habitat, which meant studying them in the field and under the microscope perhaps for years. Of course, the trend towards greater thoroughness and consequently greater specialization had been going on for some years before Darwin, but the *Origin of Species* carried that trend much further than ever before, and even professional scientists were awed by the range and depth of Darwin's research. And although Darwin himself was an amateur and an eclectic, he was the last of the line: scientists from now on would all be professionals and specialists. The days when a gentleman could, by a little reading and a little collecting and a little work at the microscope, keep abreast of current natural history research were well and truly over.

However, the most important and far-reaching effect of the *Origin* was that it demolished all the cosy tenets of natural theology that had sustained religion and science in harmony for half a century or more. Where 'Paley and co.'[3] (the term is Darwin's) saw evidence of benevolent and intelligent Design, Darwin saw evidence of natural selection. And natural selection was, by definition, not benevolent and not intelligent. It was, on the contrary, almost limitlessly wasteful and cruel. For every one useful variation that Nature might spew up in her endless random prolificity, thousands more were doomed to perish. As Darwin himself remarked privately, 'There seems to be no more design in the variability of organic beings, and in the action of natural selection, than in the course which the wind blows.'[4] Instead of the image of the skilled, benevolent watch-maker unerringly constructing his perfect watch, one now had the image of a blind, ignorant and ill-tempered mechanic haphazardly throwing cogs and springs together until one day, by pure fluke, he happened to produce a working watch. Or perhaps there was no mechanic at all: perhaps it was *all* chance. Tennyson had prefigured this awful possibility, and the spiritual doubts that would ensue, in his *In Memoriam*:

> Are God and Nature then at strife,
> That Nature lends such evil dreams?
> So careful of the type she seems,
> So careless of the single life;
>
> That I, considering everywhere
> Her secret meaning in her deeds,
> And finding that of fifty seeds
> She often brings but one to bear,
>
> I falter where I firmly trod ...[5]

Natural theology had encouraged people to 'look through nature up to nature's God', to derive their idea of God from the natural organisms around them, but now if one looked through nature with Darwin's eyes instead of Paley's, one saw everywhere signs of arbitrary cruelty, a 'Nature red in tooth and claw' where the strong prevailed over the weak, and chance prevailed over all. And even Darwin realized the horror of this vision. Though he tried to claim in the *Origin* that 'There is grandeur in this view of life ...',[6] in a private letter to Hooker he confessed, 'What a book a devil's chaplain might write on the clumsy, wasteful, blundering, low and horribly cruel works of nature!'[7]

What made natural selection an even more bitter blow was that it relied on exactly the same evidence as natural theology. Paley had laid particular stress on the minute adaptation of ends to means, of contrivances in an organism's structure that were particularly appropriate to that organism's behaviour and environment, and of course this was precisely the evidence that best illustrated natural selection. It was not that Paley had offered one set of facts about Nature to prove one conclusion, and that Darwin offered another set of facts to prove a different conclusion: Darwin used all the same facts as Paley and converted them to a new conclusion. But his conclusion was more plausible than Paley's because it also covered many phenomena (such as the existence of rudimentary organs, or the geographical distribution of species) which Paley had found inexplicable. One or two commentators tried to reconcile natural selection with Design. Asa Gray claimed that, given natural selection, Paley's watch might produce better watches and even, with a change of environment, a chronometer or a town clock. But most clear thinkers, following Huxley, recognized that natural theology had 'received its deathblow at Mr. Darwin's hands.'[8]

Among scientists, the death-blow was not quite as dramatic as it might have been, because they had been growing uneasy with natural theology for some years before Darwin, and had come to realize that this supposed compromise between science and religion might prove to be unsatisfactory both as science and as religion. The geological controversy had already shown that when religion put its trust in science, it could easily be led astray. And most scientists, it must be stressed, were also religious men who had no desire to shake the foundations of their own beliefs. They, more than most people, were alarmed when they saw that natural theology, far from acting as a handmaid to religion, was beginning to usurp its mistress's place. Edward Forbes, a highly respected marine zoologist, warned that,

It is folly and vanity to attempt to account for all the facts in nature, or to pretend to say why the Great Creator made this thing, and why He made that, and to discover in every creature a reason for its peculiar organization ... That God is all-wise is a revealed truth; and whether the organization before us seem excellent or imperfect, it matters not; we know it is perfect and good, being the work of an all-wise God.[9]

This warning may well have been directed at the writers of popular natural history books who often tended to go too far in their amateurish attempts at natural theology. As a writer in the *Popular Science Review* pointed out, 'It appears to them that, unless they drag the Creator into every second paragraph, their essay will not possess the necessary religious veneering for the public taste.'[10] Moreover, their excursions into natural theology were so frequently inept. Far from expatiating on the beauty of Design in Nature, they often ended up criticizing it, or suggesting how they might have managed things better. W.H. Harvey, for instance, had thought it was really too bad of the Creator to force the crab and lobster to 'flay themselves alive' in shedding their shells,[11] and many other writers besides Harvey had pointed out examples where the Design in Nature seemed defective, or where a better arrangement might have been envisaged. Natural theology in any case tended to encourage people to see God in man's image; carried too far, or handled too crudely, it encouraged people to put themselves in God's place. One or two of the more serious-minded natural history writers, especially Hugh Miller and Philip Gosse, noticed this tendency and began to warn their readers not to place too heavy a reliance on natural theology. It might serve as an aid to faith but only revealed religion – the New Testament – could teach the way of salvation. Miss Brightwell, author of a sentimental *Life of Linnaeus*, spoke of the sense of divine perfection in the works of Nature, but then warned:

> Good and excellent as these feelings in themselves are, they must not, however, be suffered to mislead the mind. We must not attach so much importance to them as to suppose that they constitute the whole of true religion. The heart of man is too prone to mistake natural for revealed religion. But, to suppose that the truths which this last alone can teach us, are to be learned by the most attentive regard to this lower world, and all its varied and marvellous productions, is an error, fatal to the best and highest interests of the soul.[12]

However, it was one thing to argue, with Miss Brightwell, that natural theology should not be too heavily relied on; it was another to find, from the *Origin of Species*, that the Design argument was now completely exploded. In the past, natural theology had been a prop which natural history writers could use just whenever it suited them. Some writers had used it a lot; others had merely referred to it in their prefaces to encourage new readers to take up the pursuit. But whether used at length or in passing, it was always there as the underlying justification for the study of natural history. Now natural history had no such justification. It was merely one among many forms of rational amusement which the reader could take up or discard as he or she wished. Obviously there were still many inducements to take it up. Its educational, recreational and entertainment aspects had not been diminished by the advent of Darwinism. It was still a good excuse for taking a walk. But the pious rationale, which had always been natural history's

Charles Darwin in old age

strongest claim to attention, was now removed. It carried no greater spiritual bonus than coin-collecting or antiquarianism. Indeed, it might even be claimed to carry less, since there was always the danger that in studying natural history one might be convinced by the evidence of natural selection and come to believe in the same amoral universe that Tennyson had glimpsed in *In Memoriam*. And, with Hugh Miller dead, and Philip Gosse abdicated, there were no popular writers willing to face up to these problems. The new generation, led by the Rev. J.G. Wood, merely passed over both Darwinism and natural theology in silence and concentrated on assuring their readers that natural history 'is far better than a play, and one gets the fresh air besides.'[13]

In any case, natural history was becoming dull. Once it gained universal respectability, it began to lose its charm. And once it became a school subject, as it did from the 1880s, all its last vestiges of romance were removed. The microscope became a commonplace piece of classroom equipment rather than a family treasure; and visits to the Natural History Museum or to the botanical gardens took on the aspect of an educational chore. Natural history books moved away from the personal, idiosyncratic and often highly inaccurate 'naturalist's notebook' genre towards compendious textbooks like Cassell's four-volume *Popular Natural History* or the Rev. F.O. Morris's *British Birds* – both works of unimpeachable accuracy and quite stupefying dullness. Statistics began to take the place of anecdotes; diagrams the place of vignettes. Spiders no longer appeared among the insects, nor whales among the fishes, and statements like 'The fly keeps the warm air pure and wholesome by its swift and zig-zag flight'[14] were firmly expunged.

By the end of the century, conventional natural history books had become so relentlessly dull and impersonal that a new school of nature writing arose – the 'nature lover's' essays of men like Richard Jeffries, W.H. Hudson, and, in America, John Muir and John Torrey. These were concerned, not so much with the description of Nature itself, as with the description of the writer's reactions to it, and they encouraged their readers to 'commune with' Nature, rather than to study it. Knowing the Linnaean names of things began to seem hopelessly fuddy-duddy; the important thing was to feel the wind in one's hair and thrill to the sound of the wild curlew's cry. By the end of the century, far fewer people, one suspects, could actually *identify* the natural objects they enthused over than in the 1850s when every young girl had had at least twenty names of ferns, mosses, fungi and beetles at her fingertips. The days when a poet (Tennyson) could talk about, 'Shale and hornblende, rag and trap and tuff, Amygdaloid and trachyte',[15] and expect his readers to follow him, or when a wife (Mrs Gosse) could ask her husband, 'O! Henry, do you think that can be *Boletobia*?' and receive the reply, 'No! It is only the common Vapourer, *Orgygia antiqua*!'[16] were over. Nor would any twentieth-century natural history book be likely to inform its readers that 'The legitimate mode of disposing of the cray-fish, when taken, is to put them into the hat, and the hat on the head.'[17] We would not find a modern writer including a long disquisition on the need for sanitary reform in a work on marine biology, as Charles Kingsley did in his *Glaucus*. And nor would we find, in any modern natural history book a passage like this from the Rev. C.A. Johns's *Home Walks and Holiday Rambles*:

I have been scribbling on till it is not far from midnight; but I cannot put down my pen without making yet one more note. Yesterday, April 16th, is the day on which the Nightingale is generally heard for the first time in this part of Hertfordshire. I recollected just now that I had omitted to listen for it; so, to remedy my error as far as possible, I laid down my pen, and softly unbarred the front-door, for all the household but myself were asleep. A charming calm night, a bright moon, clear starlight, no sound but the distant rumbling of a railway train: it dies away: out of its ruins rises a faint shrill piping, indicating pain rather than rejoicing; and before that is well ended, out bursts the liquid gurgling note that no instrument but the throat of the Nightingale can produce. The Nightingale is arrived, and, happy augury, I have heard his song before that of the Cuckoo.[18]

Huxley speaking at the unveiling of Darwin's statue at the Natural History Museum

NOTES AND REFERENCES

—————◆—————

1 'AS INTERESTING AS A NOVEL'

N.B. I have sometimes used 'Victorian' rather loosely to apply to books or events of the late 1820s and early 1830s because it seemed too cumbersome to keep using the phrase 'early nineteenth century'.

1 John Chancellor, *Audubon* (London, 1978) p. 199.
2 Charles Kingsley, *Glaucus; or the Wonders of the Shore* (Cambridge, 1855) p. 7.
3 E.P. Thomson, *The Note-book of a Naturalist* (London, 1845) pp. 3–4.
4 George Johnston, *An Introduction to Conchology* (London, 1850) p. 2.
5 Charles Kingsley, op. cit., pp. 7–8.
6 Quoted in G.H.O. Burgess, *The Curious World of Frank Buckland* (London, 1967) p. 21.
7 Rev. Richard Owen, *Life of Richard Owen* (London, 1894) vol. ii, p. 150.
8 Ibid., vol. i, pp. 245–6.
9 John Lubbock, 'On the Objects of a Collection of Insects', in *The Entomologist's Annual* for 1856, p. 115.
10 William Swainson, *A Preliminary Discourse on the Study of Natural History* (London, 1834) p. 125.
11 Thomas Bewick quoted on title-page of James L. Drummond, *Letters to a Young Naturalist* (London, 1831).
12 Charles Coleman Sellers, *Charles Willson Peale* (Philadelphia, 1947) vol. ii, p. 98.
13 E.P. Thomson, op. cit., p. 23.
14 George Henry Lewes, *Sea-side Studies* (Edinburgh, 1858) p. 178.
15 Ibid., p. 52.
16 Sir William Henry Flower, *Essays on Museums* (London, 1898) p. 65.
17 William Swainson, op. cit., pp. 127–8.
18 Loudon's *Magazine of Natural History*, quoted in David Elliston Allen, *The Naturalist in Britain* (London, 1976) pp. 22–3.
19 James Rennie, *Insect Architecture* (London, 1838) p. 335.
20 Charles Darwin, *The Descent of Man* (London, 1871) p. 70.
21 Charles Kingsley, op. cit., p. 160.
22 Rev. J.G. Wood, *Common Objects of the Microscope* (London, 1868) pp. 110–11.
23 Charlotte M. Yonge, *The Herb of the Field* (London, 1853) p. 72.
24 *The Naturalist's Note Book* for 1867, p. 35.
25 Rev. J.G. Wood, *Common Objects of the Country* (London, 1858) p. 33.
26 *The Entomologist's Annual* for 1856, p. 4.
27 Rev. D. Landsborough, *A Popular History of British Seaweeds* (London, 1849) p. 77.
28 William Swainson, op. cit., p. 118.
29 *The Entomologist's Annual* for 1856, pp. 9–10.
30 G.H. Lewes, op. cit., pp. 28–9.

31 Ibid., p. 179.
32 Rev. William Paley, *Natural Theology, or Evidences of the Existence and Attributes of the Deity* (London, 1802) pp. 1–4.
33 Mrs Loudon, *The Entertaining Naturalist* (London, 1850) p. 481.
34 J.L. Knapp, *The Journal of a Naturalist* (London, 1830) p. 282.
35 Ibid., p. 77.
36 Captain Thomas Brown, *The Book of Butterflies, Sphinxes and Moths* (London, 1832) vol. i, pp. xxxiii–iv.
37 E.P. Thomson, op. cit., p. 12.

2 'A NATURALIST MAY BE ANYTHING, EVERYTHING'

1 George Henry Lewes, *Studies in Animal Life* (London, 1862) p. 2.
2 Sir William Henry Flower, 'Presidential Address to the British Association, 1889', reprinted in his *Essays on Museums* (London, 1898) p. 7.
3 George Henry Lewes, *Sea-side Studies* (Edinburgh, 1858) p. 396.
4 Quoted in David Elliston Allen, *The Naturalist in Britain* (London, 1976) p. 85.
5 Leonard Huxley, *Life and Letters of Thomas Henry Huxley* (London, 1900) vol. i, p. 68.
6 Ibid., vol. i, p. 68.
7 Richard Owen, *Life of Richard Owen* (London, 1894) vol. ii, pp. 14–15.
8 Sir William Henry Flower, op. cit., p. 64.
9 Quoted in David Elliston Allen, op. cit., p. 84.
10 Charles Kingsley, *Glaucus; or the Wonders of the Shore* (Cambridge, 1855) pp. 39–42.
11 George Crabbe, *The Borough*, 1810, Letter VIII.
12 Charles Kingsley, op. cit., pp. 5–6.
13 *Chambers's Edinburgh Journal*, 23.11.1844.
14 Samuel Smiles, *Life of a Scotch Naturalist*, 1877, ed., p. 279.
15 Quoted in *The Entomologist's Annual* for 1856, pp. iii–iv.
16 Rev. W. Houghton, *Country Walks of a Naturalist with his Children* (London, 1869) pp. 10–11.
17 Samuel Smiles, op. cit., pp. 262–3.
18 Hugh Miller, *The Old Red Sandstone* (Edinburgh, 1841) p. 1.
19 William Swainson, *A Preliminary Discourse on the Study of Natural History* (London, 1834) p. 130.
20 Ibid., p. 326.
21 *The Entomologist's Annual* for 1855, p. 3.
22 E.P. Thomson, *The Note-book of a Naturalist* (London, 1845) p. viii.
23 George Henry Lewes, *Sea-side Studies*, p. 77.
24 Frank Buckland, *Log-Book of a Fisherman and Zoologist* (London, 1876) p. 74.
25 *The Entomologist's Annual* for 1855, p. 13.
26 Ibid., p. 14.
27 *The Entomologist's Annual* for 1856, p. 12.
28 Francis Hobart Herrick, *Audubon the Naturalist* (New York, 1917) vol. i, p. 422.
29 Cyril Bibby, *T.H. Huxley, Scientist, Humanist and Educator* (London, 1959) p. 185.
30 Albert E. Gunther, *A Century of Zoology at the British Museum* (London, 1975) p. 163.
31 Philip Henry Gosse, *A Naturalist's Sojourn in Jamaica* (London, 1851) p. v.
32 Rev. J.G. Wood, *Common Objects of the Country* (London, 1858) p. 33.
33 Gilbert White, *The Natural History of Selborne*, 1789, Letter I to Daines Barrington.
34 Ibid., Letter X to D.B.
35 Ibid., Letter VIII to Thomas Pennant.
36 Ibid., Letter III to D.B.
37 Ibid., Letter XXV to T.P.

38 Ibid., Letter XVII to D.B.
39 J.L. Knapp, *Journal of a Naturalist* (London, 1830) p. 425.

3 'THE MOST SYSTEMATICAL GENIUS'

1 W.H. Harvey, *The Sea-Side Book* (London, 1849) pp. 2–4.
2 D.H. Stoever, *The Life of Sir Charles Linnaeus*, trans. Joseph Trapp (London, 1794). Quoted in Wilfrid Blunt, 'Linnaeus and Botany', *History Today*, 1971, vol. xxi, 2, p. 110.
3 Quoted in Charles Singer, *A History of Biology* (New York, 1959) p. 174.
4 S. Peter Dance, *Shell Collecting: an Illustrated History* (London, 1966) p. 70.
5 Quoted in Wilfrid Blunt, *The Compleat Naturalist* (London, 1971) p. 122.
6 The French botanist Sebastien Vaillant had published an essay on the sexuality of plants, *Sermo de Structura Florum*, in 1718 which probably influenced Linnaeus.
7 Letter of 16.5.1737 quoted in Blunt, op. cit., p. 119.
8 Quoted in Blunt, op. cit., p. 34.
9 Quoted in Blunt, op. cit., p. 245.
10 Quoted in Blunt, *History Today* (see note 2 above), p. 112.
11 Quoted in Patricia Mann, *Systematics of Flowering Plants* (London, 1952) pp. 6–7.
12 Quoted in Blunt, op. cit., p. 245.
13 W.G. Maton and T. Racket, 'An historical account of testaceological writers', in *Transactions of the Linnean Society of London*, 1804, 7, pp. 119–244.
14 The Linnean Society of London officially adopted that spelling, in preference to Linnaean, in 1802. It derives from the version of his name – Carl von Linné – which Linnaeus used after his ennoblement in 1757, and by which he is still more commonly known in some European countries.
15 Miss Brightwell, *A Life of Linnaeus* (London, 1858) pp. 86–7.
16 Mrs Jane Marcet, *Conversations in Botany* (London, 1820 ed.) pp. 2–9.

4 THE DANGEROUS PLEASURE

1 Mrs R. Lee, *Memoirs of Baron Cuvier* (London, 1833) pp. 263–4.
2 Charles Kingsley, *Glaucus; or the Wonders of the Shore* (Cambridge, 1855) pp. 27–8.
3 Alfred Russel Wallace, *The Malay Archipelago* (London, 1869) vol. ii, p. 51.
4 Francis Hobart Herrick, *Audubon the Naturalist* (New York, 1917) vol. i, p. 430.
5 Ibid., vol. ii, p. 211.
6 Wilfrid Blunt, *The Compleat Naturalist* (London, 1971) p. 37.
7 Charles Waterton, *Essays on Natural History* (1871 ed.) p. 416.
8 C.S. Rafinesque, *New Flora and Botany of North America* (Philadelphia, 1836) p. 6.
9 J.J. Audubon, *Ornithological Biography* (Edinburgh, 1831–9) vol. i, p. 457.
10 C.S. Rafinesque, *Ichthyologia Ohiensis* (Lexington, 1820). Quoted in Herrick, op. cit., vol. i, p. 293.
11 Ibid., vol. ii, p. 173.
12 William Swainson, *The Bibliography of Zoology* (London, 1840) p. 339.
13 Ibid., p. 347.
14 Herrick, op. cit., vol. ii, p. 105.
15 Charles Waterton, op. cit., p. 302.
16 Ibid., p. 522.
17 Rev. Richard Owen, *Life of Richard Owen* (London, 1894) vol. ii, p. 90.
18 *The Entomologist's Annual* for 1856, p. 47.
19 Ibid., pp. 28–9.
20 Philip Gosse, *The Romance of Natural History* (London, 1860) p. 285.
21 Charles Kingsley, *The Water Babies* (1863 ed.) pp. 71–2.

5 BELIEFS ABOUT NATURE

1 Alexander Pope, *An Essay on Man*, 1733, Epistle I, V, lines 133–4.
2 *Edinburgh New Philosophical Journal*, II, 1860, p. 283.
3 Hugh Miller, *The Testimony of the Rocks* (1876 ed.) p. 97.
4 Charlotte M. Yonge, *The Herb of the Field* (London, 1853) p. 211.
5 E.P. Thomson, *The Note-book of a Naturalist* (London, 1845) pp. 37–8.
6 Robert Mudie, *A Popular Guide to the Observation of Nature* (London, 1832) pp. 177–8.
7 Ibid., pp. 94–5.
8 Thomson, op. cit., p. 68.
9 J.L. Knapp, *The Journal of a Naturalist* (London, 1830) pp. 101–2.
10 Charlotte M. Yonge, op. cit., p. 250.
11 Peter Bayne, *Life and Letters of Hugh Miller* (London, 1871) vol. i, p. 393.
12 Hugh Miller, op. cit., pp. 51–2.
13 Ibid., p. 51.
14 Quoted in Alvar Ellegard, *Darwin and the General Reader* (Göteborg, 1958) p. 223.
15 Charles Kingsley, *Glaucus; or the Wonders of the Shore* (Cambridge, 1855) p. 101.
16 Mrs Loudon, *The Entertaining Naturalist* (London, 1850) p. 338.
17 G.H. Lewes, *Sea-side Studies* (Edinburgh, 1858) pp. 365–6.
18 Charles Darwin, *Journal of Researches into the Geology and Natural History of the various countries visited by H.M.S. Beagle* (London, 1840) p. 336.
19 W.H. Harvey, *The Sea-Side Book* (London, 1849) p. 157.
20 George Johnston, *An Introduction to Conchology* (London, 1850) pp. 175–6.

6 'TO MAKE THE ACID GRIN'

1 Quoted in C.E. Jackson, *Bird Illustrators* (London, 1975) pp. 51–2.
2 Alexander Wilson to Alexander Lawson (his engraver) 22.2.1810, quoted in Francis Hobart Herrick, *Audubon the Naturalist* (New York, 1917) vol. i, pp. 203–4.
3 Ibid., vol. ii, p. 129.
4 Ibid., vol. i, p. 196.
5 Maria R. Audubon, *Audubon and His Journals* (New York, 1898) vol. i, p. 28.
6 Quoted in John Chancellor, *Audubon* (London, 1978) p. 75.
7 Audubon to his wife, 12.3.1827, quoted in Herrick, op. cit., vol. i, p. 372.
8 Ibid., vol. i, p. 213.
9 Ibid., vol. i, p. 225. The diary from which the extract is taken no longer exists, but it was quoted by George Ord in his *Sketch of the Life of Alexander Wilson* (Philadelphia, 1828).
10 Herrick, op. cit., vol. i, pp. 260–1.
11 Ibid., vol. i, p. 361.
12 Ibid., vol. i, p. 361.
13 Ibid., vol. i, p. 397.
14 Herrick, op. cit., vol. i, p. 413.
15 Ibid., vol. i, pp. 413–14.
16 Ibid., vol. i, p. 434.
17 Vivien Noakes, *Edward Lear: The Life of a Wanderer* (London, 1968) p. 29.
18 Ibid., p. 34.
19 Ibid., p. 33.
20 Ibid., pp. 39–40.
21 Herrick, op. cit., vol. ii, p. 121.
22 Ibid., vol. ii, p. 216.
23 Ibid., vol. ii, p. 221.
24 Ibid., vol. ii, p. 286.

25 Ibid., vol. ii, p. 17.
26 Philarete-Chasles, a French art critic, quoted in Herrick, op. cit., vol. i, p. 360.

7 THE ECCENTRIC SQUIRE OF WALTON HALL

1 Quoted in Francis Hobart Herrick, *Audubon the Naturalist* (New York, 1917) vol. ii, p. 91.
2 Charles Waterton, *Wanderings in South America*, 1825, ed. L. Harrison Matthews (London, 1973) p. 134.
3 Charles Waterton, *Essays on Natural History*, ed. Norman Moore (London, 1871) p. 210.
4 Waterton, *Wanderings in South America*, p. 171.
5 Ibid., p. 92.
6 Ibid., p. 70.
7. Ibid., p. 149.
8 Richard Hobson, M.D., *Charles Waterton: His Home, Habits and Handiwork* (London, 1866) 2nd ed., pp. 336–7.
9 Ibid., pp. 305–6.
10 Waterton, *Essays on Natural History*, p. 574.
11 Ibid., p. 64.
12 Hobson, op. cit., pp. 146–7.
13 Waterton, *Essays*, p. 496.
14 Ibid., p. 413.
15 R.A. Irwin, ed., *Letters of Charles Waterton* (London, 1955) pp. 71–2.
16 Waterton, *Essays*, p. 317 (*see also* p. 343 and p. 555).
17 Herrick, op. cit., vol. i, p. 415.
18 Waterton, *Essays*, p. 552.
19 Ibid., p. 347.
20 Ibid., pp. 355–6.
21 *Magazine of Natural History*, ed. J.C. Loudon (London, 1834) vol. vii, pp. 66–74.
22 Ibid., vol. vi, p. 550.
23 Waterton, *Essays*, p. 515, footnote.
24 Ibid., pp. 511–23, from which the three quotations following are taken.
25 William Swainson, *Lardner's Cabinet Cyclopaedia of Natural History*, vol. ii: *Fishes* (London, 1839) p. 111.
26 Reprinted in Waterton, *Essays*, pp. 420–7, from which the quotations in this paragraph are taken.
27 William Swainson, *Lardner's Cabinet Cyclopaedia of Natural History*, vol. xi: *Taxidermy; with the Biography of Zoologists* (London, 1840) p. 117.
28 Ibid., p. 368.

8 AN INVENTION AND ITS CONSEQUENCES

The first part of this chapter is heavily indebted to David Elliston Allen's *The Victorian Fern Craze* (London, 1969).

1 Shirley Hibberd, *The Fern Garden* (London, 1869) quoted in David Elliston Allen, *The Victorian Fern Craze*, p. 62.
2 Frances Lichten, *Decorative Art of Victoria's Era* (New York, 1950) quoted in D.E. Allen, op. cit., p. 60.
3 Charles Kingsley, *Glaucus; or the Wonders of the Shore* (Cambridge, 1855) p. 4.
4 Quoted in D.E. Allen, op. cit., p. 50.
5 John Smith, *Ferns: British and Foreign* (London, 1866) quoted in D.E. Allen, op. cit., p. 54.

6 Nona Bellairs, *Hardy Ferns: How I collected and cultivated them* (London, 1865) quoted in D.E. Allen, op. cit., p. 54.

7 Quoted in Philip Henry Gosse, *The Aquarium* (London, 1854) p. 6.

8 Quoted in David Elliston Allen, *The Naturalist in Britain* (London, 1976) p. 133.

9 Philip Henry Gosse, *A Naturalist's Rambles on the Devonshire Coast* (London, 1853) pp. 233–4.

10 Ibid., p. 441.

11 George Brettingham Sowerby, *Popular History of the Aquarium* (London, 1857) p. 8.

12 Ibid., p. 169.

13 Philip Henry Gosse, *The Aquarium* (London, 1854) pp. 256–7.

14 Ibid., p. 262.

15 Edmund Gosse, *The Life of Philip Henry Gosse, F.R.S.* (London, 1890) p. 258.

16 Quoted in S. Peter Dance, *Shell Collecting* (London, 1966) p. 152.

17 G.B. Sowerby, op. cit., p. 3.

18 Ibid., p. 66.

19 Ibid., p. 53.

20 Ibid., p. 178.

21 Arthur M. Edwards, *Life Beneath the Waters* (New York, 1858) p. 153.

22 Ibid., p. 40.

23 Mrs Margaret Gatty, *British Seaweeds* (London, 1863) quoted in D.E. Allen, *The Naturalist in Britain*, p. 132.

24 George Henry Lewes, *Sea-side Studies* (Edinburgh, 1858) p. 11.

25 Henry J. Slack, *Marvels of Pond Life; or a Year's Microscopic Recreations* (London, 1861) p. 3.

26 G.H. Lewes, op. cit., p. 115.

27 The Rev. J.G. Wood, *The Fresh and Salt-Water Aquarium* (London, 1868) pp. 3–6.

28 Quoted in G.H.O. Burgess, *The Curious World of Frank Buckland* (London, 1967) p. 203.

29 Frank Buckland, *Notes and Jottings from Animal Life* (1890 ed.) p. 359.

30 President of the Birmingham Natural History and Microscopical Society, quoted in D.E. Allen, *The Naturalist in Britain*, p. 208.

31 Edmund Gosse, op. cit., p. 348.

32 George C. Bompas, *Life of Frank Buckland* (1903 ed.) pp. 262–5.

9 THE NATURALIST OF THE BOUDOIR

1 Archibald Geikie, *Life of Sir Roderick I. Murchison* (London, 1875) vol. ii, p. 275.

2 Charles Kingsley, *Glaucus; or the Wonders of the Shore* (Cambridge, 1855) p. 50.

3 Mentioned in Hugh Miller, *The Old Red Sandstone* (Edinburgh, 1841) p. 298.

4 David Elliston Allen, *The Naturalist in Britain* (London, 1976) p. 127.

5 Rev. Richard Owen, *The Life of Richard Owen* (London, 1894) vol. i, pp. 201–2.

6 D.E. Allen, op. cit., p. 127.

7 Kingsley, op. cit., p. 54.

8 Mrs Meredith, *Romance of Nature* (London, 1833) p. 1.

9 Arabella B. Buckley, *Life and her Children* (London, 1880) 1901 ed., p. 14.

10 Mrs Loudon, *The Entertaining Naturalist* (London, 1850) p. 97.

11 Ibid., p. 344.

12 Ibid., pp. 395–6.

13 Ibid., p. 116.

14 Mrs Alfred Gatty, *Parables from Nature*, illustrated edition with additional notes (London, 1867), pp. 1–6.

15 Arabella B. Buckley, *Winners in Life's Race, or the Great Backboned Family* (London, 1882) 1923 ed., pp. 345–6.

16 Ibid., p. 179.
17 Ibid., p. 255.
18 Annual Report of the Liverpool Naturalists' Field Club, quoted in D.E. Allen, op. cit., p. 165.
19 Ibid., p. 165.
20 Rev. Richard Owen, op. cit., vol. i, p. 184.
21 L.T.C. Rolt, *Isambard Kingdom Brunel* (London, 1957). Penguin 1972 ed., p. 128.
22 Rev. Richard Owen, op. cit., vol. ii, p. 119.
23 Ibid., vol. i, p. 126.
24 Ibid., vol. ii, pp. 26–7.
25 Quoted in Wilfrid Blunt, *The Art of Botanical Illustration* (London, 1950) p. 232.
26 Cyril Bibby, *T.H. Huxley, Scientist, Humanist and Educator* (London, 1959) p. 217.
27 Peter Bayne, *Life and Letters of Hugh Miller* (London, 1871) vol. i, p. 300.
28 Jules Marcou, *Life, Letters and Works of Louis Agassiz* (New York, 1896) 1972 ed., vol. i, p. 291.
29 *The Naturalist's Note Book* for 1867, p. 186.
30 Una Pope-Hennessy, *Canon Charles Kingsley* (London, 1948) pp. 235–9.
31 Edmund Gosse, *Father and Son*, ed. James Hepburn (Oxford, 1974) p. 21.
32 William Henry Dall, *Spencer Fullerton Baird* (Philadelphia, 1915) p. 144.
33 Rev. Richard Owen, op. cit., vol. i, p. 296.
34 Ibid., vol. i, p. 122.
35 Ibid., vol. i, pp. 91–2.
36 Ibid., vol. i, p. 101.
37 Ibid., vol. i, p. 333.
38 Quoted in William Irvine, *Apes, Angels and Victorians* (London, 1955) p. 50.
39 Ibid., p. 27.

10 THE PIONEER OF ZOOPHAGY

This chapter is heavily indebted to G.H.O. Burgess's excellent and entertaining study, *The Curious World of Frank Buckland* (London, 1967). It was this book that first aroused my interest in Victorian naturalists generally, and I would like to record here my thanks to Mr Burgess.

1 Frank Buckland, *Notes and Jottings from Animal Life* (London, 1882) 1890 ed., p. 45.
2 Frank Buckland, *Curiosities of Natural History* (First Series: London, 1857) 1893 ed., p. 176.
3 Charles Darwin, *Autobiography*, ed. Gavin de Beer (London, 1974) p. 60.
4 George C. Bompas, *Life of Frank Buckland* (London, 1885) 1903 ed., p. 4.
5 Buckland's account of his schooldays for the *Temple Bar Magazine*, 1873, quoted in Bompas, op. cit., p. 13.
6 Bompas, op. cit., p. 32.
7 Ibid., p. 47.
8 Ibid., p. 70.
9 Quoted in G.H.O. Burgess, *The Curious World of Frank Buckland* (London, 1967) pp. 44–5.
10 Quoted in Burgess, op. cit., p. 59.
11 Quoted in Bompas, op. cit., p. 366.
12 Ibid., p. 23.
13 Burgess, op. cit., p. 11.
14 Buckland, *Notes and Jottings* (see note 1 above), p. 17.
15 Bompas, op. cit., p. 46.
16 Ibid., p. 99.
17 Ibid., p. 216.
18 Ibid., p. 305.

19 Ibid., p. 136.
20 Charles Waterton, *Wanderings in South America* (London, 1825) 1893 ed., p. 327.
21 Francis Hobart Herrick, *Audubon the Naturalist* (New York, 1917) vol. ii, p. 232.
22 Bompas, op. cit., p. 69.
23 Burgess, op. cit., p. 11.
24 Bompas, op. cit., pp. 100–1.
25 Ibid., p. 101.
26 Ibid., p. 118.
27 Burgess, op. cit., p. 92.
28 Ibid., p. 93.
29 Ibid., p. 93.
30 Ibid., p. 213.
31 Frank Buckland, *Land and Water*, 3, 27.4.1867.
32 Quoted in Burgess, op. cit., p. 213.

11 OMNIUM GATHERUM

 1 Quoted in J. Mordaunt Crook, *The British Museum* (London, 1972) p. 197.
 2 Ibid., p. 63.
 3 William Swainson, *Bibliography of Zoology* (part of Lardner's *Cabinet Cyclopaedia of Natural History*) London, 1840, p. 245.
 4 Ibid., p. 246.
 5 Ibid., p. 75.
 6 Charles Waterton, *Wanderings in South America* (London, 1825) p. 154.
 7 Charles Coleman Sellers, *Charles Willson Peale* (Philadelphia, 1947) vol. i, p. 249.
 8 Ibid., vol. i, p. 252.
 9 Buffon, quoted in Joseph Kastner, *A World of Naturalists* (London, 1978) p. 123.
10 Sellers, op. cit., vol. ii, p. 113.
11 Ibid., vol. ii, p. 244.
12 Ibid., vol. ii, pp. 98–9.
13 Ibid., vol. ii, p. 232.
14 This is Titian II, born 1799. He was named for Titian I, born in 1780, who had died in 1798.
15 Charles Waterton, *Letters*, ed. R.A. Irwin (London, 1955) p. 22.
16 Quoted in Albert E. Gunther, *A Century of Zoology at the British Museum* (London, 1975) p. 267.
17 Letter to Albert Gunther, 20.5.1890, quoted in ibid., p. 421.
18 E. Edwards, *Lives of the Founders of the British Museum* (London, 1870) p. 575.
19 Gunther, op. cit., p. 59.
20 Swainson, op. cit., p. 238.
21 Quoted in P. Chalmers Mitchell, *A Centenary History of London Zoo* (London, 1931) pp. 104–5.
22 Quoted in Edward Miller, *That Noble Cabinet* (London, 1973) p. 220.
23 Quoted in Gunther, op. cit., p. 84.
24 Ibid., p. 368.
25 Quoted in Miller, op. cit., p. 231.
26 Swainson, op. cit., p. 239.
27 Miller, op. cit., p. 139.
28 T. Russell Goddard, *History of the Natural History Society of Northumberland, Durham, and Newcastle upon Tyne 1829–1929* (Newcastle, 1930) pp. 45–6.
29 Rev. Richard Owen, *Life of Richard Owen* (London, 1894) vol. i, p. 170.
30 Quoted in Miller, op. cit., p. 241.
31 Mordaunt Crook, op. cit., p. 207.

12 THE BRITISH CUVIER

1 A.H. Palmer, *The Life of Joseph Wolf* (London, 1895) p. 195.
2 Sir William Henry Flower, obituary of Owen, reprinted in *Essays on Museums and other subjects connected with Natural History* (London, 1898) p. 379.
3 Leonard Huxley, *Life and Letters of Thomas Henry Huxley* (London, 1900) vol. i, p. 161.
4 Rev. Richard Owen, *The Life of Richard Owen* (London, 1894) vol. i, pp. 47–8.
5 Ibid., vol. i, p. 11.
6 Ibid., vol. i, pp. 23–5.
7 William Swainson, *A Treatise on Taxidermy* (part of Lardner's *Cabinet Cyclopaedia of Natural History*), London, 1840, p. 76.
8 Thomas Henry Huxley, essay on 'Owen's Position in the History of Anatomical Science', appended to Owen, op. cit., vol. ii, p. 332.
9 J.E. Gray, quoted in Albert Gunther, *A Century of Zoology at the British Museum* (London, 1975) p. 144.
10 W.J. Broderip, quoted in Owen, op. cit., vol. i, p. 151.
11 Frank Buckland, *Curiosities of Natural Histories* (First Series: London, 1857) p. 39.
12 Charles Waterton, *Essays on Natural History* (London, 1871) p. 168.
13 Owen, op. cit., vol. i, p. 399.
14 Ibid., vol. i, pp. 234–5.
15 Ibid., vol. i, p. 402.
16 Ibid., vol. ii, p. 101.
17 Ibid., vol. i, pp. 222–3.
18 Ibid., vol. ii, pp. 4–5.
19 J.E. Gray, quoted in Gunther, op. cit., p. 137.
20 Gideon Mantell, quoted in Gunther, op. cit., p. 127.
21 Charles Darwin, *Autobiography*, ed. Gavin de Beer (London, 1974) p. 61.
22 Ibid., p. 61.
23 Quoted in Owen, op. cit., vol. ii, p. 90.
24 Huxley's appendix to Owen, op. cit., vol. ii, p. 319.

13 THE KING OF SILURIA

1 Archibald Geikie, *Life of Sir Roderick Impey Murchison* (London, 1875) vol. i, p. 90.
2 Ibid., vol. i, p. 96.
3 Ibid., vol. i, p. 71.
4 Ibid., vol. i, p. 263 (letter to Sedgwick 19.1.1838).
5 Ibid., vol. i, p. 87.
6 Ibid., vol. i, p. 94.
7 Ibid., vol. i, p. 129.
8 Ibid., vol. i, p. 129.
9 Ibid., vol. i, p. 142.
10 Ibid., vol. i, p. 226.
11 Ibid., vol. i, p. 164.
12 Ibid., vol. i, p. 168.
13 Ibid., vol. i, p. 142.
14 Quoted in Sir Edward Bailey, *Charles Lyell* (London, 1962) pp. 68–9.
15 Ibid., p. 70.
16 Ibid., p. 70.
17 Geikie, op. cit., vol. i, p. 176.
18 Ibid., vol. i, p. 192.
19 Ibid., vol. i, p. 217.

20 Hugh Miller, *The Old Red Sandstone* (Edinburgh, 1841) p. 290.
21 Geikie, op. cit., vol. ii, p. 316.
22 Ibid., vol. i, p. 194.
23 Ibid., vol. ii, p. 13.
24 Charles Darwin, *Autobiography*, ed. Gavin de Beer (London, 1974) p. 60.
25 Geikie, op. cit., vol. ii, p. 322.

14 THE FOREIGN PROFESSOR

1 Philip Henry Gosse, *The Romance of Natural History* (London, 1860) p. 311.
2 William Swainson, *The Bibliography of Zoology* (part of Lardner's *Cabinet Cyclopaedia of Natural History*), London, 1840, p. 98.
3 Francis Hobart Herrick, *Audubon the Naturalist* (New York, 1917) vol. ii, p. 148.
4 Francis Darwin, *Life and Letters of Charles Darwin* (London, 1896) vol. ii, p. 44.
5 Jules Marcou, *Life, Letters and Works of Louis Agassiz* (New York, 1896) 1972 ed., vol. i, p. 261.
6 F.E. Melsheimer to S.H. Haldeman 17.11.1846, quoted in Edward Lurie, *Louis Agassiz, A Life in Science* (Chicago, 1960) p. 125.
7 Quoted in Lurie, op. cit., pp. 209–10.
8 Quoted in Marcou, op. cit., vol. ii, p. 132.
9 Prof. D.C. Gilman, 'Agassiz as a Teacher', in Charles Frederick Holder, *Louis Agassiz* (New York, 1893) p. 232.
10 Asa Gray to Wm C. Redfield, 13.10.1846, quoted in Lurie, op. cit., p. 125.
11 Agassiz to Rose Agassiz, 2.12.1846, quoted in Lurie, op. cit., p. 123.
12 Marcou, op. cit., vol. i, p. 289.
13 *American Journal of Science*, 2nd series IV (Nov. 1847) p. 449.
14 Maurice Desor, quoted in Lurie, op. cit., p. 159.
15 Agassiz to Rose Agassiz, 2.12.1846, quoted in Lurie, op. cit., p. 257.
16 Agassiz, 'The Diversity of Origin of the Human Races', in *Christian Examiner* XLIX (July 1850) pp. 110–45.
17 Agassiz's answer to a circular on the position of the Negro sent out by Dr Howe, philanthropist, in 1863. Quoted in Holder, op. cit., p. 115.
18 Agassiz to Edwin M. Stanton, 20.1.1865, quoted in Lurie, op. cit., p. 338.
19 Samuel H. Scudder, 'In the Laboratory with Agassiz' in *Every Saturday*, 4.4.1874, vol. xvi, pp. 369–70, quoted in Marcou, op. cit., vol. ii, pp. 94–7.
20 Agassiz to Henri Milne Edwards, 31.5.1847, quoted in Lurie, op. cit., pp. 124–5.
21 Agassiz to S.H. Haldeman, 2.5.1850, quoted in Lurie, op. cit., p. 179.
22 Elmer Charles Herber, ed., *Correspondence between Spencer Fullerton Baird and Louis Agassiz – Two Pioneer American Naturalists* (Smithsonian Institution, 1963) p. 81.
23 Theodore Lyman to Alexander Agassiz (Agassiz's son) 27.8.1872, quoted in Lurie, op. cit., pp. 377–8.

15 THE ROAD TO DARWIN

1 John W. Judd, *The Coming of Evolution* (Cambridge, 1910) p. 3.
2 Charles Darwin, *Autobiography*, ed. Gavin de Beer (London, 1974) pp. 73–4.
3 Georges Buffon, *Histoire Naturelle*, Tome IV (Paris, 1753) p. 383.
4 William Irvine, *Apes, Angels and Victorians* (London, 1955) p. 134.
5 John Chancellor, *Charles Darwin* (London, 1973) pp. 20–1.
6 Charles Darwin, op. cit., pp. 26–7.
7 *Blackwood's Magazine*, 89 (1861) p. 615.

8 Sir J. Arthur Thomson, *The Great Biologists* (London, 1932) p. 47.

9 William Swainson, *The Bibliography of Zoology* (part of Lardner's *Cabinet Cyclopaedia of Natural History*), London, 1840, pp. 230–1.

10 F. Darwin, *Life and Letters of Charles Darwin* (London, 1887) vol. 2, p. 23 and p. 29.

11 Patrick Mathew, *On Naval Timber and Arboriculture* (London, 1831) p. 384.

12 Charles Darwin, 'Historical Sketch of the Recent Progress of Opinion on the Origin of Species', appended to the third (1861) and subsequent editions of the *Origin of Species*; 1866 ed., p. xvi.

13 C.D. Darlington, *Darwin's Place in History* (Oxford, 1959) p. 79.

14 Ibid., p. 29.

15 Benjamin Disraeli, *Tancred* (London, 1847) vol. i, pp. 225–6.

16 Charles Darwin, *Origin of Species* (6th ed., 1872) pp. xvi–xvii.

17 F. Darwin & A.C. Seward, eds, *More Letters of Charles Darwin* (London, 1903) vol. ii, p. 117.

18 F. Darwin, *Life and Letters of Charles Darwin* (London, 1887) vol. ii, p. 190.

19 Wilfrid Blunt, *The Compleat Naturalist* (London, 1971) p. 179.

20 William Cowper, *The Task* (1785) Book II, lines 150–4.

21 Mrs K. Lyell, *Life and Letters of Sir Charles Lyell* (London, 1881) vol. i, p. 253.

22 Judd, op. cit., p. 72. Note of a conversation between the author and Darwin in 1880.

23 F. Darwin & A.C. Seward, op. cit., vol. ii, p. 117.

24 Mrs K. Lyell, op. cit., vol. i, pp. 417–18.

25 Ibid., vol. ii, pp. 2–3.

26 Ibid., vol. i, p. 173.

27 Ibid., vol. ii, p. 5.

28 Ibid., vol. i, p. 271.

29 P. Chalmers Mitchell, *Thomas Henry Huxley: A Sketch of his Life and Work* (London, 1900) p. 235.

30 Advertisement in back of William Buckland's *Bridgewater Treatise*, 1858 ed., vol. ii.

31 *Statesman and Record*, quoted in Hugh Miller, *The Testimony of the Rocks* (Edinburgh, 1857) 1876 ed., p. 371.

32 Quoted in ibid., pp. 353–5.

33 Alfred, Lord Tennyson, *The Princess* (1847) Book III, lines 343–4.

16 'A MUSING, MEDITATIVE STONE-MASON'

1 Peter Bayne, *Life and Letters of Hugh Miller* (London, 1871) vol. ii, p. 489.

2 Dr McCosh, quoted in ibid., vol. ii, p. 451.

3 Archibald Geikie, *Life of Sir Roderick Impey Murchison* (London, 1875) vol. ii, p. 257.

4 Hugh Miller, *My Schools and Schoolmasters* (Edinburgh, 1852) 1857 ed., p. 152.

5 Hugh Miller, *The Old Red Sandstone* (Edinburgh, 1841) 1869 ed., pp. 36–7.

6 Ibid., p. 38.

7 Ibid., p. 39.

8 Ibid., pp. 40–1.

9 Ibid., p. 92.

10 W.E. Gladstone, *Church Principles Considered in their Results* (London, 1840).

11 Baynes, op. cit., vol. ii, p. 192.

12 Report of the Proceedings of the British Association for the Advancement of Science, Wednesday, 23 Sept. 1840. Section C – Geology and Physical Geography.

13 Hugh Miller, *Footprints of the Creator* (London, 1849) p. 36.

14 Ibid., p. 279.

15 Miller, *Old Red Sandstone*, pp. 267–9.

16 Keith Lea'sk, *Hugh Miller* (Edinburgh, 1896) p. 123.
17 Hugh Miller, *The Testimony of the Rocks* (Edinburgh, 1857) 1876 ed., p. vii.
18 Ibid., p. 168.
19 Ibid., p. 229.
20 Ibid., pp. 228–9.
21 Quoted in ibid., p. 296.
22 Miller, *Footprints of the Creator*, p. ix.
23 Ibid., pp. 14–15.
24 Ibid., p. 21.
25 *Methodist Recorder*, 15.5.1863, p. 155. Quoted in Alvar Ellegard, *Darwin and the General Reader* (Göteborg, 1958) p. 47.
26 Sir Archibald Geikie, quoted in Lea'sk, op. cit., p. 149.
27 Hugh Miller, 'The Fossiliferous Deposits of Scotland', appendix to *The Old Red Sandstone*, p. 382.
28 Ibid., pp. 383–4.
29 Ibid., pp. 384–5.
30 Bayne, op. cit., vol. ii, pp. 473–4.
31 Ibid., vol. ii, p. 481.

17 A CASUALTY OF SCIENCE

1 Edmund Gosse, *The Life of Philip Henry Gosse* (London, 1890) p. 13.
2 Ibid., p. 70.
3 Ibid., p. 80.
4 Ibid., p. 87.
5 Ibid., p. 104.
6 Ibid., p. 105.
7 Philip Henry Gosse, *A Naturalist's Sojourn in Jamaica* (London, 1851) pp. 49–50.
8 Edmund Gosse, *Life*, pp. 206–7.
9 Edmund Gosse, *Father and Son* (London, 1907) p. 7.
10 Ibid., p. 11.
11 Ibid., p. 153.
12 Philip Henry Gosse, *A Textbook of Zoology for Schools*.
13 Philip Henry Gosse, *The Aquarium* (London, 1854) p. 50.
14 Edmund Gosse, *Father and Son*, pp. 116–19.
15 Ibid., p. 121.
16 Philip Henry Gosse, *Omphalos* (London, 1857) p. 111.
17 Ibid., p. 347.
18 Edmund Gosse, *Father and Son*, p. 122.
19 Quoted in Una Pope-Hennessy, *Canon Charles Kingsley* (London, 1948) pp. 184–5.
20 Edmund Gosse, *Father and Son*, pp. 122–3.
21 Edmund Gosse, *Life*, p. 301.
22 Edmund Gosse, *Father and Son*, pp. 289–90.

18 CONFESSING A MURDER

1 W.T. Thistleton Dyer in *Darwin: Memorial Notices* (London, 1882) p. 37.
2 *Patriot*, 10.9.1863. Quoted in Alvar Ellegard, *Darwin and the General Reader* (Göteborg, 1958) p. 143.
3 Edmund Gosse, *Life of Philip Henry Gosse* (London, 1890) p. 256.
4 G.J. Romanes in *Darwin: Memorial Notices*, p. 2.

5 Charles Darwin, *Autobiography*, ed. Gavin de Beer (London, 1974) pp. 83–4.
6 Ibid., p. 12.
7 Ibid., p. 23.
8 Ibid., p. 28.
9 Ibid., p. 25.
10 Ibid., p. 31.
11 Ibid., p. 31.
12 Ibid., p. 50.
13 Ibid., p. 35.
14 Ibid., p. 36.
15 Ibid., p. 40.
16 Ibid., p. 44.
17 Francis Darwin, ed., *Life and Letters of Charles Darwin* (London, 1887) vol. i, p. 207.
18 Nora Barlow, *Charles Darwin and the Voyage of the Beagle* (London, 1945) p. 96.
19 Charles Darwin, *Journal of Researches into the Natural History and Geology of the countries visited during the Voyage of H.M.S. Beagle round the World* (2nd ed., 1845) p. 316.
20 Ibid., p. 134.
21 Nora Barlow, op. cit., p. 78.
22 Charles Darwin, *Journal*, p. 173.
23 Ibid., p. 378.
24 Ibid., p. 380.
25 Ibid., p. 398.
26 Darwin, *Autobiography*, p. 45.
27 Henrietta Lichfield, *Emma Darwin, Wife of Charles Darwin* (London, 1915) vol. i, p. 277.
28 Ibid., p. 48.
29 The village is today spelt Downe, but Darwin's home, Down House, retains the older spelling.
30 John W. Judd, *The Coming of Evolution* (Cambridge, 1935) p. 125.
31 Darwin, *Autobiography*, p. 71.
32 Ibid., p. 34.
33 Ibid., p. 167.
34 Ibid., p. 167.
35 F. Darwin & A.C. Seward, eds, *More Letters of Charles Darwin* (London, 1903) vol. i, p. 41.
36 A.R. Wallace, 'On the Law which has regulated the Introduction of New Species', in *Annals and Magazine of Natural History*, Sept. 1855.
37 William Irvine, *Apes, Angels and Victorians* (London, 1955) p. 80.
38 F. Darwin, *Life and Letters of Charles Darwin*, vol. i, p. 453.
39 Ibid., vol. i, p. 466.
40 *Darwin–Wallace Celebration* (Linnean Society, 1908) p. 6.
41 F. Darwin, op. cit., vol. ii, pp. 116–17.
42 Ibid., vol. i, pp. 474–5.
43 Ibid., vol. i, p. 482.
44 Judd, op. cit., p. 131.

19 THE BATTLE FOR DARWINISM

1 Charles Darwin, *The Origin of Species*, 4th ed. (London, 1866) p. 576.
2 Ibid., p. 577.
3 Leonard Huxley, *Life and Letters of Thomas Henry Huxley* (London, 1900) vol. i, p. 176.
4 Charles Darwin, *Autobiography*, ed. Gavin de Beer (London, 1974) pp. 62–3.
5 Thomas Henry Huxley, *Autobiography* (in same volume with the above), p. 103.
6 Ibid., p. 108.

7 F. Darwin, *Life and Letters of Charles Darwin* (London, 1887) vol. ii, pp. 196–7.
8 Cyril Bibby, *Thomas Henry Huxley: Scientist, Humanist and Educator* (London, 1959) p. 70.
9 F. Darwin, op. cit., vol. ii, p. 255.
10 Leonard Huxley, op. cit., vol. i, p. 194.
11 Ibid., vol. i, p. 194.
12 For a full discussion of what was said at the Oxford meeting, see J.R. Lucas, 'Wilberforce and Huxley: A Legendary Encounter', in the *Historical Journal* 22, 2 (1979), pp. 313–30.
13 Bibby, op. cit., pp. 69–70.
14 Ibid., p. 70.
15 Ibid., p. 70.
16 Leonard Huxley, op. cit., vol. i, p. 442.
17 Ibid., vol. i, p. 190.
18 Actually they had. A young 'chimpanzee' briefly exhibited at Wombwell's Menagerie in 1855 was later found to have been a young female gorilla, but by then of course it was dead.
19 Paul Belloni du Chaillu, *Explorations in Equatorial Africa* (London, 1861) p. 71.
20 Rev. Richard Owen, *Life of Richard Owen* (London, 1894) vol. ii, p. 116.
21 Charles Waterton, *Essays on Natural History*, ed. Moore (1871) p. 582.
22 *Daily Telegraph*, 25.9.1861, quoted in Wilfrid Blunt, *The Ark in the Park* (London, 1976) pp. 140–3.
23 Philip Henry Gosse, *The Romance of Natural History* (London, 1860) pp. 258–9.
24 *Punch* XLIII, 18.10.1862, p. 164.
25 Quoted in Bibby, op. cit., p. 76.
26 Charles Kingsley, *The Water Babies* (1863) Chap. IV.
27 *British and Foreign Evangelical Review*, 9 (1860) p. 431. Quoted in Alvar Ellegard, *Darwin and the General Reader* (Göteborg, 1958) p. 49.
28 *Daily News*, 7.9.1861, quoted in ibid., p. 153.
29 *London Review*, 12 (1866) p. 516, quoted in ibid., p. 50.
30 *Popular Science Review*, July 1872, p. 291.
31 A. Hunter Dupree, *Asa Gray* (Cambridge, Mass., 1959) p. 269.
32 Louis Agassiz, 'Evolution and Permanence of Type' in *Atlantic Monthly* XXXIII (Jan. 1874) p. 101.
33 *Family Herald*, 20.5.1871, p. 44, quoted in Ellegard, op. cit., p. 101.
34 Charles Darwin, *Origin of Species*, 4th ed., p. 41.
35 F. Darwin, op. cit., vol. ii, p. 109.
36 T.H. Huxley, 'The Interpreters of Genesis and the Interpreters of Nature', in *The Nineteenth Century*, Dec. 1885, vol. XVIII, p. 856.
37 Sir George W. Cox, *Life of John William Colenso* (London, 1888) vol. i, p. 236.
38 Such as Lyell's *The Antiquity of Man* (1863) and Huxley's *Man's Place in Nature* (1863); The Duke of Argyll's *Reign of Law* (1867) and his *Primeval Man* (1869); St George Mivart's *Genesis of Species* (1870); Wallace's *Contributions to the Theory of Natural Selection* (1870); Darwin's *Variation of Animals and Plants under Domestication* (1868) and his *Descent of Man* (1871). These books all had a direct relevance to Darwinism, and tended to provoke renewed discussion of the subject in the newspapers.
39 Quoted in Ellegard, op. cit., p. 88.
40 *Daily Telegraph*, 16.8.1872, p. 3.
41 Charles Darwin, *Origin of Species*, 4th ed., p. 361.
42 *Family Herald*, quoted in Ellegard, op. cit., p. 240.
43 *Pall Mall Gazette*, 12.9.1865, quoted in ibid., p. 240.
44 Charles Darwin, *Origin of Species*, 4th ed., p. 13.
45 Charles Darwin, *The Variation of Animals and Plants under Domestication* (London, 1868) vol. ii, p. 92.

20 AFTERMATH

1 Charles Darwin, *The Origin of Species*, 4th ed. (London, 1866) p. 577.

2 Ibid., p. 84.

3 Francis Darwin & A.C. Seward, eds, *More Letters of Charles Darwin* (London, 1903) vol. i, p. 154.

4 Francis Darwin, *Life and Letters of Charles Darwin* (London, 1888) vol. i, p. 279.

5 Alfred, Lord Tennyson, *In Memoriam* (London, 1850) Canto LV.

6 Charles Darwin, op. cit., p. 577.

7 Darwin & Seward, *More Letters*, vol. i, p. 94.

8 T.H. Huxley, 'Criticisms on the Origin of Species', in Asa Gray, *Darwiniana* (New York, 1876), p. 82.

9 Edward Forbes, *A History of British Starfishes* (London, 1841) pp. 98–9.

10 *Popular Science Review*, 5 (1866) p. 215, quoted in Alvar Ellegard, *Darwin and the General Reader* (Göteborg, 1958) p. 108.

11 W.H. Harvey, *The Sea-Side Book* (London, 1849) p. 157.

12 Miss Brightwell, *Life of Linnaeus* (London, 1858).

13 Rev. J.G. Wood, *Common Objects of the Country* (London, 1858) p. 33.

14 *School Board Chronicle* (1871) II, p. 57. (Huxley spotted this howler in a zoology textbook passed for use in schools and had it deleted.)

15 Alfred, Lord Tennyson, *The Princess* (1847) Book III, lines 344–6.

16 Edmund Gosse, *Father and Son* (London, 1907) p. 36.

17 Rev. J.G. Wood, op. cit., p. 85.

18 Rev. C.A. Johns, *Home Walks and Holiday Rambles* (London, 1863) p. 53.

PICTURE CREDITS

◆

INDEX

◆

N.B. Page numbers in italics refer to illustrations

Acclimatization Society 147–8
Actinologia Britannica (Gosse) 244, 249
Agassiz, Alexander 164
Agassiz Associations 205
Agassiz, Louis 135, 161, 164, 171, 193, 194–206, *195*, 229, 230, 263, 280
Albert, Prince 168, 180, 192, 193, 214
algology 20, 21, 31, 117, 127, 244
All the Year Round 148
American Association for the Advancement of Science 203
American Association of Geologists 196
American Journal of Science 200
American Museum of Natural History 156
American Ornithology (Wilson) 86, 87, 89–91, *90*
anecdotes 18, 19, 128, 294
Annals of Natural History 116, 266
Anning, Mary *126*, 127
anthropocentric view of nature 73–9
anthropomorphism 18, 19, 42, 80–2, 131
Antiquity of Man, The (Lyell) 281
aquaria 15, 115–22, *116, 119, 122*, 136, 244, 286
  public 16, 117, 122–4, 135
Aquarium, The (Gosse) 117–19, 243, 244
Archaeopteryx 284
Ashmolean Museum 152
Atlantic Monthly 280
Audubon, Jean 88
Audubon, John James 13, 31, 39, 59, 60, 61, 62, 63, 64, 86–98, *87, 98,* 99, 107–10, 126, 145, 194, 196, 253, 276, 277

Audubon, Lucy 88–9, 91
Audubon, Victor 109
Autobiography (Darwin) 59, 140, 180, 192, 209, 222, 252–3, 254, 263, 265, 270

Bachman, Rev. John 59, 60, 95, 96–7, 194
Baird, Mary 136–7
Baird, Spencer Fullerton 30, 96–7, 145, *204*, 204–5
Banks, Sir Joseph 17, 55, 101
Barlow, Nora 254
Barnum, Phineas T. 159
Bartlett, Abraham Dee 139, 145, 276
Bartram, John 89, 196
Bartram, William 89, 196
Bateman, John 86
Bates, H.W. 59, 67, 222, 232, 266, 268
Beagle, voyage of the 30, 81, 221, 255–60, 261, 272
Beavois, Palisot de 157
Beckford, William 181
Berkeley, Hon. Grantley 147–8
binoculars 98, 287
biology: definition 28, 212
  marine 13, 16, 17, 20, *21*, 32, 37, 117–24, 243–4
Birds of America (Audubon) 59, 86, 87, 91–3, 96–8, *97,* 99, 107–10
Birds of Europe (Gould) 94, *96*
Birds of Jamaica (Gosse) 242
Birds of Paradise 40
Book of Butterflies, Sphinxes and Moths (Brown) 25
Boone, Daniel 92
botany 20, 27, 28, 30, 31, 37, 50, 52, *53,* 54, 55, *56,* 56, *66,* 68, 74, 125, 134, 262–3
Bradbury, Henry 115, *124*

Breadalbane, Marquis of 147, 148
Brewer, Mr, of Reigate 66–7
Brice, Joseph 181
Bridgewater Treatises 177, 219, 230
Brief and Complete Refutation of ... Geologists 224
Brightwell, Miss 55, 56, 292
British Association for the Advancement of Science 28, 32, 115, 132, 133, 143, 190, 192, 195, 225, 230, 273–5, 279, 282, 284
British Museum 37, 140, 152, 153, 158, 160, 161–8, *162–6,* 175, 181–2, 241, 246, 276
Brougham, Letter to Lord (Miller) 229
Brown, Capt. Thomas 25
Buckland, Frank 38, 39, 123, 139–51, *141, 142, 146,* 177, 286
Buckland, Mary (Mrs William) 126, 136, 140
Buckland, William 31, 140, 142, 143, 145, 177, 184, 187, 190, *218,* 219, 220, 230, 232
Buckley, Arabella 130–1
Buffon, Georges 155, 209–10, 212, 217
Bullock Museum 152–3, 163
Bute, Lord 139, 148

Canadian Naturalist, The (Gosse) 240–1
capybara *148,* 148
Carboniferous era *231,* 231–2
Carlyle, Thomas 232, 238
Carpenter, William 246
Cassell's Popular Natural History 294
Catastrophism 217–19, 225, 252
Catesby, Mark 196

Catlow, Maria 79
Chadwick, Sir Edwin 180
Challenger expedition 162
Chambers, Robert 214–16, 229, 233, 234, 273
Chambers's Edinburgh Journal 32, 229
Christian Examiner, the 201
cirripedia 263–4
Civil War, American 201, 204, 279
clergymen 13, 17, 18, 31, 37, 128, 140, 185, 218–19, 224, 234–5, 254, 281–2
Clift, William 174
Colenso, John William 281–2
Coleridge, S.T. 210
collecting 16–17, 35, 37, 85, 126–7, 159–61, 241, 254
Common Objects of the Country (Wood) 14, 41, 80
Common Objects of the Microscope (Wood) 19
comparative anatomy 27, 28, 30, 172, 174–7, 182–3, 273, 277–9
conservation 98, 106, 115, 288–9
Contributions to the Natural History of the United States (Agassiz) 203
Conversations on Botany (Marcet) 56
Conybeare, William 31, 184, 232
Cope, Edward Drinker 205
coprolites 224
coral atolls, Darwin's theory of 257, 260
Country Walks of a Naturalist (Houghton) 34
Cowper, William 19, 217
Crabbe, George 19, 31, 32
Creation, theories of the 71–2, 82, 209–10, 216–24, 232–3, 247–8
Cruikshank, George 86
Crystal Palace dinosaurs 177–8
Cuming, Hugh 159–61, 241
Curiosities of Natural History (Buckland) 139, 144, 151, 286
Cuvier, Georges 15, 57, *58*, 60, 63, 65, 93, 140, 157, 172, 183, 196, *199*, 200, 203, 213, 217–19, 252, 280

Cyclopaedia of Natural History (Swainson) 20, 63, 64, 109–10

Daily Telegraph 282
Dana, James Dwight 205
Darlington, Lord 100, 188
Darwin, Charles 15, 18, 25, 27, 28, 29, 30, 31, 39, 59, 65, 69, 81, 131, 134, 138, 140, 151, 162, 167, 171, 172, 179, 180, 181, 184, 192, 196, 209, 210–11, 213–16, 220–2, 235, 246, 250–68, *261*, 269–85, 287, 290, *293*, *295*
Darwin, Emma 138, 215, 260, *262*, 265
Darwin, Erasmus 54, 210–11, *211*, 213, 253
Darwin, Robert 253, 254, 255, 260
Darwinism (*see also* evolution *and* natural selection) 43, 47, 52, 72, 130–1, 167, 181, 183, 193, 196, 211, 224, 234–5, 238, 246, 249, 251, 268, 269–85, *278*, *281*, 286–94
Daubeny, Dr Charles 143, 273
David, Père Armand 68
Davy, Sir Humphry 186–7, *187*
Descent of Man (Darwin) 18, 151, 251, 281
Desor, Edward 200–1
Dick, Robert 32
Dickens, Charles 14, 238
Dillenius, Johann 52
Dinornis 176–7
Disraeli, Benjamin 215
Dixon, Charles 287
Dohrn, Anton 124
D'Orbigny, Alcide 219
Down House 171, 260, 262, *263*, 263, 275
Drake's Western Museum, Cincinnati 91, 159, 196
Dreadnought case 180
du Chaillu, Paul 59, 67, 275–7

ecology 42, 76, 259, 287–9
Economic Fish Museum 139, 149, *150*
Edinburgh Museum 162, 167
Edinburgh New Philosophical Journal 73
Edinburgh Review 162, 215, 273

education 15, 30, 31, 134, 136, 142–3, 202, 294
Edward, Thomas *33*, 33–5
Edwards, Arthur M. 120
Edwards, Henri Milne 203
Effects of Cross- and Self-Fertilisation (Darwin) 251
eland dinner 147
Eliot, George 17, 119, 281
Ellis, Sir Henry 163, 165
Emerson, Ralph Waldo 198
Entertaining Naturalist, The (Mrs Loudon) 79, 128–9
Entomological Society 37, 67, 164
Entomologist's Annual 19, 20, 37, 39, 66, 67
Entomologist's Weekly Intelligencer, 13
entomology 20, 21, 24, 25, 32, 37, 39, 59, 66, 67, 240, 254
equipment (*see also* aquarium *and* microscope) 35, 106, 119, 120, 121, 244, 287–8
Essays on Natural History (Waterton) 60, 64, 101–2, 105, 106, 107
Essays and Reviews 281
Evenings at the Microscope (Gosse) 243
evolution 27, 52, 57, 61, 71, 72, 130–1, 203, 209–16, 221–2, 233–5, 247, 251–3, 260, 266–8, 269–70, 275–85, 286–7
exchange of specimens *38*, 38, 39, 196, 240
Explorations in Equatorial Africa (du Chaillu) 59, 276–7

Falconer, Hugh 179
Family Herald 280, 284
Faraday, Michael 69, 112, 140, 181
Father and Son (E. Gosse) 239–40, 244, 246, 247, 248, 250
ferns 111–15, *114*, *124*, 286
Field 139, 149, 151
Fitch, W.H. 115
FitzRoy, Captain 255
Flower, Sir William Henry 17, 30, 168
Footprints of the Creator (Miller) 233–4, 280
Forbes, Edward 29, 140, 237, 291
fossils *see* palaeontology
Fowler, W. Warde 287

Franklin, Benjamin 153
freaks 139, 140, 148, 151, 181

Galapagos Islands 160, 258–60
Gardener's Chronicle 148, 214
Gaskell, Elizabeth 32
Gatty, Margaret 31, 120, *129*, 129–30
Geikie, Archibald 185, 191, 236
Genesis, Book of 52, 71–2, 82, 209, 216–19, 222–4, 232–3, 245–8, 281
Geological Society of London 29, 184, 187, 188, 192, 195, 220, 260
Geological Survey and School of Mines 192, 272
geology 27, 28, 32, 71–2, 77–8, 127, 184–93, 196, 216–24, *223*, 225–38, 245–8, 252, 256–9
Gladstone, William Ewart 229
Glaucus (Kingsley) 31, 32, 58, 59, 114, 119, 125, 249, 295
Goodenough, Rev. Samuel 54
gorillas 13, 68, 70, 131, 273–9
Gosse, Edmund 119, 123, 239, 240, 243, *245*, 246–50
Gosse, Emily 136, 243, 294
Gosse, Philip Henry 13, 41, 68, 82, 117–21, 123–4, 194, 239–50, *245*, *248*, *250*, 252, 277, 286, 292, 294
Gould, John 86, *95*, 94–6, 126
Gould, Mrs John 94–5, 126
Gray, Asa 196, *197*, 199, 205, 263, 268, 279–80, 291
Gray, John Edward 39, 40, 160, 164, 167, 179, 268, 276
Great Exhibition, the 111, 123, 168, 180, 233
Gressly, Armand 198
Griffiths, Mrs A.W. 127, 131
Gunther, Albert 160
Gurney, Anna 127

Haeckel, Ernst 284
Hamilton, Dr 233
Hampson, G.F. 164
Hancock Museum 166–7
Harvard Museum 161, 196, 201–3
Harvard University 195, 200, 201
Harvey, W.H. 47, 81, 127, 292
Havell, Robert *92*, 92–3
Hawkins, Waterhouse 177–8

Hemans, Mrs Felicia 19, 56
Henslow, John Stevens 31, 162, 254, *255*, 255, 260
Herb of the Field, The (Yonge) 19
Herschel, Sir John 222
Hibberd, Shirley 113
hippocampus minor controversy 273, 275–9
Histoire Naturelle (Buffon) 210
Hitchcock, Rev. Edward 196
Hobson, Dr Richard 103–6
Hooker, Joseph Dalton 140, 214, 246, 262–3, *264*, 265, 267, 268, 291
Hooker, William 262
Horsley, Sophy 133
Houghton, Rev. W. 34
Hudson, W.H. 294
Humboldt, Friedrich von 125
Hunter, John 174
Hunterian Museum 174–6, *175*, 181
Hutton, James *220*, 220–2
Huxley, Henrietta 30, 138, 272
Huxley, Thomas Henry 25, *29*, 29, 30, 40, 69, 134, 138, 144, 149, 167, 168, 172, 176, 179, 181–3, 200, 210, 215–16, 223, 254, 263, 270–81, *271*, *283*, 284, 291

Ice Age 193, 196
iguanodon dinner 177, *179*
In Memoriam (Tennyson) 290, 294
inheritance, nineteenth-century views on 212–13, 215, 284–5
Introduction to Zoology (Gosse) 241

Jameson, Robert 253
Jardin des Plantes, Paris 93, 204, 212
Jardine, Sir William 85, 94
Jefferson, Thomas 155, 156, 158
Jeffries, Richard 294
Jenner, Edward 107–8
Johns, Rev. C.A. 295
Johnston, George 14, 81
Journal of a Naturalist (Knapp) 25, 43–4, 76–7
Journal of Researches … Beagle (Darwin) 81, 256–60

Keats, John 88
Kew Gardens 28, 112, 263

Kingsley, Charles 14, 15, 31, 32, 58, 59, 69, 72, *78*, 77–9, *82*, 114, 119, 125, 127, 134, 181, 249, 279, 295
Kingsley, Mrs Charles 136
Kirby, William 31, 39
Knapp, J.L. 25, 43, 44, 76, 77
Koch, Ludwig 287

ladies 13, 37, 55, 56, 112–15, 119–22, 125–38, 172
'Labyrinthodon' *236*
Lamarck, Jean B. de 57, 65, 209, 211–14, *213*, 253, 268, 285
Land and Water 139, 149, 151
Landsborough, Rev. D. 20, 31
Lardner, Dr Dionysius 63, 64
Leach, William Elford 161, 164
Lear, Edward 94–6, *95*
lectures 133, 135–6, 144, 198, 200, 205, 275
Leicester Literary and Philosophical Society 132
Leicester Museum 167, 168
Letter to Lord Brougham (Miller) 229
Lever, Sir Ashton 152–3, 163
Lewes, George Henry 17, 20, 21, 28, 38, *80*, 81, 119–21
Life of Philip Henry Gosse (E. Gosse) 239, 241
Lilford, Lord 86
Linnaeus, Carl 15, 44, *48*, *51*, 47–57, 59, 60, 63, 65, 72, 90, 134, 212, 217
Linnean Society of London 31, 54, 55, 111, 131, 242, 268, 272
Liverpool Naturalists' Field Club 131–2
Lizars, William Home 91–2
Lloyd, Charles 143
Loddiges, George 111–12
London Review 279
Long, Stephen H. 158
Loudon, John Claudius 17, 93, 108, 109, 129
Loudon, Mrs 24, 79, 128–9
Lowell Institute 198, 200
Lowell, John Amory 198
Lubbock, Sir John 17
Lyceum movement 136, 236
Lyell, Sir Charles 130, 134, 140, 181, 184, 188, 189, *190*, 193, 196, 198, 209, *216*, 216, 219–

Lyell, Sir Charles—*contd*
  25, 246, 256, 257, 260, 262,
  266, 267, 272, 281
Lyman, Theodore 205–6

Macaulay, Thomas 30, 163
MacGillivray, William 87, 93, 253
Macleay, William Sharp 63, 65
Magazine of Natural History 93,
  108, 109
Maillet, de 233
Malthus, Thomas 209, 265, 266,
  269
Manchester Natural History
  Museum 37
Mantell, Gideon 179, *234*
Marcet, Mrs Jane 56
Marcou, Jules 195, 198
marine biology 13, 16, 17, 20, *21*,
  32, 37, 117–24, 243–4
Marsh, Othniel Charles 205, 284
Mary Barton (Gaskell) 32
mastodon 155–7, *157*, 177, 217
Mathew, Patrick 214
Maton, W.G. 54
mechanics' institutes 35, 37, 144,
  236, 275
medical training 30, 31, 143, 172,
  174, 253, 271
Melville, Herman 259
Mendel, Gregor 213, 285
Merriam, Florence A. 287
Methodist Recorder 235
microscopes 15, *16*, 16, 17, 35,
  121, 136, 243, 286, 294
Miller, Hugh 32, 35, 71, 77, 82,
  134, 191, 224–38, *226*, 280,
  292, 294
Miller, Lydia 134, 236, 238
missing links 269, 282–4
moa 176–7
Moberly, Dr George 15
Moore, Sir Norman 102
Morris, Rev. F.O. 39, 294
Moufet, Thomas 49
Mudie, Robert 74–6
Muir, John 294
Murchison, Sir Roderick Impey
  31, 69, 125, 171, 184–93, *185*,
  191, 221, 225, 230, 276
Murray, John 133, 268
museums 37, *73*, 91, 139, 140,
  149, 152–68, 174–6, 181, 182,
  195, 196, 201–3, 241, 246,
  276

My Schools and Schoolmasters
  (Miller) 225
mylodon 177

natural history: definition 27–8
  ignorance of 16, 18, 34, 43, 98,
    107, 128, 294
  popularity of 13–17, 66–70, 85,
    112–21, 125, 128, 132, 134,
    136, 165–8, 196, 205, 230,
    232, 235–6, 244, 286, 292,
    294
  virtues of 17–26
Natural History of Selborne
  (White) 15, 42–4
Natural History Review 278
natural selection 23, 27, 214, 235,
  251, 252, 265–70, 275, 280–
  5, 290–2
natural theology 16, 21–6, 72–82,
  85, 152, 219, 280–1, 289–94
Naturalist 34
Naturalist's Library series 85
Naturalist's Note Book 136
Naturalist's Rambles on the Devon-
  shire Coast, A (Gosse) 117,
  243, 244
Naturalist's Sojourn in Jamaica, A
  (Gosse) 41, 242
naturalists: definition 27–8
  field and closet 40–4, 59–60,
    107, 286–8
  status of 14, 28–31
  working-class 31–9, 66–7, 225–
    38
nature reserves 106, 288
Naval Timber and Arboriculture
  (Mathew) 214
Neanderthal man 284
Negroes 174, 201, 215, 233
New Flora of North America
  (Rafinesque) 61
Noah's Ark problem 233
Noah's Flood 156, 217–19, 223,
  233, 256
Nondescript, the 100–1
North, Marianne 126
Note-book of a Naturalist (Thom-
  son) 26
Nott, Dr Josiah Clark 201
Nuttall, Thomas 241

Ocean, The (Gosse) 241
Old Red Sandstone, The (Miller)
  35, 225–7, 230–2, 235, 237,
  238

Omphalos (Gosse) 247–8
Ord, George 91, 99, 106, 108, 109,
  158
Origin of Species (Darwin) 15, 27,
  65, 134, 171, 180, 196, 203,
  209, 213–16, 222, 235, 239,
  251–3, 256, 257, 259, 262–70,
  272–3, 280–5, 286–7, 289–
  92
Ornithological Biography (Audubon) 13, 61, 62, 64, 88, 90–
  3, 108–9
ornithology 37, 40, 42, 43, 59, 60,
  64, 65, 74, 75, 88–98, 106–8,
  287–8
O'Shaughnessy, Arthur 164
Owen, Caroline 133, 137–8, 174,
  181, 276
Owen, Richard 16, 30, 60, 65, 69,
  77, 127, 133, 134, 137, 138,
  140, 144, 147, 167, 168, 171–
  83, *173*, *182*, 273–4, 277–80

palaeontology 27, 77, 78, 127, 140,
  176–7, 196, 217, 224, 227–32,
  247–8, 256–8, 272, 284
Paley, William *22*, 22, 23, 26, 72,
  78–9, 152, 219, 290–1
Pall Mall Gazette 284
Panizzi, Antonio 163, 167
Parables from Nature (Gatty) 130
parthenogenesis 133–4, 182
Patriot 252
Peach, Charles 32–3, 37
Peale, Charles Willson 153–9,
  154, 167, 177, 217
Peale, Rembrandt 156–7
Peale, Rubens 157–9
Peale, Titian 157–9, 241
Peale's Museum, Philadelphia
  153–9, 195
Peel, Sir Robert 16
Pennant, Thomas 43
Philadelphia Academy of Natural
  Science 241, 276
Philadelphia Philosophical
  Society 155
phoenix 68, 178–9
photography 287–8, *288*, *289*
Phytologist 115
pigeon-fanciers 265
Playfair, Lyon 144
Plymouth Brethren 243–5
Poems… of a Journeyman Mason
  (Miller) 229

Poissons Fossiles (Agassiz) 196–8
Pope, Alexander 22, 23, 73
Popular Guide to the Observation of Nature (Mudie) 74–6
Popular Science Review 279, 292
Potter, Beatrix 126
Pratt, Anne 126
Priestly, Mrs 144
Princess, The (Tennyson) 224, 294
Principles of Geology (Lyell) 188, 209, 221–2, 225, 256–7, 266
prochronism 247–8
prudishness 52, 54–6, 133–4
pteridomania 112–15, 286
Punch 14, 278

Quarterly Review 133–4, 177, 268, 281
quinary system 63, 64, 93, 109–10, 215

Racket, T. 54
Rafinesque, Constantine Samuel 30, 61–3, *63,* 194
rational amusement 16, 19, 21, 123–4, *135,* 155, 168, 292–4
Rattlesnake, voyage of the 30, 272
Reeve, Lovell 85, 115, 119, 160
Romance of Natural History, The (Gosse) 242–4, 249, 277, 286
Romanes, George 252
Rothschild, Walter 160–1
Royal College of Surgeons 161, 167, 174–6, 181
Royal Institution 112, 149, 186, 276
Royal Microscopical Society 131, 242
Royal Physical Society of Edinburgh 237
Royal Society 131, 161, 186–7, 219, 244, 246, 250, 254, 272
Ruskin, John 134, 238

Samouelle, George 165
Say, Thomas 158
Scenes and Legends of the North of Scotland (Miller) 229
Scott, Sir Walter 92
Scudder, Samuel H. 202
Scudder's Museum 159, 196
sea-serpent 68–9, 180, *242,* 249
Sea-side Book (Harvey) 47, 81, 127
Sea-side Studies (Lewes) 20–1, 81, 119, 121

Sedgwick, Adam 31, 69, 140, 184, 186, 188, *189,* 215, 221, 254
Shaw, George 161, 164–5
Siegesbeck, Johann 54
Silurian System (Murchison) 190–2
Sloane, Sir Hans 161
Smiles, Samuel 33–4
Smith, James Edward 54–5
Smith, William ('Strata') 184, 190, 217
Smithsonian Institution 96, 161, 196, 203, 205
Society for Promoting Christian Knowledge 37, 241
Society for the Diffusion of Useful Knowledge *36,* 37
Sopwith's Geological Models 223
Sowerby, G.B. 119, 160
Sowerby, J.E. 115, 119
species: finding and classifying 34, 40, 42–3, 48–55, 57–60, *137,* 156–8, 202, 212, 254, 257, 286–7, 294
geographical distribution of 155, 196, 219, 257–60, 263, 268, 291
naming 34, 40, 42, 48–50, 57, 60, 65, 97, 157, 230
numbers of known 65, 233
spiritualism 167, 252, 268
Stainton, H.T. 39
Stanley, Captain Owen 272
Stanton, Edwin M. 201
stephanoceros 243
Stephen, Sir Leslie 239
Strauss, David Friedrich 281
Studies of Animal Life (Lewes) 28
Sumner, Charles 203
Swainson, William 17, 20, 35, 37, 39, 61, *63,* 63–5, 93, 107–10, 152, 153, 162, 175, 194, 213–15
swallows, hibernation controversy 14, 43

Tancred (Disraeli) 215
taxidermy 40–2, 91, 98, 100–1, 104, 107, 149–50, 153–5, 161–2
Telliamed (de Maillet) 233
Tenby (Gosse) 243
Tennyson, Alfred Lord 224, 260, 290, 294

Testimony of the Rocks (Miller) 77, 232–3, 238
Thackeray, William Makepeace 105
Thierleben (Brehm) *148, 258*
Thomson. E.P. 14, 26, 37
Thomson, Sir William 282
Thoreau, Henry 203
Thynne, Mrs Anna 115–16
The Times, 18, 273
toads in stones 14, 18, 128, 138, 181, 286
Torquay Natural History Society 223
Torrey, John 294
Tyndall, John 25

unicorn 68, 276
Uniformitarianism 193, 219–24, 256–7
Universe, The (Pouchet) *75, 86*
universities 30, 134, 143, 205, 253–4
Ussher, Archbishop James 71, 72, 216–18

Variation of Animals and Plants under Domestication (Darwin) 251, 285
Vestiges of Creation (Chambers) 71, 214–16, 224, 233–4, 265, 266, 273
Victoria, Queen 16, 147, 180
Victoria Regia water-lily 68, 70
Viviparous Quadrupeds of North America, The (Audubon) 59–60, 96–8
vulture's nose controversy 108–9

Wallace, Alfred Russel 59, 67, 209, 252, 266–8, *267,* 280, 281
Wanderings in South America (Waterton) 40, 59, 99–101, *100,* 103, 106, 108–10, 153
Ward, Nathaniel Bagshaw 111–12, 115
Wardian case 111–15, *113,* 117, 120, 124
Warington, Robert 115–17
Warrington case 116, 124
Washington, George 88, 153
Water Babies, The (Kingsley) 69, 70, 279
Waterhouse, Alfred 168

Waterton, Charles 40, 59–60, 64, 99–110, *102*, 145, 153, 158, 177, 232, 277
Wedgwood, Josiah 255
Weismann, August 213
Wernerian Natural History Soc. of Edinburgh 92, 253
Whewell, William 222
White, Adam 165
White, Gilbert 13, 15, 41–4, *42*, 59
Whymper, J.W. 241
Wilberforce, Samuel 119, 273–5, *274*

Wilkes expedition 158
Wilson, Alexander 86–91, *89*, 99, 241
Winners in Life's Race (Buckley) 131
Witness 229–30
Wolf, Joseph 40, 171
Wood, Rev. J.G. 14, 19, 20, 31, 41, 80, *102*, 103, 105, 121–2, 286, 294
World 144
wourali poison 100–1

Yonge, Charlotte M. 19, *74*, 74, 77

zoological gardens 16, *28*, 67, 68, *69*, 117, 121, 122, 133, 135, 137, 139, 140, 143, 145, 147, 176
Zoological Society of London *2*, *24*, 31, *68*, 94, 149, 153, 160, 162, 180
Zoologist 35
Zoonomia (E. Darwin) 210–11, 253
zoophagy 101, 140, 145–8